2nd edition

SOCIAL PULSE

D1920534

von
Marion Grussendorf
und Isobel Williams

unter Mitarbeit der Verlagsredaktion

Cornelsen

VORWORT

Social Pulse 2nd edition ist eine Überarbeitung des bewährten Lehrwerks, das den mittleren Schulabschluss voraussetzt und auf den Erwerb der Fachhochschulreife an Fachoberschulen, Berufskollegs und Höheren Berufsfachschulen hinarbeitet. Das Lehrwerk deckt die grundlegenden Anforderungen der Stufe B1 des Europäischen Referenzrahmens ab und führt zu Stufe B2.

Das Lehrwerk behandelt sachlich, aber dennoch sensibel die wichtigsten Themen im Bereich Soziales. Dabei steht die Kommunikation im Mittelpunkt. Insofern bildet der direkte Berufsbezug die didaktische Grundlage des Lehrwerks (handlungsorientierter Ansatz).

Die sechs Topics sind wie folgt aufgebaut:

Overview

Diese *Overview*-Seite bietet Ihnen einen direkten und kommunikativen Einstieg in jedes Topic mithilfe einer grafischen Übersicht über die zu behandelnden Themen und visuellem Input. So können Sie sich einen Überblick verschaffen und Ihre Vorkenntnisse aktivieren. Darüber hinaus gibt Ihnen diese Seite die Möglichkeit, Ihre individuellen Stärken und Interessen zu zeigen.

Ein *What's to come*-Kästchen stellt das *Scenario* vor, das Sie durch das Topic begleitet. Außerdem werden hier die wichtigsten Ziele des Topics zur Unterstützung des eigenverantwortlichen Lernens zusammengefasst.

Sections A/B/C

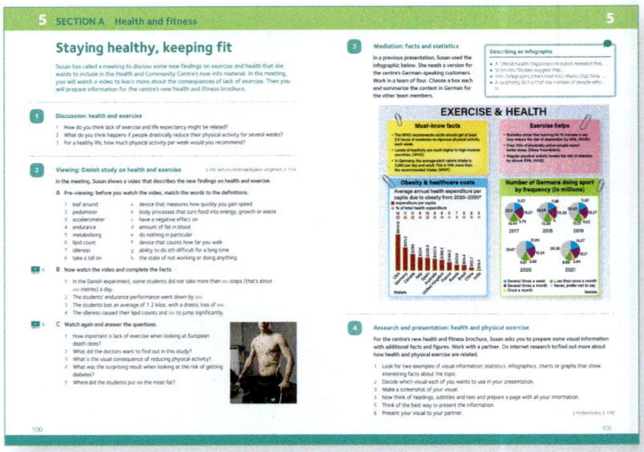

Die stark kompetenzorientierten *Sections* behandeln unterschiedliche Themen im Bereich Gesundheit und Soziales (z. B. Ernährung, Sozialarbeit, Kindererziehung, Pflege, Ergotherapie usw.). Jede *Section* ist in Doppelseiten unterteilt, die jeweils mit einem Situations-Kästchen beginnen, das den Handlungsrahmen beschreibt und Sie dazu anregt, sich aktiv mit dem Unterrichtsstoff auseinanderzusetzen. Unterschiedliche Textarten, Audios und auch Videos führen durch verschiedene Aspekte und schließen mit einem Handlungsprodukt ab.

- Alle Aufgabenüberschriften weisen die Kompetenz und den Inhalt aus, z. B. *Writing: summarizing a client conversation*
- *Situational grammar* wird in jedes Topic integriert.
- Durch gezielte Übungen wird der Wortschatz trainiert, erweitert und gefestigt.
- Binnendifferenzierung wird durch **GUIDANCE** -Karten (die mehr Unterstützung anbieten) und **CHALLENGE!** -Karten (die eine zusätzliche Herausforderung bereithalten) gefördert.

Practice

Auf dieser Doppelseite können Sie gezielt die erworbenen Kenntnisse des Topics trainieren – insbesondere Grammatik und Wortschatz, auch mit interaktiven Übungen in der PagePlayer-App.

Projects

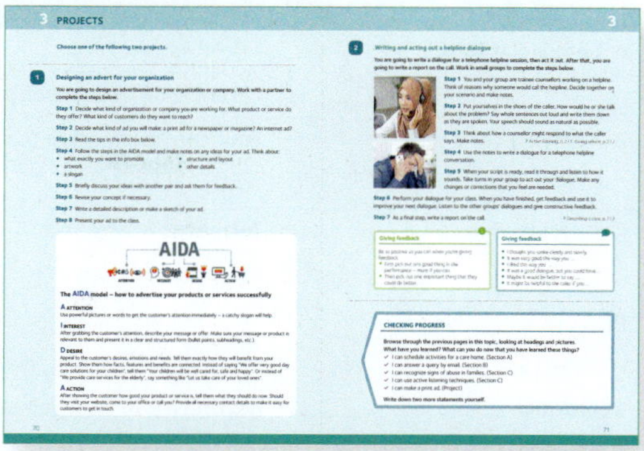

Hier wird weitere Projektarbeit angeboten, um das selbstgesteuerte Lernen zu fördern. Ein *Checking progress*-Kästchen – eine Checkliste zur Selbstevaluation – rundet das Topic ab und ermöglicht es Ihnen, über Ihren persönlichen Lernerfolg zu reflektieren.

Scenario

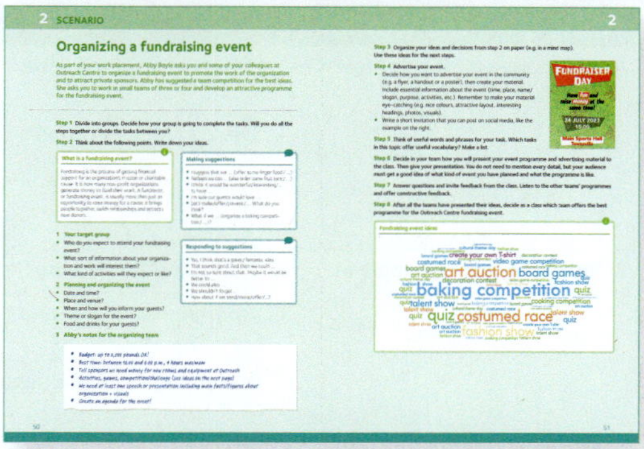

Im *Scenario* wenden Sie anhand einer komplexeren Aufgabe alle Fertigkeiten an, die Sie während des Topics erworben haben. Hier liegt der Fokus deutlich auf Berufsbezug und Praxisorientierung; dabei können Sie selbst entscheiden, welche Inhalte und Skills am besten geeignet sind, um die Aufgabe zu meistern.

Anhang

Der Anhang bietet weitere Unterstützung an. *Exam skills and strategies*-Seiten bereiten auf die Abschlussprüfung vor, indem sie mit jeweils einer Doppelseite Tipps und Aufgaben mit verschiedenen Lernstrategien unterschiedliche Fertigkeiten gezielt trainieren. Außerdem finden Sie alle *Partner* und *Guidance and challenge files* aus den Topics, wichtige Information zur Geschäftskommunikation im *Correspondence*-Teil und hilfreiche Vokabeln und Redewendungen in der *Phrase bank* sowie in den Wörterverzeichnissen.

Am Puls der Technik – mit der PagePlayer-App

weisen auf folgende Materialien hin, die Sie mithilfe der kostenlosen PagePlayer-App auf Ihr Smartphone oder Tablet laden können:

alle Audios und Videos zum Schulbuch
zusätzliche Grammatik-Erklärvideo
interaktive Übungen
die Lösungen zu den *Exam skills files*
So einfach funktioniert es:

1. Laden Sie die kostenlose PagePlayer-App im App Store Ihres Smartphones oder Tablets herunter. Sie können die Inhalte zu **Social Pulse 2nd edition** kapitelweise auf Ihrem Smartphone oder Tablet speichern und jederzeit aufrufen.
2. Scannen Sie mit Ihrem Smartphone oder Tablet die ausgewählte Buchseite. Das Material wird angezeigt und Sie können es direkt starten. Alternativ können Sie auf die Inhalte der App über das Medienmenü zugreifen.

Wir hoffen, dass Ihnen die Arbeit mit **Social Pulse 2nd edition** Freude bereitet und das Lehrwerk zu einem gelungenen und erfolgreichen Unterricht beiträgt.

Die Autorinnen und der Verlag

TABLE OF CONTENTS

A Looking at jobs

- Job adverts
- Carers in different countries

B Applying for a job

- Your curriculum vitae (CV)
- Your cover letter

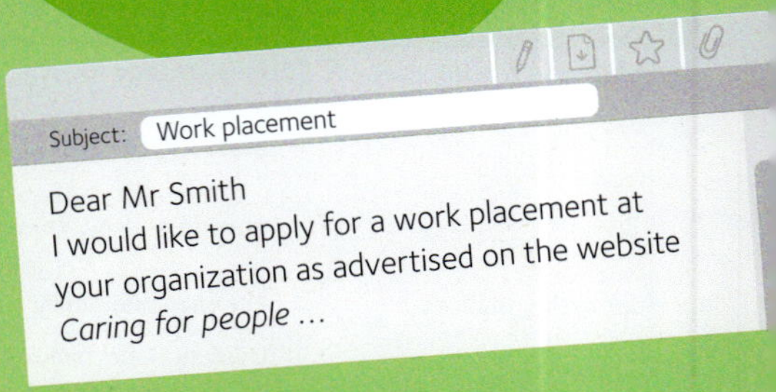

1 Finding a job

A Look at the diagram. Which of the aspects of finding a job (A–C) have you had experience with? Which activities have you not done yet? Describe your experience.

I've written a few applications, but I've never done a telephone interview.

Same here. I haven't …, but I have … .

B What jobs do people in your class want to do when they finish school or training? Walk around and collect ideas. Make a list on the board.

C Work with a partner. Pick two jobs from the list on the board. For each job, make a list of the top five skills or qualities that you think a candidate should have.

D Compare your lists in class. Add your ideas to the board under the heading "Skills/Qualities".

C Interviewing

- Telephone interviews
- Personal interviews

D Projects

- Creating a job advert
- Making a video cover letter

WHAT'S TO COME

Scenario: Everyone around you is already talking about what they want to do after they finish school. You have started thinking about where you would like to work and what kind of skills and qualifications you will need. You decide to look for a work placement abroad in order to gain some international experience in a care job while also practising your English skills. After looking around, you find an interesting job advert that you want to apply for. Now it's time to begin your job application and practise for a job interview.

But first: As you have never applied for a job in English, you will need some useful tips and practical examples before you can get started.

- You will begin by looking at different job adverts and learning about caring professions abroad. (Section A)
- Then you will practise writing a CV and a cover letter. You will also learn about creating a video cover letter as an alternative. (Section B)
- Finally you will learn about the different types of job interviews and how to do them well. (Section C)

Good luck with your application!

Job adverts

First you look at job advertisements and learn about career opportunities abroad in the care professions. You talk and write about your job preferences.

1 Brainstorming: the ideal work placement

Describe your ideal work placement. Where would you like to work and what would you like to do? Make notes.

Expressing preferences

I'd like to …
… use English in my job.
… work in the health sector / …
… gain experience in …
… work with children.

2 Pre-reading: understanding job advertisements

Before you read the job adverts, match the words (1–8) to their German equivalents (a–h).

1 impairment	5 recognized	a *Hebamme*	e *Gesundheitszustand*
2 health condition	6 volunteer	b *Ausgaben*	f *Krankenhausstation*
3 to accompany	7 midwife	c *Freiwillige/-r*	g *Beeinträchtigung*
4 expenses	8 ward	d *anerkannt*	h *begleiten*

3 Reading: three job advertisements

> *Schwierige Texte lesen, S. 154*

A Scan the adverts below and on page 9. For each, take notes on: a) the job sector, b) the skills and qualities needed, c) the types of duties, d) what the employer offers and e) career perspectives. Share with a partner.

B How should an applicant apply for each job?

Four-week work placement for trainee care worker

Who we are

Care Disability supports thousands of disabled people all over the Republic of Ireland. We help people with physical impairments, learning difficulties and long-term health conditions, as well as their carers, friends and families.

Who you are

You are reliable, motivated and flexible. You speak good English and at least one other language. You are already studying or hope to study social and health care. A full driving licence is an advantage.

Your responsibilities

- accompanying disabled people who are taking part in leisure and social activities
- helping the family of a disabled person with their daily routine

What we offer:

- a training programme for you to learn new skills
- support and supervision to help you carry out your tasks
- a small payment to help you with your day-to-day expenses

Apply now!

Send your CV and cover letter to:
Ann Haslam at a.haslam@care-disability.nex

Only Kids – The childcare experts

Are you a school leaver looking for work experience in early childhood education?
At Only Kids in Melbourne, Australia you will gain new skills and experience during on-the-job practical training, as well as an officially recognized certificate.
We offer childcare programmes for babies and children aged 6 months – 6 years.
We are looking for a friendly, cheerful person with good interpersonal skills. We provide excellent career development opportunities, as well as on-going support and mentoring.
Earn while you learn! We will provide financial support if you want to study for a diploma or university degree.

If this sounds like the perfect career path for you, apply with our online application form.

Midwives abroad

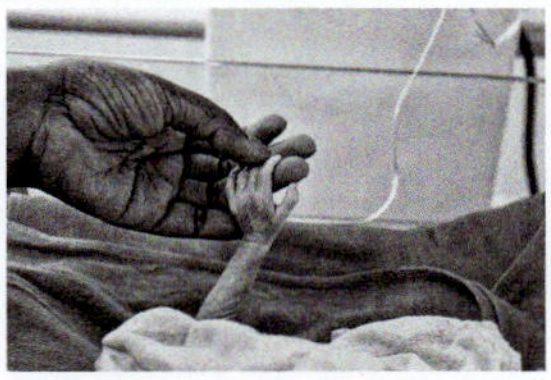

Do you want to provide healthcare to communities in a developing country?
Do you want to help those people who need our help most? Are you good in a team? Do you have a positive attitude? If so, come and join us as a **volunteer**!
Our midwifery work placement programme gives you a fantastic opportunity to gain international experience in hospital maternity wards. You will learn about healthcare for mothers and newborns from local midwives and other professionals.
Accommodation and food will be provided.
Interested? Then apply **here**

4 Writing and speaking: job preferences

A Write down the main points of one of the job adverts that you find most interesting, e.g. the job itself, the location, etc.

B Discuss with a partner why you find this job attractive.

Expressing preferences

- I'd prefer the job as a/an … because it offers/provides …
- I would apply for the position as a/an … because …
- The first job is definitely more attractive because …
- I think the second job is more suitable for me as I'm …

5 Speaking: job requirements, skills and qualities

A Copy the table and put the words and phrases into the right categories.

I can	I have	I am
	a driving licence	

~~a driving licence~~ • *a good communicator* • *a positive attitude* • *willing to learn* • *a proactive person* • *some experience in …* • *good interpersonal skills* • *deal with stress* • *hard-working* • *work well under pressure*

B What other qualities and qualifications would you mention in your own CV?

C Summarize your key skills and qualities in one minute and present them to a partner. Take turns.

CHALLENGE! *For a challenge, Partner A turn to file C1 on page 196, Partner B turn to file C5 on page 197.*

Carers in different countries

You want to learn about working conditions in other countries to help increase your job options. You find some information about social work abroad and compare working conditions for social workers in three different countries.

1 Pre-reading: social work

Match the words (1–7) from the online forum below with the correct definitions (a–g).

1 demanding	a to not have enough of
2 vacancy	b a difficult situation or question to solve
3 challenge	c to take unfair advantage of
4 violence	d to treat sb repeatedly in a cruel or violent way
5 to lack	e requiring attention, effort and time
6 to abuse	f an available position
7 to exploit	g physical force that is intended to hurt or kill sb

2 Reading: social workers around the world

> *Schwierige Texte lesen, S. 154*

A Read the comments on an online forum. Decide if these sentences are true or false. Correct the false statements.

1. Social workers in the US get a lot of help in their jobs.
2. It is usually difficult to recruit new staff in the US.
3. Violence connected with guns is a further problem for social workers in America.
4. In Russia, social workers can attend courses and learn how to stay healthy.
5. Professional supervision is generally provided both in Russia and the US.
6. In Northern Ireland, social workers are well qualified and their work is highly respected.

www.world-carers.nex

2

We all know that social workers here at home do a fantastic job helping people and that their job is very demanding, but what do we know about social work in other countries? Today is World Social Work Day so we asked social workers round the world to tell us what their work is like.

Roberto Martinez

I work in the US, where social work is pretty highly respected because people know that it's really difficult. We get a lot of support in our work, for example regular meetings with the team, formal supervision and courses where we learn how to deal with stress and look after our health and well-being. I think this is why, when there's a job vacancy, there are lots of applicants for the position. Also, social workers here are more interested in doing this work for a long time. But the challenges for social care workers are probably as big as in other countries. A more serious problem here, though, is guns and gun violence.

Tatyana Shestakova

In Russia there are about 150,000 qualified social workers who have completed a five-year degree programme. Most students feel they lack practice after finishing their studies because the study programme focuses more on psychology and theory than on practical work.
What is social work like here? Well, as in other countries, stress levels and caseloads are high, and often there are not enough social workers, or there is no budget, or both. But there's more support than in the past, mainly for learning new skills like how to prevent burnout and have a healthy work-life balance. We also get things like free medical checks and free holidays for our kids. The professional supervision isn't as good as in the US or UK – we mainly give each other feedback on a peer-group level. I think that could be better.

Arleen O'Brian

I would say social work is seen as a challenging and well-respected line of work in Northern Ireland. Our duty is to help victims of poverty, mental illness, disability and to protect people who are at risk of being abused or exploited – whether they are children or adults. The benefit of being a smaller country is that it's easier to have the same professional standards everywhere. Our academic standard is probably higher than in some other countries. That's maybe why social work is an attractive profession, and why we have such a high number of applications for our degree programmes.
We attract applicants more easily than other places.

B Compare the conditions described by Roberto, Tatyana and Arleen. Where do you find differences or similarities?

Making comparisons

Compared to …, social work/workers in … is / are …
… similar to …
… (not) as good as …
… (not much) different to/from …
… (much) better in … than …
… easier / more difficult / … than …

Comparing conditions

- When comparing things that are the same or nearly the same, we use **… as … as**.

*Social work in Russia is **as** challenging **as** in the US.*

- When comparing things that are different, we use the comparative form of adjectives + **than**.

*Professional supervision seems **more important** in the US **than** in Russia.*
*Getting qualified staff is **easier than** in the past.*

> *Comparison of adjectives and adverbs, p. 231*

C In your view, where is the best place to be a social worker? Discuss the question in small groups.

D With a partner, give a short talk about the working conditions in one of the countries described above or a country of your choice. First find out more online about social work in the country you've chosen. Make notes. Then present your findings in a three-minute talk.

GUIDANCE *For guidance, turn to file G1 on page 163.*

Giving a talk

- I'd like to give you an overview of social work in …
- My talk is based on what … says about the work and conditions in …
- Some of the benefits of working in … are …
- They also face challenges, for example …
- And finally, I want to …
- To sum up …
- Are there any questions? > *Presentations, p. 209*

Your curriculum vitae (CV)

In this part you find out what makes a good CV. Then you practise writing your own CV.

1 Pre-reading: advice on writing a CV

A What information do you think belongs in a CV? Discuss in small groups.

B Before you read some advice on CVs, match these English words to their German equivalents.

1 education	5 reverse	a *freiwillig*	e *Ausbildung*
2 training	6 voluntary	b *Erlaubnis*	f *Leistung*
3 achievement	7 permission	c *Schulbildung*	g *umgekehrt*
4 requirements		d *Anforderungen*	

2 Reading: how to write a CV in English

> *Schwierige Texte lesen, S. 154*

A You want to apply for one of the jobs on pages 8 and 9. You find this article online. Read it, then with a partner choose the correct heading for each paragraph.

Education • Interests • Personal details • Profile • References • Skills • Work experience

3

How to write your CV

A CV is a summary of your abilities, work experience, education and qualifications. There is no set format for a CV in English, and CVs may vary from country to country. Before you apply for a job in a specific country, always check the rules there first.

Your CV should be short (not longer than one page), have a clear structure as well as headings and an attractive layout. Of course, your CV must be honest and factual. Make sure you include important key words, skills and requirements mentioned in the job advertisement.

___[1]: Start your CV with your name and address, telephone number, and email address. However, in some countries it is not common practice to include a photo with your CV.

___[2]: This is a short summary outlining your skills and experience relevant to the job you are applying for. Use it to grab the reader's attention.

___[3]: This information should be given in reverse chronological order, with the most recent position first. Provide dates of the start and end of employment, employer's name and address, job title, main responsibilities and achievements.

___[4]: Give a brief description of your qualifications and the names of schools or colleges in reverse chronological order. You can use German words for qualifications and educational institutions and then say what the English equivalent is, e.g. "*Fachoberschule* is equivalent to vocational college".

___[5]: Write about what you are good at. Describe the skills you have gained. Also give the reader an idea of your main personal qualities using words like reliable, team-orientated, flexible, energetic, etc.

___[6]: This section is optional. Consider which of your activities your future employer may be interested in. Think about what your leisure activities say about your personality. Always mention voluntary or social work for a charity or in a project.

___[7]: Be careful with names or any contact details on CVs because of data protection laws. Instead offer to provide details on request. Always ask for permission before you give someone's contact details.

(334 words)

B 1 Which information in your CV should be in reverse chronological order? What do you think is the reason for this?
2 Which advice in the article surprises you? Which information do you find especially helpful?

C 1 With a partner, think of some tips on how to write a German CV. Make notes.
2 Compare your tips with those of other students. Which points are different from the CV advice given in the article?

D Use the advice from the article to make notes for your own CV.
GUIDANCE *For guidance, turn to file G2 on page 83.*

---

3 Writing: preparing your CV

A Compare the information on Leonie Kuhn's CV with the job adverts on pages 8–9. Which job is Leonie applying for? Do you think she is a good candidate for the job? Explain.

Leonie Kuhn
Domkloster 6, 50667 Cologne, Germany
Phone (+49) 0221 34589
Mobile (+49) 0176 28948
Email leokuhn@gmx.dex

Profile

Highly motivated student of social and health care seeks practical experience in Ireland.
Fluent English speaker and team player who is friendly, flexible and good at working under pressure.

Work experience

Sept. 20 .. – June 20 ..	Au pair, Münster, Germany; temporary position taking care of three primary school-aged children for visiting American professor

Education

August 20 .. – present	Fachoberschule, Cologne (equivalent to Irish vocational college) Main subjects: English, German, Biology, Health Studies, Social Studies and Home Economics
August 20 .. – June 20 ..	Kölner Realschule, Cologne (equivalent to Irish secondary school); finished with top grades

Languages
German (native speaker), English: B1/B2 (independent: oral and written), Polish (conversational)

Skills
MS Office
Good at working under pressure, team-oriented, friendly, flexible
Full driving licence, first-aid certificate

Interests
Volunteer with a local refugee organization

References
Names of referees available on request

B Prepare your own CV. Use the notes you made for **2D**. Copy the layout of Leonie's CV and use any words and phrases from her CV that are appropriate.

Your cover letter

In this part you will learn how to write a cover letter. As an interesting alternative, you analyse and compare two video cover letters.

1 Reading and writing: a cover letter

A Read Leonie's cover letter. What does she feel she can bring to the job?

1 Put your address on the top right and the address of the employer on the left.

2 If you have a contact name, use *Mr* for a man and *Ms* for a woman. Or use *Dear Sir or Madam.*

3 Always start with a capital letter and do not use short forms. Say where you saw the advert and which job you are applying for.

4 Say why you are the right person for this position.

5 Include a formal closing sentence.

6 If you start your letter with *Dear Mr/Ms,* finish with *Yours sincerely* (or *Yours faithfully* for *Dear Sir or Madam*).

Domkloster 6
50667 Cologne
Germany
leokuhn@gmx.dex

25 March 20..

Care Disability **1**
Attn: Ann Haslam
62 Calder Street
Cork City T23 T292
Ireland

Dear Ms Haslam **2**

Work placement as a trainee care worker

With reference to the advertisement on your website, I would like to apply for a work placement at your organization. **3**

I am very interested in gaining experience with disabled people and their families as this will give me the opportunity to develop both personally and professionally. I am particularly keen to work in an English-speaking country where I can apply my knowledge of English on a daily basis. **4**

Through my experience as an au pair, I know that I enjoy helping people and can fit in well with families. My language abilities will also make me an asset to your team. My English is excellent, I am a native German speaker and I also speak conversational Polish.

I hope you will consider my application and grant me an interview. I look forward to hearing from you soon. **5**

Yours sincerely **6**

Leonie Kuhn
Enc: curriculum vitae

B Look again at Leonie's cover letter and say in which order she did the following:

a ask to be considered for an interview
b refer to details on her CV
c refer to the position
d say why she is applying for the position
e state why she is the best person for the job

C Choose one of the jobs on pages 8–9 and write a cover letter.

False friends

A false friend is similar to a word in your own language but has a different meaning.

	German	English
1	*Gymnasium* = grammar school (UK), high school (US)	gymnasium = *Fitnessstudio, Sporthalle*
2	*absolvieren* = complete, finish	absolve = *freisprechen, entbinden*
3	*Noten* = grades, marks	notes = *Notizen*
4	*Chef* = boss, superior	chef = *Küchenchef/-in*

2 Viewing: a video cover letter

> *Mit Sehverstehensaufgaben umgehen, S. 144*

A video cover letter has become an attractive alternative to a written cover letter. The format is flexible, so you can be creative in the way you present yourself to an employer.

1 **A** Watch the two different video cover letters that Leonie has made. Which one do you think is more effective? Explain why.

1 **B** Watch the version that you have chosen again. Make notes on what Leonie says about:

- where she saw the advert
- education
- work experience
- skills and personal qualities
- interests
- personal details

What other information does she give?

C Talk about these elements and how Leonie uses them:

- body language
- sound effects
- visual effects

D Discuss with a partner how you think Leonie could improve her video cover letter. Share your ideas in class.

CHALLENGE! *For a challenge, turn to file C3 on page 196.*

Telephone interviews

The final step in the application process is the interview. Here you learn how to have a successful telephone interview and then role-play your own telephone interview.

---

1 Mediation: tips for telephone interviews

> *Mediation, S. 164*

Read the text below and make notes in German. Use your notes to explain the tips to a friend who is going to do a telephone interview.

No sweat! It's only a telephone interview

Your first telephone interview needn't be scary. Just make sure that your interviewer hears that this phone call is as meaningful to you as if it were a face-to-face interview. Follow the tips below.

Always dress carefully for a telephone interview
Even though the interviewer cannot see you, you will feel and sound more confident and will make a better impression.

Understand the questions
By asking just a few questions, an interviewer can quickly decide if you are a likely candidate for the job. Here are the top five interview questions, and what the interviewer really wants to find out.

	Question	What the interviewer wants to find out
1	Can you tell me something about yourself?	What kind of person are you?
2	What are your strengths?	If we take you on, where can you work most effectively?
3	What are your weaknesses?	Are you aware of your weaknesses and willing to work on them?
4	Why are you applying for this position?	Why do you think you're the right person for this job?
5	What would you like to be doing five years from now?	If we take you on, will we be making an investment in the future of the company?
6	Is there anything you'd like to ask me?	Have you done any research on our company?

Be prepared!
Have these things ready beside your phone:
- a copy of the job description
- a copy of your cover letter and your CV
- a notepad and pens to take notes during the interview
- a list of questions you want to ask the interviewer
- a smiley to remind you to smile (the interviewer will hear it!)

Practice makes perfect!
Before the interview, role-play a telephone interview with a friend.

2 Listening: a telephone interview

> Mit Hörverstehensaufgaben umgehen, S. 144

4

A Listen to the interview. Then answer the questions.

1 What does Thomas say about his personal background?
2 Why does he want to work for *Volunteers Abroad?*
3 What are his strengths?
4 What are his weaknesses?
5 What does the interviewer say will happen as a next step?

4

B Listen again and complete the sentences.

1 ___ Franca Miller from *Volunteers Abroad.*
2 ___ the opportunity to talk to you today.
3 Could you tell me ___?
4 And what made you ___?
5 What about you? What are you ___?
6 But ___ and I believe I could fit in very quickly.
7 Do you ___ for us, Mr Hermann?
8 Thank you again for your time. I really look forward ___.

3 Role-play: a telephone interview

Use the flow chart and the phrases in **2** and below to role-play a telephone interview.

CHALLENGE! *For a challenge, Partner A turn to file C4 on page 197; Partner B turn to file C2 on page 196.*

Partner A: Interviewer	Partner B: Candidate
	Answer the phone.
Greet the candidate and give your name. Say that you would like to ask a few questions.	Greet the interviewer and say you will be happy to answer his/her questions.
Ask five or six questions and respond appropriately to the replies.	Ask the interviewer to repeat something.
	Give your own answers to the questions.
	Thank the interviewer for the opportunity to talk.

Telephoning

- Hello, this is … (speaking)
- I'm calling from …
- Can I speak to …, please? / Is that …?
- Speaking. / This is …
- Could you repeat that, please?
- Sorry, I didn't catch that.
- Can I ask you another question?
- I'm sorry, you're breaking up.
- Thank you for giving me the opportunity to talk to you.
- Thank you for calling.

> *Telephoning, p. 205*

Personal interviews

Here you learn what to do in a face-to-face interview, whether it is in person or in a video conference call. Then you role-play an interview and get feedback.

---

1 Viewing: getting it right

> *Mit Sehverstehensaufgaben umgehen, S. 144*

A When preparing for a job interview, what do you need to think about? With a partner, make a mind map.

2 **B** Watch part 1 of the film. How well has Mike prepared for the interview?

2 **C** Watch part 1 again. Make a list of mistakes Mike has made. Add any new ideas to your mind map above and discuss them.

3 **D** Watch part 2 of the film. What does Mike do better this time?

3 **E** Watch part 2 again. What questions does the interviewer ask? Write them down.

---

2 Dealing with interview questions

A With a partner, think of at least five typical questions that you would expect at an interview. Then watch the interview in 1 again, if you like, for other questions. Make notes.

GUIDANCE *For guidance, turn to file G3 on page 184.*

B Prepare answers to these questions individually.

C Take turns asking and answering the questions.

Interview questions

- Where did you ...?
- When did you first ...?
- How long have you been ...?
- If you could ..., what would you ...?
- Tell me about your ...
- What would you say is/are your ...?
- What would you like to ...?

- My first ... was ...
- I've been ... for/since ...
- If I could ..., I would (probably) ...
- I would say my ... is/are ...
- I would like to ...

3 Role-play: an interview

You are going to take part in an interview for a work placement.

A Choose one of the job adverts on pages 8–9.

Think about these questions:

a What skills are required?
b Why are you a good / the best candidate for the job?
c Why are you applying for this job?
d What questions do you want to ask about the company and job?

B Practise the interviews.

> *Job interviews, p. 208*

Work in groups of 3–4 students. Each member of the group will be interviewed for the job. The others will take turns to be the interviewer or observers.

The interviewer	
Greet the candidate	Good morning, Mr/Ms .... Pleased to meet you. Please have a seat.
Ask at least three questions	Can you describe yourself? What are your strengths? What are your weaknesses?
If possible, ask follow-up questions	Can you give me an example of some past goals and how you achieved them? How did you first become interested in this field of work?
End the interview politely	Do you have any other questions? Thank you for coming. We'll contact you within the next two weeks.

The observers			
How did the candidates present themselves? (body language, voice, appearance, confidence, etc.)	☺	😐	☹
How well did they answer questions?	...	...	...
Did they ask good questions?	...	...	...

C Decide who should get the job.

The observers use their notes to give feedback to the candidates. The group then decides who performed best in the interview. Then tell the class who got the job and why.

1 PRACTICE

1 Using verbs in job adverts

Complete the sentences with the correct verbs from the box.

apply • earn • gain • give • include • join • provide • supply

1 We ___ excellent training opportunities.
2 With our traineeship you will ___ new skills for your future career.
3 In your role, you will ___ elderly people with their daily routine.
4 If you are a team worker and have a positive attitude, come and ___ us as a volunteer!
5 This placement programme will ___ you a fantastic opportunity to work abroad.
6 Your responsibilities will ___ helping elderly people and their families.
7 We provide financial support for students, so you can ___ while you learn.
8 If you are interested in this position, ___ now by clicking here.

---

2 Using prepositions

Choose the most suitable preposition in the brackets to complete the sentences.

1 This job description sounds great. You should apply (on / to / for) this job.
2 I am good (with / in / at) working with children.
3 You should be able to work (on / with / under) pressure.
4 I refer (on / to / at) your offer of a traineeship in your care home.
5 After studying social care (for / during / in) five years, I finished with a degree.
6 I am interested (on / in / for) gaining experience in this field.
7 I look forward (for / on / to) your response.
8 Any references are available (after / under / on) request.
9 I'm not used (for / to / on) being interviewed.
10 The interviewer said she had waited (since / for) 20 minutes.

---

3 Describing skills and qualifications

Match the sentence halves.

1 During my work placement, I was able to
2 I would like to practise
3 Last month, I completed
4 After finishing school, I trained
5 I grew up in Hamburg where I attended
6 To learn more about midwifery, I
7 My experience abroad taught me about
8 Helping my older sister with her baby

a took a course for mothers and newborns.
b convinced me of this career path.
c a secondary school.
d practices in other cultures.
e gain valuable experience in this field.
f as an assistant nurse.
g my language skills.
h a training course at a local hospital.

4 Understanding interview advice

Complete the text with the correct words and phrases from the box.

applying • do some research • preparation • qualities • took a course • very good with • weaknesses • you're interested

Whether an interview is done over the telephone, in a video call or in person: the key to success is ___[1]. It is important to think about what questions the interviewer may ask and how you're going to answer. That's why you should ___[2] into the company by checking out their website. Write down questions you want to ask about the company or the job you're ___[3] for. This shows ___[4] and have done your 'home-work'. Questions about strengths and ___[5] are very popular. When asked about weaknesses, you should mention skills or ___[6] that are not absolutely necessary for the job. If you apply for a job in a kindergarten, then you could say "I'm not ___[7] technology and computers". After that, you should say what you have done to improve: "Last summer I ___[8] to improve my skills in office software."

---

5 Comparing jobs

> *Comparison of adjectives and adverbs, p. 231*

Complete the sentences using the words in brackets to form the correct comparative phrase.

1 The support we get in our job is much ___ it was in the past. (good, than)
2 I think a healthy work-life balance is ___ working with nice colleagues. (important, as … as)
3 Our case loads are extreme, but not much ___ those of other social workers. (extreme, than)
4 Quality standards today are not ___ 20 years ago. (high, as … as)
5 Working in social care is a lot ___ doing an office job. (difficult, than)
6 Most people don't work ___ we do every day. (long, as … as)

---

6 Writing a cover letter

Complete the extract from a cover letter with the phrases from the box.

a certificate • advertised • doing a work placement • attach • I am currently studying • I studied • I look forward to • qualified

I refer to the offer of a work placement as a Trainee Nursery Nurse ___[1] on your website.
___[2] Social and Health Care at Dortmund Vocational College. Part of my course involves ___[3].
As I hope to work in childcare after I have ___[4], a work placement at your nursery would be ideal for me.
___[5] English for six years at school and did a first-aid course with ABC Insurance through my swimming club. I received ___[6] showing details of the course. A copy is available on request.
I ___[7] a copy of my CV.
I believe I can add value to your nursery. ___[8] hearing from you soon.

1 PROJECTS

Choose one of the following two projects.

1 Creating a job advert

You are going to write a job advertisement. Work with a partner to complete the steps below.

Step 1 You and your partner work for a local organization which offers work placements to social and health care students. Write an advertisement in English for the organization's website. Include the following points:

- the name of your organization
- details of the work placement (number of weeks, what the student will have to do, etc.)
- how to apply (post, email, website, etc.)
- a request for a CV

Step 2 Proofread your advertisement. Then show it to the class.

Job advertisements

• The candidate will be responsible for …-ing … • The job responsibilities (also) include …-ing …	dealing with disabled children. arranging appointments with doctors and hospitals.		
• As a part of his/her job, the candidate will … • In this role, he/she will also be expected to … • One of the duties is to …	talk to carers on the phone. deal with questions about our services. observe local professionals at work.		
• The job requires … • The candidate should have …	strong good excellent	communication people language	skills.

2 Making a video cover letter

Create your own video cover letter by following the steps.

Step 1 Read the following tips on making a video cover letter.

How long?
As a general rule, your video should be between 1 and 3 minutes long.

Appearance
Dress in the same way you would for a face-to-face interview. Think of the job you are applying for and wear clothes that are appropriate for this role.

How to grab your viewer's attention
You want to get your viewer interested in what you are going to say – don't forget you only have a few seconds to do that. Introduce yourself and tell them why you are the best person for the job. At the end of your little talk, say something positive and thank the viewer for their time.

How to speak
Never read from a script while you are speaking. The viewer will notice that you are looking away to read your notes.

Body language
Maintain eye contact with the camera, look friendly, stand or sit in a relaxed position and do not move your hands or arms too much.

What to avoid
Don't film in an untidy or unclean room. Make sure that there is no background noise or people or pets entering the room behind you.

Step 2 Make notes about what you want to say, then practise saying it a few times.

Step 3 Use your phone to film your cover letter.

Step 4 Work in groups of three or four.
Show your video cover letter to your group.
Ask for feedback.

Step 5 Give constructive feedback and discuss what is good and what could be improved.

Giving feedback

- What I like about your cover letter is …
- I think you could perhaps work on your body language / …
- I think you did a great job. The only think I would suggest changing is …
- In my opinion, your cover letter was a bit short/long.

CHECKING PROGRESS

Browse through the previous pages in this topic, looking at headings and pictures. What have you learned? What can you do, now that you have learned these things?

- ✓ I can read and understand job advertisements. (Section A)
- ✓ I can talk about caring professions around the world. (Section A)
- ✓ I can complete the paperwork needed for a job application. (Section B)
- ✓ I can take part in a simulated job interview. (Section C)
- ✓ I can write a job advert. (Project)
- ✓ I can create a video cover letter. (Project)

Write down two more statements yourself.

Getting a job: from advert to interview

You are looking for a work placement abroad to gain experience in an international care job and to practise your English skills. You decide to apply for one of the jobs advertised in this topic (see pages 8–9) or one that you have found on the internet.

---

1 Write your job application

Step 1 Before you write your application, think about:

1 The job advert

- What are the job activities and duties described?
- What skills and personal qualities are expected?
- What benefits does the company offer?
- Does the company provide any career development opportunities?
- How do you apply? (e.g. by email, letter, application form, on a website)

2 The CV and cover letter

- structure, layout, length
- polite, professional, formal language
- what details you want to provide (education, work experience, etc.)
- if the requirements in the job advert and your application match

Step 2 Think of the vocabulary and phrases you need. Find exercises in this topic to help you with your task. List vocabulary and phrases that you find useful.

Step 3 Write your CV and cover letter.

Step 4 With a partner, check spelling and grammar.

More useful phrases for a cover letter

- I am writing in response to your job listing in …
- I am particularly interested in this job because …
- I am training to be a/an …
- I am very good at …
- My strengths are …
- I would have no problem working/speaking/…
- My experience working as a/an … has taught me …
- During my time as a/an …, I improved/furthered/extended my …

2 Plan and practise your job interview

> Job interviews, p. 208

Step 1 First think about:

Planning your interview

- What kind of interview will it be, e.g. in person, by video or telephone?
- Where will it take place, e.g. at a company or remotely?
- If it is a remote interview, do you have the necessary technical equipment?
- Who will be your interviewer?
- What are you going to wear?
- How are you going to deal with nervousness?

The interview

- What questions could be asked?
- How will you answer the questions?
- Have you practised talking about your strengths and weaknesses?

Step 2 Think of the vocabulary and phrases you might need. Find exercises in this topic to help you with your task. Make notes on tips, vocabulary and phrases that you find useful.

Step 3 Practise your interview with a partner.

Step 4 Work in groups to say how the interview went.

- Did the candidate handle the questions confidently?
- Could he or she communicate effectively (vocabulary, grammar, sentence flow)?
- What about body language?
- How could the candidate improve his/her interview techniques?

A Working in caring professions
- Different fields of care
- Two care organizations
- Introducing yourself

B Reaching out to people in trouble
- Working with the homeless
- Programmes and strategies
- Presenting facts and figures

2 In the workplace

A Look at the overview above and say which of the topics interests you most. Explain why. In which of these areas can you expect to learn the most for your future work?

B Do you know of or have you worked in organizations that provide support to people in need? What kind of organizations are they (for example, non-profit, church, social, health, etc.)?

C Answer these questions. If you don't know, discuss with a partner and take a guess.

1 How many people do you think have a severe disability in Germany?
a 2.5 million b 5.7 million c 7.9 million

2 How many people with severe disabilities are integrated into the labour market?
a 34% b 57% c 63%

Compare and discuss your answers in class.

D Talk about your experiences with people with special needs in or outside the context of work. What challenges do those people face? What kind of help do they need?

C Working with people with special needs

- Inclusion
- Equal employment opportunities
- Attending a work event

D Projects

- Presenting facts and figures
- Creating an inclusive concept

WHAT'S TO COME

Scenario: You are doing a work placement with Outreach Centre, a large organization in Cardiff, Wales. Outreach provides support for care professionals as well as services for different groups in the community: young people from difficult family backgrounds, people with drug problems, homeless teenagers and people with disabilities.
Abby Boyle, who runs the organization, has asked you and a group of colleagues to organize a fundraising event. The purpose is to promote the work of your organization, to get media attention and to attract more funding from private sponsors. Abby has suggested a team competition to develop an attractive programme for the event.

But first: You need to learn about the different services that Outreach provides.

- You start by getting to know different fields of care and two care organizations. You attend a workshop where you introduce yourself and your workplace. (Section A)
- You then learn about working with homeless people. You also work with statistics on people with drug problems. (Section B)
- After that you focus on the rights and concerns of people with disabilities. (Section C)
- Finally, you attend an open day during a visit to a partner organization in Germany. (Section C)

You're ready to create the perfect fundraising event for Outreach Centre!

Different fields of care

You have begun your work placement at Outreach Centre, where you work in different areas of care. There you meet several caring professionals and find out what they do and what they like about their jobs.

1 Speaking: caring professionals at work

> Job titles, p. 204

A Look at this extract from a job advert in a magazine for carers and choose the best heading.

a Ready to work hard? Become a carer!
b Motivated? Committed? We need YOU!
c Carers in demand
d Social support services

In the UK today, around 2.5 million people receive social care. This care ranges from children's services to support for teens and adults of all ages. With people working harder and living longer, the demands on our social support services are immense. That's why we continually need highly motivated and committed carers to provide support to the people who need it most. Could one of these carers be you?

B Which caring professionals from the box below work with adults, which work with children, and which with both? Draw a table with three columns and sort the jobs into the right categories.

child welfare worker • community support worker • day care centre assistant • geriatric carer • midwife • nurse • nursery nurse / nursery (school) teacher • occupational therapist • paediatric assistant • physiotherapist • psychiatric assistant • social administrator • social worker • telephone counsellor

C Who does what? Match the caring professionals to the tasks they might do.

1 support people with mental problems
2 help people live in their community
3 help people do everyday things
4 manage a team of care workers
5 work with young children
6 assist the elderly with day-to-day needs
7 help people with mobility problems
8 help pregnant women and mothers with newborns

Talking about what people do

- We use the simple present to describe what someone does regularly.
  *Midwives **work** with pregnant women.*
  *A nursery nurse **works** with children.*
- *He, she, it* – das „*s*" muss mit!

> *Simple present, p. 219*

I think a geriatric carer assists the elderly.

I agree. He or she also works with people and helps them do everyday things.

2 Listening: three caring professionals

> *Mit Hörverstehensaufgaben umgehen, S. 144*

The Social Pulse team talks to people from all sectors of the caring professions and brings you information, opinions and tips that will be useful for you at work. In this week's podcast, Fran and Mark interview three carers: Adya, Bill and Cass. Our first question: "Why did you decide to work as a carer?"

5 **A** Listen to the interviews and note down at least one interesting thing about each speaker.

5 **B** Collect the information on the board and reconstruct the carers' stories. Listen again and check.

C Which of the speakers says the following personal qualities are necessary for their work? Make a list of other qualities that carers need.

1 being able to stick to decisions
2 being easy-going
3 being pragmatic
4 being sensitive
5 being strict
6 having patience

D Work with a partner. Can you remember the questions that Fran and Mark asked? Write down three more questions you would like to ask the carers.

Asking for information

- Question words (*who / what / where*, etc.) come at the start of the question.

Where *are you from? – I'm from Birmingham.*

- We use *do / does* to ask questions and give short answers in the simple present and *did* in the simple past.

Do *carers* ***work*** *long hours? – Some* ***do****, but some* ***don't****.*
Did *you* ***go*** *to college full-time? – No, I* ***didn't****.*

- For negative statements we use *don't / doesn't* or *didn't*.

> *Simple present, p. 219; Simple past, p. 220*

3 Interaction: introductions

A Talk to a partner. Ask what he/she hopes to do and where he/she would like to work. Discuss which personal qualities will help your partner at work.

B Introduce your partner to the class.

Introducing people

- I would like to introduce … / This is …
- He/She decided to be a carer because …
- He/She hopes to work as a/an …
- He/She would like to work with …

> *Introductions, p. 230*

Two care organizations

It's a new week at Outreach and the senior social worker, Radha, introduces you to two care organizations that Outreach works with. You talk about their visions, goals and services.

1 Reading: caring organizations

> Schwierige Texte lesen, S. 154

A First, look at the web pages and study the headings and photos. Work with a partner and predict what you will learn from the pages. Make notes.

B Now skim the texts (= read them quickly). Which points on your list have been covered?

a http://www.talkitover2.nex

TALK IT OVER

We are a charity providing relationship support to couples and families.
Our vision is a future in which healthy relationships are the basis of a thriving society. Our highly skilled counsellors support clients at times of crisis and help them make decisions about their relationships. This support has an impact on people's ability to work or go to school, to maintain a stable home life and to get involved in their community.

Our mission is to:
- help couples, families and individuals to make relationships work better.

Our organization was founded in Edinburgh in 1962 when its aim was to help married couples with relationship problems. Today, we help people in all kinds of relationships. We have over 50 centres all over the UK and a network of trained counsellors working face-to-face as well as by phone and online.

b http://www.elderlycare.nex

Culturally sensitive support in a caring community.

MULTICULTURAL ELDERLY CARE, Birmingham

We are a non-profit organization offering advice and assistance to the elderly. We provide activities in our day care centre, as well as home support or home help services, and undertake crisis management for clients who are isolated or ill.

Our aims are to:
- establish culturally appropriate care services for elderly people from Birmingham's black and minority ethnic communities.
- respond to needs for personal care, domestic care, carer support and crisis care.

Our centre was set up in 1994 to help the many ethnic families who have problems dealing with bureaucracy. Our day care facilities are aimed particularly at those from the black and minority ethnic (BME) communities. We train our hand-picked team to respond to the needs of BME elders. We also aim to recruit and train more people from BME communities as home carers.

C Do the tasks below using your own words as much as possible. > *Umgang mit Operatoren, S. 158*

1 Describe the target group each of the organizations is aimed at.
2 Explain the purpose or goal of each organization.
3 Outline the services each organization offers.
4 Find evidence to show that each organization offers a competent and professional service.

D Find words or phrases on the web pages (a and b) to describe the following:

1 a an organization which is funded by gifts of money given by private individuals
  b an organization which does not earn any money
2 a people who know how to give advice
  b employees who have been carefully chosen for the job
3 a people living and working together successfully
  b a group of people that help and respect each other

E Find synonyms for the following words and phrases:

1 effect – to keep – to set up
2 help – goal – to handle

2 Talking about aims, goals and visions

Describe the aims, goals and visions of the two organizations to a friend who would like to apply for a job in the UK.

GUIDANCE *For guidance, turn to file G4 on page 184.*

Both organizations aim to …

The purpose of the first organization is to …

This particular charity was founded in order to …

This organization's/charity's main purpose is to …

3 Writing: a caring organization

At the end of the day, the senior social worker asks you to describe a caring organization you would like to work for. It can be one you already know or one that you research. Write a description that includes information about what your organization does, who it serves and what its purpose and mission is.

GUIDANCE *For guidance, turn to file G5 on page 184.*

Introducing yourself

The Outreach Centre has organized a workshop about helping teenagers in trouble. You are attending the workshop. You introduce yourself and tell the others about your work and organization.

1 Listening: greetings and small talk

Colin Young, senior social worker at Outreach, is greeting some new trainees. When you arrive, two other trainees are already there.

Outreach Centre, Cardiff

Trainee social workers

6 **A** Listen to the conversation and find out the names of the trainees, where they live and how they got to work.

6 **B** Listen again and make a note of the phrases used for greetings, introductions and small talk.

> **Making small talk**
>
> Making small talk is one important way of making a good, friendly impression when you meet someone for the first time. You can talk about the weather, how you got to the meeting and where you live.

C Complete the examples of small talk from the listening text.

1. Do you ___ from ___ here?
2. Did you come here ___?
3. I'm ___ to see you both.
4. So, you had ___ finding us, then?
5. That's a nice ___ to live, isn't it?
6. It's ___ weather for a walk.

2 Role-play: introducing yourself

> Introductions, p. 203

Work in groups of four. Take it in turns to play different members of the Outreach team and introduce yourselves, then make small talk.

Hi, I'm … / my name is … / I'm from …

Nice to meet you.

Nice to meet you too. / You too.

Hello. How are you?

Fine thanks. And you?

3 Reading: my workplace

Fiona was asked to explain more about her job, what she does and the organization she works for. Read her statement, then answer the questions.

I work as a community outreach worker for a local organization. It's a pretty tough job, but I like it a lot. I mostly work in the office but sometimes also outdoors when there is a community event. My responsibilities include planning, organizing and carrying out community outreach programmes and community events.
I also organize workshops, conferences and discussion groups to promote health education.
A lot of my work is administrative, that means paperwork, filing and normal office tasks. I also help the office manager compile and maintain records, reports and statistical information.
A big part of my job is assisting customers at the counter and by phone. We get a lot of questions about education programmes regarding health and healthy lifestyles, so I also prepare and give presentations on assigned topics. (132 words)

A Read Fiona's statement. Match these German words to their English equivalents in the text.

1 *durchführen* carrying out
2 *Büro- oder Schreibtätigkeit* administrative work
3 *Ablage* filing
4 *zusammenstellen*
5 *Unterlagen*
6 *Schalter*

B Discuss what kind of skills Fiona needs for her job.

---

4 Talking about your workplace

After the introductions, Colin asks you to prepare a short talk about your workplace. Introduce yourself, say what you do and describe the organization you work for. Choose one of the options below.

Option 1 If you have done practical training or have work experience, make notes about one of the places where you have worked. Use your notes to describe that workplace.

Option 2 If you have no work experience, imagine you work for one of the places mentioned on these pages. Use information from the web page to describe your place of work. Invent more information where you need to, e.g. *There are 16 carers and three therapists.*

Talking about yourself and your workplace

- My name is …
- I'm a/an *(job title)* at *(name of organization).*
- It's located in …
- I work for … (*e.g. the city council*)
- *(Name of organization)* was set up in … by … to …
- We help/assist/support …
- We have a staff of *(number).*
- I'm responsible for …
- My responsibilities include …

> *Introductions, p. 203*

Remember!

I work **for** the NHS (National Health Service).
NOT: ~~I work by the NHS.~~

Working with the homeless

During the workshop at Outreach, you find out more about the organization's work with homeless people. You summarize a German article for the other participants.

1 Pre-listening: Outreach and their work

Match the English words (1–6) with their German equivalents (a–f).

1 abuse	4 to overcome	a *(eine Straftat) begehen*	d *Opfer*
2 to cope	5 poisoning	b *bewältigen*	e *zurechtkommen*
3 victim	6 to offend	c *Vergiftung*	f *Missbrauch*

2 Listening: Outreach's mission and a personal success story

> *Mit Hörverstehensaufgaben umgehen, S. 144*

Colin gives a short talk about Outreach and introduces a client.

7 **A** Listen to the first part of Colin's talk and take notes to complete the gaps below.

Outreach Centre, Cardiff
- *Typical client problems:* ___ [1]
- *Mission:* ___ [2]
- *Four main activities:* ___ [3]
- *Number of participants in the education programme:* ___ [4]

Success rates – percentage of clients who have made progress in these areas:

mental health: 82.8%
anger management: ___ [5]
self-harm: ___ [6]
alcohol abuse: ___ [7]
drug abuse: ___ [8]
offending: 71.1%

8 **B** Listen to Tony's story, then do the tasks below.

1. Explain the circumstances that led to Tony's homelessness.
2. Explain when and why Tony started to smoke and drink.
3. Describe how Tony was introduced to Outreach. Say what the result was.
4. Describe Tony's situation now.

8 **C** Colin and Tony use the following expressions in their talks. Explain their meaning.

1. to be entitled to sth
2. to get to grips with sth
3. to chuck sb out
4. to vandalize sth
5. to go right off the rails
6. to sleep rough

GUIDANCE *For guidance, turn to file G6 on page 185.*

3

Speaking: telling someone's story

Work with a partner. Use the notes in your files to tell the story of two more Outreach clients. Discuss similarities and differences between all three cases.

Partner A: file 1, page 166 Partner B: file 21, page 174

4

Viewing: Lockers lighten load for Lisbon's homeless

> *Mit Sehverstehensaufgaben umgehen, S. 144*

4

A partner organization in Portugal has just sent a video showing their latest strategy for helping the homeless. Colin, the senior social worker, hopes the video will give Outreach some new ideas for helping homeless teenagers. Watch the video and make notes. Then write a short summary for Colin.

5

Mediation: street kids in Germany

> *Mediation, p. 164*

You have found an interesting article in a German magazine that you want to share with the team. Make notes about the main points in English, then summarize the text.

GUIDANCE *For guidance, turn to file G7 on page 185.*

Straßenkinder

Bei dem Begriff „Straßenkinder" denkt man meist an Entwicklungsländer. Aber auch hierzulande gibt es immer mehr junge Menschen, die ohne festen Wohnsitz sind und sich von Familie, Heim und Schule abgewandt haben. Darunter fallen nicht nur diejenigen, die auf der Straße schlafen, sondern auch temporär in Notschlafstellen, Jugendhilfeeinrichtungen und bei Freunden unterkommen.

Die Gründe dafür sind vielfältig und komplex. Schwerwiegende Probleme im Elternhaus, wie z. B. psychische oder physische häusliche Gewalt, Missbrauch oder Verwahrlosungstendenzen sind die häufigsten Ursachen für die Entscheidung, auf der Straße zu leben. Aber auch Armut, Arbeitslosigkeit oder Suchtproblematik wie Alkoholismus bei den Eltern können eine Rolle spielen.

Auf der Straße zu leben, klingt für viele der Jugendlichen zunächst sehr verlockend, weil oft Zusammenhalt und Anerkennung in den Herkunftsfamilien fehlten. Doch es birgt auch viele Schwierigkeiten und auch gesundheitliche Gefahren. Mangelnde Privatsphäre, eingeschränkte Hygienemöglichkeiten, finanzielle Probleme, dadurch entstehende Kriminalisierung durch Diebstähle, Drogenhandel oder Betteln sowie Haus- und Platzverbote durch Polizeikontrollen sind die häufigsten Probleme, die zum Alltag der wohnungslosen jungen Menschen gehören. Oft suchen jungen Mädchen Unterschlupf bei älteren Bekannten, was zu sexuellen Übergriffen führen kann.

Eine wichtige Herausforderung besteht also darin, den Jugendlichen angemessene Beratungsangebote bereitzustellen und ihnen langfristige sowie verlässliche Hilfen zur Verfügung zu stellen.

Programmes and strategies

You look at some of the strategies that Outreach uses for working with homeless teenagers. You also get an insight into the work schedule at Outreach.

1 Reading: supporting homeless teenagers

> Schwierige Texte lesen, S. 154

A Read the article from Outreach's online newsletter. Copy and complete this chart about the problems and challenges the Outreach team faces and the strategies they are using.

Challenges and problems	Strategies
persuading teenagers to talk	▬

B Trust, respect, dignity: define the three terms in your own words, and say why they are important when working with homeless teens.

9

http://www.outreachcardiff.nex

TRUST, RESPECT, DIGNITY

A new programme and a project for Cardiff's homeless teenagers

The Outreach bus is well known in Cardiff wherever young homeless people have made their shelters.

TRUST

One of our main challenges is persuading homeless teenagers to trust us. Some of the young people we are trying to reach have chosen to live rough because they have had disagreements with their parents. As a result, they are unwilling to talk to us in case we send them back home. Moreover, many of them have had negative experiences with social services, so they are suspicious of us. It takes a lot of persuasion to get people to talk to us and trust us. We gain their trust by making it clear to them that we won't force any help on them if they don't want it.

RESPECT

Once we've made contact, a specific social worker looks after his or her own particular homeless youths. Everyone we talk to has a name and a face for us – we don't just view them as case numbers. By recognizing that our clients are individuals with their own specific problems, needs and hopes for the future, we treat our clients with the respect they deserve.

DIGNITY

One of the biggest challenges for homeless teenagers is retaining their dignity. Thus, one of the purposes of our bus is to give homeless teens a place to meet privately if they want to talk to us. A qualified nurse travels with us when the bus goes out, so anyone with a medical problem can be examined in privacy and given medication if needed. We are also in the process of putting together individual "street kits" of hygiene and medical items that will be distributed to homeless teenagers to help them cope with their circumstances.

Get clean, stay clean

To help homeless teens get healthy and off drugs and alcohol, Outreach works hand-in-hand with medical services and rehabilitation clinics. Unfortunately, many teenagers fall back into old habits once they leave the clinic or rehab and return to the streets. In order to tackle this problem, Outreach is setting up a new programme: "Get clean, stay clean". With this programme, we hope to help those teenagers who have made up their minds to get off drugs to stay off drugs for the rest of their lives.

2 Speaking: talking about current activities and schedules at work

It's Monday morning and there is a lot going on at the Outreach centre. Read the schedule and say what the staff does every Monday, what they are doing now and what they are doing later.

Who?	What?	When?
Mary	speak to case manager	right now
Colin	read case reports	on Monday afternoons
Ahmed	meet with AA group	in the afternoon
Jenny	plan a prison visit	today
Ian	on bus duty	every Friday
The team	a meeting	at 3 p.m.

What is Mary doing at the moment?

Where is Ahmed going this afternoon?

What does Colin do on Monday afternoons?

Talking about current activities and regular schedules

- We use the simple present to talk about things that happen on a regular basis. > *Simple present, p. 219*
  *The therapy session **takes place** on Mondays.*
- We use the present progressive to talk about what is happening now. > *Present progressive, p. 219*
  *What **is** Mary **doing** at the moment?*
- We also use the present progressive to say what you have already arranged to do. > *The future, p. 222*
  *When **is** the AA group **meeting** this week?*

3 Writing: your working schedule

A week later, you are helping with a newsletter update about Outreach's work with homeless teens. Describe some of your work activities and those of your team this week (120 words). Answer the questions – Who? What? When? You can use the information in the box and in **2** or make up your own work activities.

Work activities

- Read case reports
- Put together street kits
- Distribute street kits
- Meet with rehab staff
- Visit clients
- Make phone calls

Presenting facts and figures

Outreach also offers support to people with drug problems. Today you look at statistics about drug-related hospital stays and give a short presentation.

1 Describing a chart: drug-related hospital stays

Mary, a case worker who works with street kids with substance-abuse problems, shows you a bar chart which depicts drug-related hospital admissions in England and Wales in 2020.

A Read the statements and compare them with the information in the chart. Choose the right word or phrase in **bold** that Mary uses to describe the trend shown in the chart.

1 The chart shows us how many people were admitted to hospital for drug-related reasons by **year** • **age**.
2 The **blue** • **green** bar gives us the number of people who were treated for drug-related mental and behavioural disorders.
3 What we can see is that hospital admissions are **highest** • **lowest** for younger people.
4 In the age group **16 to 24** • **25 to 34**, the number then rises to more than 3,000, which is a drastic **decrease** • **increase**.
5 The numbers remain at a **low** • **high** level in the age groups 35 to 44 and 45 to 54.
6 Hospital admissions **decrease** • **rise** to just **under** • **over** 750 for those aged between 65 and 74.

10 **B** Now listen to Mary and check your answers.

C Mary asks you to describe the trends for the blue bar, which shows hospital admissions for drug-related mental and behavioural disorders. In groups of three, use the chart and phrases from **1A** to prepare your description.

Partner A: Analyse and describe the first four age groups from under 16 to age 44.
Partner B: Analyse and describe the last four age groups from age 45 to 75 and over.
Partner C: Look at the complete chart and summarize its main findings.

> *Schaubilder beschreiben und analysieren, S. 152*

Admissions for drug-related mental and behavioural disorders, and for poisoning by drug misuse by age

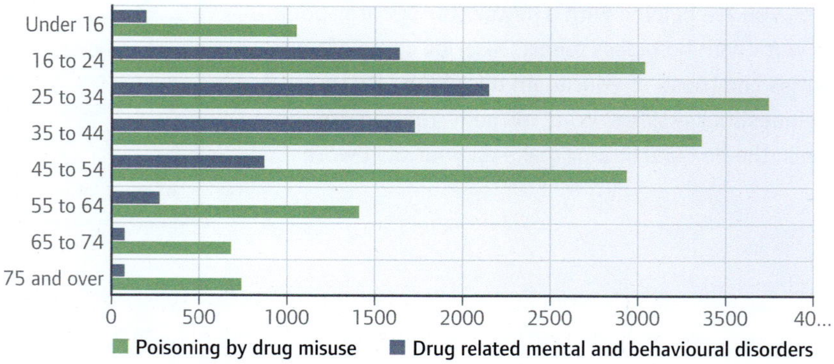

Source: NHS Digital

2 Reading: drug policies across Europe

> Schwierige Texte lesen, S. 154

You want to find out how other EU countries deal with drug problems. You find an article online.

A Read the article. Decide if these statements are true or false. Correct the false statements.

1. Some European countries work together to implement a central drug strategy. ✗ There is no common European drug strategy
2. The Netherlands has a liberal drug policy and drug consumption is legal. ✗
3. In the Dutch model, police mainly focus on hard drugs and drug crime. ✓
4. Portugal has completely changed the way they think about and treat drug addicts. ✓
5. Sweden is not as strict as Portugal when it comes to drugs. ✓

Drug policies across Europe

Open borders in Europe mean that people and goods can move freely. Unfortunately, this is often also true for drugs, so all European countries face drug problems. As there is no common European drug strategy, each country has a different approach to drug policies, ranging from criminalizing the possession and distribution of drugs to decriminalizing them completely. Basically, the question is: how does one regard drug abuse? Is it a criminal offence which must be punished or a public health problem which must be solved?

The Netherlands is known for its coffee shops and its tolerance of the use of soft drugs. That is why many people think soft drugs are legal there, which is not the case! The Dutch policy is to focus on harder substances such as heroin and cocaine and drug-related crime, but using soft drugs is not a criminal offence. This strategy seems to be working well as the level of drug use for both hard and soft drugs is one of the lowest compared with other EU countries.

Portugal had one of the worst drug problems in Europe. In 1999, the health system reported between 60,000 and 100,000 heroin addicts, which is why a new strategy was urgently needed. The central idea of the new 'National Drug Strategy' was to treat drug offenders as patients, not criminals. This required funding for prevention, treatment and support for drug addicts and their families, including education, medical treatment, safe houses, etc. This approach has been a massive success: Portugal now has the lowest number of cannabis and cocaine users compared with the other two countries.

Sweden has one of Europe's most restrictive drug policies. It wants to achieve a drug-free society based on a 'zero-tolerance' approach to drug use. Sweden invests heavily in its drug policy, which includes prevention, drug treatment and strict law enforcement. It has been praised for its hard-line policy internationally. However, so far the Swedish strategy has not solved the drug problem: the use of hard drugs has increased considerably and, in 2016, Sweden reported the second-highest death rate as a result of overdoses. (350 words)

B Rewrite the sentences using relative pronouns and the information in brackets.

1. Europe has open borders. (It means that drugs often move across countries).
2. Addiction is a serious problem. (It can be treated as a health issue or a criminal offence.)
3. In 1999, Portugal registered a very high number of drug addicts. (They took heroin.)
4. Sweden has a zero-tolerance policy. (It aims at a drug-free society.)

Adding extra information

- We often join sentences by putting *who*, *which* or *that* in place of *he, she, it* or *they*.

There are many people ***who/that*** *think soft drugs should be decriminalized.*
Countries ***which/that*** *have a zero-tolerance approach have been praised in the media.*
Portugal introduced a new drug policy, ***which*** *has been very successful.*

> Relative clauses and contact clauses; Defining and non-defining relative clauses, p. 232

3 Debate: the pros and cons of legalizing drugs

> An Diskussionen teilnehmen, S. 148

In two groups, hold a debate on the legalization of drugs. One group is pro-legalization, the other is anti-legalization. Prepare and present your arguments, hold the debate and then decide which group had the better arguments.

Inclusion

Many people with special needs come to Outreach for help, advice and education. This week Outreach is focusing on the rights and concerns of people with disabilities. You attend a number of talks and discussion groups.

1 Reading: rights and opportunities for people with disabilities

A Scan the text. Summarize briefly what it is about.

From the UN Convention on the Rights of Persons with Disabilities, 2006

Article 3 – General principles

- **a** Respect for inherent dignity, individual autonomy including the freedom to make one's own choices, and independence of persons
- **b** Non-discrimination
- **c** Full and effective participation and inclusion in society
- **d** Respect for difference and acceptance of persons with disabilities as part of human diversity and humanity
- **e** Equality of opportunity
- **f** Accessibility
- **g** Equality between men and women
- **h** Respect for the evolving capacities of children with disabilities and respect for the right of children with disabilities to preserve their identities

Work opportunities for disabled people

According to the latest World Report on Disability (WRD), more than 1 billion people in the world have some form of disability. This corresponds to about 15% of the world's population. Globally, between 110–190 million people have very significant physical or mental difficulties. The report states that disabled people of employment age are more likely to be unemployed than non-disabled people. In OECD* countries, the employment rate for people with disabilities (44%) is slightly over half that for people without disabilities (75%).

Despite anti-discrimination laws, many people with disabilities have difficulties finding employment.

**Organization for Economic Cooperation and Development*

B Look at the text again. Describe two important facts from each of the two parts of the text.

C Choose the right meaning (a–c) for these words from the UN Convention.

1	inherent	a *erworben*	b *angeboren*	c *erlernt*
2	diversity	a *Auswahl*	b *Vielfalt*	c *Abwechslung*
3	accessibility	a *Barrierefreiheit*	b *Chancengleichheit*	c *Wahlfreiheit*
4	to evolve	a *weiterbilden*	b *entstehen*	c *sich weiterentwickeln*
5	to preserve	a *erwerben*	b *bewahren*	c *erkennen*

D Discuss in small groups what the principles described by the UN Convention could mean in practice, for example in the workplace. Give examples.

2 Reading: for and against inclusion in school

You would like to work as a paediatric assistant. Inclusion is a topic that interests you, so you look online for more information. You find a forum where people have posted comments.

A Read the posts and say which writers are for and which are against inclusion.

http://www.lets-talk.nex

12

Alan *Liverpool, England*
My son has trisomy 21 (Down's syndrome). He's been at a mainstream school all his life. Now, the secondary school he attends says his development will suffer if he continues in mainstream education. I just can't understand this as he's doing so well. Academic expectations are higher in a mainstream school, and my son has achieved much more as a result.

Barbara *Sydney, Australia*
Sorry. The idea of inclusion is very nice for differently abled children, but what about the able children? There are children with developmental problems in my son's class. He's a very bright child, but is not getting the attention he deserves as his teachers spend far too much time assisting the less able children. I realize that differently abled children have a right to an education, but every time I see them, I think "Why this school?"

Carmen *Madrid, Spain*
I completely agree with Alan's point of view. My daughter, who has cerebral palsy, attends a regular primary school. I believe that inclusion is not only the best thing for children with special needs, it is also good for society. My daughter's school friends are helping her to grow up normally. She goes to their parties and they come to us for parties and sleepovers. It is great for both the abled and people with disabilities to live in a community which adapts to people with special needs.

Don *New York, NY*
I'd like to add something to Barbara's statement. Day after day, we hear there is no money for education. So why is a specialist teacher being brought into our local school? Is it fair to other children that schools are allocating resources to train teachers to look after differently abled children?

Eve *Vancouver, Canada*
As a teacher, I know that many schools include differently abled children very well, but at the school where I work, we do not have the time or the ability to adapt lessons to suit the needs of the differently abled child. Resources are limited, and teachers have not been trained to cater for children with special needs.

(355 words)

B You want to make sure you understand what the people have written, so you look up these words and phrases in a bilingual dictionary. Find the English equivalents in the posts.

1 *Regelschule*
2 *Sekundarschule*
3 *Leistungserwartungen*
4 *Aufmerksamkeit*
5 *Recht auf Bildung*
6 *Grundschule*
7 *Ressourcen zuteilen*
8 *jds Bedürfnissen gerecht werden*

C Read the posts again. Which argument do you find most convincing? Explain your answer.

CHALLENGE! *For a challenge, turn to file C6 on page 197.*

---

3 Writing: inclusion – both sides of the story

> *Eine Stellungnahme schreiben, S. 162*

Use information from these pages to write a comment on the issue of differently abled children in mainstream schools. Include the points of view of all parties concerned.

GUIDANCE *For guidance, turn to file G9 on page 186.*

Equal employment opportunities

Abby Boyle gives you some information about terminology for people with special needs and about employment for less severely impaired clients.

1 Reading: disabilities – definitions

> *Schwierige Texte lesen, S. 154*

A Read the definition and the information on common terms used in the UK that Abby has given you. Talk to a partner about:

- why the principle of equal opportunity is important for people with disabilities.
- why disabled people don't like being referred to as "handicapped".

B Read about disabilities and impairments. Describe what each term means in your own words.

equal opportunity *n.* Absence of discrimination (in the workplace), based on race, age, gender, sexual orientation, national origin, religion, or mental or physical disability.

Which word?

In the UK, the expression "disabled people" is generally preferred to "people with disabilities". The term "disabled people" is widely used by international organizations, such as Disabled Peoples' International (DPI). You will also hear "people with impairments" (e.g. "people with visual impairments"), and most people would rather be referred to as a "disabled person" or a "person with a disability" than as a "handicapped person".

13

DEFINING DISABILITIES AND IMPAIRMENTS

Intellectual disability

This term refers to a group of disorders characterized by a limited mental capacity. Social interaction and activities such as managing money, schedules and routines are often difficult. Intellectual disability originates before the age of 18 and may result from physical causes, such as autism or cerebral palsy. Non-physical causes, like lack of stimulation and lack of responsiveness in adults towards the developing child, might also lead to intellectual disability.

Physical disability

This describes the total inability to use one or more parts of the body completely because of a physical condition, illness, injury, etc. Examples of physical disabilities are motor neuron disease, multiple sclerosis, cerebral palsy, paraplegia, quadriplegia, amputated limbs, total deafness and total blindness.

Physical impairment

Any problem which limits the physical function of limbs or motor ability is a physical impairment. If someone's ability to see, speak or hear has been damaged but not destroyed completely, they are described as having an impairment, e.g. vision impairment (sometimes called "visual impairment"), speech impairment (sometimes called "a speech impediment") or hearing impairment. Mild hearing loss is not always considered a disability.

Invisible disabilities

Several chronic disorders, such as diabetes, asthma, inflammatory bowel disease or epilepsy, are counted as invisible disabilities, as opposed to disabilities which are clearly visible, such as those requiring the use of a wheelchair.

(219 words)

C Find these words and phrases in the texts on page 42.

1 two phrases that mean "the same chances of employment for everyone"
2 two general terms to describe "people who are differently abled"
3 two terms for physical causes that may lead to intellectual disability
4 two phrases that describe non-physical causes which may lead to intellectual disability
5 one phrase that means "a long-lasting condition that is difficult to cure"

D Do the following tasks with a partner.

1 Point out to what extent the chronic conditions mentioned in the texts are disabling.
2 Talk about someone you know with a disability or impairment and the challenges he or she faces.

E With a partner, make a mind map. Collect words from the texts about different types of disabilities and add other words you know. When you have finished, compare your mind map with those of others in your class. Use a bilingual dictionary if you like.

GUIDANCE *For guidance, turn to file G10 on page 186.*

---

2 Listening: assisting disabled people looking for work

> *Mit Hörverstehensaufgaben umgehen, S. 144*

Abby suggests you listen to a podcast with further useful information.

In our podcast today, Mark from the Social Pulse team talks to Angela Rankin about helping disabled people to enter the workplace.

Angela is a Disability Employment Adviser (DEA) who works in a Job Centre.

A In the podcast, Angela talks about a "positive about disabled people" symbol. Before you listen, read the list of topics covered in the interview and decide which part of the interview Angela might talk about it in.

- what a DEA does
- disability-friendly employers
- matching disabilities to jobs
- prejudices against hiring people with disabilities
- a success story

14 **B** Make a table with the list of topics above, then listen to the interview and take notes. Write down anything you find interesting.

C Work with a partner. Pool your notes from **2B** and summarize the interview.

---

3 Presentation: employment opportunities for people with disabilities

> *Präsentieren, S. 146*

For one of the discussion groups, Abby asks you to give a presentation on employment opportunities for disabled people. Use what you have learned in this section (pages 40–43) to prepare and give your presentation.

Attending a work event

Outreach works together with several organizations across Europe. Abby has received an invitation to an open day at a partner organization in Germany. You travel there with her and take a tour of the place.

Open day for professional care workers – 25 October
The Eider Werkstatten GmbH runs sheltered accommodation, workshops and day care facilities for adults with disabilities. Self-esteem, independence and empowerment are our aims for our employees. You can see these aims being put into action at our open day.

1 Reading and mediation: preparing for the visit

> *Mediation, S. 211*

A First, look at the invitation. What do the terms "self-esteem", "independence" and "empowerment" mean? Why do you think these are important aims for adults with disabilities? How do you think the workshop can help the employees achieve these aims?

B Abby gives you a list of questions. Look at the organization's "About us" page below and find the answers.

1 What kind of organization is Eider Werkstätten?
2 Who works there?
3 What sort of jobs do the differently-abled employees do?
4 Why is there such a variety of jobs?

PROFIL

Wer sind wir?
In der Eider Werkstätten GmbH arbeiten Kolleginnen und Kollegen mit und ohne Behinderung zusammen, die sich mit vielfältigen Problemen auseinandersetzen, welche ihre gemeinsame Arbeit aufwirft.

Was wollen wir?
Wir gestalten im Rahmen der Eingliederungshilfe den Alltag von Produktion und die Produktion von Alltag. Der ideologische Gegensatz von individueller Förderung und betrieblicher Produktivität wird durch die Praxis von Kollegialität und Leistung aufgehoben.

Im Arbeitsbereich arbeiten ca. 12 Kolleginnen und Kollegen mit dem Gruppenleiter / der Gruppenleiterin in einer Produktionsgruppe zusammen. Als Werkstatt für Menschen mit Behinderung bieten wir ein breites Angebot an verschiedenen Arbeitsplätzen in unterschiedlichen handwerklichen und industriellen Bereichen an (u. a. Metallbearbeitung, Autopflege, Gartenbau, Montage usw.), um den Interessen, Neigungen und Fähigkeiten aller Mitarbeitenden mit Behinderung gerecht zu werden. Darüber hinaus ist jeder Bereich in Tätigkeiten mit unterschiedlichen Schwierigkeitsgraden gegliedert.

Nicht alle unsere Angestellten stellen neue Produkte her; manche packen lediglich z. B. Süßigkeiten um, deren Verpackung während des Transports beschädigt worden ist, und befüllen neue Tüten mit der richtigen Menge. Dies ermöglicht jeder Kollegin und jedem Kollegen, an dem Arbeitsplatz zu arbeiten, der ihrem bzw. seinem Leistungsvermögen entspricht.

C Abby needs this information for her files. Summarize the text for her in English.
GUIDANCE *For guidance, turn to file G11 on page 186.*

2 Listening: a tour of the workshop

> Mit Hörverstehensaufgaben umgehen, S. 144

You have arrived at the workshop in Germany. The senior supervisor, Jana Dalk, welcomes you and the other visitors at reception and takes you on a tour of the building.

15

A Look at the floor plan and listen to the tour. Take notes on what each room is used for.

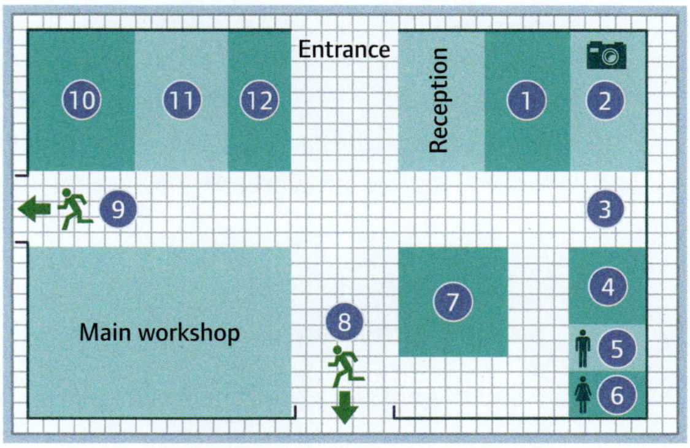

B Work in groups and do the tasks below.

1. Describe how the building has been designed. Explain why.
2. Outline the feeling that one of the visitors describes. Explain what provokes this feeling.
3. Explain what the glass cube is normally used for and how the visitors will use it later.
4. Give an example of how the company encourages empowerment.
5. Describe the kind of work the employees do.

3 Listening: on the job

> Mit Hörverstehensaufgaben umgehen, S. 144

During your visit to the workshop, Olli, an assistant carer and one of the team leaders in the workshop, talks about his work.

16 Listen and make notes on the following points:

1. the room Olli and his team work in and the job they are doing
2. the team's favourite goods
3. Olli's experience with disabled people before he joined the company
4. what Olli likes about the work and his motivation for working there
5. what is important for the employees at the workshop

CHALLENGE! *For a challenge, turn to file C7 on page 198.*

4 Giving an oral report: the Eider Werkstätten GmbH

When you and Abby return to Outreach, she asks you to tell the colleagues there about the workshop to help her decide if she should start one in Cardiff. Describe the workshop using the floor plan. Point out how the employees benefit from the work they do. Say what the Cardiff enterprise can learn from your visit.

GUIDANCE *For guidance, turn to file G12 on page 187.*

Showing someone around

- This is where the employees …
- This area is used for …
- The kitchen is opposite / next to / on the right/left of …
- Over there, in the corner, is the …

> *Showing someone around, p. 204*

1 Saying what people do

> *Simple present, p. 212*

Put the verbs into the simple present. Be careful with questions and negative statements.

1 Ian ___ (work) hard all day at the nursery so he ___ (not go out) in the evenings during the week.
2 Bob and Mary ___ (be) trainee social workers. They ___ (go) to college once a week.
3 ___ (you / get on) well with old people? A geriatric nurse ___ (need) a lot of patience.
4 David ___ (enjoy) his job. He ___ (be) a physiotherapist.
5 Claire ___ (be) a nurse, but she ___ (not work) in a hospital. She ___ (have) a job in a private clinic.
6 ___ (the youth worker / know) what Tommy ___ (do) every evening?

---

2 Asking questions

> *Simple present, p. 219; Simple past, p. 220*

Read the answers that one carer gave in an interview about her job. Use the question words in the box and the words in brackets to formulate the questions that she was asked.

How • What (x2) • Where • Who • Why

1 I like helping people. (become a carer)
2 I work in a residence for the elderly. (work)
3 I serve meals, I make beds and I help the residents get washed and dressed. (do at work)
4 I am patient and I have respect for older people. (personal qualities help at work)
5 I go running and I meditate. (cope with stress at work)
6 My colleagues give me support. (give support)

---

3 Odd one out

Which personal quality does not fit with the others? Say why.

1 friendly • good • sociable
2 gentle • happy • kind
3 balanced • calm • talkative
4 helpful • interested • supportive

---

4 Writing a profile

You did an internship with Beth, an English carer in a residence for the elderly. She asks you to describe her on her Xing page. Use your notes to write a short description of Beth in English.

- *engagierte Altenpflegerin*
- *unkompliziert, aber auch sensibel*
- *verantwortungsbewusst und fleißig*
- *hat Geduld und Respekt gegenüber Senioren*

5 Talking regular schedules, current activities and future arrangements

> *Simple present, p. 219; Present progressive, p. 219; The future, p. 222*

Talk about people at Outreach. Use the prompts below to say what they usually do and what they are (not) doing at the moment. Say what they plan to do later in the day.

1 Colin ___ (run) the AA meeting at the moment.
2 What ___ (the trainees / do) later? – They ___ (sit in) on the drug counselling session.
3 Jennifer and Patsy always ___ (enjoy) basketball training with the girls.
4 Mary ___ (write) a report about the visit to the shelter, so don't bother her.
5 Why ___ (Ian / not take part) in the meeting this afternoon? – He ___ (visit) a client in hospital.
6 Ahmed usually ___ (work) at home one morning a week. He ___ (come) in to the office later.

---

6 Describing an infographic

Choose three points or details in the chart to describe. Write down words you will need to talk about them in English. Then describe them to a partner.

Describing an infographic

- What we can see here is …
- The infographic is about …
- It shows that …% of people with disabilities …
- The number of people who … is …
- Look at the percentage of places which …
- We can see that …
- The quota of people in … is …

Choose one of the following two projects.

1 Presenting facts and figures

You are going to prepare a presentation about homeless people in your area. Work with a partner to complete the steps below.

Before you start, decide how you are going to share the tasks. Will you do all the steps together, or divide the tasks between you?

Step 1 Do internet research to find out about homelessness in your area (or another place of your choice). Find facts explaining homelessness or specific problems related to it, for example who is particularly affected by homelessness. Look for relevant statistics, charts or graphs and decide which one(s) you would like to use in your presentation.

Step 2 Make notes in English about what you would like to say. Refer to pages 34–37 in this topic to help you prepare your talk.

Step 3 Upload your graph(s) and any other visuals onto slides. Make sure the slides support what you want to tell your audience. Remember that your slides should not be too full.

Step 4 Prepare a handout that gives your audience an idea of the topic and the main points of your presentation and includes any visuals (graphs, charts, photos, etc.) that you want to talk about. Don't forget to mention the exact sources of the facts and charts on your handout.

Step 5 Give your presentation. Then answer any questions from the audience. > *Präsentieren, S. 146*

Step 6 After your presentation, ask the other teams for feedback.

Giving a presentation

- Today we'd like to talk about …
- We've divided our presentation into three/ four main parts …
- In the first part of our talk, …
- First, … / Second, …
- Then, … / After that, …
- Finally, …
- Moving on, …
- The next topic we're going to talk about is …
- To sum up, …
- In summary, we think it is clear that …
- Thank you for listening.
- Are there any questions?

> *Presentations, S. 209*

Giving and receiving feedback

- I thought your presentation was clear / well structured / …
- It was very good the way you …
- I liked how you used/said/presented …
- I had a bit of trouble understanding what you meant by …
- Maybe you could have said …
- Another good way to say it might be …
- The way you talked about the graph/chart/ was …

- That's a good point.
- That's true.
- I'll/We'll have to remember that (for our next presentation).
- Thanks, that's very helpful.
- Thank you for your feedback.

2 Creating an inclusive concept

You are going to develop a concept for activities to offer at an after-school care centre for differently abled children.
Work in a team to complete the steps below.

Before you start, decide whether you want to do all the steps together as a team or divide the individual tasks amongst you.

Step 1 Think about your target group. For example: How old are the children who will take part in the activities? What kind of disabilities might they have?

Step 2 Write a mission statement (i.e. a summary of your organization's aims and values). Why are you offering an inclusive programme? How do you want to help your clients and society?

Step 3 Brainstorm ideas for activities you might offer. Make a list.

Step 4 Think carefully about whether the activities are appropriate for your target group. If you are not sure, don't include them.

Writing a mission statement

- As an after-school care centre, we want to …
- We feel it is important to …
- The purpose of this care centre is to …
- Our goal/aim/intention/objective is to …
- It is our responsibility to …
- We will work hard to provide an environment that …
- We will work/strive to help children …

Step 5 Decide on your final list of activities.

Step 6 Discuss how much assistance the clients in your target group will probably need. Decide how many assistants will be needed to keep the after-school programme running smoothly.

Step 7 Present your concept to the class and ask for feedback. (See the language box on page 48.)

CHECKING PROGRESS

Browse through the previous pages in this topic, looking at headings and pictures. What have you learned? What can you do, now that you have learned these things?

- ✓ I can describe a caring organization. (Section A)
- ✓ I can introduce myself and make small talk. (Section B)
- ✓ I can mediate a German article in English. (Section B)
- ✓ I can present facts and figures. (Section B / Project)
- ✓ I can comment on a controversial issue. (Section C)
- ✓ I can understand and use terminology for people with special needs. (Section C)
- ✓ I can create and present a concept. (Project)

Write down two more statements yourself.

Organizing a fundraising event

As part of your work placement, Abby Boyle asks you and some of your colleagues at Outreach Centre to organize a fundraising event to promote the work of the organization and to attract private sponsors. Abby has suggested a team competition for the best ideas. She asks you to work in small teams of three or four and develop an attractive programme for the fundraising event.

Step 1 Divide into groups. Decide how your group is going to complete the tasks. Will you do all the steps together or divide the tasks between you?

Step 2 Think about the following points. Write down your ideas.

What is a fundraising event?

Fundraising is the process of getting financial support for an organization's mission or charitable cause. It is how many non-profit organizations generate money to fund their work. A fundraiser, or fundraising event, is usually more than just an opportunity to raise money for a cause: it brings people together, builds relationships and attracts new donors.

1 Your target group

- Who do you expect to attend your fundraising event?
- What sort of information about your organization and work will interest them?
- What kind of activities will they expect or like?

2 Planning and organizing the event

- Date and time?
- Place and venue?
- When and how will you inform your guests?
- Theme or slogan for the event?
- Food and drinks for your guests?

3 Abby's notes for the organizing team

- *Budget: up to 2,500 pounds OK!*
- *Best time: between 12:00 and 6:00 p.m., 4 hours maximum*
- *Tell sponsors we need money for new rooms and equipment at Outreach*
- *Activities, games, competition/challenge (see ideas on the next page)*
- *We need at least one speech or presentation including main facts/figures about organization + visuals*
- *Create an agenda for the event!*

Making suggestions

- I suggest that we ... (offer some finger food / ...)
- Perhaps we can ... (also order some fruit juice / ...)
- I think it would be wonderful/interesting/... to have ...
- I'm sure our guests would love ...
- Let's make/offer/present/.... What do you think?
- What if we ... (organize a baking competition / ...)?

Responding to suggestions

- Yes, I think that's a great / fantastic idea.
- That sounds good. And then we could ...
- I'm not so sure about that. Maybe it would be better to ...
- We could also ...
- We shouldn't forget ...
- How about if we send/make/offer/...?

Step 3 Organize your ideas and decisions from step 2 on paper (e.g. in a mind map). Use these ideas for the next steps.

Step 4 Advertise your event.

- Decide how you want to advertise your event in the community (e.g. a flyer, a handout or a poster), then create your material. Include essential information about the event (time, place, name/slogan, purpose, activities, etc.). Remember to make your material eye-catching (e.g. nice colours, attractive layout, interesting headings, photos, visuals).
- Write a short invitation that you can post on social media, like the example on the right.

Step 5 Think of useful words and phrases for your task. Which tasks in this topic offer useful vocabulary? Make a list.

Step 6 Decide in your team how you will present your event programme and advertising material to the class. Then give your presentation. You do not need to mention every detail, but your audience must get a good idea of what kind of event you have planned and what the programme is like.

Step 7 Answer questions and invite feedback from the class. Listen to the other teams' programmes and offer constructive feedback.

Step 8 After all the teams have presented their ideas, decide as a class which team offers the best programme for the Outreach Centre fundraising event.

Fundraising event ideas

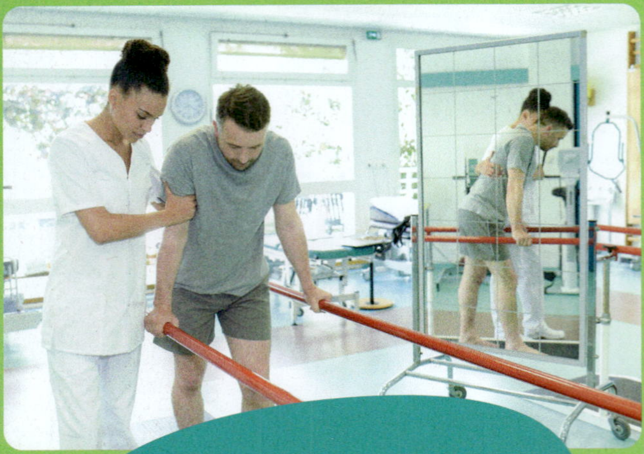

A Care professionals at work

- On the job with two carers
- Planning a day in a care home
- Helping with personal care

B Promoting your services

- Finding the right service
- Promoting with ads and video

3 Services and processes

A Care professionals are needed in many places around the world. After looking at the topics above, what places can you think of where care professionals work? Which of them are you most interested in? Explain why.

B Check how much you already know about care services.

1 How many people do you think needed care services in Germany in 2020?
a 3.5 million b 4.1 million c 5.5 million

2 How many people live in care facilities in Germany?
a 500,000 b 620,200 c over 730,000

What impression do you get from these numbers?

C Discuss how these quotes relate to the care profession and what qualities they refer to.

"If you want others to be happy, practise compassion. If you want to be happy, practise compassion."
— Dalai Lama

"Care is a state in which something does matter; it is the source of human tenderness."
— Rollo May, psychologist

C Giving advice

- Identifying warning signs
- Helpline advice

D Projects

- Designing an ad for your organization
- Writing and acting out a helpline dialogue

WHAT'S TO COME

Scenario: Care professionals are needed all around the world. A group of care professionals has launched an initiative called PEOPLE FOR CARE to promote the field of care and attract more people to the profession. As part of their campaign, they want to produce a promotional film for their website and for the upcoming International Care Fair in Berlin. The film will highlight the many different areas of care work.

The organizers want to involve young people like you who have done work placements in care organizations. They have asked you to share your experiences by working in groups to develop a promotional film segment. These segments will then be combined into one film.

But first: You will assist two care workers from PEOPLE FOR CARE, Jason and Angela, and attend a seminar organized to give more insights into care work.

- Jason documents the work of care professionals as part of an online campaign. (Section A)
- Angela explains scheduling and work processes at a care home for the elderly. (Section A)
- In a seminar, you examine how care organizations can effectively promote their services, and study print ads and promotional videos. (Section B)
- You also learn about the job of a counsellor in the seminar and practise giving advice on a telephone helpline. (Section C)

Ready to shoot?

On the job with two carers

You are assisting Jason, a care professional, at the Outreach Centre. Outreach is looking for qualified care professionals in different areas. Jason manages an online campaign that asks professionals to share insights into their work.

1 Reading: a physiotherapist at work

> *Schwierige Texte lesen, S. 154*

A The organization's online campaign has attracted entries from different professionals. Before you read one of them, match the words (1–8) to their German equivalents (a–h).

1	stroke	5	consultant	a	*Fortschritt*	e	*Wahrnehmung*
2	ward	6	progress	b	*Facharzt/-ärztin*	f	*Behandlung*
3	assessment	7	limb	c	*Gliedmaße*	g	*Schlaganfall*
4	treatment	8	cognition	d	*Krankenstation*	h	*Beurteilung*

B Now read the entry from the campaign's blog page and answer the questions below.

www.outreach-dublin.nex

17

Helen, 29, Lucas Hospital, Dublin

I'm a physiotherapist in a stroke unit. My day usually starts at 7:30 in the morning. After printing off the handover from the ward, I meet with the team at 8:00. As every day, we go through each of our patients and decide who needs to be seen by whom.

We usually do integrated therapy assessments and treatments, which means that the patients will be seen by a physiotherapist and an occupational therapist (OT) at the same time. That way, we make sure the patients get the best possible support. The daily round starts at 9:00. That's when two consultants, a physio or an OT, go around the ward and see the patients. From time to time, a speech therapist is involved as well. Together they check on the patients, see what progress they have made and decide who can leave hospital soon.

Twice a week I join the board round, but not yesterday. I went to see a stroke patient who is new to the ward. After reviewing the notes and checking her CT scan, I tried to get a better idea of the patient's general condition. That normally involves looking at the function of limbs, cognition and the patient's mood, etc.

I always need to think about further treatment options and rehabilitation. Our patients rarely return home straight after leaving hospital. We often refer them to a rehab clinic so that they can carry on with therapy to speed up the recovery process.

After every single patient contact, we have to write notes to keep a record of what we've done. We also note down treatment plans and what we want to do with the patients next time for the MDT – that's the multidisciplinary team.

Lunch is at 12:00, but I rarely manage to have it on time. (307 words)

1 What does Helen do after arriving at work?
2 How does the team make sure patients get good support?
3 What happens at 9:00 a.m.?
4 What did Helen do yesterday?
5 Why do patients often go to a rehabilitation clinic?
6 What does Helen need to record in her notes and why are they important?

C Look at the blog entry again and collect words and expressions that describe how often things happen in Helen's work. Sort them under the following headings:

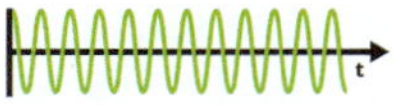
HIGH FREQUENCY (happens frequently/regularly)

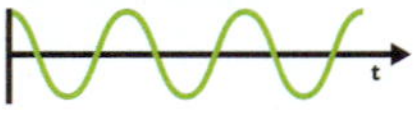
LOW FREQUENCY (doesn't happen frequently/regularly)

Talking about frequency

- We use adverbs of frequency to describe how often activities are done. We put them before the verb.
*I **always** start work at 8:00 a.m.*
- We use longer expressions of frequency at the beginning or end of the sentence.
***Every morning**, I have a team meeting.*
*We discuss treatment plans **once a week**.*

> *Adverbs of frequency, p. 231*

2 Listening: working at a women's refuge

> *Mit Hörverstehensaufgaben umgehen, S. 144*

18

A The campaign's blog page includes audio entries by care professionals. Listen to one carer, Sophia, and answer the questions.

1 What is Sophia's job title?
2 How does she feel about her job?
3 What is the main purpose of Sophia's and her team's work?

B Say whether the sentences about her work are true or false. Correct the false statements.

1 Sophia doesn't usually get home before 8 p.m.
2 When she arrives at the refuge, she never knows what is waiting for her.
3 Her day always starts with a team meeting.
4 Support plans for residents are discussed several times a week.
5 In the late morning, Sophia organizes the transfer of women to new homes.
6 External appointments usually take place in the afternoons.

3 Writing: a job description

A Outreach is preparing online job ads for the jobs in **1** and **2**. First choose one or more adjectives that best describes each job. Share and discuss your answers.

challenging • stressful • exciting • rewarding • attractive • tiring • frustrating • uninteresting

Describing jobs

- As a physiotherapist, you often …
- There is a daily/weekly …
- One of your regular tasks is …
- Your day typically starts with …
- Once a week, …

B Write a short job description for one of the jobs. Include the following points:

- job title or position
- location
- regular tasks and activities and their frequency

Planning a day in a care home

You now get the opportunity to assist Angela, head nurse at Glenville House, a long-term care home. On the first day, Angela explains how the day is structured. Later she asks you to create a schedule of activities for the afternoon.

The future of long-term care

People are getting older and living longer, and with this, the risk of chronic disease and age-related disabilities is rising. Typical age-related medical conditions include diabetes, loss of hearing, sight and movement, as well as cognitive illnesses such as dementia and Alzheimer's. Injuries from falls are also common. As the number of older people grows, the need for long-term care will increase significantly, especially for the over 80s. Their numbers are estimated to grow from 125 million worldwide in 2015 to 434 million in 2050.

---

1 Listening: different types of care services

> *Mit Hörverstehensaufgaben umgehen, S. 144*

Angela is going to describe different care settings and services, some of which play a role in the schedule of activities. Before she starts, she gives you an info sheet.

19

A Look at the info sheet. Then listen and decide on the correct heading (a–e) for each description. Compare your answers with a partner's.

a nursing home
b residential home
c adult day care
d assisted living facility
e home care

Care options for the elderly

1 This type of facility offers help with personal care, such as washing, dressing, going to the toilet and taking medication. It may also offer social activities such as day trips, music sessions or outings.

2 This is an arrangement for people who want to live independently in a safe environment with personal care services.

3 This type of care provides the highest level of care including medical care and assistance from nurses and medical professionals.

4 This type of care includes any professional support services which allow a person to continue living in their own home.

5 This is a programme for people who need supervised professional care during the day. It offers both physical and social activities for adults with health challenges.

B Find the German equivalents for the headings in A.

C Talk in small groups about care facilities and services. List and compare the different kinds of care assistance that you have experienced or know about.

2 Reading and discussion: a residential home schedule

A Angela asks for ideas to include social interaction, physical activities or entertainment in the afternoon schedule. First find the words and phrases in the morning schedule that mean the following:

1 *Wäsche ausgeben*
2 *Medikamente verabreichen*
3 *Bewohner begleiten*
4 *auf der Station bleiben*
5 *Getränke reichen*
6 *Grundpflege durchführen*
7 *Übergabe*
8 *Aufgaben unter der Belegschaft verteilen*

6:30 – 7:00 a.m.	7:00 – 10:00 a.m.	10:00 – 11:30 a.m.	11:30 – 1:00 p.m.
• handover • distribute care tasks among staff	• perform basic body care tasks • administer morning medication **9:30 – 10:00 a.m.** • break for Nurses 1 and 2 • Nurse 3: • remain on the unit • distribute breakfast to residents with service staff	• breakfast break for Nurse 3 (10:00 – 10:30) • help residents go to toilet • distribute laundry (Mon, Wed, Fri) • gymnastics • prepare medicines for noon and late service • serve drinks	**11:30 – 12:30 p.m.** • escort residents to lunch • or distribute and serve food to residents in their rooms **12:30 – 1:00 p.m.** • escort residents to nap time

B In small groups, discuss and plan activities for the rest of the day. Think about 1) social, physical or other activities, 2) time period, 3) tasks for the care staff and 4) things for active residents to do, e.g. outings, music sessions, walks, etc. Make notes. Then share your ideas in class.

GUIDANCE *For guidance, turn to file G13 on page 187.*

3 Writing and role-play: planning activities and tasks

A Using ideas from **2B**, work with a partner and write your own schedule for the care home. Decide what activities and tasks you want to include.

B A relative of a resident calls and would like to know how the afternoons are organized in the care home. Role-play the situation with a partner.
Partner A: You are the caller (file 2, p. 166)
Partner B: Use your schedule and answer A's questions.

Describing schedules

- Between … and …, there is time for …
- During the next … minutes, the main activities are …
- From … to …, the nurses/ residents …
- The time between … and … can be used for activities like …
- … takes place between … and …

Helping with personal care

With two new employees joining the care home, Angela explains the steps in a typical work process and why they are done.

1 Listening: personal hygiene and care homes

> Mit Hörverstehensaufgaben umgehen, S. 144

20

A Angela begins by talking about hygiene. Listen and find out why personal hygiene is important in the context of a care home. Make notes. Compare your answer with a partner's.

20

B Listen again. Then do the tasks.

1 Describe what PADL means.
2 Explain why it can be difficult to help people with their personal care.
3 Outline what Angela says about people's bathing practices.
4 Think of other personal activities elderly people might need help with.

2 Reading and listening: helping people with personal hygiene

21

A Complete the information below using the phrases in the box. Then listen and check.

lead to accidents • make sure the bathroom • getting in and out • prepare the person • helps distract • completely dry • allow the person • be gentle • use a sponge • put a towel

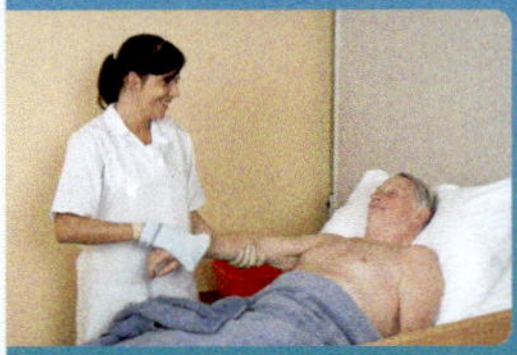

BEFORE
- Get the shampoo, soap, washcloth and towels ready.
- ___[1] is well lit and warm.
- ___[2] for what's about to happen. Say "It's time to have a bath/shower now."
- Tell the person what you are going to do, step by step.
- Make sure the water temperature is comfortable.

DURING
- ___[3] over the person's shoulders or lap.
- Then ___[4] or washcloth to wash under the towel.
- Talk to the person while you wash them. It ___[5] them so they won't get upset.

AFTER
- Make sure the person is ___[6].
- Pat the person's skin with a towel. It will prevent rashes or infections.
- If the person has trouble ___[7] of the bath, do a sponge bath instead.
- Apply skin lotions or creams to avoid dry skin.

MORE TIPS
1 ___[8] to do as much as possible: this helps them feel more in control.
2 Be matter-of-fact about bathing.
3 Play soft music. This may help the patient to relax.
4 ___[9] and respectful.
5 Don't use bath oils as they may cause infections or ___[10] by making the bath slippery.

B Read the information again and do the tasks. > *Umgang mit Operatoren, S. 158*

1 Explain why you should talk to a person while you wash them.
2 Outline what you should do to avoid dry skin.
3 State why it is good for people to do as much as possible on their own.
4 Describe the effect that music may have.
5 Explain why you shouldn't use bath oils.

---

3 Reading and discussion: helping with meals

Angela has posted some information in the staff room about assisting people with meals.

A Read the information and discuss possible reasons for each rule. Make notes.

Talking about possible actions and expected results

- We can use type 1 *if*-sentences to talk about possible actions or situations and the results you can expect from them.

*If you **give** the patients privacy, they **will not be** distracted while eating.* > *If-sentences, p. 228*

Helping with meals

Sometimes people have trouble feeding themselves. This may be the result of an accident or due to a medical condition such as poor vision or dementia. Keep these six basic rules in mind when you help somebody with their meals.

1 Provide a private setting for feeding.
2 Offer food that is suitable for the patient.
3 Allow the patient to feed himself or herself if possible.
4 Make sure the patient wears eyeglasses if required.
5 Place the patient in a comfortable position.
6 Provide wide-grip utensils, a straw, etc.

B Angela is explaining how she helps with meals. Match the sentences with rules 1-6 in **3A** and then complete them.

a … chew and swallow more easily.
b … not feel embarrassed if they spill food.
c … see all the food on the plate.
d … feel better and more in control.
e … easier for the patient and the nurse.
f … easier to hold a cup, knife or fork.

Explaining why you do things in a certain way

- it will make it simpler/easier for them to …
- it allows them to …
- they can … if they need to
- it will prevent/stop/avoid …

---

4 Speaking: describing a work process

Describe a work process from pages 56–57, or one you know, to a partner. Use the phrases in the language box.

Describing steps in a process

- The first thing I do is …
- The next step is to … / After that, I …
- Once I have finished …, I will begin …
- The last step is to …

Finding the right service

You are at a seminar organized by PEOPLE FOR CARE. Lisa Simmons, the organization's advertising expert, and Peter Barlow, the communication adviser, use the example of day care nurseries to talk about how care organizations can promote their services.

1 Brainstorming: a good nursery

A As a class, talk about what is important to know about a day care nursery before choosing one as a parent. Create a mind map or make a list with points that you find important.

B With a partner, rank the points according to their importance. (1 = least important – 5 = very important). Share and discuss your ideas in class.

2 Reading: two day care nurseries

> *Schwierige Texte lesen, S. 154*

A With a partner, scan the web pages and say how they compare with your points from **1A**. Explain if they provide the information you need to make a choice. Which nursery do you prefer? Why?

https://www.littletreehouse.nex

Home | About us | Get involved | News | Contact us

Little Tree House is a day nursery offering outstanding services to children aged 6 weeks to 5 years. We are a small homely nursery. Little Tree House's absolute highlight is our large and wonderful garden.

For over 50 years, we have opened our doors to families who live or work in this area. We offer a wide range of services and provide high-quality child care, which we are very proud of.

Our nursery is child-centred, family-focused and affordable. We have highly experienced and qualified staff.

Open Monday – Friday, 7:00 a.m. – 5:30 p.m.

We are flexible: sessions can be arranged to suit your needs.

The first session is free!

Contact: info@littletreehouse.nex

https://www.kidsspace.nex

Home | About us | Programme | Team | Contact us

Kid Space Day Care

WHERE YOUR CHILD WILL BE HAPPY, SAFE AND WELL CARED FOR

Our nursery, established in 1985, offers an efficient, professional and caring service.

Opening hours are:

- Monday to Friday: 8:00–18:00
- Open all year round apart from bank holidays

Nursery fees are:

- £29.00 all-day session / £17.50 halfday session
- Extra hours on top of half-day session will be charged at £3.85 per hour

Meals are included:

- lunch time: hot main meal and dessert (delicious homemade dishes!)
- tea time: light snack, e.g. cheese or jam sandwiches, etc. and fruit or BYO (bring your own): your child is welcome to bring their own healthy cold packed lunch or tea from home (no chocolate or sweets, please!)

B Read the two offers again. Find adjectives in the texts that mean the following:

1 excellent or very good
2 comfortable and cosy
3 not costing too much
4 having particular skills or training
5 able to adapt to the situation
6 working quickly and in an organized way
7 being kind and supportive
8 having a very nice taste

3 Role-play: services and features

Choose one of the web pages for a role-play.

Partner A: You are a parent who calls the nursery with some questions. Prepare by writing down three or more points you would like to ask about.

Partner B: You work at the day nursery. You answer the caller's questions.

When you have finished, swap roles and follow the steps again with the other web page.

Talking about services and features

- We offer a wide range of services including …
- The nursery provides high quality …
- They offer caring/efficient/professional/affordable/… child care.
- This includes meals / free trial session / …

4 Writing: answering a query

> *Writing emails, p. 202*

Kid Space Day Care has received an email from a parent. Ms Miller is interested in a place for her son and writes with some questions. Write an email informing Ms Miller about your nursery's services. She is particularly interested in: the service quality, the staff, fees and meals.

GUIDANCE *For guidance, turn to file G14 on page 187.*

Promoting with ads and video

In the next part of the seminar, you learn about print adverts and how to choose the best promotional video for your organization. Then you create a concept for a promotional video.

1 Listening: an interview about advertisements

> Mit Hörverstehensaufgaben umgehen, S. 144

Lisa, the advertising expert, is going to share some advice in an interview with Peter.

A Before you listen, match these words from the interview with their correct definition.

1	to promote	a	a scheduled time to try something and see how good it is
2	technique	b	an illustration or a photo as part of an advert
3	message	c	an idea that an organization wants to communicate
4	catchy	d	instantly attractive and memorable
5	artwork	e	a skillful or an efficient way of doing something
6	trial session	f	to help sell a product or service by advertising it

22

B Now listen to the interview and answer the questions.

1 How different are public and commercial advertisements?
2 Why is a catchy headline or slogan important?
3 What does Lisa say about the importance of pictures?
4 What is a 'call to action'?

C Describe an advertisement that you have seen or heard. What made it memorable? How did it use at least one of the features that Lisa describes?

2 Discussion: a print ad

> An Diskussionen teilnehmen, S. 148

A With a partner, look at this print ad from an organization promoting a helpline service. Describe what you see and what the ad is about.

> Bilder und Cartoons beschreiben, S. 150

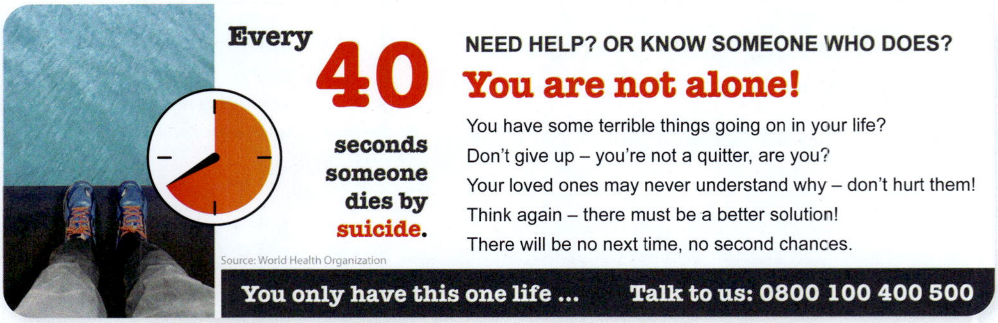

B Look at the ad again. With a partner, discuss the message and how well it works together with the photo. Would the ad work without any photos or graphics? Does it reflect Lisa's advice? Give examples.

C Discuss what other words and/or pictures could help convince people to call a helpline.

3 Reading and discussion: what kind of video?

> Einen Text zusammenfassen, S. 156

Peter is talking about producing a short promotional video for a website. Lisa gives you an info sheet.

23

A Read the text and summarize the main facts about each type of promotional video.

Promotional videos – choose the best type for your purpose!

A promotional or promo video is a short video whose purpose is to promote a company's product or service. In the best case, it tells an interesting story that can educate, inspire or motivate customers. Choose the right type of video for your product and purpose.

Explainer video

As its name suggests, an explainer video explains how something works. According to a recent survey, 91% of customers said they have watched one to learn about a product. It should also show the customer how your product is different from your competitors' or how it stands out from the crowd.

Customer testimonial video

A customer testimonial video shows a happy customer telling the story of how your product helped them solve their problems. This can be very effective as the customer talks highly of your product, which will help convince other prospective customers to buy it too.

Product demo/tour video

A product demo video is different from an explainer video in that it *shows* your product in action and doesn't just *talk* about it. You take the viewer through a particular process step by step, from beginning to end. Of course, it is the same for services.

Product review video

A product review video features a reviewer, often a well-known person, who shows the product in action and says what they think about it. Viewers feel they are getting an honest opinion about the product.

Event video

Companies use event videos to build up excitement before an event, or during the event to show highlights. Later, the videos are often posted on social media for people who could not attend. (287 words)

B If you were going to produce a promotional video, which type would you choose? Explain.

---

4 Viewing: a promotional video

> Mit Sehverstehensaufgaben umgehen, S. 144

5

A Watch this promotional video from a health care service provider and then answer the questions.

1 What kind of services do they offer?
2 What is included in their home care service package? Give three examples.
3 How can they support people who need medical care? Give two examples.
4 Why do they call their work "coordinated care"?
5 How long has the company been around?

B What type of video have they chosen to promote their services? Explain and give examples.

---

5 Writing: a promotional video concept

With a partner, develop a concept for a promotional video for an organization or company. Before you begin, decide what kind of organization and product or service you want to promote.

Identifying warning signs

In the last part of the seminar, Adrian Hunt, a counsellor, explains the work of counsellors and how to recognize warning signs of domestic abuse. You summarize what you learn.

1 Reading: understanding unspoken signs

Adrian gives you a handout describing the unspoken signs of domestic abuse.

A With a partner, read the handout and use sentence parts (a–h) to complete it.

a depressed, anxious or suicidal.
b with their partner to report where they are and what they're doing.
c clothes or accessories which might hide bruises or scars (e.g. wearing sunglasses indoors).
d in public without their partner.
e everything their partner says and does.
f access to money, credit cards or the car.
g work or social occasions, without giving an explanation.
h major personality changes (e.g. an active person becomes passive and withdrawn).

Understanding unspoken signs of abuse

General warning signs

Someone who is being abused could:

- seem anxious to please their partner.
- often check in ___[1]
- go along with ___[2]

Warning signs of physical violence

Someone who is a victim of domestic violence may:

- have frequent injuries, and say they were caused by accidents.
- wear ___[3]
- frequently miss ___[4]

Warning signs of isolation

Someone who is restricted by their abuser might:

- be kept away from family and friends.
- have limited ___[5]
- rarely appear ___[6]

Psychological warning signs

Someone who is being emotionally abused could:

- have very low self-esteem, even if they used to be confident.
- be ___[7]
- exhibit ___[8]

B Use the correct form of the words from the box to say how an abuser behaves. Add your own ideas too.

- Abusers often seem/appear/look …
- When they are alone with their victims, they act …
- When they are with other people, they often behave/react …

Talking about how people look and behave

- We use adjectives to say how something or somebody is, looks, etc.

In front of others, an abuser often appears to be ***normal****.*

- We use adverbs to say how something happens or is done.

Abusers treat their victims ***badly****.*

> *Adjectives and adverbs, p. 230*

aggressive • angry • anxious • bad • calm • confident • excited • friendly • kind • normal • sorry • unhappy

2 Listening: the cycle of violence in domestic abuse

> *Mit Hörverstehensaufgaben umgehen, S. 144*

Adrian is going to talk about the stages in the cycle of violence from the point of view of the abuser. Before he starts, he gives you another handout and asks you to complete it.

Asking for and giving opinions

- I think that .... What about you?
- I don't agree. How do you feel about ...?
- Yes, you're probably right.
- I'm not sure. How about ... instead?

> *Discussions, p. 211*

24 **A** Work with a partner and look at the six slides. Decide on the order in which you think the abuser would do these things. Then listen and check.

24 **B** Work in small groups. Listen to the trainer again and make notes on the points below, then discuss the cycle of violence together, adding your own ideas.

1 the reasons why the abuser feels sorry
2 the usefulness of blaming the victim
3 how physical violence is like taking drugs
4 the purpose of the trap

---

3 Writing and presentation: domestic abuse

Adrian advises you to review what you have learned so far before you present your organization in a video. Write a summary in German of the main points. Then present it to a partner.

GUIDANCE *For guidance, turn to file G15 on page 188.*

Helpline advice

Continuing the theme of counselling in this final part of the seminar, Adrian focuses on the work of a telephone helpline. You learn about active listening skills and how to give advice. Then you role-play a dialogue between a counsellor and a caller.

1 Discussion: making referrals

Adrian begins the session today by explaining the need to respect a caller's anonymity. However, there are times, he says, when a counsellor must make a decision to call in one of the emergency services or suggest that the caller contact another professional.

A Adrian gives you the list below and asks you to sort the situations into categories a or b.

a immediately get help for the caller
b give the caller details of who to contact

The caller
1 is a woman who has been raped.
2 is a young child who says he has been alone for two days.
3 is an alcoholic and says he would like to stop drinking.
4 is a teenager who is the victim of cyberbullying.
5 tells you that she has swallowed a whole bottle of sleeping pills.
6 would like to get off drugs.

B Brainstorm more situations where clients need to be referred to other services. Say what services you would contact or suggest to the caller.

the police • a counsellor • a doctor • youth protection services • his/her therapist • his/her general practitioner

Making referrals

- I would recommend that the person call …
- I'd suggest the client get in touch with …
- I think he/she should call …
- I would contact …

> *Making referrals, p. 214*

2 Listening: a helpline call

> *Mit Hörverstehensaufgaben umgehen, S. 144*

Encouraging clients to talk can help them get in touch with their feelings. The trainer plays a recording which shows how active listening works.

25 **A** Listen to the call and describe the situation. Identify the problem and the suggestion the counsellor makes.

25 **B** Listen again and pay attention to the counsellor's language. Choose guidance or challenge and follow the instructions in your file.

GUIDANCE *For guidance, turn to file G16 on page 188.*

CHALLENGE! *For a challenge, turn to file C8 on page 198.*

3 Reading and mediation: skills for active listening

Adrian is planning to hold a seminar for German trainee counsellors next month and needs some information in German. He asks you to read some information about active listening.

A With a partner, discuss the questions below and make notes. Then read the text and compare your answers.

> *Schwierige Texte lesen, S. 154*

1 What is active listening?
2 How do you listen actively?
3 Why should you listen actively?
4 How can you show a client that you are interested?
5 How will your feedback help the client?

26

Skills for active listening when working with clients

Have you ever told somebody a story and got no reaction? The person you were talking to was present, but you knew that they were not actually listening to you. Not a nice feeling, is it? Now imagine you wanted to talk about a problem and hoped that the listener could help you solve it. What if your problem was a matter of life and death? As counsellors, we are often told about serious issues. We need to listen actively to our clients, whether face-to-face or over the phone.

Active listening

Active listening means giving your full attention to the client and showing that you are listening. If you don't do this, they may think that what they are talking about is uninteresting to you. By using verbal and non-verbal messages you can reassure the client that you are indeed interested. Your "feedback" helps make the client feel more at ease and enables them to communicate more easily, openly and honestly. Active listening is a skill every counsellor has to learn. It can be difficult, but with practice, you will master it.

Tips

- Show you are listening and that you understand by using appropriate words and making sounds like "uh-huh", "mmm, mmm", "yes", "OK".
- Repeat some of the client's words to encourage them to say more.
- Repeat in your own words what the client says.
- Use silence and be patient. Give the client time to explore their thoughts and feelings and to work up to what they want to say. Don't feel you have to jump in with questions or comments every time there are a few seconds of silence.
- Judge when to use questions to help the client to open up and tell you more.
- If you are in a face-to-face situation, use non-threatening, open body language to make the client feel comfortable. Nodding your head will indicate that you are listening.
- Always remain neutral and non-judgemental. Never take sides or offer your personal opinion. Remember, only the client really knows what's best.

(391 words)

B Adrian wants a shorter German version of the text with clear instructions for a seminar. Write a step-by step guideline in German with a headline, an introductory sentence and 8–10 tips.

4 Role-play: helpline calls

> *Mediation, S. 164*

Your trainer ends the session by having you practise active listening techniques using role-plays.

A Work with a partner. Take turns playing the roles of a counsellor and a caller. In the role of the counsellor, use skills for active listening to encourage the caller to talk. **Partner A:** file 4, page 167, **Partner B:** file 22, page 174

B CHALLENGE! Record your version of a successful counselling session and share it with the class.

Active listening

- Tell me about your problem.
- Shall we talk about it?
- I understand.
- Take your time.
- So, you feel as if …?
- If I understand you correctly, …
- Is it true that …?

> *Active listening, p. 211*

3 PRACTICE

1 Talking about frequency

> *Adverbs of frequency, p. 231*

A Rewrite the sentences with the adverb or adverbial phrase in the correct position.

1 We meet to discuss the schedule. (every day)
2 There's someone there when a patient needs help. (always)
3 I take time to talk to my colleagues. (in the morning)
4 She checks the job ads online. (sometimes)
5 The older residents need our attention. (twice a day)
6 I have my lunch in the staff room. (usually)

B Use the prompts to make sentences. You may have to change the form of the verbs.

1 appointments • take place • in the mornings • usually
2 always • my day • start • with checking my email
3 once a week • have lunch • in the restaurant • they
4 I • not • have time • always • for breakfast
5 Tina • from time to time • work late
6 at the end of the day • I • update • always • my colleague

---

2 Solutions to problems

> *If-sentences, p. 228*

Complete the sentences with the correct form of the verbs in brackets.

1 If you ___ bath oil, the shower or bath ___ slippery. (use • become)
2 If the patient ___ to have a bath, then you ___ wash him or her with a sponge. (not want • have to)
3 People who need help with a meal ___ it more if they ___ some privacy. (enjoy • have)
4 If she ___ trouble drinking, then she ___ a straw. (have • prefer)
5 It ___ relaxing if a carer ___ too loudly. (be • not speak)
6 If we ___ our patients to do more things on their own, it ___ them feel more in control. (allow • help)

---

3 Finding the right service

Complete the text with words and expressions from the box.

affordable • family-focused • fantastic garden • highly qualified • opening hours • wide range

Our day nursery offers a ___[1] of services and provides outstanding childcare for children aged 12 weeks to 6 years. We are proud to work with very experienced and ___[2] staff. Our nursery is situated in Mount Pleasant and we have a ___[3] for our kids to play in. We are ___[4] and our fees are ___[5]. We can arrange flexible sessions to suit your individual needs. Our ___[6] are 7:00 a.m. to 7:00 p.m.

4 Completing a report

Complete the report with words and phrases from the box.

abusing • abusive • apologizes • apology • back to normal • cycle of violence • excuse • excuses

Client A is married to a woman who has a son from a previous marriage. Client A has come for counselling as he is ___[1] to his partner. He hits her in the face and on the back of the head. When he has finished ___[2] her, he ___[3] for his behaviour. During counselling, he has admitted that he is afraid that his partner will go to the police.

Not long after the ___[4], Client A starts to make ___[5] for his behaviour. He says that his partner takes her son to visit his father so that she can have an affair with her ex-husband.

Once he has said this, life gets ___[6] for a few weeks but, soon, the ___[7] continues. Client A dreams about hitting his partner again and he thinks up another ___[8] for doing so.

---

5 Using adjectives and adverbs

> *Adjectives and adverbs, p. 230*

Choose the correct word to complete the sentences.

1 The client grew up in a **(violent / violently)** household.
2 His father behaved **(aggressive / aggressively)**.
3 His father was always **(sad / sadly)** after he had been abusive.
4 Counselling is helping him to **(slow / slowly)** understand his behaviour.
5 The client feels **(bad / badly)** about the way he treats his children.
6 He feels that the counselling sessions are doing him **(good / well)**.

---

6 A jumbled helpline call

Put this helpline call between a counsellor (A) and a young caller (B) in the right order.
Start like this: c – h – b …

a **A** Do you know of anything that might have made your mum depressed?
b **A** Have you tried talking to her?
c **A** How can I help you?
d **A** I'm glad that you called. I hope things will get better soon.
e **A** I see, she won't talk to you. Is there anyone in the family your mum could talk to?
f **A** You know, even when people argue with each other, they are sometimes more unhappy when they're apart. What about talking to the family doctor about your mum? There are organizations like marriage guidance where your mum and dad could go for counselling.
g **B** No. There's only me and mum.
h **B** My mother is depressed and I am very worried about her.
i **B** Yes. I'll talk to the doctor. Maybe she can get them to go to marriage guidance. Thank you for your help.
j **B** My dad moved out a few months ago, but I don't think that's the problem. Mum wanted him to leave. She and dad were arguing a lot.
k **B** She won't talk to me. She always tells me she's OK.

Choose one of the following two projects.

1 Designing an advert for your organization

You are going to design an advertisement for your organization or company. Work with a partner to complete the steps below.

Step 1 Decide what kind of organization or company you are working for. What product or service do they offer? What kind of customers do they want to reach?

Step 2 Decide what kind of ad you will make: a print ad for a newspaper or magazine? An internet ad?

Step 3 Read the tips in the info box below.

Step 4 Follow the steps in the AIDA model and make notes on any ideas for your ad. Think about:

- what exactly you want to promote
- artwork
- a slogan
- structure and layout
- other details

Step 5 Briefly discuss your ideas with another pair and ask them for feedback.

Step 6 Revise your concept if necessary.

Step 7 Write a detailed description or make a sketch of your ad.

Step 8 Present your ad to the class.

The AIDA model – how to advertise your products or services successfully

A ATTENTION
Use powerful pictures or words to get the customer's attention immediately – a catchy slogan will help.

I INTEREST
After grabbing the customer's attention, describe your message or offer. Make sure your message or product is relevant to them and present it in a clear and structured form (bullet points, subheadings, etc.).

D DESIRE
Appeal to the customer's desires, emotions and needs. Tell them exactly how they will benefit from your product. Show them how facts, features and benefits are connected. Instead of saying "We offer very good day care solutions for your children", tell them "Your children will be well cared for, safe and happy". Or instead of "We provide care services for the elderly", say something like "Let us take care of your loved ones".

A ACTION
After showing the customer how good your product or service is, tell them what they should do now. Should they visit your website, come to your office or call you? Provide all necessary contact details to make it easy for customers to get in touch.

2 Writing and acting out a helpline dialogue

You are going to write a dialogue for a telephone helpline session, then act it out. After that, you are going to write a report on the call. Work in small groups to complete the steps below.

Step 1 You and your group are trainee counsellors working on a helpline. Think of reasons why someone would call the helpline. Decide together on your scenario and make notes.

Step 2 Put yourselves in the shoes of the caller. How would he or she talk about the problem? Say whole sentences out loud and write them down as they are spoken. Your speech should sound as natural as possible.

Step 3 Think about how a counsellor might respond to what the caller says. Make notes. > *Active listening, p. 211; Giving advice, p. 212*

Step 4 Use the notes to write a dialogue for a telephone helpline conversation.

Step 5 When your script is ready, read it through and listen to how it sounds. Take turns in your group to act out your dialogue. Make any changes or corrections that you feel are needed.

Step 6 Perform your dialogue for your class. When you have finished, get feedback and use it to improve your next dialogue. Listen to the other groups' dialogues and give constructive feedback.

Step 7 As a final step, write a report on the call. > *Describing a case, p. 213*

Giving feedback

Be as positive as you can when you're giving feedback.

- First pick out one good thing in the performance – more if you can.
- Then pick out one important thing that they could do better.

Giving feedback

- I thought you spoke clearly and slowly.
- It was very good the way you …
- I liked the way you …
- It was a good dialogue, but you could have …
- Maybe it would be better to say …
- It might be helpful to the caller if you …

CHECKING PROGRESS

Browse through the previous pages in this topic, looking at headings and pictures. What have you learned? What can you do now that you have learned these things?

- ✓ I can schedule activities for a care home. (Section A)
- ✓ I can answer a query by email. (Section B)
- ✓ I can recognize signs of abuse in families. (Section C)
- ✓ I can use active listening techniques. (Section C)
- ✓ I can make a print ad. (Project)

Write down two more statements yourself.

Creating a promotional video

The care professionals at PEOPLE FOR CARE are producing a promotional video that will highlight the many different areas of care work. They have asked you to work in a small group and to use your work placement experience in care organizations to develop your own video segment. The group segments will later be combined into one film.

Step 1 Before you work on your task, think about the following:

1 Your target group
- Who will watch the video?
- What aspects will they be interested in?
- What age group are you targeting?

2 Content and message
- What field of care, aspect or service do you want to promote?
- What is your message and aim?

3 Planning, concept and script
- How long should your video be?
- Who will appear in the video?
- What type of video is it (see page 63)?

Step 2 Think about the words and phrases you will need. Which tasks in this topic offer helpful vocabulary? Make a list. The language boxes will give you some ideas.

Promoting your product or service
- This … is ideal for people who …
- … is designed for customers who …
- This is the perfect solution for everyone who needs/wants …
- If you're looking for …, … is what you need.
- And what's more, we offer …
- And, on top of that, we offer outstanding/excellent …

Describing and promoting your job
- My day usually starts with …
- This job is about … (supporting people / giving advice / …).
- What is really interesting/exciting in my job is …
- The best part of my job is … because …
- If you're looking for a job in which you can …, this is what you should do.
- What I like/love about this kind of work is …
- My organization offers …, which really helps people …

Step 3 Follow these steps (1–9) to make your video segment.

1 Prepare your equipment
Make sure you have the right equipment for filming and editing (e.g. a camera and editing software). In most cases a mobile phone camera will do the job.

2 Define your message and goal
Decide what message you want to communicate and what exactly you want to achieve with your video.

3 Create a concept
Brainstorm ideas and discuss what kind of video you want to make. Think about structure, tone, style, etc.

4 Write a script

The script includes the text that will be spoken, who is speaking, the location and the tone or mood.

5 Create a storyboard and a shot list

Use a storyboard to sketch and describe how you want each scene to look. Then use a shot list to plan when, where and how you will film each shot.

Shot	Location (exterior/interior, etc.)	What happens?
Shot 1: taken from behind care worker	inside the entrance to the care home	care worker is greeting older woman
Shot 2: seated at a table	inside the care home, at a table	care worker is describing her day

6 Rehearse

Everybody involved in the video should practise their lines and what they do in each scene.

7 Shoot

Lights, camera, action! Stick to your storyboard and follow the schedule in your shot list.

8 Edit

Edit your footage using editing software. Only keep a shot if it adds value to your video – not just because it is nice.

9 Add music and sound

Music and sound effects can help to make your visual message stronger. Use them to support your message but not if you feel they distract the viewer's attention from the message of the video.

Rights and permissions

Before you start filming, it is important to think about rights and permissions.

Permission to shoot a video
Generally, it is OK to film in public places, but in private locations, first get permission from the owner – in writing if possible.

Privacy rights
Before shooting, prepare a model release form and ask each person who will appear on camera to sign it. If the video includes underage people, the parents have to sign the form. The form will protect you against legal problems and allow you to use the video for commercial purposes or personal use.

Music rights
If you want to include music, you can do one of the following things:
- Compose your own music.
- Ask the composer, record company or musician of the music you want to use for permission.
- Use rights-free music, which can be found online.

A A special event in a nursery school

- Enquiring about services
- Making further enquiries

B At the Outdoor Experience Centre

- Helping in the office
- Dealing with an emergency

4 Work-related communication

A Look at the six small illustrations and match them to the means of communication in the box.

business letter • email • landline • smartphone • sticky note • text message

B Add any other means of communication that you can think of.

C Which of these means of communication do you use yourself and how often?
Rank them from 1 (rarely) to 5 (very often).

D What do you think? Match these characteristics to the different means of communication.

correct spelling • easy to use • formal • informal • quick response • slow

C A new hospital catering concept

- Hospital food and catering
- Comparing catering concepts

D Project

- Creating communication guidelines for your organization

WHAT'S TO COME

Scenario: Organizing company events is a normal part of every business organization. To do this, organizers have to communicate with business partners such as service providers and product suppliers. You are working for one of the organizations presented in this topic – Little Rascals Nursery School, The Outdoor Experience Centre or St Mary's Hospital – and have been asked to organize an event.
The first step is to collect event ideas and decide what is appropriate for your organization. Then you need to research these activities and services to find suitable providers. The next step is to make enquiries, choose the best offer and place an order. Lastly, you need to write an email to invite guests to the event.

But first: To help you, you will practise business communication in different settings.

- In Little Rascals Nursery School, you will assess event offers online, write a formal email request for information and practise making telephone enquiries. (Section A)
- In the Outdoor Experience Centre, you will take messages, make and change appointments by phone and use mediation skills to communicate information. You will also write an accident report. (Section B)
- At St Mary's Hospital, you will assess offers for a new catering concept and learn how to write a formal letter. You will also write a report and recommendation. (Section C)

Good luck organizing the event!

Enquiring about services

You work for Little Rascals Nursery School, a bilingual nursery, which is planning a special summer event for its children and their families. You write an email to a company asking for more information about their event packages.

1 Brainstorming: planning a party for children

Discuss which activities would be suitable for a children's event or party.

I think a bouncy castle would be fun.

Yes, and face painting is always a good idea.

2 Reading: an online offer

Your nursery school has asked you to research possible services for the summer event. You have come across this ad on a website. Read it and answer these questions.

1 We don't have a garden, but would like an outdoor party. How can you help us?
2 We have some ideas regarding games at the party. Could we integrate them in your package?
3 We are planning a party for 50 children, but there aren't enough parents to help. Can you support us?

www.kids.entertainment.nex

KIDS ENTERTAINMENT

We are committed to your child's party and offer hassle-free kids party packages, so you can enjoy the party with your family and friends. We plan and manage your party or even search for a suitable venue in your area.
We completely run the whole event from start to finish and take your ideas on board to personalize the experience for you.

Our kids parties are child-centred and are based on interaction and play – and fun! If you want the best kids party in this area, get in touch with our event manager Mike Bott.

mike.bott@kids.entertainment.nex

Our most popular party formats:

Nature treasure hunt: an unforgettable outdoor teamwork experience for your kids!

Mini artist: let your child discover their inner artist!

3 Reading: asking for more information

> Schwierige Texte lesen, S. 154

You ask a colleague for help writing an email and she gives you one she has written recently. Read the email and match the sentences (a–f) to the numbers (1–6) in the email.

a Say what the email is about.
b Ask for information.
c Say where you found the ad.
d Give contact details.
e Say why you are writing.
f End the email in a polite way.

To: info@slidesforkids.nex

From: little.rascals@mail.nex

1 Subject: Enquiry about your outdoor slides Date: 14 March 20xx

Dear Mr Carlson

2 We saw on your company's website that you have children's outdoor slides for hire. We would like to receive more information about your slides and your conditions.

3 We are a nursery school for children up to 6 years of age. In June this year, we will be celebrating our 10th anniversary. We are planning a special programme for our children and their families. This will include a number of games and play activities for the children, so we are especially interested in more details about your inflatable bouncy castle with a water slide.

4 Could you please send us your price list and catalogue?

5 We look forward to your reply.

Best regards

6 Lisa Mann

Little Rascals Nursery School

---

4 Listening: how to write formal emails

> Mit Hörverstehensaufgaben umgehen, S. 144

27

You still feel unsure about writing emails, so you look for more information and find this podcast. Listen and say whether the sentences are true or false. Correct the false statements.

1 The words email and mail have the same meaning.
2 The subject should be as specific as possible.
3 After the salutation, your letter or email always starts with a capital letter.
4 Formal letters and emails are quite different.
5 In formal letters, contractions and short forms should be avoided.
6 An email normally consists of two parts.

---

5 Writing: requesting more information

> Writing emails, p. 202

Write an email to Kids Entertainment asking for more information about their event packages. You should include the following:

- Say who you are.
- Say where you saw the advert.
- Ask them for details of the packages and prices.
- Also ask if they can help with catering for the event.
- Say what you expect them to do.
- Give your contact details.

GUIDANCE *For guidance, turn to file G17 on page 189.*

Making further enquiries

You have received a reply from Kids Entertainment and need more information. You make a follow-up call to ask some questions.

1 Reading: a reply to an enquiry

A Read the reply and find the equivalents of the following words and phrases in the email.

1 *wir freuen uns*
2 *wir hängen auch ... an*
3 *der Preis ist*
4 *können zwischen ... und ... wählen*
5 *dieses Paket kostet*
6 *für Ihr Interesse an*
7 *zögern Sie nicht, uns anzurufen*
8 *wir freuen uns darauf, von Ihnen zu hören*

CHALLENGE *For a challenge, turn to file C9 on page 198.*

B Read the email again. Answer these questions and compare your answers with a partner.

1 What exactly is the Nature Treasure Hunt?
2 What is included in the Mini Artist package?

C Discuss the offer and any open questions before you decide whether to accept.

To: little.rascals@mail.nex
From: mike.bott@kids.entertainment.nex
Subject: Your enquiry about our kids event packages
Date: 21 January 20xx

Dear ...

Thank you for your interest in our kids party packages.

We are pleased to give you more details about our two most popular formats. We also attach our current price list and latest catalogue.

In our Nature Treasure Hunt, the kids go on a special adventure through woodlands with the help of a treasure map, while they fill their own treasure bag as they go.

This package costs €55.00 per child and includes the treasures (bracelets, bouncy balls, small toys) as well as transport, soft drinks, maps, a snack and an experienced guide.

Our Mini Artist package offers a range of activities that encourage your kids to be creative. The rate is €21.00 per child if you arrange a venue for the event yourself.

Please feel free to call me if you have any further questions or ideas you would like to suggest. I am sure we can create an unforgettable experience for your children and their families!

We look forward to hearing from you.

Best regards

Mike Bott
Event Manager

2 Listening: A follow-up call

> *Mit Hörverstehensaufgaben umgehen, S. 144*

You discuss the email with your colleague Lisa, who then phones Mike with some follow-up questions.

28

A Listen to the call and answer the questions.

1 Which party or entertainment package is the nursery school interested in?
2 How long is the standard programme?
3 How many activities does it include? Name at least two.
4 Who will help the kids with the games and activities?
5 What about weekend rates?
6 What will happen next?

B Match the sentence beginnings (1–8) to the endings (a–h). Then listen again and check.

1	I'm calling about the email	a	I help you?
2	Great to hear from you, Ms Mann. How can	b	have the party on a Saturday or a Sunday?
3	Would it be OK to	c	how long the programme would be?
4	Could you tell me	d	like us to find one for you?
5	And could you tell me know what kind of	e	you sent us.
6	And would it be more expensive to	f	activities are included in the standard package?
7	Well, yes, I'm afraid the rates	g	would be a little higher in that case.
8	Will you organize the venue or would you	h	talk about those points now?

3 Reading and discussion: polite communication

A You want to prepare for a phone call by learning more about work-related communication. With a partner, read the tips and compare how you would say this in German. Discuss any similarities or differences between German and English regarding politeness or directness.

Polite communication – What you need to know!

1 Indirect questions Indirect questions are often used in work-related communication to make them more polite.	
less polite: *How much does it cost?*	more polite: *Could you tell me how much it costs?*
2 Modal verbs Words like *can, could, will, may* and *might* make a big difference in the tone.	
less polite: *Explain the problem to me in more detail.*	more polite: *Could you explain the problem to me in more detail, please?*
3 Giving bad news Always use *I'm afraid* … when you have bad news or something negative to say.	
less polite: *We don't offer that service.*	more polite: *I'm afraid we don't offer that service.*
4 Polite key words Always use *please, thank you* and *sorry* in polite communication.	

B With a partner, look at the sentences and questions. Use the tips above to rewrite them as politely as possible. Compare with another pair and discuss the level of politeness.

1 How much is the party package?
2 It's more expensive at weekends.
3 I want to ask a question.
4 Call me again tomorrow.
5 I need more information about the offer.
6 What do you want?

4 Role-play: asking and answering questions politely

Partner A works for Little Rascals Nursery School and Partner B for Catering Plus, which offers catering packages. Use the role cards to prepare and act out a telephone call. Then swap roles.

Partner A: file 5, page 167 Partner B: file 38, page 181

Helping in the office

You are interested in doing volunteer work for an international organization. After looking around, you find an organization that also gives you the opportunity to work in the office and gain experience in business communication.

1 Reading: the Outdoor Experience Centre

> Schwierige Texte lesen, S. 154

A Skim the text and answer the following questions.

1 Where is the organization located?
2 What three areas does the organization focus on?
3 Where do the volunteers work?

Theme 1 **Youth leisure**
Theme 2 **Education through sport and outdoor activities**
Inclusion **Cultural differences, economic difficulties, geographical difficulties**

Our volunteers have the opportunity to learn many different things with us. You will be actively involved in duties in our office and in our Outdoor Experience Centre.

1 In the office. Here, you will assist staff in preparing and organizing international projects. Office work includes working on the website, taking telephone calls, working with Word and Excel, making flyers and posters and mailing them to international participants, as well as writing grant proposals. You will also participate in the weekly staff meeting.

Duties include:
- assisting the centre manager with administrative duties.
- working in the medical room.
- preparing and cleaning equipment.

2 In the Outdoor Experience Centre. Here, you will assist our instructors in activities like mountain biking, hiking, white-water rafting and cross-country skiing.
While working as a volunteer, you will learn various outdoor skills, as well as techniques for effective facilitating and debriefing. You will attend local staff training sessions and have the chance to attain the qualifications you need in order to become an accredited instructor. The accreditation is recognized on an international level.

(179 words)

B Find words and expressions in the text which match the German words below.

1 *Freizeit*
2 *Erlebnispädagogik*
3 *Zuschussanträge*
4 *Verwaltungsaufgaben*
5 *Outdoor-Fähigkeiten*
6 *anerkannt*
7 *Moderation*
8 *Nachbesprechung*

C Now read the text again and do these tasks.

1 List the volunteers' duties while working in the office.
2 Describe what goes on in the Outdoor Experience Centre and explain what the volunteers do.
3 Discuss how working at this site might help the volunteers later in life.

2 Listening: taking a message

> *Mit Hörverstehensaufgaben umgehen, S. 144*

You are working as a volunteer in the office of the Outdoor Experience Centre alongside Kate Flynn, the office manager. She receives a phone call from the head of a Finnish vocational school, who would like some information.

29 **A** Listen to the phone call and make a note of:

1 the caller's name.
2 the name of the person he should speak to.
3 the caller's phone number.
4 details of what he would like to know.

29 **B** Listen again and make a note of what Kate says to:

1 indicate how she will deal with the caller's request.
2 ask for the caller's name.
3 check the caller's name.
4 indicate that the caller should wait.
5 confirm that the caller is still on the line.
6 explain that someone is not available.
7 make a suggestion.
8 ask for contact details.
9 confirm details.
10 close the call.

GUIDANCE *For guidance, turn to file G18 on page 189.*

---

3 Making and changing appointments

A The following verbs can all be used with *appointments* or *meetings*. Copy the table and match the words under the following headings.

(neu) vereinbaren	verschieben	vorverlegen	absagen
___	___	___	___

1 postpone
2 cancel
3 reschedule
4 arrange
5 bring forward
6 call off
7 fix
8 put off

B Complete each sentence with a verb from **A**. Sometimes more than one verb is possible.

1 I'm afraid something urgent has come up. We'll have to ___ tomorrow's meeting.
2 Can we ___ an appointment to talk about the job offer in more detail?
3 I'm afraid the meeting on August 3rd won't work for me. Can we perhaps ___ it ___ to August 1st or 2nd?

---

4 Role-play: making and changing appointments

Work with a partner and take and make some calls.
Partner A: file 7, page 168
Partner B: file 26, page 176

Changing appointments

- I'm afraid I've had to change my plans.
- I'm going to have to cancel the appointment.
- How about Friday afternoon instead?
- Would that suit / be convenient for you?

> *Telephoning, p. 205*

Dealing with an emergency

The Outdoor Experience Centre is planning to host an outdoor first aid workshop. Unfortunately, there is an accident. You write a report of the accident.

1 Packing a first-aid kit

Emil, the medical officer in charge, asks you to pack a first-aid kit for an outing. With a partner, sort the items on the right under the following headings: wound care, medication and extras.

adhesive tape • antibiotic ointment • antihistamine • aspirin • bandages • emergency shock blanket • iodine • roll of gauze • safety pins • scissors • tweezers

2 Listening and discussion: being prepared

> Mit Hörverstehensaufgaben umgehen, S. 144

Emil notices that some items are missing from the kit and explains why they must be included.

A Before you listen, think about what the items below are used for. Match the sentence halves.

1 Paracetamol
2 An EpiPen® needle
3 Hydrocortisone cream
4 Latex gloves
5 A SAM splint

a relieves the symptoms of bites, stings and rashes.
b can save the life of someone having an allergic reaction.
c helps stabilize breaks and sprains.
d relieves pain and reduces fever.
e prevent wound infection.

30

B Listen to Emil describing the items and check your answers. Explain why the items are important.

3 Mediation: first aid workshop for outdoor activities

> Mediation, S. 164

Kate Flynn has received requests for a first-aid training as part of the outdoor experience. You find a suitable offer on a German website.

A Work with a partner. Read the offer and discuss or look up any words you do not understand.

B Discuss which details you think are important. Make notes.

C Take turns telling Kate about the offer.

ERSTE-HILFE-KURS FÜR OUTDOOR-FANS

Sie verbringen gerne Ihre Freizeit in der Natur? Das ist gesund und macht natürlich Spaß, aber was ist, wenn dabei etwas passiert?

Was tun, wenn …
- … die Rettungswege weit sind?
- … es sehr heiß, sehr kalt oder sehr nass ist?
- … kein Verbandsmaterial vorhanden ist?

In unserem Kurs lernen Sie, mit schwierigen Szenarien umzugehen und mit einfachen Mitteln Erste Hilfe zu leisten. In Rollenspielen sind Sie selbst Teamführer/-in, Helfer/-in oder Verletzte/-r.

Unser Lehrgang umfasst:
+ **Unfälle** im Wald, beim Wandern, Klettern, Fahrradfahren usw.
+ **Erste Hilfe** im Outdoor-Bereich, Notfallsets speziell für draußen
+ **Beurteilung** des Gesundheitszustands
+ **Herz-Kreislauf-Stillstand**
+ **Wunden** und Verbände, stark blutende Wunden
+ **Unterkühlung/Erfrierung, Hitzeschäden**
+ **Kopfverletzungen/Helmabnahme**

Der Lehrgang dauert 6 Stunden und kostet € 45 pro Person. Bitte tragen Sie feste Schuhe und bringen Sie wetterfeste Kleidung und eigene Verpflegung mit.

4 Role-play: emergency!

At the end of the day, you and a supervisor accompany a group from the Finnish vocational school on a cross-country skiing tour. One student, Virpi Hakala, hits a rock and injures her leg. You help your supervisor administer first aid and make Virpi comfortable while you wait for an ambulance.
Work in groups of four. Do all of the tasks together and take turns playing the different roles.

A At the hospital, the admissions nurse asks what happened and what first-aid measures were taken. Look at her questions and write a dialogue. Be prepared to act it out.

GUIDANCE *For guidance, turn to file G23 on page 180.*

Can you describe what happened?

What had she been doing before the accident?

Did she lose consciousness at any time?

Have you given her any medication?

Was the patient wearing a helmet?

Describing past actions and events

- We use the past progressive and simple past together to describe how an action that was already in progress was interrupted by a second action or event.

*We **were skiing** in the forest when it **started** snowing.* *> Past progressive, p. 220; Simple past, p. 220*

- We use the past perfect (progressive) to talk about events that had happened (or were happening) before other events in the past.

*Virpi **had lost** consciousness before I **got** to her.*

*Before the accident **happened**, she **had been skiing** at a normal pace.* *> Past perfect, p. 221; Past perfect progressive, p. 222*

- We use the present perfect to talk about past events which have an effect on the present.

*I **have learned** first aid so I know what to do.* *> Present perfect, p. 221*

B The admissions nurse asks you to help Virpi complete some forms. Use information in the role cards to prepare and then act out the dialogue.
Partners A and B: "You" (file 8, page 168) Partners C and D: Virpi (file 27, page 177)

31 **C** The doctor, who speaks a bit of German but no English, assesses Virpi's injuries and explains what will happen next. Listen to the doctor and mediate for Virpi in English.

5 Writing: a report of the accident

Emil has to submit an accident report to the Finnish school. He asks you to write a short summary of the accident and the outcome. Summarize the information from your role-play and make up the rest of the story. What happened after the doctor spoke to you?

Hospital food and catering

You work at St Mary's Hospital in Dublin. The hospital has had problems with their food and catering. You are part of the admin team that has been asked to introduce a new catering concept. You begin by studying facts about hospital food and catering. Then you read a formal letter from a hospital caterer.

1 Brainstorming: hospital food

Discuss what comes to mind when you think of hospital food. Have you ever eaten food in a hospital or a similar institution? If so, what was it like? What could be improved and how?

2 Discussion: facts about hospital catering

A Read the facts about hospital food and catering. Match them to the following key words.

costs per meal • dietary needs • environmental impact • food quality • handling of product packaging • quantity of meals served • safety and hygiene • unhealthy food

1 Six patients tragically died in Leeds after eating hospital sandwiches contaminated with bacteria.
2 In a recent survey, 39% of NHS staff said food and catering services in their hospital were poor.
3 Major allergens are often not mentioned on the menu – a risk for people with food intolerances.
4 Some patients have trouble opening plastic tubs or sandwich packs.
5 In 2019, the NHS served 141 million meals to about 125,000 patients a day.
6 Hospital vending machines sell sugary drinks and foods high in salt, fat and sugar.
7 One hospital reports it generates between 45 and 55 tonnes of food waste a year.
8 In 2019, the NHS spent £4.56 on a patient meal per day (including labour costs and overheads).

B Discuss how important you find the facts mentioned in **2A**. Rank them on a scale from 1 (= not important) to 5 (= very important).

3 Reading: a formal business letter

Your admin team has contacted several hospital caterers and asked them to send you proposals. Read the first letter you receive and match the parts (1–12) to the descriptions (a–l).

a salutation
b subject line
c date
d enclosure(s)
e inside address
f signature
g letterhead
h reference initials
i body of the letter
j copies
k salutation
l complimentary close

1 **Catering Solutions Ltd.**

381 The Serpentine
Market Harborough
LE16 8QE • Great Britain

Tel +44 1858 44564
Fax +44 1858 44565
info@catering-solutions.nex
www.catering-solutions.nex

2 Our ref: NK/CM

3 15 May 20..

4 St Mary's Hospital
Clough Road
DO1 X2XO
Dublin
Ireland

5 Dear Mr Thomas

6 **Catering concept for your hospital**

7 Thank you for your interest in our catering concepts for hospitals.

We are sure we can offer you a concept that fits the needs of your patients, their families and your medical staff.
As requested, we are sending you our information pack including details of our catering services. A brochure and copy of our latest price-list are also enclosed for your information.

If you have any further questions, please do not hesitate to contact me.

8 Yours sincerely
9 Catering Solutions Ltd.
10 *Nina Khan*

Nina Khan (Ms)
Sales Manager

11 cc Chris Mason
12 Encs: Catering info pack, price list

4 Mind map: preparing a decision

> *Visualisierungs- und Lernhilfen erstellen, S. 160*

Before studying the catering proposals in detail, look at your answers to **2B** again and think about which aspects are important when you are deciding on the best offer. With a partner, create a mind map with the most important aspects.

GUIDANCE *For guidance, turn to file G20 on page 190.*

Comparing catering concepts

You have received two concept offers from two different hospital caterers. You evaluate them and then write a report with your findings and recommendations.

---

1 Reading: two catering concepts

> *Schwierige Texte lesen, S. 154*

A Read the two offers below. Say which sentences are true for offer a, which for offer b, and which for both.

1 The hospital needs to buy some equipment.
2 The company offers tasty, healthy and nutritious food.
3 Patients can say what they want to eat in the morning.
4 The caterer has high safety and hygiene standards.
5 Special dietary needs will be considered.
6 The caterer wants to reduce its environmental impact.
7 The meals are delivered to the hospital.
8 The caterer offers organic and sustainable food options.

B Discuss in small groups which offer you think is best and why.

Expressing opinions

- I'd prefer the first solution because ….
- The second option provides more/better …
- I would choose/recommend the first caterer because the … options are much better.
- The advantage/disadvantage of the [meal pack solution] is …
- As far as [prices] are concerned, the first option seems …

a

Top chefs for healthcare: our offer

We provide healthy and nutritious food options to hospital staff, patients and visitors.
We understand the importance of mealtimes in hospitals so we offer:

Best quality food
We use fresh food and first-rate quality ingredients.

Sustainable food
- 100% cage-free eggs
- 60% salt reduction
- no palm oil
- organic products

Top chefs
Highly qualified cooks and their team prepare excellent meals in high tech kitchen.

Timely delivery
Your meals will be delivered on time every day of the week.

Food hygiene
We follow strict hygiene and safety standards.

Prices for hot meals range between €1.20 and €2.50. Snacks, pastries, desserts and sweets are priced between €0.35 and €1.20 per item. Please contact us or visit our website for further details.

www.topchefs-for-healthcare.nex (129 words)

b

OUR OFFER

Catering Solutions

Our new cost-effective catering concept, which has successfully trialled at several hospitals in the Dublin area over the past three years, provides patients, staff and visitors with food that is fresh, hot, safe, nutritious and tasty.

We offer complete meals with a nutritionally balanced mix of ingredients. We provide a choice of 15 hot meals per day plus an additional menu that caters to vegetarian, vegan, kosher, halal and special dietary requirements.
At mealtimes, the meal packs are taken from the fridge, put on a plate and then microwaved for 3–4 minutes. The food in the meal pack is pressure-steamed, which ensures maximum retention of nutrients, colour and texture.

All you need in your hospital ward is a large refrigerator to store the meal packs and three to four standard microwave ovens to heat them. The chilled meal packs are delivered daily – you just tell us when suits you best.

We care about the environment! All used packaging will be collected daily. We have our own composting programme for food waste and recycle about 80% of packaging.

The typical cost for the required equipment in the ward would be around €2,000. The hot meal packs cost between €0.90 and €1.50 and snacks and desserts range from between €0.20 and €1.00 per item. For more details, please see our price-list. (255 words)

2

Writing: replying to an offer

After reading the offers, the admin team have decided to meet the suppliers. They have written a draft of a letter they want to send.

A Complete the sentences in the letter with words from the box.

1 Your catering and meal packs solution ___ very interesting.
2 Would Monday 3 June be ___?
3 Thank you for your ___.
4 We ___ hearing from you soon.
5 Before we make any decision, however, we ___ to learn a little more about your concept.
6 My colleagues and I are ___ in the solutions you offer for different dietary needs.
7 For this reason, we would like to arrange a meeting to discuss ___.

convenient • further details • look forward to • offer • particularly interested • sounds • would like

B Now put the sentences in **A** in the correct order.

3

Writing: a report to the hospital management

Write a brief report informing the hospital management of the offers you have received. Say which offer you think would be best for the hospital and give reasons. Then compare your report with a partner's.

GUIDANCE *For guidance, turn to file G21 on page 190.*

4 PRACTICE

1 Correcting mistakes in an email

Read the email and say what is wrong or missing. Then rewrite the email.

To: jo.smith@carnival-outfit.nex
From: frank.miller@first.fun.nursery.nex
Subject: Carnival outfits
Date: 14 February 20xx

Hi Mr Smith

we are a pre-school in Germany and we saw on your website that you offer carnival outfits.
We're very interested in your carnival costumes for young children.
Send us your catalogue and price list.

We look forward hearing from you.

Many greetings.

Frank Miller

GUIDANCE *For guidance, turn to file G22 on page 190.*

---

2 Replying to an enquiry

Complete the sentences with words from the box. There are some words you do not need.

actual • are pleased • arrange a venue • attached • current • feel free • Thank you very much for • This package offers

1 ___ your interest in our kids party packages.
2 We ___ to give you further information about our two most popular formats.
3 ___ activities that encourage your kids to be creative.
4 The price per child is €30.00 if you ___ for the event yourself.
5 Please ___ to give me a call if you have any further questions or ideas.
6 Please find our ___ price list attached.

---

3 Asking polite questions

Look at the following polite question beginnings (1–8). Match them to the correct category (a–c).

a offering help or information
b asking for help or information
c asking for permission

1 Could you give/tell me …?
2 Would you like me to …?
3 Could you please give us …?
4 Shall I send you …?
5 Could you let us know …?
6 Would you mind telling me …?
7 Would it be OK if we …?
8 Could I ask you to …?

4 Using the telephone

Use words from the box to complete the telephone phrases.

1 I'd like to ___ to someone in administration, please.
2 Just ___ on one minute and I'll try to ___ you.
3 ___ you still there? I'll ___ you through.
4 I'll ___ on your message.
5 How can I ___ you?
6 I'd like to ___ an appointment, please.
7 Can you ___ your name, please?
8 I'm sorry, but I have to ___ my appointment.
9 You're ___ up. I can hardly ___ you.

are • breaking • change • connect • hear • help • hold • make • pass • put • speak • spell

---

5 Talking about what happened earlier

> *The past tenses, pp. 220–222; Present perfect, p. 221*

Complete the sentences using the correct form of the verbs in brackets.

1 The organization ___ (run out) of money long before they ___ (leave) the country.
2 The people ___ (suffer) for weeks before the relief organization ___ (arrive).
3 I ___ (just decide) to volunteer when I ___ (see) the advert for assistants in Romania.
4 We ___ (hike) for an hour when it ___ (start) to rain.
5 Where ___ (you / be)? The patient ___ (lie) here for two hours.
6 When we ___ (reach) the hospital, the patient ___ (already recover).
7 The volunteer ___ (work) here for six months, so she ___ (take charge) immediately after the accident.

---

6 Leaving a message on voicemail

Complete the voicemail message with the phrases from the box.

a message for • forward to hearing • have to reschedule • I'm calling • perhaps get back • this is

Hello, ___[1] Carla Helm from the Outdoor Experience Centre. ___[2] on behalf of Kate Flynn, our office manager. I'd like to leave ___[3] Gordon Boxhall. It's about your video appointment with Kate. I'm afraid we ___[4] this video call as something urgent has come up. Could you ___[5] to us so that we can arrange a new date and time? Thank you very much. We look ___[6] from you. Goodbye.

---

7 Understanding words

Look again at the two offers on pages 86 and 87. Find the English equivalents for these words.

1 *nahrhaft*
2 *nachhaltig*
3 *Bioprodukte*
4 *Sicherheitsstandards*
5 *erfolgreich erprobt*
6 *Erhaltung*
7 *Konsistenz*
8 *gekühlt*

Choose one of the following two projects.

1 Creating communication guidelines: tips and rules

You work in your organization's communications department and have been asked to create guidelines for the different means of communication in your organization. The guidelines should set out rules and include instructions for how to act and what to say or write, depending on the means of communication.

Divide into three groups. Each group will create rules for one of these three means of communication:

- making telephone calls
- writing emails
- writing formal letters

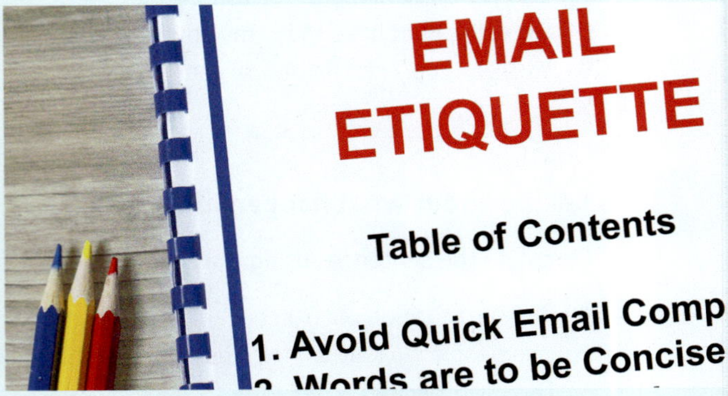

Follow the steps below in your group.

Step 1 Skim topic 4 again to find useful advice or tips for your group's part of the guidelines. Then do research on the internet to find more ideas. Make notes.

Step 2 Write a list of aspects that are important for your group's means of communication, e.g. spelling, politeness, etc.

Step 3 Discuss which of the tips or rules are most important. Choose the top five that you want to include in your guidelines.

Step 4 Formulate your top five tips or rules. Remember that they should be short, easy to understand and memorable. Include examples of how to do things correctly.

Step 5 Prepare to present your guidelines. Decide who in your group will speak and what they will say.

Step 6 Present your guidelines to the rest of the class. Get the other groups' feedback and make any necessary changes.

> *Präsentieren, S. 146*

Presenting your project

- We'd like to present …
- We chose to create …
- As you can see, we have …
- The first/second/third/… point/tip/rule is …
- We'd like to point out that …
- We thought this is important because …
- So, those are our guidelines.
- Are there any questions or comments?
- That's a good point.
- Thanks for listening.

> *Presentations, p. 209*

Giving feedback

- Your tips are well structured.
- All of the most important points were covered.
- I would add … to the list.
- I think … would be better.
- There are some important parts missing.
- You forgot to include …
- Check your text next time, there were a few mistakes in it.

2 Creating communication guidelines: a poster

Now that you have discussed the tips and rules that should go into your communication guidelines, make a poster that displays them in an attractive way.

Step 1 Decide what size and format you want your poster to be.

Step 2 Decide what kind of layout, design and colours you want to use. Think about how you want to format your guidelines to give them a clear structure, for example using headings, subtitles, bullet points (•), etc.

Step 3 Think of visuals or graphics that could make your poster more attractive and support your tips and rules, for example pictures or icons.

Step 4 When you have finished, hang up your poster in the classroom.
Gallery walk: look at the other groups' posters. Ask any questions you might have. Give constructive feedback. Answer questions about your own poster.

CHECKING PROGRESS

Browse through the previous pages in this topic, looking at headings and pictures. What have you learned? What can you do now that you have learned these things?

- ✓ I can write an email request for information. (Section A)
- ✓ I can make telephone enquiries. (Section A)
- ✓ I can communicate appropriately and politely. (Section A / Project)
- ✓ I can make and change appointments. (Section B)
- ✓ I can take and leave phone messages. (Section B)
- ✓ I can write a report. (Sections B and C)
- ✓ I can write a formal letter. (Section C)

Write down two more statements yourself.

Organizing an event

You are working for one of the organizations presented in this topic:
– Little Rascals Nursery School,
– The Outdoor Experience Centre
– or St Mary's Hospital.
Together with a group of colleagues, you have been asked to organize an event for your organization. Follow the steps on these pages to organize your event.

Step 1 Choose an event.

Divide into three groups. Decide which group will plan an event for which organization: the nursery school, the Outdoor Experience Centre or the hospital. Each group should choose a different organization.

Your organization's management has asked you to include catering and a special highlight when planning the event.

Think about the following points:
- What type of event are you planning? (e.g. party)
- Who will attend this event? (e.g. elderly people)
- Where will it take place? (e.g. indoors or outdoors)
- What goods and services do you need? (e.g. music)

You can use a placemat to gather everyone's ideas.

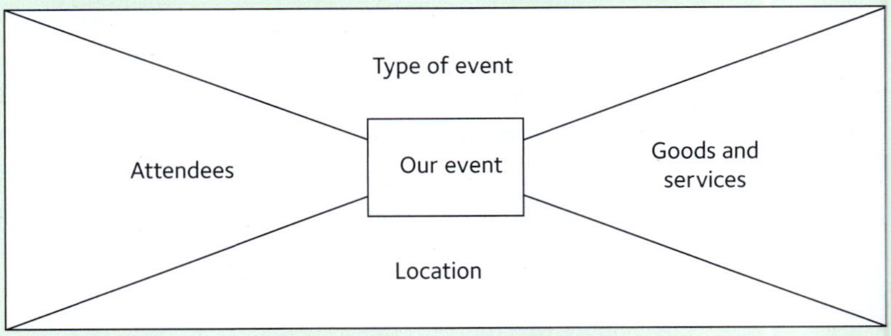

Step 2 Find suitable services and offers.

Once you have decided on the type of event and the goods and services you will need, research suitable service providers and suppliers on the internet. Find offers that match the criteria you defined in Step 1. Select the best offers.

Discussing offers

- Of all of the offers, I think offer 1 is …
- This one offers … but it doesn't offer …
- This one is the best value for money.
- I think this one would be the most suitable because …
- I see your point but I think …

Step 3 Role-play a telephone enquiry. > *Telephoning, p. 205*

After studying the offers that you've selected, act out a dialogue with a partner.

Partner A: You are an employee of one of the companies offering goods or a service.
Before you receive the call, make notes on what the caller might ask.

Partner B: You are interested in the company's offer.
Before you make the call, make notes on further details you would like to ask about.

When you are both ready, begin your role-play.

Making a telephone enquiry

- I'm calling about …
- How can I help you?
- Could you tell me …?
- I'd like to know if …
- I'd like to know more about …
- That's very helpful. Thank you.
- Thank you for calling.

Step 4 Place an order. > *Placing an order, p. 217*

After your telephone enquiry, you decide to place a written order. With a partner, write an email to the service provider or supplier explaining what kind of service or product you would like to have for your event.

Decide what details you want to include, e.g. how many people are expected to come, dates and times, details about delivery, food, etc.

Step 5 Write an invitation. > *Writing emails, p. 202*

Now that the planning process is completed and you have ordered everything that you need, write an email invitation to the people you would like to attend your event. Include the place, venue and time and details about the event. The phrases in the box may help you.

Writing an invitation

- We are planning a special event on … (date) to celebrate …
- We would like to invite you to our … that will take place on …
- The event will be an excellent opportunity to …
- We have a special highlight planned for our guests: …
- There will also be a buffet with different hot and cold dishes, salads, …
- We would be pleased if you could attend this event.
- We look forward to your positive response.

Now swap your emails and respond to another group's.

A Health and fitness

- Healthy food for kids
- Diets and chronic conditions
- Staying healthy, keeping fit

B Supporting families

- The changing family
- Dysfunctional families
- Making decisions

5 Communication inside and outside work

Over 22 million people in Germany have an immigrant background.

Fifteen per cent of children in Western Europe grow up in single-parent households.

Only three in ten teenagers get the minimum recommended amount of daily exercise.

Between six and ten million children in the US are of bisexual, lesbian and gay parents.

Each year, 678,000 people in the US die from nutrition-related diseases.

A Look at the topics in sections A–C above. Think of situations relating to these topics where you as a carer would communicate with people. Who would you communicate with and how?

B Look at the facts in the bubbles. Which topics in sections A–C do they relate to?

C Choose the fact that you find most interesting. Explain why.

D Look at the cartoon on page 93 and describe the situation. Explain the issue that the cartoon addresses. Summarize the cartoonist's viewpoint in one or two sentences.
> *Cartoons beschreiben, S. 150*

E Think of three tips for staying healthy and fit. Make notes. Then compare your notes in class. Decide on the three best tips.

C Starting a new life

- Settling in a new country
- Cultural awareness
- Supporting migrants

D Projects

- Making a poster or video
- Writing a scene for a reality show

WHAT'S TO COME

Scenario: You are working for the Health and Community Centre (HCC) which supports people of different ages with questions relating to fitness and nutrition as well as families struggling with difficult situations. About 200 refugees from different parts of the world will arrive in town soon. Among the refugees, the organization expects families, pregnant women and people with health problems. HCC wants to offer the best possible support for the refugees. Together you will:

- update the website information describing HCC's services,
- have a team meeting to discuss how to organize support for the refugees,
- record the results and prepare an action plan,
- contact local organizations and individuals and ask for support and funding.

But first: Your work in HCC's different areas of activity will help prepare you.

- In the area of health and fitness, you will practise advising people on a healthy diet and look at new research on exercise and health. (Section A)
- In the area of family support, you will give a talk on dysfunctional families and deal with a case of teen pregnancy and adoption. (Section B)
- And in the area of migrant support, you will work to develop your cultural competence and practise receiving and leaving messages. (Section C)

Now you are ready to prepare to welcome the refugees.

Healthy food for kids

In your first week at HCC, you assist Susan Hill, a health and nutrition expert, in a workshop for pre-teens.

1 Reading and discussion: facts about health and fitness

A Look at the fact file and answer the questions.

1. What trends in the past and projections for the future do the statistics show?
2. What measures are being taken to tackle the problem?

B Work in pairs. Describe one of the statistics to your partner.

>Statistiken beschreiben und analysieren, S. 152

C What thoughts or questions come to mind when you look at the information? What do you find interesting or surprising?

D Collect words and phrases used to talk about staying healthy and keeping fit, for example getting exercise, having a balanced diet, etc.

Overweight and obesity worldwide

1 **Since the 1970s** In 1975, fewer than 1% of children and adolescents aged 5–19 were obese. In 2016, 6% of girls and 8% of boys were obese.

2 **2016** Nearly 18% of girls and 19% of boys were overweight.

3 **2019** Over 150 million children and adolescents worldwide were obese. In Africa, the number of overweight children had risen by almost 24% since 2000.

4 **2030** By this date, more than 250 million children worldwide will be obese.

5 **What to do** The World Health Organization (WHO) has developed a “global action plan on physical activity 2018–2030”. It is about “active people for a healthier world” and promotes policy actions to increase physical activity worldwide.

Expressing opinions

- It’s interesting that …
- It’s hard to believe that …
- I wonder how/why …
- I’m surprised that …
- I can’t imagine that …

2 Discussion: the types of food children eat

After Susan has described a balanced diet, the children talk about the food they eat.

A Match the types of food the children mention (1–8) to the descriptions (a–h).

1. “My stepmum and dad both work, so we eat a lot of **convenience food** in our house.”
2. “My mum never buys **factory-farmed** meat. She says it’s full of chemicals.”
3. “I always eat **fast food** with dad.”
4. “Some of my schoolmates mostly eat **organic** food, but we can’t afford that.”
5. “We can’t get **free-range** eggs in our local supermarket.”
6. “I get the shopping with my sister. She only ever buys **processed food**.”

a a way of farming in which animals can move around in natural conditions
b food which can be cooked quickly in a microwave oven
c food which has been treated in order to make it last longer
d frozen or canned food that you can prepare quickly and easily
e livestock kept in small spaces and fed special food so they produce more eggs, meat, etc.
f food grown or raised without the use of chemicals and genetic manipulation

B Give the children advice on healthier types of food.

GUIDANCE *For guidance, turn to file G23 on page 190.*

If you ate less fatty meat, you would lose weight.

Talking about making changes

- We use type 2 *if*-sentences to describe what the future would be like if the present were different.

*If you **ate** less salt, you **could lower** your blood pressure.*
*Your skin **would look** better if you **drank** more water.*

> If-sentences, p. 228

3 Interaction: planning a healthy meal

The children would like to cook a meal from scratch. You choose a suitable recipe and organize the cooking equipment you will need. Work in groups of three. Use information in the files below to reconstruct a recipe you can use with the children.

Partner A: file 9, page 169 Partner B: file 28, page 177 Partner C: file 24, page 175

4 Mediation: what is in a chicken nugget?

> Mediation, S. 164

One of the children said that they eat a lot of chicken nuggets. What parts of the chicken do you think are used to make them? Read the description in file 10 on page 169 and summarize the German text in simple English for the children.

5 Listening: an interview with a nutritionist

> Mit Hörverstehensaufgaben umgehen, S. 144

In this week's podcast, Fran from the Social Pulse team talks to Andrew Ferrie, a nutritionist who analyses fast food products.

A Susan plays a podcast on a similar topic. Before you listen, read the description and speculate about the contents.

32

B Read the tasks below, then listen and take notes.

1 Define the word "derivative" and give examples.
2 Explain what TBHQ and PDMS are.
3 Explain what Andrew means by: "Nothing is wasted".
4 Point out what can be found in factory-farmed meat.
5 Explain what Fran means by: "What are the costs to our health?"

GUIDANCE *For guidance, turn to file G24 on page 191.*

6 Writing: the impact of fast food

> Eine Stellungnahme schreiben, S. 162

Based on the information given in this section, comment on the impact of fast food on people's health and life. Take the point of view of a parent, an educator or an employee in the food industry.

Diets and chronic conditions

Susan Hill also advises people with chronic diseases on improving their diet. She has scheduled an appointment with a client to discuss his diet plan.

1 Discussion: diet facts and myths

Clients often have their own opinions about eating when they come to see Susan. She gives them some typical statements that she hears from other clients. Look at the statements and say what you think.

Which word?

In English, the word *diet* can mean two things: the food people normally eat (= *Ernährung*) or a special eating plan to reduce weight or for medical reasons (= *Diät*).

Diets don't work.

Overweight is a genetic thing. There's nothing you can do about it.

A healthy lifestyle and diet won't prevent chronic diseases.

Eating at night will make you gain weight.

You are what you eat.

Eating should be fun. Counting calories isn't.

2 Discussion: talking about food

Susan often uses this illustration to talk to clients about eating a balanced diet.

A Look at the illustration and say what kind of foods you can eat a lot of and what kind you should only eat in small quantities.

B Draw a food plate showing your own daily diet. Describe your diet to a partner and ask them to comment on it.

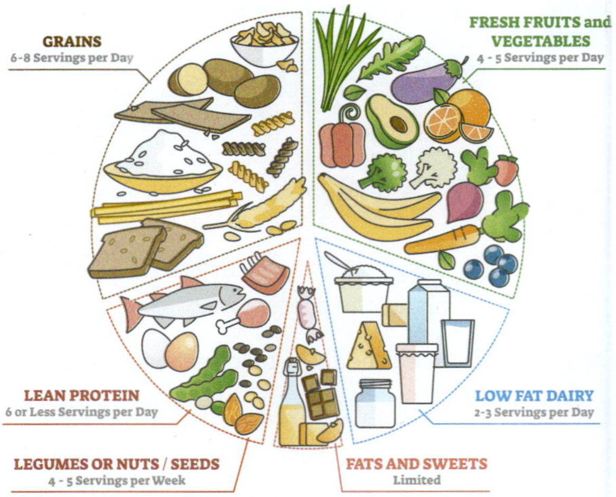

3 Reading: a healthy diet plan

Read Susan's article and answer the questions that clients often ask her.

1 What exactly is DASH?
2 I have diabetes. Why should I try a diet that was designed for people with high blood pressure?
3 Why are high cholesterol levels and high blood pressure dangerous?
4 How will I benefit from this diet?
5 If I use this eating plan, what should or shouldn't I eat?
6 How long will I have to follow this eating plan?

33

A HEALTHY EATING PLAN FOR PEOPLE WITH CHRONIC CONDITIONS

by Susan Hill

Diabetes is a health problem that affects people from all age groups and cultural backgrounds. In fact, people who move to Germany from other countries have an increased risk of type 2 diabetes. An unhealthy diet and insufficient exercise often play a major role. It seems that many people only adopt the unhealthy lifestyle after arriving in Germany.

A healthy eating plan is key to managing diabetes. If you want to keep your blood sugar in check, it is not enough to change your eating habits for a short time. What you need is a long-term nutrition plan.

Our recommendation is the DASH diet. It is not like other diets you may have tried. DASH stands for *Dietary Approaches to Stop Hypertension* as it was originally designed to help treat or prevent high blood pressure. High blood pressure and high LDL (low-density lipoprotein) cholesterol levels are two major risk factors which cause heart disease and strokes.

Hypertension and diabetes often go hand in hand. Studies show that more than 50% of diabetes patients have high blood pressure. Scientists found out that the DASH diet also works well for people with type 1 and type 2 diabetes. It may even reduce the risk of getting diabetes by 20%.

Apart from lowering blood pressure, the diet may also improve blood glucose levels and lower the concentration of fats in the blood. It also helps reduce weight. When treating diabetes, controlling blood glucose levels is vital to prevent any heart damage.

The DASH diet is a flexible and balanced eating plan that is easy to start and to follow throughout your life. DASH is about healthy eating habits with less processed food and more whole foods. You should eat fruits, vegetables, lean meat, low-fat dairy, whole grains, beans and nuts. At the same time, you should limit sugary foods and drinks, salt, red meat and full-fat dairy products.

To reduce your blood pressure, we recommend cutting back on salt drastically. Instead of salt, use spices and reduce your sodium intake to half of a teaspoon of salt per day. (350 words)

4 Role-play: a conversation with a prediabetes client

Mr Ares Kasanidis, originally from Greece, needs advice about his diet. His doctor has diagnosed him as a risk patient with prediabetes. Susan is in a meeting and asks you to take the call.
Work with a partner. Role-play a conversation using information from these pages. If possible, record your conversation using your phone.
Parter A: file 11, page 170 Partner B: file 29, page 178

GUIDANCE *For guidance, turn to file G25 on page 191.*

5 Writing: summarizing a client conversation

Susan has asked you to summarize the conversation for her. If you recorded it, listen and write down what you discussed. If not, try to remember the main points.

Staying healthy, keeping fit

Susan has called a meeting to discuss some new findings on exercise and health that she wants to include in the Health and Community Centre's new info material. In the meeting, you will watch a video to learn more about the consequences of lack of exercise. Then you will prepare information for the centre's new health and fitness brochure.

1 Discussion: health and exercise

1 How do you think lack of exercise and life expectancy might be related?
2 What do you think happens if people drastically reduce their physical activity for several weeks?
3 For a healthy life, how much physical activity per week would you recommend?

2 Viewing: Danish study on health and exercise

> *Mit Sehverstehensaufgaben umgehen, S. 144*

In the meeting, Susan shows a video that describes the new findings on health and exercise.

A Pre-viewing: before you watch the video, match the words to the definitions.

1	loaf around	a	device that measures how quickly you gain speed
2	pedometer	b	body processes that turn food into energy, growth or waste
3	accelerometer	c	have a negative effect on
4	endurance	d	amount of fat in blood
5	metabolizing	e	do nothing in particular
6	lipid count	f	device that counts how far you walk
7	idleness	g	ability to do sth difficult for a long time
8	take a toll on	h	the state of not working or doing anything

6 **B** Now watch the video and complete the facts.

1 In the Danish experiment, some students did not take more than ___ steps (that's about ___ metres) a day.
2 The students' endurance performance went down by ___.
3 The students lost an average of 1.2 kilos, with a drastic loss of ___.
4 The idleness caused their lipid counts and ___ to jump significantly.

6 **C** Watch again and answer the questions.

1 How important is lack of exercise when looking at European death rates?
2 What did the doctors want to find out in this study?
3 What is the usual consequence of reducing physical activity?
4 What was the surprising result when looking at the risk of getting diabetes?
5 Where did the students put on the most fat?

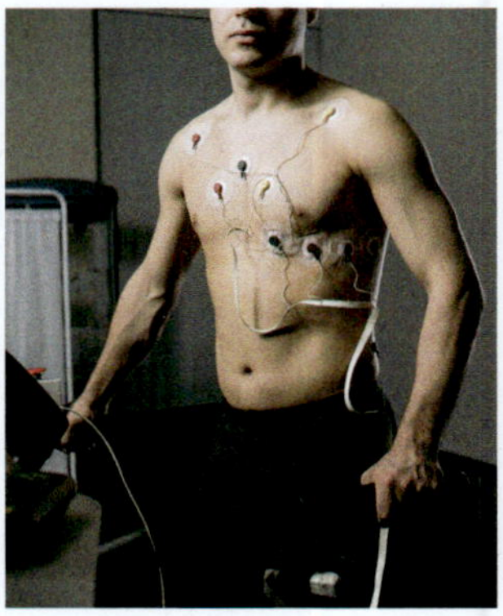

3 Mediation: facts and statistics

In a previous presentation, Susan used the infographic below. She needs a version for the centre's German-speaking customers. Work in a team of four. Choose a box each and summarize the content in German for the other team members.

Describing an infographic

- A (World Health Organization) report revealed that …
- Scientists/Studies suggest that …
- This (infographic/chart/statistic) shows that/how …
- A surprising fact is that the number of people who … is …

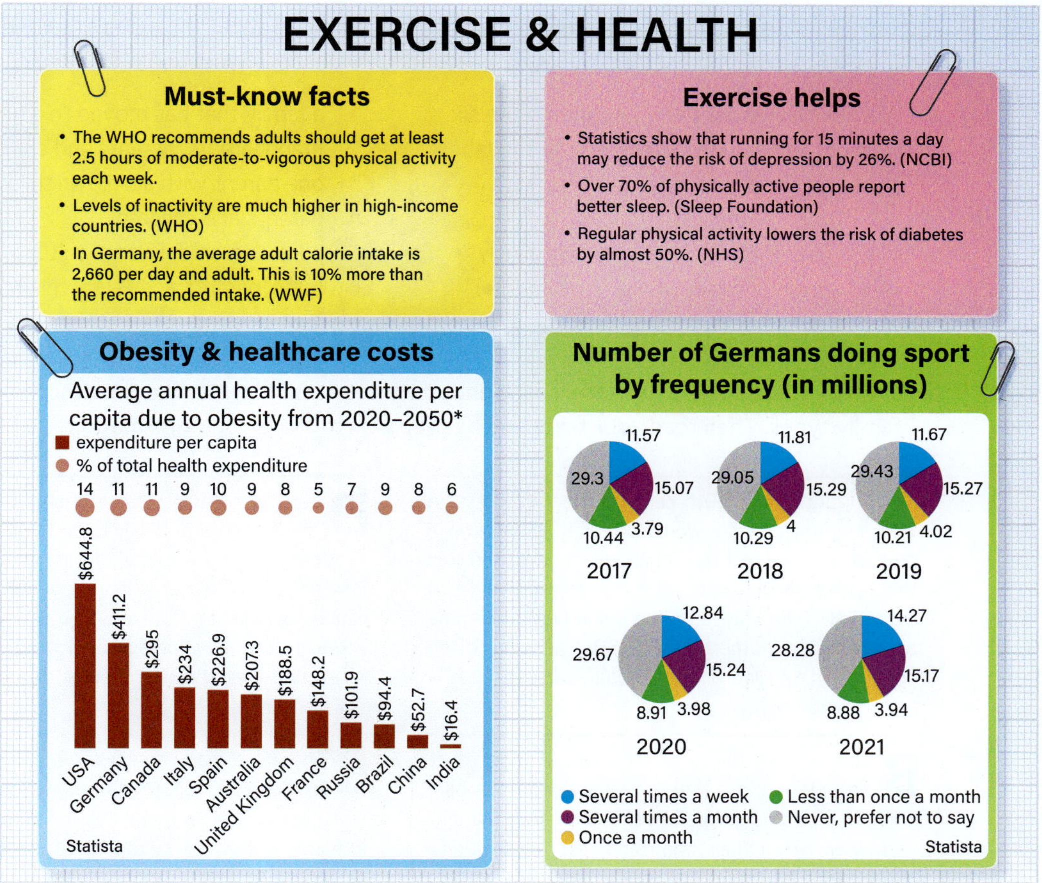

4 Research and presentation: health and physical exercise

For the centre's new health and fitness brochure, Susan asks you to prepare some visual information with additional facts and figures. Work with a partner. Do internet research to find out more about how health and physical exercise are related.

1 Look for two examples of visual information: statistics, infographics, charts or graphs that show interesting facts about the topic.
2 Decide which visual each of you wants to use in your presentation.
3 Make a screenshot of your visual.
4 Now think of headings, subtitles and text and prepare a page with all your information.
5 Think of the best way to present the information.
6 Present your visual to your partner.

> *Präsentieren, S. 146*

The changing family

The Health and Community Centre also helps families in difficult situations. Alice May, the senior social worker, asks you to look into the problems different family types face.

1 Reading: defining the family

> Schwierige Texte lesen, S. 154

Alice shows you and two other trainees a folder with information about the types of families they are dealing with at the moment. She wants to prepare for her upcoming meeting with some council officials.

A Work with two partners and match the six types of family units in the box to the labels (1–6) given to them by social workers.

extended family • intercultural family • migrant family • nuclear family • single-parent family • stepfamily

1 a family that has moved to a new country
2 grandparents, parents and children
3 one parent with a child or children
4 parents and children
5 parents from different cultural backgrounds
6 (step)parents and (step)children

B In your group, choose two labels each and scan the texts below to find the description of "your" family types. Then read your texts and be prepared to share your information.

A Until the mid 20th century, a typical western European family would probably have been a mother, a father and their children. The husband was the "breadwinner" who went out to work to earn money. His wife stayed at home and was a full-time housewife and mother. In the 1950s, the media often presented this type of 'ideal' family in adverts. It is less common today.

B This type of family hasn't changed much over time. Wherever they live, the family members hold on to traditional set-ups that they have brought with them from their homeland, e.g. a patriarchal household in which women stay at home and men go out to do business. In some cases, the children marry within their own culture; sometimes the marriages are arranged. However, some families are fully "integrated" and look and behave the same as "native" families in the new country.

C Until the early 1960s, this type of family was usually the result of the death of one parent. Today, these families are more often the result of separation or divorce. The mother or father looks after the children. The other partner has access on certain days. Statistically, in most cases the mother is the carer. Some parents split the caring down the middle, and the children live part of the week with one parent and the rest of the week with the other.

D It is less common than it used to be, but you still see this type of family today: a man or a woman – or both – living with one of their children and their child's family. If the grandparent is still fit, he or she can be a real help to a working mum. Sometimes, however, the older person is in need of care. You'll often find that the daughter or daughter-in-law is the main carer.

E There are many couples with different cultural backgrounds today in Germany. Some find it hard to adjust to the partner's cultural difference and to integrate into a new culture and society. But cultural diversity can have a very positive effect: their children grow up in a culturally-rich environment and can experience the best of both parents' worlds. They might learn both parents' languages and get to know both parents' countries.

F This family, in which at least one parent brings a child from a previous relationship, is a common set-up today as a result of the rise in divorce. Making the set-up work is not easy, especially when parents from different cultural backgrounds take their children into a new relationship. When it does work, close bonds can develop between family members. The experience of growing up in such a family can be very beneficial to a child.

C Copy the table. Work together to complete the table using keywords from your texts.

Type of family	Family members	How this type of family comes into being	How this type of family has changed over the years
…	…	…	…

D CHALLENGE! Choose one family type. Point out the problems that may arise among the members.

2

Discussion: talking about change

Some trainee social workers from other parts of the country are visiting. Exchange information about families you know. How have things changed over the last ten years?

There used to be fewer …

Ten years ago, it was unusual to see …

Lately, there have been more …

Describing change

- We use the present perfect to connect the past with the present.

*Things **have changed** over the years.*
*Since the beginning of the millenium, families **have grown**.*

> *Present perfect, p. 221*

- We use the simple past to talk about a state or action in the past. With *used to / didn't use to* + infinitive we can contrast a past habit with what we do now.

*In the 1950s, women usually **stayed** at home. They **didn't use to work**.*

> *Simple past, p. 220*

3

Listening: households with children and single parents

> *Mit Hörverstehensaufgaben umgehen, S. 144*

34

Listen to a podcast in which two journalists talk about the situation of parents and children in different countries. Complete the statements.

1 Between 2010 and 2020, most EU states saw a … in the average number of people per household.
2 In 2020, the EU recorded 195 million households with an average of … members per household.
3 According to data from 2020, there were single parents in … of all EU households.
4 In Germany in 2020 there were just over 2.1 million single mothers and ….
5 In 2019, the European countries with … rate of single mothers who couldn't afford shelter were Lithuania and Estonia (36%).
6 In the US, 40% of single mothers struggled to … and 27% had trouble affording shelter.

4

Writing: the changing family

> *Eine Stellungnahme schreiben, S. 162*

Alice has asked you to report on what you have learned about families. Write a text describing how families have changed over the years. Describe the potential problems modern families could have and why. Point out how these changes influence the problems social workers have to deal with.

GUIDANCE *For guidance, turn to file G26 on page 192.*

Dysfunctional families

Alice, the senior social worker, would like you and the other trainees to give a talk on dysfunctional families.

1 Reading: what is a dysfunctional family?

Alice first asks you to consider what makes a family dysfunctional and gives you some tasks to do in small groups.

A Decide if the statements are true or false. Find evidence for your choice in the text below.

1. A dysfunctional family is not a healthy family.
2. A crisis often turns a healthy family into a dysfunctional family.
3. Many dysfunctional families start to behave better after the stress is over.
4. Children who grow up in a dysfunctional family could take their problems with them when they have a family of their own.
5. Every dysfunctional family behaves in the same way.

When we describe a family as being "dysfunctional", we mean that something continually happens in the family which stops the family functioning in a healthy way.
Almost every family is faced with stressful events at some time, e.g. a serious illness or a death in the family, but healthy families usually get back to normal after the crisis has passed. In dysfunctional families, problems are always there and are never dealt with in a healthy way. Negative patterns of behaviour are repeated on a regular basis and are often handed down from generation to generation.
There are many types of dysfunctional families. Some parents neglect their children. Other parents control their children's lives and never allow them any independence. In some families, children are the victims of sexual and/or physical abuse.

(130 words)

B Copy the diagram and sort these common behaviour patterns of dysfunctional families into the correct sections.

adultery • alcoholism • bullying • lying • manipulative behaviour • mental abuse • physical abuse / battering • playing truant • promiscuity • sexual abuse • stealing from parents • substance abuse

C What TV series do you know? Describe some of the families in them.

- What are the relationships like between parents and children, and between siblings?
- What behavioural patterns do the family members often/sometimes/never show?
- Say how the families might be described as dysfunctional.

If you do not watch any series, ask other people to describe them.

2 Listening: describing the dysfunctional family

> *Mit Hörverstehensaufgaben umgehen, S. 144*

Next, you listen to a podcast as part of your preparation for your talk.

In this week's podcast from the Social Pulse team, Fran talks to Jim Allan about working with dysfunctional families. Jim is a senior social worker who works in a London family support centre.

35

A Before you listen, explain what these phrases from the interview mean. Then listen and check.

1 cope with the situation alone
2 afraid to go to a women's refuge or seek assistance
3 break out of the pattern
4 lack of empathy
5 marginalized
6 denial
7 stand by and do nothing

GUIDANCE *For guidance, turn to file G27 on page 192.*

35

B Listen again and answer these questions.

1 Why does everyone in a dysfunctional family accept bad behaviour as normal?
2 Why does an abused child often have to cope with the situation alone?
3 What kind of help does Jim offer to the families he works with?
4 How can someone who was brought up in a dysfunctional family break out of the pattern?

---

3 Discussion: two cases

Alice gives you two summaries of cases that the centre has dealt with and asks you to explain what is happening.

A Work with a partner and read the case notes in your file. Look up any words you don't know. Use the information you have about dysfunctional families to describe and explain the case to your partner.
Partner A: file 12, page 170 Partner B: file 30, page 178

B Where would you recommend that the families get assistance?

> **Getting help**
>
> The following offer help to families in trouble. Here are just a few:
> - family pastoral care *Familienseelsorge*
> - women's refuge *Frauenhaus*
> - youth welfare services *Jugendhilfe*
> - welfare department *Sozialamt*
> - family doctor *Hausarzt/-ärztin*
> - district nurse *Pflegekraft in der ambulanten Pflege*

C CHALLENGE! Describe a case currently featured in the news. Say how you would support the family in question.

---

4 Presentation: supporting dysfunctional families

> *Präsentieren, S. 146*

Now it is time to give your talk on dysfunctional families and offer suggestions on how to support them. Focus on dysfunctional families in general or describe a particular family you know. If you like, you can talk about a family you have seen on TV.

Making decisions

This week, you deal with cases of pregnancy and adoption. Alice asks you to describe one of your cases: a pregnant teenager who has decided to give her baby up for adoption. In a team, you assess prospective couples who would like to adopt the baby.

1 Reading: case notes

> *Schwierige Texte lesen, S. 154*

A Read the case notes below and do these tasks with a partner.

1 Describe the areas of conflict and dysfunctional behaviour in Molly's family.
2 Identify the patterns you see running through the family.
3 Explain Molly's reasons for putting the baby up for adoption.
4 Describe how things are proceeding.

Termination of pregnancy

Medical professionals refer to induced (= *eingeleitet)* abortions as "termination". It sounds less traumatic to the patient than "abortion".

Case# 358 Pregnant teenager

Molly P. is 15 years old. She is pregnant. She lives with her mother, stepfather and two half-brothers. The family has changed neighbourhoods frequently to avoid paying rent, and Molly "thinks" she attended six different primary schools. In November, the family moved to London's Brixton area and Molly started to attend the Holy Cross Secondary School.
Molly was referred to us by the school social worker who had a chat with her when she noticed changes to Molly's figure. Molly is not sure who the father of the baby is. The only person who knows about her pregnancy is her 16-year-old best friend.
Since moving to Brixton, Molly has stayed with her friend a couple of times because there was trouble at home. Examples she gave included her stepfather's aggressive behaviour when drinking, verbal abuse from her mother and one brother's hostility.
The family has been known to the family support team for a while. Molly's mother was also a single, teenage mother. She decided to keep her child and she continued to live with her own (single) mother. Molly was brought up well by her grandmother and insists that she was never neglected. When Molly was eight years old, she and her mother moved in with her current stepfather.

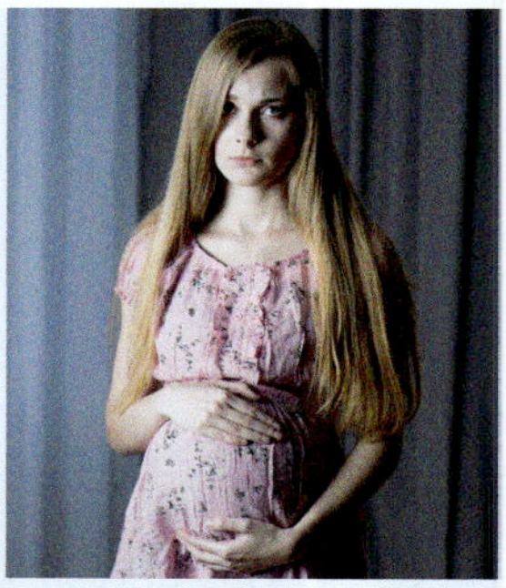

The couple have two common children, both boys. According to Molly, her two half-brothers "are treated like gods". Molly is realistic about her situation and does not want to bring up her child in her current circumstances. Apart from the fact that she is now in her 26th week of pregnancy and cannot legally have a termination, Molly is from a Roman Catholic family. She has decided to give her child up for adoption as she would like to see it grow up in a nice family and be well looked after.
She is attending an antenatal clinic regularly and the pregnancy is developing normally and she should be able to give birth without any problems.
We are liaising with the adoption agency and are assessing potential adoptive couples. (343 words)

B You want to check some key vocabulary. Find the equivalents of these German words in the text.

1 *schwanger*
2 *jdn überweisen*
3 *Schwangerschaft*
4 *(ein Kind) großziehen*
5 *einen Schwangerschaftsabbruch legal vornehmen lassen*
6 *ein Kind zur Adoption freigeben*
7 *vorgeburtlich*
8 *entbinden*
9 *mit jdm zusammenarbeiten*
10 *potenzielle Adoptivpaare*

C Summarize the case for the senior social worker.

Partner A: You are the trainee. Use phrases from the box to describe the case.
Partner B: You are the senior social worker. Ask questions to get more information and to check the facts, e.g. "What's her name?", "How old is she?", "Can you tell me a bit about her family?"

Describing a case

The client
- The client's name is …
- He/She is … years old.
- He/She lives …

The family background
- The client's family is …
- He/She was looked after by his/her …
- When he/she was … years old, …

Client's assessment of the situation
- The client is (not) able to understand his/her situation.
- He/She would like to / doesn't want to …

The current situation
- We are looking into …
- We have spoken to … and are currently …

> *Describing a case, p. 198*

2 Discussion: assessing adoptive parents

> *An Diskussionen teilnehmen, S. 148*

You are on a team assessing possible adoptive parents for Molly's baby. Follow the steps below.

A **Think:** In groups of six, brainstorm family situations and other criteria which should be taken into account when assessing adoptive parents, such as whether both parents work, etc.
Discuss which of the aspects might negatively affect the potential adopters' application.

B **Pair:** Divide into three pairs. With your partner, read the notes on the candidates in your file.
Partners A and B: file 13, page 170
Partners C and D: file 25, page 176
Partners E and F: file 31, page 178

C **Share:** In your group, describe "your" couple and point out the agency's recommendations. Decide which (if any) of the candidates might be suitable. Explain why.

Tom and Julie Laurence, with children

Kevin and Gale Jameson

Evan and Helen Fletcher

3 Writing: termination or adoption?

> *Eine Stellungnahme schreiben, S. 162*

During your time with the family support team, you have counselled many couples on the pros and cons of termination and adoption and supported them in their choice. Before you leave the team, Alice asks you to write a short text for the trainee file.

GUIDANCE *For guidance, turn to file G28 on page 193.*

Settling in a new country

You are now working alongside Tim Parsons, who is responsible for supporting migrants. He is preparing an international conference which will deal with a number of topics around migration, including the problems migrant children face in Germany where some of the participants are based.

1 Reading: schooling for young immigrants

> Schwierige Texte lesen, S. 154

Tim asks you to prepare for the conference by reading the following article.

A Read the article and say where these sentences go in the text.

a A 78% increase in migrants from Greece is one of many examples.
b Germany is the second "new start" for many immigrants.
c His teacher says he is more or less fully integrated.
d "Living in Germany will give me better chances for work too," she adds.
e The challenge for the education system is huge.
f This is where volunteers from Teach First Deutschland come in.

36

INCREASE IN NUMBER OF MIGRANTS MEANS EXTRA WORK FOR SCHOOLS

Germany has seen a boom in immigration from countries that have been hit by the euro crisis or that are experiencing conflict. This has resulted in an increase in the number of children and young people entering German schools without German language skills. ___[1] *One way to cope with these overwhelming numbers is to offer special classes.*

In 2012, as a consequence of the euro crisis, there was a sharp rise in immigration compared to the previous year. ___[2] Since the most recent enlargement of the EU, migrants from Bulgaria and Romania have also come to Germany in large numbers. In 2015, refugees fleeing the conflict in Syria began arriving in huge numbers. Beginning in 2022, Germany has seen a further wave of refugees fleeing the war in Ukraine.

Alongside skilled workers, academics and professionals looking for employment, there are also many working-class families. The children of these families, no matter what their background, are putting a huge burden on the education system.

Most of these newly arrived students start school with no German. While some learn quickly and can soon be integrated into regular classes, others need months to learn the language. With their growing numbers, many schools just do not have enough qualified staff to teach German as a second language, nor the budget to contract any new teachers. ___[3] The non-profit organization supports schools in Baden-Württemberg, Berlin, Hamburg, Hesse and North Rhine-Westphalia. With the help of volunteers, students can get extra hours of specialized German language instruction.

In a classroom in Berlin, a young student named Jamal from Syria explains that his parents had a successful business in Damascus, but when the war started, the family moved to Germany, where Jamal's aunt was already living. Jamal is a fast learner and aims to go to technical college. ___[4] "I feel happy in Germany but I don't expect to live here forever," he says. "My main goal is to return to Syria and use my German qualifications to get work there."

An interesting trend in German schools is the number of students who have also spent time living with their families as immigrants in other countries. ___[5] Turkish students who have grown up in Bulgaria, and Algerian children born in France are two examples.

Elena, a Greek teenager who grew up in Portugal, moved to Stuttgart four months ago. "I was lost when I came here first but now that I can speak German and have made some friends it's more like home," she says. ___[6]

(443 words)

B Find expressions in the text that have the same meaning as the German expressions below.

1 *steigende Einwandererzahlen*
2 *eine starke Zunahme der Einwanderung*
3 *Erweiterung der EU*
4 *gut ausgebildete Arbeitskräfte*
5 *unabhängig von ihren Verhältnissen*
6 *eine starke Belastung*
7 *vor kurzem angekommene Schüler/-innen*
8 *steigende Wachstumsrate*

C Outline the information presented in the text.

---

2 Listening: coping with problems

> *Mit Hörverstehensaufgaben umgehen, S. 144*

Tim has called a meeting to discuss problems that migrant children may have when they first arrive. He plays you a recording of four students describing how they felt when they arrived.

37

A Listen and take notes. What were the problems that Adam, Lee, Rosa and Nikita faced? How did they cope with them?

B Use your notes to write a memo with complete sentences for the colleagues who can't join the meeting today.

C The strategies below were taken from an online manual for students who are unhappy at school. Use the correct form of the verbs in the box to complete the sentences. Then decide which strategies you might have recommended to each of the four students.

change • do • feel • go • ignore • take (×2) • talk • work

1 A boy or girl who starts ___ physically threatened by others might decide ___ judo lessons.
2 A child who dislikes ___ homework might want ___ on it with some friends.
3 Some students enjoy ___ things over with other students from the same cultural background.
4 It is best if you can manage ___ people who tease you.
5 If a student refuses ___ to school because of bullying, we suggest ___ to another school.
6 Some students plan ___ revenge on people who have hurt them. Luckily, most students don't.

Talking about strategies

- In a sentence with more than one verb, the main verb can be followed by the *to*-infinitive or the *-ing* form (gerund). There are no rules on why certain verbs require a particular form. All you can do is learn them.

*Cem **likes playing / to play** chess, so he **decided** to join a chess club.*
*He **hopes to make** some new friends.*
*I **suggest talking** to an adult about your problems.*
> *Gerund/Infinitive, p. 229*

D Think of other strategies, then prepare and act out a dialogue in which a student explains his or her problem and a counsellor suggests possible ways of dealing with it.

---

3 Writing: towards successful integration

Discuss the problems young immigrants face. Present a list of strategies to promote successful integration.

Cultural awareness

Tim is preparing the part of the conference that deals with cultural awareness and cultural competence. As your trainer, he gives you some tasks to do.

1 Reading and writing: reports from the field

First, Tim asks you to read what some care professionals say about working with older clients from other cultures.

A Read the cards and sort what the people say under the following headings. There is one more than you need.

cultural knowledge • cultural skills • cultural encounters • cultural background

38

1 « I work in a community centre. We have regular "getting to know you" events in which people from different cultures can mix. A lot of the older people tell their stories and talk about where they lived as children. We also have musical evenings and folk dancing evenings. The ladies prepare the food for these evenings. The events are part of an integration programme aimed at the local community, and I've learned a lot from them too. »

2 « People have different beliefs about God and religion. Some people believe you die and go to heaven. Other people say that you come back to Earth as something else after you die. In some countries, talking about death is a taboo subject, mourners cry and a funeral is often very sad. In other countries, they celebrate a person's death in a happy way. Other people do not want to have a funeral as we know it. It doesn't matter what we think, we have to respect our clients' wishes and the wishes of their families. »

3 « We deal with a lot of migrants in the hospital I work in. In some cultures men and women are strictly separated. They attend different schools, sit in different parts of their place of worship, or eat apart from each other. Some of our clients are very strict about who can touch them. The men will only accept a male carer, and female carers look after women. Immigrants with dementia are an additional challenge. Even though many of them have lived here for years and can speak the language, they slowly start to lose it until only their mother tongue remains. It's fortunate that we have a multilingual staff. »

B **Think:** Which of the three topics above interests you most?
Pair: Pool your ideas with a partner who has the same topic and write a card like the ones above.
Share: Read out your card in groups or in class. Say what you think of the ideas. How far will they help you to become a culturally competent caring professional?

2 Reading and discussion: Who are the older migrants?

Before you can work with older migrants, Tim would like you to talk about the background of some of the older clients.

A Work in pairs and discuss the photos. Where are the people from? When did they probably migrate to Germ? Why did they come here?

B You and your partner are going to read two different texts to find out if your ideas from **A** are correct. Once you have read your texts, you will exchange information with your partner.
Partner A: file 14, page 171 Partner B: file 32, page 179

C After you have exchanged information, get into groups with other pairs. What options might there be for care professionals working with older migrants or their children?

3 Listening: developing cultural competence

> *Mit Hörverständnisaufgaben umgehen, S. 144*

Tim wants to include the topic of cultural competence at the conference. To find out more about the topic, you and Tim attend an interview organized by a local vocational college. Liam Kelly, who teaches intercultural competence in Germany, is talking about its importance in the caring profession.

A Before listening, make sure you know the meanings of the words below. Give synonyms or definitions and use a dictionary if necessary.

1 ethnic
2 diverse
3 sensitive
4 differ
5 prejudice
6 impose sth on sb
7 agnostic
8 atheist

GUIDANCE *For guidance, turn to file G29 on page 194.*

39 **B** Now listen to the interview and answer the questions.

1 What is cultural competence?
2 What is its place in the caring business?
3 What might the expression "diverse cultural and ethnic backgrounds" mean?
4 What is cultural knowledge and how might someone acquire it?
5 How does a carer become sensitive to the way of life of other cultures?
6 What are cultural skills?
7 What are cultural encounters?
8 What is Liam's advice?

C Work in groups. Use your answers to the questions above to start a mind map on cultural competence in care work. Brainstorm more ideas and add them to the mind map.
> *Visualisierungs- und Lernhilfen erstellen, S. 207*

4 Role-play: an interview with a carer

> *An Diskussionen teilnehmen, S. 148*

To prepare for the conference, you put what you have learned into practice in an interview role-play. In groups of four, use the information in your files to prepare and act out the interview.
Partners A and B: file 15, page 171 Partners C and D: file 33, page 179

Supporting migrants

As part of the conference, Tim wants to talk about asylum seekers and how the centre can help them. He has prepared a couple of activities.

---

1 Brainstorming: ideas about asylum seekers

A As a class, write a list of countries and nationalities of people seeking asylum in Germany. For each nationality, brainstorm why someone might leave their country. Think about who the asylum seekers are, e.g. age, qualifications, etc. Put yourself in the shoes of an asylum seeker: what would make you want to leave your home country?

B Now focus on the thoughts that local people have about asylum seekers. Are these positive or negative? Supportive or harmful? True or false? Where do these ideas come from?

C Talk in groups. What kind of care assistance might asylum seekers need?

---

2 Mediation: looking for a volunteer mentor

> *Mediation, p. 164*

Tim would like to attract multilingual volunteers to work with asylum seekers and migrants. He asks for your help in developing an advertisement in English for the centre's website. He gives you the German version of the advertisement.

A Work with a partner. Read the job advertisement and discuss which parts you need to convey.

B Use a dictionary to find the correct translation of any words you do not know.

C In English, describe the project and what they are looking for.

Mentorenprojekt

HELFER WILLKOMMEN!

Seit 1986 hilft unsere Einrichtung traumatisierten Flüchtlingen und Opfern von extremen Menschenrechtsverletzungen. Wir sind eine politisch und religiös unabhängige, nichtstaatliche Menschenrechtsorganisation. **Unser Ziel ist es**, Opfern von Folter, Krieg und anderen schweren Menschenrechtsverletzungen sowie ihren Familienangehörigen einen geschützten Raum und psychotherapeutische Hilfe wie auch soziale Begleitung anzubieten.

Dafür suchen wir freiwillige und ehrenamtliche Helfer, die Geflüchteten, Migranten und Migrantinnen beratend, unterstützend und ermutigend zur Seite stehen. Leisten Sie praktische Hilfe bei der Orientierung in der Stadt, bei der Wohnungssuche, im Umgang mit Behörden und Bürokratie und bei Bildungs-, Ausbildungs- und Arbeitsangelegenheiten. Auch beim Aufbau neuer Kontakte und beim Umgang mit anderskulturellen Lebensgewohnheiten können Sie helfen.

Wir suchen: Helfer, die Kenntnisse in der englischen, arabischen oder einer osteuropäischen Sprache haben. Deutsch sollten Sie mindestens auf dem Sprachlevel B1 sprechen.

Zeitlicher Rahmen: 1× pro Woche, 2–3 Stunden nach Absprache

vorbereitende Einzelgespräche • kostenfreie Informationsbroschüre • Beratung bei allen aufkommenden Fragen • Leitfaden zur Vorbereitung auf Ihre zukünftige Tätigkeit • Internetforum für alle Ehrenamtlichen

Bitte setzen Sie sich telefonisch mit uns unter folgender Nummer in Verbindung …

3 Listening: voicemail messages

> *Mit Hörverstehensaufgaben umgehen, S. 144*

40

A few days after the English advert appears, there are four messages from potential volunteers. Listen to the messages and take notes.

Name of caller:
Languages:
Contact details:
Experience (if any):
Nationality:

---

4 Speaking: voicemail messages

Tim has asked you to call two of the people back to arrange a meeting. As neither is at home, you have to leave a message both times.

Bitte Olena Melnyk und Daniel Mills zurückrufen und jeweils einen Termin vereinbaren.

Telephoning

Spelling names

- "Müller. That's M–U with an umlaut–double L–E–R."
- "Pabst. That's papa–alpha–bravo–sierra–tango."

> *International spelling alphabet, p. 193*

Saying phone numbers

0176 33816745. "That's oh–one–seven–six, double three–eight–one, six–seven–four–five."
NOT: "~~thirty-three, eighty-one~~ …"

Leaving a message

- My name is …
- I'm calling on behalf of … about your application to …
- We were pleased … and would like to …
- If that date and time is not possible, …
- If you are still interested in …, perhaps you would …
- The number is …
- Thank you.

> *Telephoning, p. 205*

Work with a partner. Follow the steps below to prepare and then leave your messages.

1 Decide together on a phone number for the centre.
2 Think about a good way to start the message (stating your name, job title, why you are calling) and make sure you know how to end the message politely.
3 Now turn to one of the files below, read the social worker's notes and leave the message.
Partner A: file 16, p. 172 **Partner B:** file 34, p. 180
4 Evaluate your partner's message. Was it clear and effective?

---

5 Role-play: interviewing prospective volunteers

> *An Diskussionen teilnehmen, S. 148*

The senior social worker has asked you to sit in on an interview with two prospective volunteers. Use the information in your file to prepare and then do the role-plays.
Partners A and B: file 17, page 172 **Partners C and D:** file 35, page 180

---

6 Writing: benefits of living abroad

> *Eine Stellungnahme schreiben, S. 162*

Comment on the following statement: Every student who wants to work in the field of caring should have to work in another country for at least six months.

1 Mind mapping: living a healthy life

> Visualisierungs- und Lernhilfen erstellen, S. 160

Make a mind map showing how we can live a healthy life. Collect words from the topic and add any other words you think are important.

2 Odd one out

Say which word or phrase does not fit in the sets of words and phrases below. Explain why.

1 factory-farmed • free-range • home-cooked
2 balanced diet • fast food • fresh ingredients
3 anorexia • bulimia • a respiratory problem
4 body mass index • eating disorders • height and weight
5 active • slow • sluggish
6 exercise plan • fitness programme • weight-reducing products

3 Talking about health and fitness

> If-sentences, p. 228

Complete these type 2 *if*-sentences with the correct form of the verbs in brackets.

1 If you ___ (take) more exercise, you ___ (feel) much better.
2 If I ___ (lose) weight, I ___ (fit) into my favourite jeans.
3 You ___ (be) healthier if you ___ (follow) the recommendations on the food plate.
4 If the fitness club ___ (not cost) so much, I ___ (go) there more often.
5 ___ (you / enjoy) exercising more if you ___ (do) it in a group?
6 What ___ (you / say) to your friend if she ___ (have) an eating disorder?
7 If I ___ (be) a vegetarian, I ___ (eat) mostly salad and fruit.
8 I ___ (enjoy) the Australian boot camp if I ___ (go) there.

4 Talking about intercultural competence

> Gerund/Infinitive, p. 229

Rewrite these sentences using the sentence beginnings given and a gerund or an infinitive. Sometimes both forms are possible.

1 I think you should attend a workshop on intercultural competence.
I suggest ___
2 I think I will try and learn more about different cultures.
I have decided ___
3 I was talking to a patient but then answered the phone.
I stopped ___
4 I like to talk to people from all over the world.
I enjoy ___
5 She won't let a male nurse look after her.
She refuses ___

5 Describing change

> *Simple past, p. 220; Present perfect, p. 221*

A Put the verbs in brackets into the correct form.

1 The definition of "family" ___ (change) over the decades.
2 Intercultural families ___ (always be) common in London.
3 Many years ago, most mothers ___ (not go out) to work; instead they ___ (stay) at home and ___ (take care of) the house and children.
4 Divorce rates ___ (rise) over the years, which ___ (mean) an increase in single-parent families and stepfamilies.
5 Over the last ten years, more and more gay couples ___ (adopt) children.
6 Until recently, single-parent families ___ (not get) enough help from the social services.

B Make sentences with *used to* and *didn't use to* about couples and families fifty years ago.

1 bigger families
2 marry more than once
3 take leave after childbirth
4 share household duties
5 take care of elderly parents at home

---

6 Saying how often things happen

> *Adverbs of frequency, p. 231*

Decide where to put the adverbs of frequency in the following sentences.

1 The Browns are a dysfunctional family. The neighbours hear them fighting. (often)
2 If Mr Brown comes home drunk, he beats his wife. (sometimes)
3 The family eats together.(never) The children look hungry. (always)
4 In the old days, single mothers left home to give birth to their babies in secret. (sometimes)
5 The grandmothers brought up the babies as their own children. (frequently)
6 Single mothers have more choices nowadays. (usually)

---

7 Leaving a voicemail message

Complete the voicemail message with words and phrases from the box.

application • behalf of • call • look • looking • volunteer • volunteering

Good morning, my name is Ben Grant. I'm calling on ___[1] the Care and More Agency about your ___[2] to join our team as a ___[3]. If you are still ___[4] to play a role and are interested in ___[5], perhaps you would give me a ___[6]. My number is 0758 764809.
I ___[7] forward to hearing from you.

Choose one of the following two projects.

1 Making a poster or video: options for working with migrants in your area

You are going to make a poster or a video showing local options for caring professionals and/or volunteers who would like to work with migrants. Work in small groups.

Step 1 Walk through your neighbourhood or town and look for places which might offer possibilities for migrants to meet. These could be community centres or multicultural cafés. Find out if there are any homes for asylum seekers in your area. In some cities, you will find information in *Stadtteilmanagement* offices.

Step 2 Choose one or two of the places and get information about what happens there. (You will have to do this in German.) Find out about the clientele and the roles carers play there. If it is appropriate, you might like to get this information from someone in charge. Send an email enquiry first, explaining who you are and why you would like to visit the place and talk to somebody personally.

Step 3 Once you have done your research, gather all your information and decide what you are going to present in English on your poster or in your video.
For the poster: Think about texts, photos, illustrations and graphs.
For the video: Think about what it will show: only places or also people? Look at the tips on pages 72–73 for producing a video and information about privacy rights and permissions.

Step 4 Design your poster. / Film and edit your video.

Step 5 Present your work.
For the poster: Hang all the posters on the classroom wall and do a gallery walk.
For the video: Show your video and watch the other teams' videos.
Take notes and give feedback to the other teams. Decide as a class on the best option. Perhaps even take action by contacting the organization.

Giving feedback

- I think your poster/video looks ...
- The information you presented was very interesting/surprising/...
- It was well made and kept my attention.
- You should check the language thoroughly for mistakes.
- I didn't notice any mistakes in the language.
- The poster could be a bit more colourful / structured a little better /...

2 Writing a scene for a reality show

Your task is to work in groups and develop a scene from a scripted (or semi-scripted) reality show in which a carer or counsellor is helping a family cope with difficulties.

Step 1 Talk about which reality shows on TV focus on the family. What support are families given? Who supports them? How are conflicts shown? Make a mind map.

> *Visualisierungs- und Lernhilfen erstellen, S. 160*

FAMILIES IN SCRIPTED REALITY SHOWS

- *Zuhause im Glück*
  Families with problems are helped to renovate their house. Supported by Eva Brenner and John Kosmalla
  …
- *Teenie-Mütter*
  …
- *Familien im Brennpunkt*
  Families who are having problems bringing up their children are given advice.
  …

Step 2 Choose one of the shows and brainstorm ideas for an episode. Make notes.

Step 3 Use your notes to produce a list of characters. One of the characters should be a carer or counsellor. Imagine an important scene showing how the carer or counsellor supports the family.

Step 4 Now write the scene for your episode in the form of a storyboard or film script. Explain the situation, say who is involved and say how the characters are supported.

Step 5 Present your episode to the class and act out the scene you have chosen.

CHECKING PROGRESS

Browse through the previous pages in this topic, looking at headings and pictures. What have you learned? What can you do now that you have learned these things?

- ✓ I can identify what a healthy diet means for children (Section A)
- ✓ I can help people with chronic conditions plan their diet. (Section A)
- ✓ I can talk about dysfunctional families. (Section B)
- ✓ I can practise cultural competence. (Section C)
- ✓ I can take and leave messages. (Section C)
- ✓ I can present options for working with migrants. (Project)

Write down two more statements for yourself.

Preparing for the arrival of refugees

The Health and Community Centre (HCC) is expecting 200 refugees from different countries in a few weeks. In order to prepare for their arrival, the centre has decided to:

- create a new webpage with all relevant information for the refugees,
- hold a meeting to discuss the next steps for supporting the refugees,
- document these steps and create an action plan and
- contact local organizations and private individuals and ask for support and funding.

Follow the steps below to begin your preparation.

Step 1 Create a website.

- In small teams, look at the three Sections in topic 5 again. Make notes and summarize the services, help and support that your organization offers.
- Compare your findings with those of the other teams.
- As a group, decide how you can best present HCC's services on an info page (e.g. as a text, mind map, infographic, etc.).
- Create the content for a webpage with the most relevant services.

Step 2 As a class, hold a meeting to discuss how to organize support for the refugees. Remember to take notes. Talk about the following points:

> *An Diskussionen teilnehmen, S. 148*

- What kind of people will come (e.g. children)?
- What kind of help will they need most urgently (e.g. accommodation)?
- What activities can you offer to children and young people (e.g. entertainment)?
- How can you prepare the migrants for life in a new country? (e.g. cultural awareness)
- What would be a nice event to welcome the refugees? (e.g. picnic)
- How will you divide the tasks?
- Who are you going to contact for support (e.g. which local organizations/individuals might help you)?
- How are you going to contact them (e.g. by phone)?

Exchanging ideas and suggestions

- They will probably / most likely / … be / need / …
- For the kids, we could organize a …
- A good activity for the young people might be …
- I suggest that we …
- What about …?
- I think a good idea would be to …
- I don't mind helping with …
- I can …, if you could …

Step 3 Depending on the results of the meeting and how the tasks were allocated:

- Give a brief summary of what was discussed in the meeting.
- Create an action plan for your team that describes the concrete steps you are going to take.
- Include information on who you will contact and how.

Step 4 Contact local organizations and individuals to ask for help or funding.

- First, decide what form of communication you will use to ask for support.
- Then work in teams of two to role-play a phone call, leave a message or write a letter or an email. Each team should do two different tasks.

Which tasks in this topic offer relevant vocabulary? List the words and phrases that you will need. The language box will also help you.

Asking for support or contributions

- I am writing on behalf of … [name of organization], where I work as a …
- We are preparing for the arrival of 200 refugees in …
- In a few weeks, 200 refugees from different countries will arrive in …
- We are writing to ask if you could help us support the newcomers by …
- In order to help them, we will need …
- We are looking specifically for … [items/services].
- As a major manufacturer/provider of … [product/service], perhaps you would like to contribute …

1 Role-play a telephone call. > *Telephoning, p. 205*

Partner A: As a team member of HCC, you call an organization to ask for support for the refugees. You need help with language classes and support with translating. Before you make the call, make notes on what you want to tell and ask the other person.

Partner B: You work for an organization offering language classes and translation services. Before you receive the call, make notes on what you can offer.

2 Leave a message on voicemail.

Partner A: As a team member of HCC, you call a big international company to ask for support for the refugees. Before you make your call, make notes on what you want to tell and ask the other person.

Partner B: You work for a big international company and are out of office today. Before you receive the call, write a text for your own recorded message. If possible, record it. When the phone rings, read it aloud or play it for the caller.

3 Write a letter or an email. > *Correspondence, p. 199*

- Explain who you are and why you are writing.
- Describe the situation and say what support is needed.
- Decide how many details you want to include about your organization, the refugees and the kind of help you are asking for.
- Also include your contact and bank details if necessary.

A Dealing with conflicts

- Harassment
- Case assessment
- Downsizing

B Handling complaints

- Telephone complaints
- Dealing with problems in writing

6 Solving problems at work

A Look at the topics listed in sections A and B above. What information do you think each topic includes? Discuss with a partner.

B Skim the points on the notepad. With your partner, sort the points under the three section A headings: harassment, case assessment and downsizing. Compare your answers in class.

C Look at these statements about workplace problems and conflicts. Which topics in sections A and B do you think deal with these problems? One of the statements has no match.

1 "Our organization has been taken over by a big company and they're planning to reduce staff."
2 "I often have to email customers and explain what went wrong."
3 "Unwelcome behaviour that threatens employees and creates a hostile workplace is not tolerated."
4 "We use social media to discuss workplace problems."
5 "In my job, I speak to clients who are unhappy. It's all the support we can offer them."
6 "We look at each person individually and try to understand their needs and how we can help them."

D Describe and analyse the cartoon. What does it say about resolving conflicts?

> *Cartoons beschreiben und analysieren, S. 210*

- supervision
- sexual harassment
- mobbing
- mediation
- stress
- alcoholism
- counselling
- burnout
- conflict
- racial discrimination
- face-to-face discussion
- legal advice
- intimidation
- depression
- inner resignation

C Projects

- Solving a problem through mediation
- Creating a flow chart for handling complaints

"A mediator hasn't worked, so I brought in everyone's moms."

WHAT'S TO COME

Scenario: You are doing a work placement at Workplace Counselling Services (WCS), which advises businesses in aspects related to conflicts and complaints in the workplace. WCS has been contacted by the human resources (HR) department of the German IT company SystemTec. HR is concerned about a rise in the number of complaints about workplace harassment and unacceptable behaviour among staff. Also, employees at SystemTec's Dublin office are stressed and unhappy as a result of recent restructuring.
The unresolved conflicts and dissatisfaction have had a negative effect on the work with clients, which is why the company's management has asked WCS to create a new concept for preventing and dealing with conflicts within the company. Your team will work on this concept.

But first: You will assist Claudia Weber. She has been assigned to work with SystemTec.
- At SystemTec you will mediate in a case of workplace harassment; analyse the source of stress and dissatisfaction that an employee is experiencing and help employees deal with the effects of company restructuring. (Section A)
- While assisting Claudia in a communication training seminar for the organization Jugendforum, you will practise handling telephone complaints and formulate a written response to an unhappy client. (Section B)

Now you are ready to start working on your concept!

Harassment

As part of your work placement at Workplace Counselling Services (WCS), you are assisting Claudia Weber, who has been assigned to work with the IT firm SystemTec. The first session is with Vera Lebedeva, a 45-year-old electronics engineer. Vera has complained to HR about being harassed by male colleagues.

1 Mediation: understanding what harassment is

> *Mediation, S. 164*

Claudia Weber would like you to prepare yourself for the session, which is to be held in English. She gives you the information below.

A Read the document and match the English words and phrases (1–10) to their equivalents in the text.

1 intimidation
2 jokes about sexual orientation
3 offensive remarks
4 picking on someone
5 sexually suggestive emails
6 sexual gestures
7 sexual harassment
8 staring in a sexually suggestive manner
9 telling sexual or lewd jokes
10 touching in an inappropriate manner

B Summarize the document in English.

Konfliktmanagement § 35: Beispiele für Belästigung

Einige Beispiele sexueller Belästigung

- Anstößige Bemerkungen zum Aussehen, zur Kleidung, zu Körperteilen
- Witze über die sexuelle Ausrichtung
- Das Anstarren auf geschlechtlich betonte Weise
- Unangemessene Körperberührung
- Das Erzählen von sexuellen oder anzüglichen Witzen
- Erotikbetonte Bilder am Arbeitsplatz; sexuelle Gesten
- Die Versendung, Weiterleitung oder Anforderung aufreizender oder zweideutiger Briefe, Schriftstücke, E-Mails oder Abbildungen

Beispiele für andere Arten von Belästigung

- Einschüchterung
- Jemanden andauernd kritisieren
- Negative Bemerkungen über das Alter von Kollegen und Kolleginnen machen, die 40 Jahre oder älter sind.

2 Listening: scenes from a session

> *Mit Hörverstehensaufgaben umgehen, S. 207*

41

A Listen to the first part of the session and answer the following questions.

1 How does Claudia introduce herself?
2 How does she introduce you? What is your function at the session?
3 What does Claudia say and do to make Vera feel comfortable?

42 **B** Listen to the second part of the session and take notes on Vera's description of the harassment.
GUIDANCE *For guidance, turn to file G30 on page 194.*

C Use the information from the document in **1B** to describe the situation as Vera perceives it. Which examples of sexual harassment does she report?

43 **D** Listen to the conclusion of the session. Take notes so that you can do the following tasks.

1. Describe what happened when Vera opened the email.
2. Outline the options Claudia offers Vera.
3. Explain Vera's decision. Point out her reasons for the decision.

E CHALLENGE! Listen "between the lines" to the complete session. What observations of your own can you make about the situation?

---

3 Mediation and role-play: dealing with harassment

> *Mediation, S. 164*

Vera has decided to wait and see how things develop. Claudia gives you the German document below and asks you to use it to give Vera some advice.

Konfliktmanagement, § 36: Mobbing

Ratschläge für angemessenes Verhalten bei Mobbing

Sprechen Sie den Kollegen / die Kollegin, von dem/der Sie sich gemobbt fühlen, auf sein/ihr Verhalten an – am besten unter vier Augen. Fordern Sie ihn/ihr auf, dieses Verhalten zu beenden – aber sprechen Sie dabei keine Drohungen aus. Allerdings funktioniert ein solches Gespräch nur, wenn sich die Situation nicht schon zu weit zugespitzt hat.
Lassen Sie sich durch Kritik oder Nörgelei nicht einschüchtern. Nehmen Sie keine Verteidigungshaltung ein.
Schreiben Sie Vorfälle, die Ihnen als Mobbingversuche erscheinen, mit Datum, Beteiligten und eventuellen Zeugen genau auf. Pflegen Sie, wo immer das möglich ist, gute Kontakte zu Ihren Kollegen und Kolleginnen. Nehmen Sie weiterhin aktiv am betrieblichen Alltagsleben teil.
Schreiben Sie auf nachprüfbare Weise Ihre laufenden Arbeitsleistungen auf, um gegen mögliche Vorwürfe gewappnet zu sein. Protokollieren Sie auch, falls Ihnen unzumutbare Arbeiten zugewiesen werden.
Überdenken Sie Ihre bisherigen Verhaltensweisen im Betrieb: Könnte es sein, dass Sie durch unangemessenes Verhalten auch selbst zur Mobbing-Situation beigetragen haben?

A First make sure you know what the highlighted words mean in English. (Use your dictionary if necessary.) Then make notes in English for your meeting with Vera.

B Now work with a partner. One of you takes on Vera's role while the other gives her advice.

Giving advice

- It's a good idea to …
- If you can, you should …
- Try not to …
- Perhaps you could think about …
- Have you ever considered talking …?
- Why don't you try speaking …?

> *Giving advice, p. 212*

Case assessment

The second session today is with Glen Carter, a 36-year-old American employee who works in IT Support at SystemTec. The company doctor believes that Glen is suffering from stress.

1 Reading: analysing a stress checklist

> Schwierige Texte lesen, S. 154

Glen has completed a two-page stress checklist. Claudia would like you to go through the pages with her before the session, which is to decide how to support Glen. It will be in English.

A Work with a partner. Read "Before you start", do your task, then compare your information.
Partner A: After reading, study how Glen has evaluated the statements.
Partner B: After reading, turn to file 39 on page 182 and read Glen's comments.

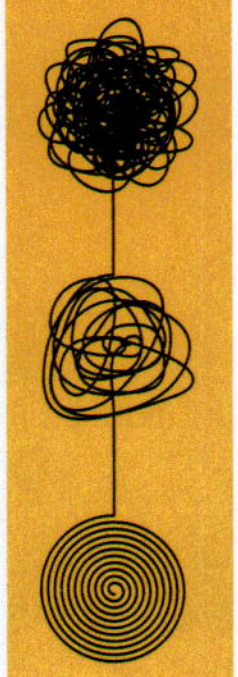

Stress Checklist

page 1

Before you start ... This checklist will help us find out if your stress level is too high. It will also help you to recognize some of the conditions that cause you to feel stressed. Evaluate the statements below as they relate to your experience: from 0 = never to 5 = always. When you have completed the checklist, please use page 2 for comments.

Statement		Evaluation
1	I have too much responsibility.	0
2	My work situation is unclear; there are too many people to satisfy.	5
3	There is a great deal of time pressure at work.	3
4	I have trouble focusing on a given task.	0
5	I have difficulty communicating with my spouse, children, family, boss or co-workers.	5
6	I handle most things alone with little support from family, friends or co-workers.	5
7	I do not have enough say in decisions that affect me.	5
8	I regularly have headaches; I have muscle tension in my shoulders, neck or back.	5
9	I have stomach pains, indigestion or other digestive problems.	4
10	I regularly take aspirin, indigestion medication, sleeping pills or tranquilizers.	5
11	I drink a great deal of coffee or other caffeinated beverages.	4
12	I drink alcohol every day / regularly.	0

B Add up the numbers and compare the result with the table in file 40 on page 182. Discuss the advice given and decide what recommendations might be suitable.

2 Listening: the challenging client

> Mit Hörverstehensaufgaben umgehen, S. 144

Glen arrives 15 minutes late for his appointment and takes a while to settle down.

44

A Listen to an excerpt from the first part of the session and do the tasks below.

1 Point out how Glen feels about counselling.
2 Describe Claudia's response.
3 Explain what Claudia would like to do.

45 **B** Listen to the conclusion of the session and answer the questions.

1 Why is Glen not motivated?
2 How would he like things to change at work?
3 How might he achieve his aims?

3 Reporting what someone says

Look at what Glen, his boss and colleagues said. Use the dialogue extracts to report what was said.

Start like this:
Glen told his boss that he wanted …. He asked his boss if …

1 Glen: "I want to take on more responsibility. Can I take on another project?"
Boss: "No, I think it's better if you just take it easy and focus on your current tasks."
2 Glen: "I studied at MIT, Boston and graduated at the top of my class."
Boss: "I know that. But what year was that?"
3 Colleague A: "Do you know what is wrong with Glen? He always eats alone at his desk and looks so unhappy."
Colleague B: "I don't know. I think he's angry that he didn't get the promotion. I'll ask him to join us at the canteen, but he'll probably just say no. He never takes a proper break."

GUIDANCE *For guidance, turn to file G31 on page 194.*

Reporting what someone says

- If we report what someone said with a reporting verb (e.g. *tell sb, ask*) in the simple past, the verbs in the original sentence move back in time.

Glen: "I wrote down what my colleagues said."
*Glen **told** Claudia that he **had written down** what his colleagues **had said**.*

> *Reported speech, p. 224*

4 Role-play and writing: the follow-up appointment

> *An Diskussionen teilnehmen, S. 148*

Claudia has arranged a follow-up meeting with the aim of mediating between Glen and his supervisor. She asks you to sit in on the meeting and take notes.

A Work in groups of four.

Partner A: You are Glen (file 19, page 173).
Partner B: You are Claudia (file 23, page 175).
Partner C: You are Glen's boss, Janice (file 36, page 180).
Partner D: You are the trainee. Your task is to take notes which can be used to write a record of the meeting. While the others are preparing, write the names of the participants in your notebook, with space beside each for notes.

B In your group, read the trainee's notes and add anything else from the meeting which you think is important. Write the record of the meeting together.

Writing a record of a meeting

As a professional in the field of caring, you may be asked to produce a record of a meeting for a client's file. This record will include specific details so that everyone who is involved with the client knows what has been discussed and agreed. It is important to record everything carefully and accurately. Include the date, time and place of the meeting, who was present (+ job titles if appropriate) and any decisions which have been made.

Useful phrases

- X explained/suggested/recommended that …
- It was decided/agreed that …
- Y is to talk to / meet with …

> *Writing a record of a meeting, p. 213*

Downsizing

SystemTec is restructuring its office in Dublin. Tomorrow you will accompany Claudia to Ireland and will meet some of the employees. In preparation, you read some entries from a forum with comments from users around the world.

1 Reading: effects of downsizing

> Schwierige Texte lesen, S. 154

46

Has your company been restructured & your job affected? Tell your story.

ALVIN

I've just been told that I'm being laid off at the end of the year. The HR manager explained very fully about why the cuts were necessary and described how badly the market was doing in our sector. She explained how my severance package would be calculated. I kept waiting for her to say: "Thanks for the 22 years of your life that you've invested in the company." She didn't.

CLARA

In my firm here in the US, it was all done very quickly. On the Monday morning, a notice was pinned up on the bulletin board to inform the staff that there would be some lay-offs, and staff who were affected would be invited to a meeting later in the week. On the Wednesday, an email was sent out to 127 people, announcing a 5 p.m. meeting. Fifteen minutes into the meeting, our boss broke the news: "You will all be leaving in two weeks' time".

DEAN

I gave my life to my work. I worked overtime to meet delivery dates and I worked during my holiday. Where am I now? After 28 years as a company man, I am now back to square one: 52 years old and standing in line at the job centre with kids just out of university. I've heard that my old company is already hiring new staff – university graduates. No experience, but, hey, they're cheap and they're keen to show how smart they are. I'd be happy to take my experience and know-how to any of our rivals, but I'm too expensive.

EVELYN

When my company downsized last year, social factors were used to decide who would be fired and who would be kept on. I'm a single parent with two school-aged children so I had enough points and could stay on. In the downsizing process, the company was forced to offer me another position. I was retrained as a teleworker and work from home. The work is OK, but I miss my colleagues and the atmosphere in the office.

JOHN

The company I worked for behaved insensitively too. My boss was great, though. She let me use the rest of my time and the office resources to look for new work. I'm well qualified and I would have found a job in my sector easily, but I decided to go freelance. That was six years ago, and my business is now doing so well that I have to outsource some of my work. (435 words)

A Scan the text to find:

1 five words or expressions that have to do with being made unemployed.
2 the term for the conditions offered to employees when their work contracts are ended.
3 three words to describe alternative ways of working or getting work done.

B Use the following points to talk about the cases.

1 Describe the "insensitive" behaviour experienced by Alvin and Clara.
2 Analyse Dean's point of view: "After 28 years as a company man, I am now back to square one: 52 years old and standing in line at the job centre with kids just out of university."
3 Explain why Evelyn is doing telework; say how she feels about it and what she intends to do.
4 Describe the positive experience John had just after he had been told he was being laid off; say what he did and describe how things are now.

2 Discussion: who said what?

Claudia asked you to take notes during the talks with employees at the company.

A Complete the original quotes with the missing verbs.

have been given • have been laid off • have been made • is being outsourced • was respected • will all be given

1 My entire staff ___ overseas starting next month. At least they ___ a good severance package.
2 These cuts ___ to keep the company running and to provide workplaces for people abroad.
3 For me this is great news. I ___ the chance to do my own thing and start my own business.
4 I always thought I ___ by my superiors and colleagues, but clearly I was mistaken.
5 So many good employees ___ so far. The news hasn't been easy to give, nor to receive.

B Now match the quotes to the people who said them.

CEO • employee • future freelancer • HR manager • senior manager

Talking about circumstances beyond your control

- We use the passive when we do not know the subject of the sentence or it is not important.
- We use *by* to say who does the action.

Work ***is being outsourced****.*
Many people ***have been laid off by*** *ABC Engineering.*

> *The passive, p. 227*

3 Discussion: socially sensitive restructuring

Claudia emails you a list of tools firms can use to restructure in a socially sensitive manner.

A There is a problem and the tools have become jumbled. Match 1–7 with a–g.

1 counselling in order to work through
2 skills assessment to assess the benefits
3 training to prepare an employee for
4 mobility assistance to help an employee
5 alternative work schedules and/or ways
6 severance packages as compensation for
7 survivor round tables to provide the

a of working e.g. part-time, flexitime, teleworking
b feelings of anger and find acceptance
c who has to move away to find work
d loss of earnings
e of retraining people
f opportunity for those still employed to talk openly about the change
g a move to another department

B Sort the tools into the categories a and b below (some will be in both). Which tools would have been useful to help the people who posted on the forum?

a support for employees who will be kept on under different conditions
b support for employees who have lost their jobs

4 Writing: how (not to) restructure

> *EIne Stellungnahme schreiben, S. 162*

Take on a point of view of your choice, e.g. of a mediator or an employee, and comment on how staff are affected by restructuring and downsizing. Give examples.

Telephone complaints

Claudia has organized a communication training seminar for Jugendforum, an organization which has been getting more English calls recently and also some complaints. You assist her. On day one, the focus is on conflict management strategies for telephone complaints.

1 Discussion: dealing with conflicts

What conflict management strategies do you think the seminar will cover?

2 Reading: advice about conflict management strategies

> Schwierige Texte lesen, S. 154

Claudia gives you a printout with some tips from WCS's communication guidelines.

A Read the telephone tips. Match the sentences (a–f) with the correct tip.

a Present a solution.
b Give the client your full attention.
c Thank the client.
d Show you care and apologize.
e Take action immediately.
f Summarize the client's concerns.

47

Tips for dealing with unhappy customers

1 People who are angry need to be heard. Upset clients or patients want to express their feelings. Stay calm and let the clients talk – don't interrupt them. While they are talking, don't think about what you are going to say next. And don't forget that the caller can hear what you are doing. Avoid any noises that show the client you are not giving them your full attention, for example eating or typing on your computer. If you type, let the client know that it is related to the conversation you are having.

2 Once the client has explained what went wrong, repeat what he or she said in your own words. This allows you to check if you have identified the problem correctly. It also shows that you are listening and take their problem seriously. Use the client's name to show respect and be more personal.

3 Show you understand why the client is upset and empathize. Say that you are sorry for what happened. Understand that even if the situation isn't your fault, the client is unhappy and wants you to show empathy.

4 Explain what you can and what you can't do. If possible, suggest a solution that will make the client happy. If that is not possible, show your willingness to help the client as best as you can.

5 Now you need to act quickly and let the client know what will happen. Explain how exactly you are going to fix the problem and when it will be solved.

6 Thank the client for sharing his or her problem with you. Let them know that their feedback is welcome and that you were glad to be of help.

(315 words)

B Read these phrases for handling complaints. Sort them under the correct tips (1–6) above.

1 I understand how annoying that must be.
2 I'd be happy to offer you …
3 What I will do right now is …
4 Let me suggest a way we can resolve this for you.
5 I'm typing some notes on my computer as we speak.
6 I'm sorry to hear that.
7 OK, let me just summarize what happened.
8 As a solution, may I suggest …
9 Right, I'll just enter this into our files.
10 So what you're saying is that …
11 The next steps are …
12 I'll deal with this matter straight away
13 Let me make sure I've got this right.
14 Thanks for bringing this to my attention.

3 Mediation: a youth adventure camp

> *Mediation, S. 164*

Before you listen to a complaint, the Jugendforum employees show you some iinfo on their website. Read the text and answer these frequently asked questions that customers have sent.

1 Where exactly is the camp and what does it offer?
2 How do we pay and when?
3 What documents do we need to travel?
4 What is your cancellation policy?

www.jufo-nordost.nex

Abenteuer-Camp: Jugendfreizeit in Portugal

Sonne, Meer, Sport und Abenteuer in Portugal? Kommt in unser Abenteuer-Camp an der portugiesischen Algarve! Hier auf unserer 5 Hektar großen Anlage umgeben von Wäldern bieten wir euch Spiele, Outdoor-Erlebnisse und Entdeckungen in der Natur.

Teilnahmebedingungen Mit Vertragsabschluss wird eine Anzahlung von 50 % des Teilnahmebetrags fällig. Die Restzahlung ist 30 Tage vor Veranstaltungsbeginn zu begleichen.

Ausweis- und Einreisebestimmungen Für deutsche Staatsbürger/-innen ist ein gültiger Kinderausweis, Personalausweis oder Reisepass notwendig. Nicht deutsche Staatsbürger/-innen wenden sich zur Beratung bitte an die jeweilige Geschäftsstelle.

Gruppengröße und Mindestteilnehmer/-innenzahl Die Reise wird unter Vorbehalt einer Mindestteilnehmer/-innenzahl von 10 angeboten und ist für eine Gruppengröße von 10 bis 25 Personen konzipiert. Bei Nichterreichen bis spätestens 30 Tage vor Reiseantritt ist der Veranstalter berechtigt, vom Reisevertrag zurückzutreten.

4 Listening: an angry client

> *Mit Hörverstehensaufgaben umgehen, S. 144*

Claudia plays a recording in which Hannes Schmidt from Jugendforum handles a call from a client who booked the adventure camp.

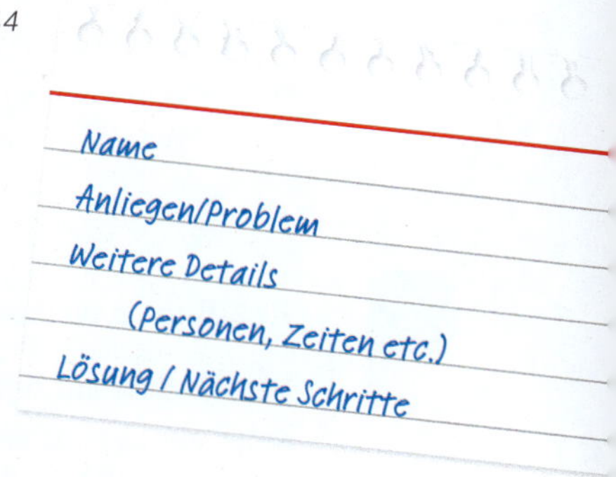

48

A Listen and take notes in German on these points.

B Which information did the client get wrong?

C Match the sentence parts from the dialogue. Then listen again and check.

1 What exactly can
2 Let me just make sure
3 Let me see what I
4 Could you give me
5 I understand how annoying
6 I'm sure we can resolve
7 How does
8 I'm glad I was

a this issue for you.
b I understand you correctly.
c able to assist you.
d the trip details, please?
e that must be for you
f I do for you?
g that sound?
h can do for you.

5 Role-play: an unhappy client

Now it is your turn to deal with some complaints on the phone. Work with a partner.
Partner A: file 20, page 173 **Partner B:** file 37, page 181

Dealing with problems in writing

During the seminar, Claudia talks about various problems that Jugendforum employees may need to address. Then she helps you formulate a written response to an unhappy client.

---

1 Handling different types of problems

Claudia gives you some words you will need when you practise writing to clients.

A Match the words (a–h) to their definition (1–8).

a	delay	1	different people have different ideas of what was said
b	error	2	sth stopped working or isn't working as it should
c	failure	3	a wrong decision or sth that goes wrong in a computer system
d	fault	4	sth went wrong because sb didn't notice sth
e	mistake	5	a wrong action that causes confusion
f	misunderstanding	6	sth for which sb is to blame, or a weakness in a system or technical device
g	mix-up	7	an action by a person that has an unpleasant result
h	oversight	8	sth happens later than planned or agreed

B Complete the sentences with words from **A**.

1. It will take a few more days to look into your application. We're sorry about this ___.
2. We didn't notice that your address had not been updated. This was an ___ on our part.
3. There has been a ___. I said that I would call you *tomorrow*, not today.
4. I'm very sorry that you haven't received the information. That was my ___.
5. Due to an administrative ___, the payment was rejected.
6. We couldn't send any emails yesterday because of a complete system ___.

---

2 Reading: a written complaint

Hannes Schmidt has received an email about another holiday trip that Jugendforum offers for teenagers. Read the email, then answer the questions.

1. What details does Kevin Fox give about who is travelling, the destination and the travel dates?
2. What is the problem he mentions?
3. What does he ask Hannes Schmidt to do?

GUIDANCE *For guidance, turn to file G32 on page 195.*

From: Kevin.Fox@email.nex
To: hannes.schmidt@Jugendforum.ger
Date: 15 July 20xx
Subject: Issue with documents for summer camp

Dear Mr Schmidt

A few weeks ago, I booked the summer camp in Austria for our daughter Kira (10–24 August). We paid the 50% deposit and when we spoke on the phone, you promised to send an info package about the trip and a booking confirmation.

It is now only a few weeks until the beginning of the summer camp and we still haven't heard from you or received anything. I'm getting worried that there is a problem with our booking!

Please look into this and let me know what you plan to do.

I look forward to hearing from you soon.

Regards

Kevin Fox

3 Writing: replying to a customer complaint by email

Claudia asks you to draft a reply. You need to check the German expressions in italics to complete your email. Match them with the correct phrases in the box.

It looks as if • Please accept my apologies • I am very sorry to hear • Due to an error • Unfortunately, we did not notice our mistake • I will make sure • I have looked into this matter • it was an oversight on our part

Dear Mr Fox

Thank you for your email. ___[1] *(Es tut mir sehr leid zu hören)* that you have not received any response from us. ___[2] *(Ich habe diese Angelegenheit geprüft)* and would like to give you an update on the current status. ___[3] *(Es sieht so aus, als ob)* the information package and confirmation was sent to the wrong address. ___[4] *(Wegen eines Fehlers)* in our database, your address details were incorrect. It appears the street name was wrong. This is why the package was returned to us a few days later. It was sent a second time a week later, but I am afraid the same thing happened again. After that, no further action was taken.
___[5] *(Leider bemerkten wir unseren Fehler nicht)* until we received your email including your address. When I checked it against our database details, I found that this mix-up had caused the problem.
Let me say again that ___[6] *(dies ein Versehen unsererseits war)*, which should not have happened. ___[7] *(Ich bitte Sie für … um Entschuldigung)* for the delay and inconvenience that this has caused you. ___[8] *(Ich werde sicherstellen)* that you receive your info package and booking confirmation within the next few days.
If you have any further questions, please feel free to contact me at any time.

Yours sincerely

Hannes Schmidt
Jugendforum

---

4 Role-play: dealing with complaints

> *An Diskussionen teilnehmen, S. 148*

With a partner, practise handling a complaint.

A Each of you writes down a complaint that you want to make on a card or piece of paper. Include brief notes outlining:

- what went wrong
- when it happened
- what action you expect

Then give your card to your partner.

B Study the details of your partner's complaint and make notes on how you plan to respond. Remember the strategies and language you have learned in this unit.

C Act out your dialogues.

Giving explanations

- I'm afraid we are having problems with …
- Due to a computer problem/…, we / our customers were not able to …
- Unfortunately, there has been a mistake/ mix-up regarding …
- The problem/delay was caused by …
- It appears/seems that …
- I'm afraid there has been a misunderstanding/ mix-up …

6 PRACTICE

1 Problems at work

A Use words from the box to form collocations for talking about clients who have problems at work. You can use some of the words in more than one collocation.

> conditions • discrimination • discussion • level • manner • orientation • pains • pressure • problems • remarks • session • tension

1 digestive	4 muscle	7 sexual	10 stomach
2 face-to-face	5 offensive	8 sexually suggestive	11 time
3 follow-up	6 racial	9 stress	12 working

B Which collocations can be used to talk about the following topics?

a counselling / giving advice
b harassment
c medical problems
d work

---

2 Reporting what people said

> *Reported speech, p. 224*

Change the direct speech into reported speech.

1 "I've had enough of this company. I'm leaving," Vera said.
2 "Ms Lebedeva does not speak German well. This causes some problems," the supervisor explained.
3 "We would like to apologize if we have hurt Vera's feelings. We really thought she would see it as a joke," one of her colleagues said.
4 "I'm one of the best in my field," Glen stated.
5 "I'm willing to give him a chance, but he has to adopt a more positive attitude," the boss explained.
6 "We are trying to include Glen in some of our after-work activities," one of his colleagues said.
7 "The economic situation at the moment is not good," a spokesperson for the company reported.
8 "We have given our workers excellent severance packages," the CEO claimed.

---

3 Talking about being laid off

Complete the forum entry with words from the box.

> downsize • laid off • lay-offs • meeting • overworked • rumours • sector • severance package • trends

Before we heard the news from management, my colleagues and I had read about the proposed ___[1] in *Business Online*. The news didn't come as a big surprise. There had been ___[2] that the company had problems. Once the news was out, management called a ___[3]. The CEO began by saying that the company had been forced to ___[4] because of market conditions in our ___[5]. He went on to say that the company had been keeping a close eye on ___[6] for several months and had tried all they could to avoid it but, sorry, some people would have to go. I got a good ___[7] and I found another job quite quickly. I met some of my old colleagues last week and they complained about being ___[8]. I'm happy with my new job, and glad I was ___[9].

4 Changing active to passive

> *The passive, p. 227*

Change these active sentences into passive sentences. Remember to use *by* when necessary.

1 Some male colleagues harassed Vera.
2 Vera's supervisor has advised her to have counselling.
3 The doctor told Glen about the effects of stress.
4 They will assess Glen's case next week.
5 The company employs a lot of highly-qualified workers.
6 They have laid off 200 people.
7 The boss gave the staff reasons for the lay-offs.
8 Most of the workers have accepted the severance pay offer.

5 Different types of problems

Match how people describe problems in speaking (1–6) with how they summarize the same problems in writing (a–f).

1 "We got a new computer system last week. For a few days after that, we weren't able to see and use our patients' data."
2 "Last week, three people were off sick in our centre and there were just two people left to deal with the clients. We didn't have enough time to answer all the emails, so people will have to wait a bit longer."
3 "The client paid for the physiotherapy sessions by bank transfer and used a wrong account number. It was probably a typing error."
4 "We sent a letter to customers informing them about our new help desk, but unfortunately, we got the telephone number wrong."
5 "We always ask our customers to use the online form to contact us, but our system was down for one day and customers couldn't use any of our online services."
6 "We have two customers who have the same surname. We accidentally sent the letter to the wrong customer."

a incorrect contact details
b no access to customer data base
c incorrect bank details
d online services unavailable
e customer name mix-up
f office understaffed

6 Complaints

Complete the sentences with the correct preposition.

1 I'm calling to complain ___ your service.
2 Let me apologize once again ___ this delay.
3 Thank you for bringing this problem ___ my attention.
4 We could not send any emails yesterday due ___ a technical problem.
5 I'll take care ___ this matter straight away.
6 The delay was caused ___ a delivery problem.
7 I'll make sure you receive an offer ___ the next three days.
8 If you need further assistance, feel free to call me ___ any time.

Choose one of the following two projects.

1 Role-play: solving a problem through mediation

You are going to role-play a mediation session between people who are dissatisfied with a situation or have a problem.
Form groups of at least three. Choose one of the four situations.

Situation 1: a conflict among colleagues
Situation 2: employees unhappy with changes
Situation 3: a conflict with a line manager
Situation 4: employees dissatisfied because of too much work

Step 1 Discuss what the problem or conflict could be in the situation you have chosen. Decide on a concrete problem.

Step 2 Look at the problem in detail and make notes.
- Discuss what exactly happened.
- Decide how many people and who is involved in the conflict (name, position in the company, exact role in the conflict).
- Talk about how the people involved in the conflict felt when it happened or how they feel now (e.g. sad, disappointed, angry, upset).

Step 3 Plan your mediation session.
- Choose your roles: Who is an employee? Who is the mediator? Who is an observer? There should be just one mediator to help solve the conflict.
- Make notes individually about what you want to say in the role-play.
- On a separate piece of paper, write down what you think the best solution or result should be. Don't show the others what you have written.

Step 4 Now role-play your discussion. The mediator should not give direct advice but instead help clients find ways to solve the problem themselves.

Step 5 After the role-play, compare your expected solution or result with the one you achieved in the mediation session. Rate your experience below and explain your rating.

How happy are you with the result of your mediation session?

Rate your experience on a scale of 1-5.

☹☹	☹	😐	☺	☺☺
1	2	3	4	5

2 Creating a flow chart for handling telephone complaints

You are going to create a flow chart that shows how different telephone complaints are handled in your organization.

Step 1 Work in small groups. Identify what kind of complaints your organization would typically deal with. For each kind of complaint, what points would be discussed on the phone? Sort the points in the order you would deal with them.

Step 2 Before you work on your flow chart:

- Think about the steps of a typical conversation and create a flow chart that shows the sequence of steps.
- Decide what kind of format or design your flow chart will have. You can draw it yourself or use software to create it on your computer.
- Discuss what you want to write in the flow chart: are you going to give direct instructions to the employees or just describe what happens step by step?

Then complete the flow chart.

Step 3 Peer-review the work of at least two other groups. Use the feedback on your own flow chart to make any necessary changes.

Step 4 Present your flow chart to the class. Describe in complete sentences what happens step by step.

Describing how a complaint is handled

- When someone calls with a complaint …, first we ask …
- Then the complaint gets passed on to …
- He or she tries to find out if …
- … if so/not, then …
- … in that case …
- After that, …
- At this point, we …
- Once we have …, then we …

Giving feedback

- I think the flow chart covers all the steps.
- You forgot to include …
- I would add … to the chart.
- It is clearly presented / a little confusing / …
- I like how you …

CHECKING PROGRESS

Browse through the previous pages in this topic, looking at headings and pictures. What have you learned? What can you do, now that you have learned these things?

✓ I can mediate for an unhappy employee or client. (Section A / Project)
✓ I can analyse and assess a workplace problem. (Section A)
✓ I can report what someone says. (Section A)
✓ I can handle telephone complaints. (Section B)
✓ I can formulate a written response. (Section B)
✓ I can create a flow chart for handling complaints. (Project)

Write down two more statements for yourself.

Concept: dealing with conflicts and complaints

The human resources department at SystemTec has asked Workplace Counselling Services (WCS) to create a new concept for preventing and handling conflicts within their company. You and a small group are going to create a concept and then present it in class.

Step 1 Think about the following points:

1 Identifying conflicts or difficult issues

- What kind of conflicts or problems typically arise at the workplace?
- How can you sort these conflicts into different categories? (e.g. conflicts among colleagues, problems with superiors)
- What could be reasons for conflicts?
- What emotions are typically involved in conflicts?
- How do colleagues become aware of conflicts between other people?
- What effects can unresolved conflicts have on employees and how they work?

2 Possible areas or aspects which you could look at

- the company's feedback and evaluation culture
- conflict and complaints management process
- conflict awareness
- training and supervision
- communication and language
- respect and trust among staff and superiors
- team-building activities
- whistleblower policy

Step 2 Discuss the points in your group. Choose one area of conflict to deal with in your concept.

Talking about problems

- We are having problems/difficulties with …
- We are going through a difficult phase at the moment.
- One reason for this could be …
- This is a problem we need to tackle.
- There are some urgent issues we need to resolve.
- We need to sort out this problem quickly.
- This company is experiencing a lot of problems related to …
- Do you think we could solve this conflict by …?

Step 3 Now prepare your concept. You may want to consider the following points:

Preventing and handling problems

- What measures do you suggest for the area of conflict you chose?
- Where can people go when they want to talk about problems or want to make a complaint?
- Is there a defined process for handling complaints?
- Do all employees know what they should do when they have a problem in the workplace?
- Who is responsible for dealing with conflicts and complaints (e.g. one person or a whole team)?
- How can you make sure an employee's complaint or problem is treated confidentially?
- How does the organization actively help solve conflicts (e.g. by mediation)?

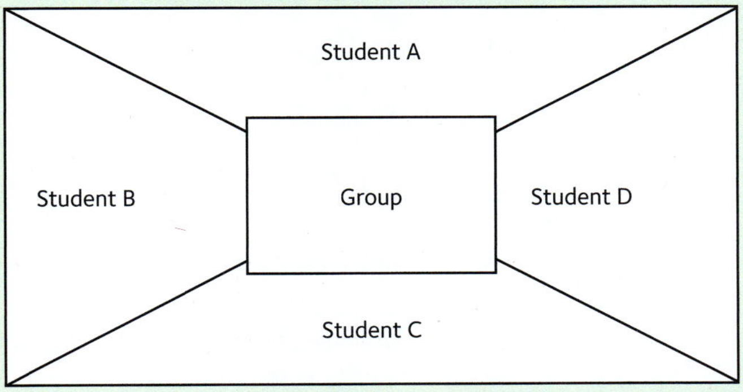

You can use the placemat method (see the illustration) to gather everyone's ideas on individual points.

Or you can use the jigsaw method: each group member focuses on a different point or area, then you combine the results.

Step 4 Once you have discussed and agreed on the main ideas and measures for your concept, plan your presentation. How would you like to present your concept to the others? Find the way that suits your group best. The following questions might help you.

- How is your concept structured?
- How many parts does it have?
- What about headings, subtitles, paragraphs?
- What kind of format will you use (e.g. a Word document, a PowerPoint presentation, a poster)?
- What kind of language will you use (e.g. formal, less formal)?

Step 5 Present your concept and give each other feedback.

> *Präsentieren, S. 146*

EXAM SKILLS AND STRATEGIES

Lösungen zu den *Skills*-Aufgaben finden Sie in der PagePlayer-App.

1 Strategien zum Vokabellernen

Es gibt viele Arten und Möglichkeiten, Vokabeln zu lernen. Wichtig ist dabei herauszufinden, welche Methode für Sie am besten funktioniert. Helfen können Ihnen Online-Programme, in denen Sie Ihren Wortschatz effektiv und oft spielerisch erlernen und trainieren können. Aber auch altbekannte Methoden wie das Vokabellernen mit Karteikarten helfen. Häufige, kürzere Trainingseinheiten sind sinnvoller als seltene lange Einheiten.

TIPPS

Vokabel im Kontext

Einzelne Wörter isoliert zu lernen ist wenig effektiv. Folgende Methoden bringen mehr Erfolg:
- Assoziationen: Lernen Sie das Wort in Verbindung mit anderen Dingen, die Ihnen spontan dazu einfallen.
- Visualisierung: Eine Veranschaulichung hilft dabei, sich Vokabeln besser zu merken.

Thematische Vokabellisten

Sortieren Sie Vokabeln zu einem bestimmten Thema, zum Beispiel in einem Kapitel im Buch oder einem Thema, das im Rahmen Ihres Unterrichts öfter besprochen wird. Sammeln Sie Wörter, die im Zusammenhang mit dem Thema wichtig sind.

Beispiel: Thema Pflege
- *care home*
- *nursing care*
- *to care for*
- *home care*
- *medical care*
- *carer*

Wortgitter

Zur besseren Strukturierung können Sie die Vokabel in ein Wortgitter sortieren und einen Beispielsatz einfügen.

Word	Word form	Opposite	Synonym	Word in context
increase	verb	decrease	rise, go up	The number of obese adults is increasing.

Lernkarten und Lernkartendatei

Lern- oder Karteikarten sind einfach herzustellen und praktisch. Sie können sie nach Bedarf erweitern und sich eine Lernkartendatei anlegen. Schreiben Sie auf die eine Seite das englische Wort oder die Redewendung, auf die andere die deutsche Übersetzung. Ergänzen Sie die deutsche Übersetzung mit einem deutschen Beispielsatz. Sortieren Sie die Karten so, dass Sie Vokabeln, die Sie noch nicht beherrschen, öfter wiederholen.

Auch viele Vokabeltrainer-Apps nutzen Lernkarten, die Sie selbst erstellen, bearbeiten und speichern können. Hier gibt es meist einen integrierten Wiederholungszyklus.

2 Mit Wörterbüchern umgehen

Wörterbücher sind sehr nützliche Werkzeuge. Ihr Gebrauch erfordert jedoch etwas Übung. Ob in Buchform oder online - Sie sollten auf die Art des Wörterbuches und dessen Qualität achten. Außerdem sollten Sie immer die angebotenen Übersetzungen und Möglichkeiten sorgfältig prüfen und abwägen, was am sinnvollstem im jeweiligen Kontext erscheint.

Wichtig für:

- Arbeit mit Texten
- Erweiterung des eigenen Wortschatzes
- Lernen neuer Redewendungen

TIPPS

Mit Wörterbüchern arbeiten

Machen Sie sich mit den ein- und zweisprachigen Wörterbüchern vertraut, die an Ihrer Schule benutzt oder empfohlen werden.

1

Beantworten Sie für diese Wörterbücher folgende Fragen:

1. Gibt es eine 'Benutzungsanleitung' und wie ist diese strukturiert?
2. Welche Symbole und Abkürzungen benutzt das Wörterbuch? Wo werden diese erklärt?
3. Wo gibt es eine Liste mit unregelmäßigen Verben?
4. Welche anderen Listen oder Verzeichnisse bietet das Wörterbuch?
5. Welche Grafiken oder Schaubilder gibt es im Wörterbuch?
6. Findet man Hilfen zur Aussprache?

Andere Übersetzungshilfen

Außer Wörterbüchern in Buchform und als Online-Angebote von namhaften Verlagen können auch andere Online-Übersetzungshilfen hilfreich sein.

benutzerbasiert	Kontext-Übersetzer online	Übersetzungssoftware
die Nutzer/-innen können selbst Einträge vornehmen oder verändern	Suchmaschinen finden das entsprechende Wort im Internet, oft auf Webseiten	eine Software übersetzt mit hilfe von großen Datenbanken einzelne Wörter oder ganze Texte

Auch hier gilt: Prüfen Sie genau und wählen Sie nicht die erstbeste Übersetzung!

Zweisprachige Wörterbücher

Das zweisprachige Wörterbuch lässt die gesuchte Bedeutung oft schnell finden, erfordert jedoch große Genauigkeit. Bevor Sie sich auf eine Bedeutung festlegen, beantworten Sie diese Fragen:

- Nach welcher Wortart suche ich (Verb, Nomen, Adjektiv etc.)?
- Habe ich alle Möglichkeiten gründlich geprüft und die für meine Zwecke passende Übersetzung ausgewählt?

2 Suchen Sie im Wörterbuch die englische Übersetzung für das Wort "erreichen" und übersetzen Sie folgende Sätze:

1 Ich habe die Kundin leider nicht erreicht.
2 Wie können wir diese Ziele erreichen?
3 Er hat den Zug um 8.00 Uhr erreicht.

Einsprachige Wörterbücher

Üblicherweise finden Sie folgende Bestandteile und Merkmale in jedem Eintrag:

- Wortart – als Abkürzung: *verb (v), noun (n), adjective (adj), adverb (adv), etc.*
- unregelmäßige Verbformen: *take – took – taken*
- phonetische Aussprache: /ˈdɒktə/
- Sprachvarianten: *British English, American English, etc.*
- Grammatikhinweise
- Beispiele im Kontext
- Verwendung von Präpositionen
- Redewendungen bzw. idiomatische Ausdrücke, in denen das Wort vorkommt

3 Sie schlagen im Wörterbuch das Wort *care* nach.

A Finden Sie unter dem Eintrag die folgenden Bestandteile und Angaben:

1 Definitionen
2 Redewendungen
3 Kollokationen (Wortverbindungen)
4 Aussprache und Sprachvarianten
5 Wortarten
6 Beispielsätze
7 Grammatikinformationen
8 Präpositionen

care ⊶ *noun, verb*

▪ ***noun*** **1** ⊶ [U] the process of caring for sb/sth and providing what they need for their health or protection: medical/patient care ◊ How much do men share the housework and the care of the children? ◊ the provision of care for the elderly ◊ **skin/hair care** products ➲ see also COMMUNITY CARE, DAY CARE, EASY-CARE, HEALTH CARE, INTENSIVE CARE **2** ⊶ [U] attention or thought that you give to sth that you are doing so that you will do it well and avoid mistakes or damage: *She chose her words with care.* ◊ *Great care is needed when choosing a used car.* ◊ *Fragile – handle with care* (= written on a container holding sth which is easily broken or damaged) **3** [C, usually pl., U] (formal) a feeling of worry or anxiety; something that causes problems or anxiety: I felt free from the cares of the day as soon as I left the building. ◊ Sam looked as if he **didn't have a care in the world.**

IDM **ˈcare of sb** (*NAmE* also **in ˈcare of sb**) (*abbr.* **c/o**) used when writing to sb at another person's address: Write to him care of his lawyer. **in ˈcare** (*BrE*) (of children) living in an institution run by the local authority rather than with their parents: *The two girls were **taken into care** after their parents were killed.* in the care of sb/in sb's care being cared for by sb: *The child was left in the care of friends.*

WORD FAMILY
care *noun, verb*
careful *adj* (≠careless)
carefully *adv* (≠carelessly)
caring *adj* (≠uncaring)

B Beantworten Sie folgende Fragen:

1 Für welche Wortarten kann das Wort *care* stehen?
2 Welche Wörter zählen zur Wortfamilie?
3 Welche Abkürzung wird benutzt, wenn der Empfänger unter der Adresse einer anderen Person erreichbar ist?
4 Auf welche Verbindungen mit dem Substantiv *care* wird verwiesen?
5 Welchen Ausdruck benutzt man in Transport und Logistik beim Versenden empfindlicher Waren?
6 Was bedeutet *in care* im britischen Englisch, wenn es um Kinder geht?
7 Ist *care* in den Ausdrücken *day care* und *health care* zählbar oder nichtzählbar?
8 Was heißt „Er war völlig unbekümmert." auf Englisch?

3 Mit unbekannten Wörtern umgehen

Mit unbekannten Wörtern umgehen zu können ist eine sehr wichtige Kompetenz. Sie werden öfters auf Wörter stoßen, die Sie nicht kennen. Denken Sie daran, dass man nicht jedes einzelne Wort kennen muss, um den ganzen Text zu verstehen. Wenn Sie ein Wort nicht verstehen, denken Sie über die allgemeine Aussage des Satzes nach und wenden Sie eine der folgenden Worterschließungsstrategien an:

Wichtig für:

- Leseverstehen
- schriftliche Mediation
- rollenbasierte Stellungnahme

TIPPS

METHODE 1: Erschließung aus dem Kontext

Betrachten Sie umliegende Wörter, die vielleicht Hinweise auf die Bedeutung geben können.

Hinweis	Die Zahlen zeigen Ihnen, dass das Verb „steigen" heißen muss.
Textbeispiel	*Unemployment crept from 10.9% last year to 12% this year …*

METHODE 2: Erschließung eines Teils einer Wendung

Sie können einen Teil des Wortes identifizieren.

> *Schwierige Texte lesen, S. 154*

Hinweis	Betrachten Sie Präfix (Vorsilbe) oder Suffix (Nachsilbe).
Textbeispiel	*counterproductive*; *counter* = kontra, gegen

METHODE 3: Erschließung eines Teils einer Wendung

Sie können ein Wort als Bestandteil einer Wendung identifizieren.

Hinweis	Sie kennen das Wort *budget* und können dann daraus schließen, dass es um Geld gehen muss.
Textbeispiel	… *bringing budget deficits below 3%.* (*budget deficits* = Haushaltsdefizite).

METHODE 4: Erklärung im Text suchen

Oft werden schwierige Wörter oder Wendungen im Text erklärt.

Hinweis	Sie kennen *austerity policies* nicht, aber bekommen die Erklärung *to save money.*
Textbeispiel	*Austerity policies have been introduced in many countries to save money …* Der Zweck von *austerity policies* (Sparpolitik) wird genannt.

METHODE 5: Erschließung durch die Wortform

Oft ist es möglich, die Wortform (Verb, Adjektiv, Substantiv, Adverb) zu bestimmen und so die Bedeutung zu verstehen.

Hinweis	*introduce* muss ein Verb sein und steht im *present perfect*
Textbeispiel	*… have been introduced in many countries…*

METHODE 6: Großschreibung

Im Englischen findet man Großschreibung bei Eigennamen von Personen und Organisationen.

Hinweis	Sie können auf einen Eigennamen schließen.
Textbeispiel	*… according to Eurostat, the European statistics office.*

1 Lesen Sie nun die Wörter im Zusammenhang. Die Zahl hinter dem hervorgehobenen Wort gibt die angewendete Regel (1–6) an.

Apprenticeships on the rise to combat unemployment
The European Commission has made plans to **boost**[5] training and apprenticeships for young people across Europe. This decision was reached after the jobless[2] rate in Europe reached new and unacceptable levels in February. Unemployment **crept**[1] from 10.9% last year to 12% this year, according to **Eurostat**[6], the European statistics office. Approximately 26.3 million young people are out of work across the EU. Austerity **policies**[4] have been introduced in many countries to save money and help the economy by bringing budget **deficits**[3] below 3%. Unfortunately, these policies have been **counterproductive**[2], and have had a negative effect on economic growth and employment.

2 Lesen Sie nun den Rest des Artikels. Wenden Sie die Regeln auf die hervorgehobenen Wörter (a–f) an. Eine der Regeln kann nicht angewendet werden.

Natalia Aivazova[a], from the Peterson Institute for International Economics, stated that one reason many economies are still struggling with **sluggish**[b] growth and high unemployment is that young people do not have the skills that employers are looking for. Implementing apprenticeship programmes could help to solve this problem. Brussels has started a **"Youth Guarantee" programme**[c], in which all EU member states give young people the possibility to get work within four months of leaving school or college, or to get more education. This **ensures**[d] that all young people have either employment, or an apprenticeship or **traineeship**[e].
Natalia Aivazova reported that Germany, Austria and Switzerland, three countries with low youth unemployment and high levels of apprenticeship education, offer valuable **insights**[f] into the training of young people. (230 words)

3 Entscheiden Sie, ob die folgenden Aussagen jeweils richtig, falsch oder im Text nicht erwähnt sind. Begründen Sie Ihre Antworten.

a Since February last year, unemployment levels have risen by 5%.
b Unemployment rates in the UK rose in February 2013.
c Natalia Aivazova blames unskilled young people for slowing down economic growth.
d Many young people leave school or college and go abroad in search of work.
e Brussels has put a limit on the number of apprenticeships available to young people.
f Aivazova believes that many countries could learn from Germany, Switzerland and Austria.

4 Mit Aufgaben zum Hör- und Sehverstehen umgehen

Trainieren Sie Ihr Hör- und Sehverstehen von gesprochenem Englisch auch außerhalb des Unterrichts. Dafür bieten sich zum Beispiel Radio, Podcasts, TV-Serien oder Dokumentationen an. Wenn Sie sich dabei aktiv auf das Gesprochene konzentrieren, können Sie Ihr Hörverstehen schnell verbessern.

Wichtig für:

- Hör-/Sehverstehens-aufgaben

BEISPIEL-AUFGABE

Sie hören einen Text über die Selbstmordraten bei Männern in Großbritannien. Die Aufnahme wird zweimal vorgespielt. Lesen Sie zuerst die Fragen und hören Sie aufmerksam zu. Beantworten Sie danach die Fragen.

49

1 Um wie viel höher ist die Selbstmordrate bei Männern (verglichen mit der Selbstmordrate bei Frauen) in Großbritannien?
2 Welche Gruppe von Männern ist am meisten gefährdet?
3 Was sind, so Jane Powell von Calm, die Gründe, warum Männer keine Hilfe bekommen, wenn sie Selbstmordgedanken haben?
4 Welcher Teil Großbritanniens hat die höchste Selbstmordrate bei Männern?
5 Was wird als Reaktion auf diese Zahlen erwartet?

TIPPS

Textsorten

Folgende Textsorten können in Ihrer Prüfung vorkommen.

Medium	Format
• Radio • TV • Internet	• Nachrichten, Hintergrundberichte • Interviews, Gespräche • Diskussionen

Ablauf

Hör-/Sehverstehensaufgaben werden üblicherweise zweimal abgespielt. Der erste Durchgang ist dazu bestimmt, eine allgemeine Vorstellung vom Inhalt zu bekommen oder die Kernaussage zu verstehen. Beim zweiten Hören/Sehen sollten Sie sich mehr auf bestimmte Details konzentrieren.

Methoden

1 Vor dem ersten Hören

- Achten Sie auf den **Titel:** Welche Hinweise gibt er auf das Thema?
  z. B. Suicide rates in men in the UK

- Aktivieren Sie **Vorwissen** zu dem Thema.
  z. B. *Was wissen Sie bereits über diese Themen? Worüber könnten die Personen sprechen?*
- Lesen Sie die **Aufgabenstellung** sorgfältig durch.
- Markieren Sie **Schlüsselwörter.**
  z. B. *higher than, risk, gender*
- Achten Sie auf **Zusammenhänge, Gründe und Auswirkungen.**
  z. B. *cause, result, consequence*

2 Während des Hörens

- Schreiben Sie beim Hören mit, notieren Sie **Stichpunkte**.
- Vor dem zweiten Hören lesen Sie die Fragen noch einmal schnell durch. So wissen Sie, auf was Sie im zweiten Durchgang achten müssen.

Men 40–45
NE of England

- **Vervollständigen Sie Ihre Notizen** im zweiten Durchgang. Kürzen Sie Wörter ab, um Zeit zu sparen, aber schreiben Sie leserlich.
- **Bleiben Sie gelassen**, wenn Sie nicht jedes einzelne Wort verstehen und hören Sie weiter aufmerksam zu. Erschließen Sie Unverstandenes aus dem größeren Zusammenhang.

3 Nach dem Hören

- Wenn Sie wenig notiert oder viel gekürzt haben, formulieren Sie Ihre Stichpunkte jetzt so aus, dass der Inhalt eindeutig zu verstehen ist.

Videos verstehen

Wenden Sie die gleichen Fertigkeiten wie beim Hören einer Aufnahme auch beim Anschauen eines Videos an und nutzen Sie die Methoden 1–3 wie beim Hörverstehen. Achten Sie auf den Titel des Videos, der Ihnen wichtige Informationen zum Thema gibt.
Der Vorteil eines Videos ist, dass Ihnen zusätzlich die Bilder und Texte helfen. Lesen Sie jeden Text, der auf dem Bildschirm erscheint, um so viele nichthörbare Informationen wie möglich zu erhalten. Achten Sie außerdem auf Körpersprache, Mimik, Gestik und Schauplatz – Sie können Ihnen Hinweise auf die Handlung geben.

1 (Video 7)

Sie sehen ein Video mit dem Titel *Obesity*. Das Video wird zweimal gezeigt. Entscheiden Sie, ob die Aussagen (a–e) richtig oder falsch sind. Begründen Sie Ihre Antwort. Beantworten Sie danach die Fragen (f–h) auf Deutsch.

a Fettleibigkeit (Adipositas) hat sich weltweit seit 1980 verdreifacht.
b Mehr als zwei Billionen Menschen sind übergewichtig.
c Adipositas wird definiert als übermäßige Fettablagerung, welche die Gesundheit schädigen kann.
d Die Ursache ist ein Ungleichgewicht in der Energiezufuhr.
e Fettleibigkeit ist das zweitgrößte Todesrisiko weltweit.
f Ab welchem BMI gilt man als übergewichtig?
g Welche Krankheiten werden durch Fettleibigkeit verursacht oder begünstigt? Nennen Sie mindestens zwei.
h Wie viele Menschen sterben jährlich an den Folgen von Übergewicht und Fettleibigkeit?

2 (Audio 50)

Jim Constantin works in a community outreach centre. He has received three voicemail messages. Listen to the information and complete the form on the right. You will hear two messages.

Message for: Jim Constantin
Name of caller: …
Date and time of call: …
Message: …

5 Präsentieren

Die Kompetenz, eine wirkungsvolle Präsentation vor einem Publikum zu halten, ist in fast jedem Lebensstadium von Bedeutung – in der Schule wie auch im Arbeitsleben. Dabei kommt es sowohl auf den Inhalt als auch auf Klarheit und Verständlichkeit an.

Wichtig für:

- Präsentieren
- mündliche Prüfung
- Analyse und Kommentieren einer visuellen Vorlage

BEISPIEL-AUFGABE Halten Sie eine Präsentation zum Thema *Have fun while getting fit*.

TIPPS

Recherchieren und planen

Bereiten Sie Ihr Thema sorgfältig vor und stellen Sie sicher, dass die Webseiten, die Sie wählen, **glaubwürdige Quellen** darstellen.

Nutzen Sie präzise Suchbegriffe, um passende Seiten zu finden. Verlassen Sie sich nicht auf die ersten Informationen, die Sie finden. Wenn eine URL auf *.org*, *.edu* oder *.gov* endet, ist sie wahrscheinlich eine glaubwürdige Quelle. Prüfen Sie auch den *About us*-Link und finden Sie heraus, wer für den Inhalt verantwortlich ist.

Erstellen

- Denken Sie bei der Erstellung immer an Ihre **Zielgruppe** und wie Sie Ihre Präsentation so gestalten können, dass Ihr Publikum bestmöglich angesprochen wird.
- Notieren Sie auf Englisch **Stichwörter** zu den wichtigsten Punkten/Aspekten/Aussagen, die Sie für Ihre Präsentation verwenden. Nutzen Sie dabei **Moderations- oder Karteikarten**, die Ihnen helfen werden, frei und in Ihren eigenen Worten zu sprechen.

Fitness – things to think about re:
– age/weight/general health
– what is realistic?

- Prüfen Sie die Korrektheit Ihrer Notizen in Bezug auf Informationsgehalt und Sprache.
- Wenn Sie bei der **Aussprache** nicht sicher sind, hören Sie sich Beispiele in einem Online-Wörterbuch an.
- Nutzen Sie geeignetes **Anschauungsmaterial**, um Ihren Vortrag visuell zu unterstützen. Auch Gegenstände können effektives Anschauungsmaterial sein. Besorgen Sie für Ihre Präsentation, wenn möglich, reale Gegenstände, wie z. B. Souvenirs, Flyer, Broschüren etc.
- Wählen Sie eine **Darstellungsform** für Ihre Präsentation.

Flipchart/Whiteboard	Präsentationssoftware
• Wie soll es am Ende aussehen? • Schrift sauber und leserlich?	• übersichtliche, klar strukturierte Folien? • Schrift gut lesbar?

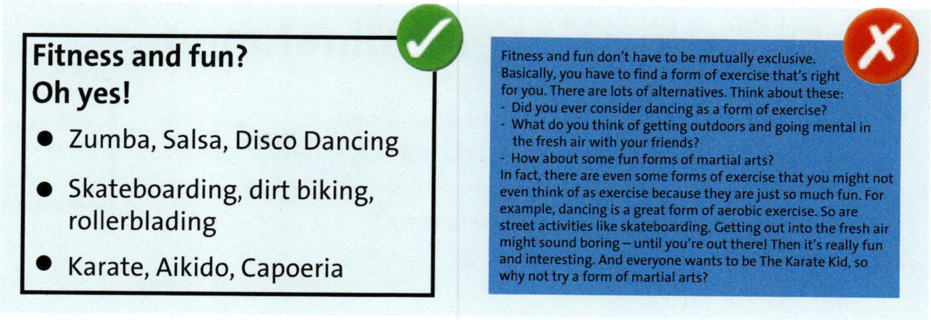

- Verwenden Sie **Fakten, Zahlen und Daten sparsam**, um Ihr Publikum nicht zu überfordern. Während Sie sprechen, zeigen Sie relevante Zahlen und Fakten in schriftlicher Form. Visuelle Elemente sollten nur als Verstärkung, nicht als Dekoration dienen.
- Strukturieren Sie Ihren Vortrag durch **orientierende Redewendungen** (*signposting*), zum Beispiel *Now I'd like to talk about …* , damit Ihr Publikum zu jedem Zeitpunkt weiß, wo genau Sie sich im Vortrag befinden und was als Nächstes passiert.

Üben

- Üben Sie so oft wie möglich. Am besten proben Sie Ihre Präsentation zunächst vor einem Spiegel oder machen Sie ein Video von Ihrem Vortrag; Sie können gar nicht oft genug üben!

Vortragen

- **Interagieren** Sie mit Ihrem Publikum. Halten Sie Blickkontakt und stellen Sie ab und zu Fragen. Stehen Sie ruhig und aufrecht und achten Sie auf Ihre **Körpersprache** (Gestik und Mimik).

Giving a presentation

Introducing yourself and your topic
- Good morning/afternoon. My name is …
- Today I am going to talk about …
- The subject of my talk is …
- My topic today is …
- If you have any questions, please don't hesitate to interrupt me.
- I'd like to ask you to please save your questions for the end of the presentation.

Beginning your first point
- I'd like to begin by saying something about …
- I want to start by explaining …

Guiding your audience through your presentation
- There are a number of points I'd like to make.
- I'll start with …. Then I'll talk about …
- Firstly … / Secondly … / And finally, …
- The next topic I'd like to focus on is …
- Now I'd like to discuss / we'll move on to …
- Let's look at …
- Why is this important? Because …
- The significance of this is …

Ending your presentation
- Let's summarize briefly what we've looked at.
- Let me remind you of the issues we've covered.
- In conclusion, …
- I would like to finish by saying …
- Thank you very much for your attention.
- I'm happy to answer any questions now.

1 Halten Sie nun die Präsentation über das Thema *Have fun while getting fit*.

6 An Diskussionen teilnehmen

In einer Gruppendiskussion, Debatte oder einem Rollenspiel ist es wichtig, sich aktiv zu beteiligen und auf die anderen Teilnehmer/-innen zu reagieren. Diskussionen bieten eine gute Möglichkeit, freies Sprechen zu trainieren.

Wichtig für:

- Interaktion

BEISPIEL-AUFGABE

Discuss this statement with your partner or in small groups: "Germans must realize that immigrants are their country's only hope for a successful future."

TIPPS

Vorbereiten und planen

- Bereiten Sie sich inhaltlich vor, indem Sie sich einzelne Aspekte des Themas noch einmal ins Gedächtnis rufen und Schlüsselbegriffe auf Englisch notieren.

Why is immigration important to Germany?
- *Low birth rate in Germany – ageing population*
- *Wealthy country – can afford to take new people*
- *Benefits of cultural diversity on society*

What about negative factors of immigration?
- *Do people ever really accept immigrants?*
- *Cost of integration programs*

- Legen Sie sich, falls genügend Zeit ist, ein paar Fragen/Antworten zum Thema zurecht.

Can you think of any examples of good or bad integration from real life?
Imagine you left Germany. How would you integrate into another culture?

An der Diskussion teilnehmen

1 Über Aussage nachdenken, aber spontan sprechen

Sie können sich nicht auf alles vorbereiten! Denken Sie kurz nach, bevor Sie anfangen zu sprechen, aber versuchen Sie, spontan zu sein.

- *My spontaneous reaction to your question is …*
- *I've thought about this, and my opinion is …*

2 Meinung äußern und begründen

Äußern Sie Ihre Meinung und begründen Sie das, was Sie sagen.

- *Personally, I think/believe/feel that …, because …*
- *I'm convinced that …*

3 Andere Meinungen hören

Fragen Sie andere nach ihrer Meinung und ob sie Ihnen zustimmen oder nicht.

- *What do you think about …?*
- *What's your opinion on …?*
- *Would you agree that … is right/wrong/better/worse?*

4 Zustimmen oder widersprechen

Stimmen Sie anderen zu oder seien Sie anderer Meinung.

- *I absolutely agree with what you said.*
- *That's exactly how I see it.*
- *I'm afraid I can't go along with you on that.*
- *I'm not sure I agree with you.*
- *Do you really think so?*

5 Das Gehörte oder Gesagte überprüfen

Prüfen Sie, ob Sie inhaltlich verstanden wurden und ob Sie die anderen richtig verstanden haben.

- *Do you see what I mean?*
- *Does that make sense?*
- *So, you were saying that …*
- *If I understand you correctly, the general idea is …*

6 Andere Teilnehmer/-innen unterbrechen

Haben Sie keine Hemmungen, jemanden zu unterbrechen.

- *I'm sorry to interrupt, but …*
- *Sorry, can I come in here?*
- *Can I stop you there for a moment?*
- *Hold on a second.*

7 Andere Teilnehmer/-innen ins Gespräch einladen

Versuchen Sie, schüchterne oder ruhige Teilnehmer/-innen in das Gespräch miteinzubeziehen.

- *What do you think about that?*
- *What's your opinion, [name of the person]?*

8 Interesse zeigen

Verwenden Sie genügend Ausdrücke, um Interesse, Überraschung oder andere emotionale Reaktionen auszudrücken. Die macht die Diskussion lebhafter.

- *I see. / Right. / OK then.*
- *Oh dear! / You're joking!*
- *Really? / Is that true? / Unbelievable!*

9 Beim Thema bleiben

Bleiben Sie beim Thema und schweifen Sie nicht ab.

10 Interaktion und Körpersprache

Gehen Sie auf Ihre Gesprächspartnerin/Ihren Gesprächspartner ein und halten Sie Blickkontakt.

1 Paired discussion: Discuss the difficulties faced by people migrating to Germany from Spain, Greece and Italy. Why do they make the decision to move in the first place? Do you think they have the intention of staying temporarily or permanently? If they intend to go back to their own country one day, should they try to integrate into German society?

2 Role-play: In a group of four, role-play the following situation.
Partners A and B are social workers who help migrants integrate into German society.

> *Turn to file 3 on page 166.*

Partners C and D are siblings from Greece and have been living in Germany for a short time.

> *Partner C turn to file 6 on page 167. Partner D turn to file 18 on page 172.*

7 Bilder und Cartoons beschreiben und analysieren

Wenn Sie ein Bild oder einen Cartoon beschreiben, sollten Sie sich auf die Hauptaussage konzentrieren und sich nicht in Details verlieren. Vermeiden Sie, 'um die Ecke zu denken', sondern bleiben Sie im Rahmen des Themas.

Wichtig für:

- Analysieren und Kommentieren einer visuellen Vorlage
- rollenbasierte Stellungnahme

BEISPIEL-AUFGABE

Beschreiben Sie und analysieren Sie den Cartoon. Vergleichen Sie ihn mit dem Text.

Couch potatoes don't need to exercise like crazy
A new study reveals that it doesn't take longer than 30 minutes a day to become healthy if you're a moderately overweight man aged between 20 and 40. The study found that 40% of Danish men in this age group do not lead very active lives – they are couch potatoes. The good news is that exercising 30 or 60 minutes a day brings the same health benefits.

TIPPS

Bildbeschreibung

Wen oder was sieht man? (Personen, Objekte) Schauen Sie sich alle Aspekte der Abbildung an, beschreiben Sie jedoch nur die Elemente, die für die Aussage wichtig sind.	*a potato* *a sofa/couch* *a TV set*
Welches Objekt / Welche Person beschreiben Sie? Wo befinden sich Objekt oder Person? Geben Sie an, was Sie beschreiben, indem Sie genau bestimmen, wo es sich im Bild befindet.	*In the middle of the picture, there is a potato on a couch.*
Verwenden Sie das ***present progressive*** für Tätigkeitsverben (*sit, hold, watch*), um zu beschreiben, was gerade geschieht. Bei **Zustandsverben** (*be, seem, describe*) verwenden Sie das ***simple present***.	*The potato* ***is eating*** *something.* *The potato* ***seems*** *to be watching TV.*

Interpretation

Interpretieren Sie, was Sie sehen. Wenn Sie der Meinung sind, dass die Darstellung nicht viel aussagt, erwähnen Sie dies. Bezeichnen Sie die Abbildung als mehrdeutig oder unklar.	*The message of the cartoon is clearly that…* *The message of the cartoon is not clear. It could be that… or…*

Wirkung und Meinung

Stellen Sie dar, welche **Auswirkung** das Bild auf Sie hat: Fassen Sie die Hauptaussage zusammen und geben Sie Ihre **eigene Meinung** wieder.	*I (don't) think this cartoon is very funny.* *I (don't) agree with the message of this picture.*

Bezug zwischen Bild und Text

Falls es einen Text zum Bild gibt, **vergleichen** Sie die Abbildung mit dem Inhalt des Textes: Sagen Sie, ob das Bild die Aussage des Textes unterstützt oder ihr widerspricht.	*The cartoon supports/illustrates the information in the text, which says that…* *What is shown in the picture contradicts the text.*

Describing the picture
- The cartoon shows …
- The picture seems to show …
- The scene depicts …
- In the foreground/background/centre there is …
- On the left/right there is …
- The person seems to be (holding something / writing / walking away)

Interpreting the picture
- The picture/cartoon deals with …
- The cartoon is intended to create …
- The (person in the centre) represents/shows/symbolizes …
- This shows/reveals/indicates …
- The impression of … is created.
- The point of the cartoon is / seems to be …

Commenting on the picture
- I think … / In my opinion …
- The cartoon makes a fair point.
- The cartoon convinces / doesn't convince me.
- I agree with the cartoonist, but …
- The cartoonist is partly right.
- The cartoonist exaggerates a little / a lot.
- It forces you to think about …
- It has the effect of …

Comparing the picture with the text
- Although the picture shows … , the text says …
- In the text we found out that …
- The cartoon/picture supports the information in the text in the following way.
- The cartoon/picture gives a completely different opinion about the information in the text.

1 Describe and analyse the cartoon below. Write at least 150 words.

2 Compare the cartoon with the text.

Do you know this situation?
A horrible feeling spread through my stomach. My head began to spin, my heart was sinking. I was on the phone. On the other end of the line was an angry client. I could almost feel steam coming out of his ears. A simple misunderstanding and now the client was furious. He raised his voice and refused to listen to a word I was saying. How can I deal with a situation like this?

8 Schaubilder und Statistiken beschreiben und analysieren

Wichtig für:

- Analyse und Kommentieren einer visuellen Vorlage
- Präsentationen

Schaubilder und Diagramme werden oft benutzt, um Zahlen und Statistiken anschaulich darzustellen. Sie machen es Betrachtern leichter, Informationen zu erfassen und zu verstehen. Die Wahl des Schaubilds hängt von den Informationen ab, die veranschaulicht werden sollen. Lernen Sie Phrasen, die Sie zur Beschreibung und Erläuterung verschiedener Schaubilder brauchen.

BEISPIEL-AUFGABE

Briefly describe and analyse the following statistics.

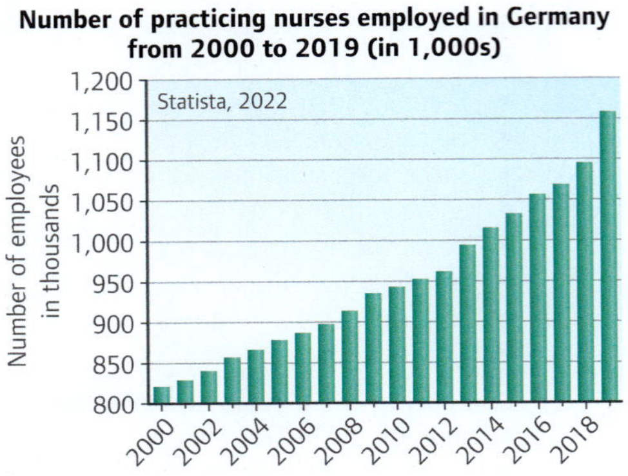

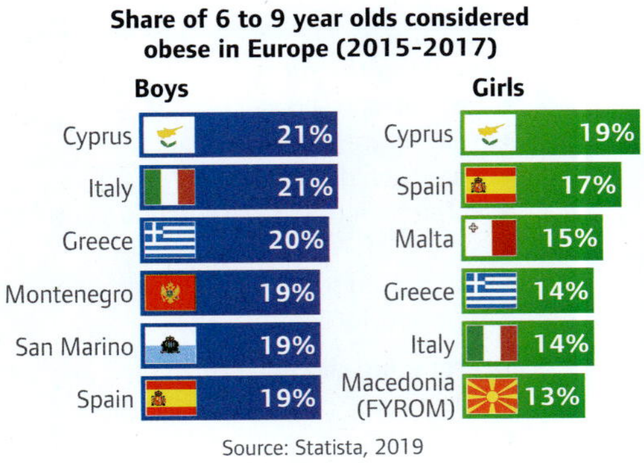

TIPPS

Beschreiben des Schaubilds

1 Überblick

Nennen Sie zunächst kurz Art, Inhalt und Zweck des Schaubilds. Erwähnen Sie auch Herkunft, Urheber/-in und Datum der Publikation.	*The chart/graph shows/provides information about / gives an overview of the number of practising nurses in Germany from 2000 to 2019.* *This chart was published by Statista in July, 2021.*

2 Aufbau und Struktur

Erklären Sie, wie das Schaubild aufgebaut ist.	*The chart is divided into two sections/parts/segments …* *One part stands for boys, one for girls.*
Fassen Sie dann kurz die Entwicklungstendenz zusammen. Vereinfachen Sie dabei komplexe Zahlen.	*Since 2000, the number of practising nurses in Germany has increased steadily, reaching 1,159 million in 2019.* *Better: … reaching* ***just over 1.1 million*** *in 2019.*

Using approximate numbers

roughly, nearly, approximately, around, about, just under/over, well under/over

3 Vergleichen

Wenn es mehrere Informationen gibt, vergleichen Sie diese.	*Compared with / In comparison with a 21% share of obese boys, there are 19% obese girls in Cyprus.*

4 Trends und Entwicklungen

Nennen Sie die wichtigsten Merkmale und Höhe- und Tiefpunkte von Entwicklungen. Nutzen Sie ausdrucksstarke Verben, Adjektive und Substantive, um sie genauer zu beschreiben.	*In 2019, the number of practising nurses in Germany reached a peak.* *The number of employed nurses increased considerably between 2000 and 2019.*

Describing trends

- Use words like *rise, increase, surge, soar,* and *improve* for upward movement.
- Use *decline, decrease, dip, drop, fall, plummet* and *slump* for downward movement.
- *Fluctuate/fluctuation* expresses frequent change.
- *Remain stable/constant, stay at / maintain / keep the same level* and *stabilize* all indicate no change.
- Adverbs and adjectives give variation to how much or how quickly something moves: *considerable/ly, gradual/ly, rapid/ly, sharp/ly, significant/ly, slight/ly, steep/ly, substantial/ly*

Analysieren und Schlussfolgerungen

Schreiben Sie eine kurze Schlussfolgerung der Informationen. Äußern Sie nicht Ihre Meinung. Achten Sie auf die richtige Zeitform: **past tense** *für* abgeschlossene Zeiträume, **present perfect** für anhaltende Zeiträume.	*The general trend is that the number of nurses in Germany is growing.* *…the number of health and social workers* ***rose steadily until 2019***. *This trend* ***has continued*** *until today.*

1 Complete the text about the line diagram with words from the box.

considerable fluctuation • dipped • gradual increase • rising • slowly decreased • generally considerably higher • remained stable • dropped suddenly • peaked • rise sharply

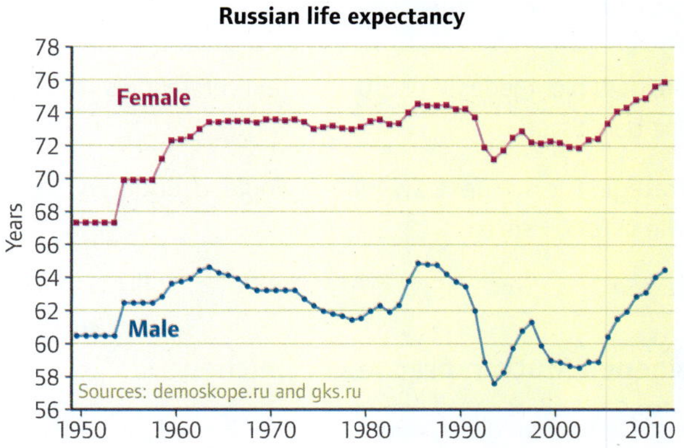

This line graph shows life expectancy in Russia since the 1950s. Life expectancy for females there is ___[a] than for males. For both male and females, there was a ___[b] between 1950 and 1965, then the male life expectancy ___[c] while the female life expectancy ___[d]. There was ___[e] between 1980 and 2005: Life expectancy ___[f] for both sexes in the early 1990s, then began to ___[g] until it ___[h] again in 1998, and ___[i] again in the early 2000s. Since then, it has been ___[j] slowly.

9 Schwierige Texte lesen

Es kommt vor, dass man beim ersten Lesen eines schwierigen Textes nicht gleich alles versteht. Das ist kein Grund, aufzugeben! Oft konzentrieren wir uns fälschlicherweise auf das, was wir nicht kennen, statt auf das, was wir verstehen. Mit einer Lesestrategie, die schrittweise vorgeht, ist es möglich, die eigene Lese- und Dekodierungskompetenz zu stärken und auch schwierige Texte selbstständig zu erschließen.

Wichtig für:
- Leseverstehen
- Mediation
- rollenbasierte Stellungnahme

BEISPIEL-AUFGABE

Read the text *Sweden vs England: differences in supervision style* on the opposite page.

TIPPS

INHALTLICHE EBENE
METHODE 1: Verschiedene Lesestile anwenden

Abhängig von Ihrem Ziel beim Lesen können Sie außer dem genauen und intensiven Lesen folgende Lesestile anwenden:
- *Skimming:* Text überfliegen, um schnell den groben Inhalt zu erfassen
- *Scanning:* Text gezielt nach bestimmten Informationen durchsuchen

1 Benutzen Sie für Text *Sweden vs England* den passenden Lesestil für die folgende Frage:
In Erik's experience, what are the main differences between social work in England and Sweden?

METHODE 2: Texterschließungsstrategien nutzen

Wählen Sie eine Strategie aus, mit der Sie den Text gut erschließen können.

Abschnitte zusammenfassen	Notizen machen	Fragen stellen	Zusammenhänge visualisieren	Positivlesen

Positivlesen bedeutet, dass Sie den Text mit drei Farben markieren:
grün: alles verstanden
gelb: Bedeutung kann aus dem Kontext erschlossen werden
rot: nicht verstanden
Durch Positivlesen kann man erkennen, dass nicht jedes Wort für das Textverständnis wichtig ist und wie hoch die eigene Wortschatzkompetenz bereits ist.

2 Nutzen Sie eine Texterschließungsstrategie für den Text *Sweden vs England*. Erklären Sie, warum Sie diese Methode gewählt haben und wie effektiv sie ist.

DEKODIERUNG WORTEBENE

> *Mit unbekannten Wörtern umgehen, S. 142*

METHODE 3: Wörter mit der eigenen Muttersprache vergleichen

Oft gibt es im Englischen Wörter, die im Deutschen gleich oder sehr ähnlich sind, zum Beispiel *cultural* (kulturell), *result* (Resultat), *colleague* (Kollege/Kollegin).

METHODE 4: Wortbildungsmuster nutzen

Aus Vor- und Nachsilben lassen sich oft Rückschlüsse auf die Bedeutung eines Wortes ziehen.

Vorsilben *(prefixes)*	**mis-** (e.g. misunderstanding) bad, wrong	**re-** (e.g. review) back, again	**un-** (e.g. uneducated) not
Nachsilben *(suffixes)*	**-ful** (e.g. successful) full of	**-less** (e.g. hopeless) without	**-able** (e.g. affordable) can be done

METHODE 5: Einsprachige Wörterbücher nutzen

Einsprachige Wörterbücher helfen, den Wortschatz zu erweitern und sind besonders bei Redewendungen nützlicher als zweisprachige Wörterbücher.

3 Nutzen Sie passende Dekodierungsmethoden bei den im Text hervorgehobenen Wörtern.

4 Lesen Sie den Text und beantworten Sie dann die Fragen.

Sweden vs England: differences in supervision style

I left Sweden and moved to England a year ago. After I started working in England, I became aware of cultural differences in the field of social work, especially in the approach to supervision. In Sweden, supervision focuses on reflection and self-awareness. In England, it focuses more on procedure.

In Sweden, I often talked to my supervisor about the feelings that came up as a result of my work. This helped me develop both self-confidence and my relationships at work. Twice a month, my colleagues and I also met an external facilitator, and discussed our work in a group. The facilitator gave us independent, unbiased opinions, which we all found very useful. We learned a lot from these sessions.

In England, when I meet my line manager every month, I usually talk about what I do and how I do it. My line manager then gives me feedback and useful tips about how to do my job better. This is very helpful, but we rarely talk about how I feel or how I am coping on a personal level. There is some reflective supervision in England, but little time is given to it.

Process-oriented supervision is important to everyone in our profession, but social work is so complex and demanding, and the decisions we make can change people's lives forever. We often worry ourselves with the question: "Did I make the right decision?" For this reason, we need to reflect on our feelings.

(260 words)

a Was fehlt, dem Autor zufolge, bei Mitarbeitergesprächen in England?
b Wer führt die Mitarbeitergespräche in Schweden durch?
c Was macht der/die englische Vorgesetzte?
d Warum sei es, so der Autor, wichtig für die Menschen in einem sozialen Beruf ihre Gefühle nachzudenken?

10 Einen Text zusammenfassen

Die Kompetenz, einen Text zusammenzufassen, ist wichtig, um einen Text vollständig zu verstehen und um ihn auf seine wesentlichen Informationen zu kürzen.

Wichtig für:

- Schreiben einer Stellungnahme
- Leseverstehen
- Mediation
- rollenbasierte Stellungnahme

BEISPIEL-AUFGABE Lesen Sie den Text *Number of street kids rising in Germany* und schreiben Sie eine kurze Zusammenfassung auf Englisch.

Number of street kids rising in Germany

According to the online news portal Expatica, there are more than 7,000 kids living on the streets of Germany and more than a third of those are living in the nation's capital. Poverty, troubled family backgrounds, violence, drugs and alcohol are just some of the reasons that the German street kid scene is growing.

The charity Terre des Hommes reports that life is getting tougher for these young people, especially because of increasing violence. In the past, the average age of Berlin's street kids was 18. Now it's down to 16, with some among them only 14. Without family or friends, some street kids end up addicted to drugs.

They mostly come from broken homes or poor family backgrounds. After they arrive in the city, they have no idea where they should go to seek help.

Various organizations have been set up to help deal with this problem. The biggest aid organization in Berlin is the Karuna Association, which helps up to 800 homeless teenagers annually find work and shelter. Some youngsters get "one-euro jobs", and later, those without school-leaving certificates are encouraged to study for them. After that, they are helped to find apprenticeships.

Other organizations include Off Road Kids, which is active in Berlin, Hamburg, Dortmund and Cologne, and Klik in Berlin. These offer advice and guidance for street kids.

The question is, will these organizations be able to help the kids before it is too late?

(248 words)

TIPPS

Planen

1 **Lesen Sie den Text gründlich.** Behalten Sie während des Lesens die Kernideen im Kopf – schauen Sie sich dafür die hervorgehobenen Abschnitte an. > *Schwierige Texte lesen, S. 154*

2 Lesen Sie und **machen Sie sich Notizen.** Um sicherzugehen, welche Informationen wichtig sind, formulieren und beantworten Sie die W-Fragen:

→ ***Who?*** *Young people who are living on the streets and organizations who try to help them*
→ ***What?*** *Youth homelessness getting worse – organizations trying to help*
→ ***Where?*** *Germany, especially Berlin and other big cities*
→ ***When?*** *Nowadays*
→ ***Why?*** *Poverty, bad family background, violence, drugs and alcohol are all reasons that kids end up on the streets. Kids need help urgently.*

Schreiben

Schreiben Sie nun Ihre **Zusammenfassung anhand Ihrer Notizen**. Beachten Sie dabei Folgendes:

- Beschreiben Sie in einem oder zwei einleitenden Sätzen, um was es geht.
  → *This article is about young people who live rough on the streets of big cities in Germany, and the organizations that try to help them.*
- Weniger ist mehr: Lassen Sie alles weg, was nicht von Bedeutung ist. Die sind unter anderem Beispiele, Auflistungen, Namen, Zitate und Statistiken.
  → *The text states that young people come to big cities like Berlin, Hamburg, Dortmund and Cologne and become involved with drugs and violence.*
- Legen Sie dar, was im Text steht. Bewerten Sie keine Aussagen, äußern Sie nicht Ihre Meinung.
  → *According to the author, many young people have no idea where to get the help they need.*
- Benutzen Sie Ihre eigenen Worte.
  → *The biggest aid organization in Berlin is the Karuna Association.*
  The Karuna Association is the largest organization in Berlin.
- Wenn Sie jemanden aus dem Text zitieren möchten, wandeln Sie Aussagen in indirekte Rede um.
  → *"The question is, will these organizations be able to help before it is too late?"*
  Finally, the author asks whether the organizations would be able to help before it was too late.

› *Reported speech, p. 224*

Überprüfen

Überprüfen Sie Ihre Zusammenfassung auf Fehler, und stellen Sie sicher, dass Sie alle relevanten Aspekte des Textes miteinbezogen haben.

→ *This article is about young people who live rough on the streets of big cities in Germany, and the organizations who try to help them. The text states that young people come to Berlin and become involved with drugs and violence. Often, they have no idea where to get the help they need. This is why various organizations have been set up to help deal with this problem.*

1 Read the following text and write a summary of it.

Teens living rough

Eighteen year old Sascha stands at a subway station every day, playing his guitar, trying to earn a few euros. "When I make enough money to get a night in a hostel, it's great, because I get food and a shower too," says Sascha. "A lot of the time I sleep on a park bench."

Paying for a bed is just one of the problems faced by Sascha and the other 2,000 young people sleeping rough in Berlin. Many turn to drugs as a way of dealing with their situation. Many face increasing violence. There are many health risks. Some kids get Hepatitis or HIV from using dirty needles. If they get injured in a fight, they can have major problems with their bones. If they are sleeping outdoors, they can get illnesses because they are run down from lack of sleep. Often, they get infections because they can't wash properly.

But help is at hand. Teams of social workers from Off Road Kids are going onto the streets to find young people and help them find places in shelters and hostels. Their mission is to educate these kids on the importance of looking after themselves. The kids need to know about the importance of hygiene. Although the aim is to stay away from drugs, if that isn't possible, they are told to use clean needles and not to share them. These basics stop the spread of diseases and prevent a lot of unnecessary deaths.

(263 words)

11 Textproduktion - Umgang mit Operatoren

Textproduktionsaufgaben enthalten sog. „Operatoren“, d.h. Arbeitsanweisungen, wie Sie die Aufgabe genau bearbeiten sollen. Es ist deshalb wichtig, sich mit diesen Begriffen vertraut zu machen. Operatoren sind in drei „Anforderungsbereiche“ unterteilt.

Wichtig für:

- Textproduktionsaufgaben, die Operatoren enthalten

BEISPIEL-AUFGABE

Read the text on the opposite page and complete the tasks a–d.

a **State** the author's main idea in your own words.
b **Outline** the aspects of diversity that are mentioned in this text.
c **Analyze** the author's use of informal language to engage readers.
d **Discuss** possible reasons that TV programmes are made about non-stereotypical families.

TIPPS

Anforderungsbereich I (Wiedergabe von Sachverhalten) **+ II** (Erklären, Verarbeiten und Übertragen bekannter Sachverhalte basierend auf neuen Fragen)

Operator	Übersetzung	Sie sollen
describe	beschreiben	Aspekte präzise und strukturiert beschreiben
illustrate	veranschaulichen	Aspekte (mit Textbelegen) veranschaulichen
outline	darstellen, umreißen	Aspekte auf das Wichtigste reduzieren und darstellen
point out	aufzeigen	auf zentrale Aspekte hinweisen
state	angeben	Aspekte klar herausarbeiten
summarize	zusammenfassen	die wichtigsten Punkte zusammenfassen
analyze *examine*	analysieren untersuchen	Aspekte eingehend beschreiben und erklären, wie ein bestimmter Zweck erreicht wird

Anforderungsbereich III (selbstständiges Erarbeiten von Argumentation, Deutungen, Lösungen)

Operator	Übersetzung	Sie sollen
assess *evaluate*	bewerten	nach Abwägung aller Argumente eine ausgewogene Meinung ausdrücken
comment on *give your opinion of*	Stellung nehmen zu	die eigene Meinung klar und strukturiert darlegen und mit Beispielen untermauern
discuss *weigh the pros and cons*	erörtern	ein komplexes Thema aus unterschiedlichen Perspektiven beleuchten, implizite und explizite Absichten und Bedeutungen erfassen und erörtern

1 ***State*** und ***outline*** sind Operatoren aus dem Anforderungsbereich I. Es geht also um Textreproduktion in Ihren eigenen Worten. Strukturen Sie Fakten mit Visualisierungshilfen, z. B. einer Mindmap.

> *Visualisierungshilfen und Gliederungen erstellen, S. 160*

2 Der Operator ***analyze*** in Aufgabe c gehört zum Anforderungsbereich II. Sie untersuchen, wie der Autor / die Autorin den Text aufgebaut hat und welche Mittel verwendet werden, um einen bestimmten Zweck zu erreichen (z. B. informieren, überzeugen, ein Thema erörtern).

→ **c** *The author uses informal language to talk directly to the reader. For example, when he asks questions like "What is a 'normal family'?" at the start of the text.*

3 Operatoren aus den Anforderungsbereichen I und II verlangen sachliche Antworten, keine persönliche Meinung über den Text.

→ *It is surprising that television families were non-stereotypical even in the 1950s.*

4 Der Operator ***discuss*** in Aufgabe d gehört zum Anforderungsbereich III. Hier zeigen Sie Vor- und Nachteile auf und es kann auch vorkommen, dass Sie eine persönliche Beurteilung geben müssen.

> *Einen Aufsatz oder eine Stellungnahme schreiben, S. 162*

→ **d** *TV production companies need to make money. Therefore, they make programmes that people want to watch. Clearly, TV shows about unusual families are more interesting to viewers.*

Television as the mirror of family life

What is a "normal family" – is that a mother, father, two children, a pet, that all live together in a house in the suburbs? But, were families ever really like this? Television programmes often mirror real life. Let's look at different families from popular American TV shows and see how many of them reflect this stereotype.

Right back at the start of commercial television in the 1950s, the most popular American TV show was I Love Lucy. This featured Lucille Ball and her real-life husband, Desi Arnaz, who was from Cuba, and six years younger than her. This intercultural, older-woman-younger-man couple were childless when the series began and later had a child. In general, the family was very different to the stereotypical family of this era.

Let's skip ahead to the 1970s and the Brady Bunch, the story of a single man with three boys who met a single woman with three girls. The couple married, and all of them lived together happily. The writer of the show read that around 20–30% of marriages had at least one child from a previous marriage, and wanted to represent that on television.

The 1980s gave audiences The Cosby Show, which was about a wealthy family with five children. Both parents were well-educated and had successful careers, but always had time for their children. The Cosbys were the epitome of a perfect family. There was just one unexpected aspect – the family was African-American.

One of the few famous stereotypical families in TV history is The Simpsons. They fulfil every cliché about a traditional family. They live in a house in the suburbs with two children and their pets. The mother stays at home, and the father works. And they have provided audiences with numerous examples of family dysfunction.

So, the most famous TV families starting from the 1950s have not been homogeneous, nuclear or perfect. They've been culturally diverse, patchwork, and problematic. Family diversity is nothing new and has been represented on television since the first shows were broadcast.

(344 words)

1 Describe the stereotypical family the author says is not shown on television.

2 Discuss a television family you know but which is *not* mentioned in the text, and whether or not it is really representative of modern family life.

12 Visualisierungs- und Lernhilfen erstellen

Mit Visualisierungshilfen kann man Informationen und Zusammenhänge zwischen verschiedenen Aspekten strukturieren. Sie helfen dabei, Ideen zu sammeln, in Sinnabschnitte zu gliedern und damit Inhalte übersichtlicher zu strukturieren.

Wichtig für:
- Schreiben einer Stellungnahme
- Präsentieren

TIPPS

Mindmap

Diese 'Gedanken-Landkarte' eignet sich für ein Brainstorming und um einen Überblick zu bekommen. Sie kann als Grundlage für das genutzt werden, was Sie schreiben oder präsentieren wollen.

Mindmaps sind eine nützliche Lernhilfe für folgende Aufgaben und Zwecke:
- Vorbereitung von Vorträgen und Referaten
- komplexe Themen erarbeiten
- Strukturierung schwieriger Texte und Themen
- Brainstorming-Ergebnisse strukturieren

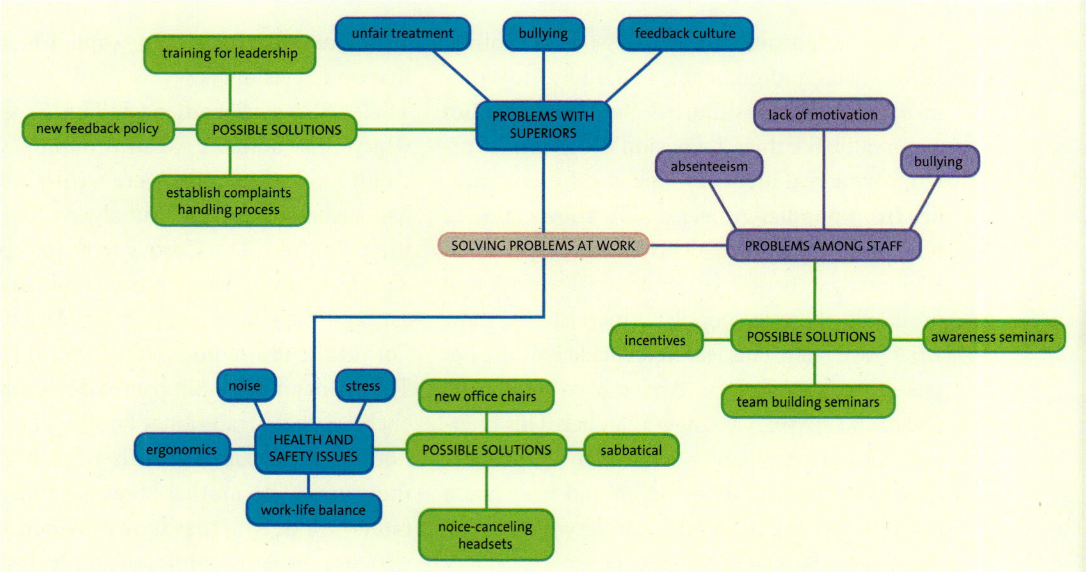

1. Schreiben Sie das zentrale Thema in die Mitte eines Blatt Papiers.
2. Notieren Sie die wichtigsten Gedanken zu diesem Thema ringsherum und verbinden Sie diese jeweils mit dem Hauptthema durch Linien. Die Begriffe dieser Verästelungen können die Grundlage für die einzelnen Paragraphen Ihres Textes darstellen.
3. Fügen Sie jedem Unterbegriff weitere Wörter und Gedanken hinzu. Die ist das Gerüst, das Sie benötigen, um Ihre Ideen auszuarbeiten.

1 Vervollständigen Sie die Mindmap mit weiteren Ideen.

Flussdiagramm (*flowchart*)

Diese Form der Visualisierung eignet sich für die Darstellung von Abläufen, Entscheidungsprozessen und der Darstellung von Ursache und Wirkung. Pfeile verbinden die jeweiligen Handlungen oder Stationen.

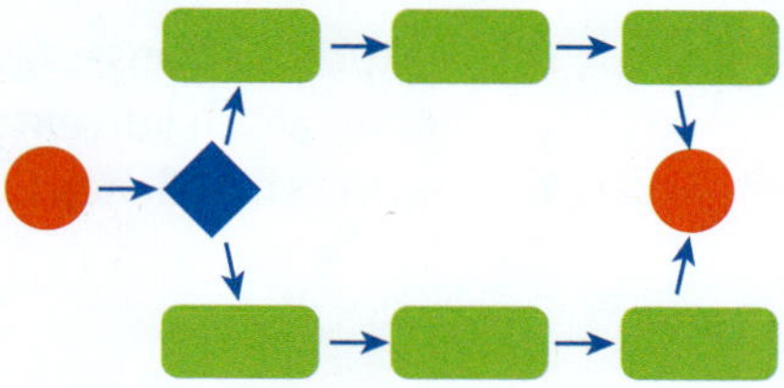

Es gibt folgende Formsymbole:

Kreis: Anfang/Ende

Rechteck: Vorgang/Handlung/Station

Raute: Ja/Nein-Entscheidung

Andere Visualisierungshilfen

Zur Darstellung von Prozessen und Abläufen eignen sich auch folgende Hilfen:

Zyklus

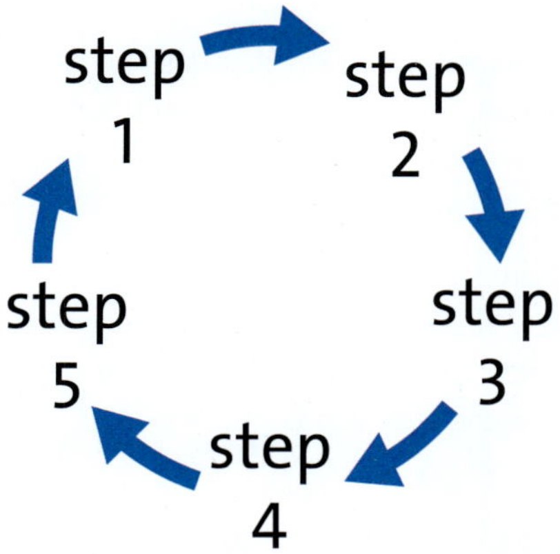

Für zeitliche Abläufe können Sie auch ein Zeitleisten-Diagramm nutzen.

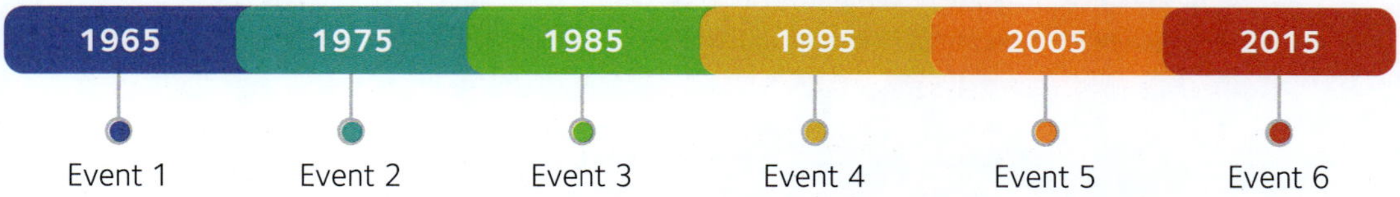

2 Welche Visualisierungsform würden Sie für die folgenden Themen wählen?

- Auswirkungen der Erhöhung des Mindestlohns auf Firmenkosten
- Vor- und Nachteile von Gesundheitskursen für Mitarbeitende
- Entwicklung Ihrer Organisation seit deren Gründung (mit Zeitangaben)
- Darstellung eines typischen Ablaufs eines Beratungsgesprächs
- Im Team Ideen für bessere Serviceleistungen eines Pflegedienstes sammeln

3 Create a graphic organizer to prepare a report on the pros and cons of remote working. Decide which form of organizer suits your purpose best. Look at the box for some aspects you might want to include.

more flexibility for employees • difficult to work from a small flat • saves time • no commute • no contact with colleagues • no separation between work and home • need for more technology • difficult for single parents

13 Einen Aufsatz oder eine Stellungnahme schreiben

Bei Textproduktionsaufgaben geht es darum, nicht nur grammatikalisch korrektes, sondern auch gut strukturiertes und verständliches Englisch zu verwenden.

Wichtig für:

- Schreiben eines Aufsatzes oder einer Stellungnahme
- rollenbasierte Stellungnahme

BEISPIEL-AUFGABE Write an essay / a comment on this statement: "The costs of hiring people with disabilities outweigh the benefits."

TIPPS

Vorbereiten und planen

1 Brainstorming

Schreiben Sie alle Gedanken auf, die Ihnen in den Sinn kommen, wenn Sie über das Thema nachdenken, und ordnen Sie diese in einer Struktur an. Grobgliederungen, Mindmaps und Flussdiagramme eignen sich dafür sehr gut.

> *Visualisierungshilfen und Gliederungen erstellen, S. 160*

2 Strukturieren

Die oben gesammelten Gedanken müssen nun in eine klare Struktur gebracht werden.

Einleitung: kurze Darstellung der Situation/Aufgabe bzw. des Problems

Hauptteil: Darlegen der Argumente, und Belegen derselben mit Fakten und Beispielen

Schlussteil: Schlussfolgerung und Zusammenfassung, eigene Meinung

My opinion: Disagree strongly – social benefits of diversity outweigh the costs
Argument 1: Costs of inclusion not very big – maybe some new equipment, or some training
Argument 2: Benefit to company: tax breaks
Argument 3: Benefit to company: good PR

Schreiben (Beispiel bewertende Schreibaufgabe)

1 Einleitung

Schreiben Sie einen Einleitungssatz, der das Thema und die darauf zurückzuführende Situation darstellt. Beschreiben Sie dann das Thema mit anderen Worten und äußern Sie Ihre Meinung. Geben Sie Ihren Lesern/-innen abschließend einen Überblick der Argumente, die Sie anführen wollen.

- *Some employers are still reluctant to hire disabled workers. They argue that the costs of doing so will be too high.* (Stellungnahme:) *This excuse is unreasonable and I will argue against it.*
  I will also name some benefits that come with employing disabled workers.

2 Hauptteil

Behandeln Sie im Hauptteil jedes Argument in einem eigenen Abschnitt. Stützen Sie Ihre Argumente mit Fakten und Beispielen. Stellen Sie sicher, dass Ihre Argumente logisch und leicht nachvollziehbar sind. Verwenden Sie Wörter und Wendungen, welche die Struktur Ihres Textes klarer machen.

- *First, let's look at the "expense" excuse. Is it really very expensive to modify a workplace for a disabled person's needs? Not unless the company is so poor it cannot, for instance, afford a small amount of training, or some equipment – like a handrail. In other words, if any adjustments need to be made, the cost of these will probably be minimal. Therefore, concerns about the cost are not a good argument against hiring a disabled person.*

3 Schlussteil

Schreiben Sie in der Schlussfolgerung eine Zusammenfassung dessen, was Sie bereits geschrieben haben. Führen Sie hier keine neuen Argumente ein. Unterstreichen Sie Ihren Standpunkt kurz und knapp in einem Schlusssatz. Dieser sollte in einer Stellungnahme Ihre eigene Meinung ausdrücken.

- *In conclusion, employers who are willing to challenge prejudice benefit in many ways. They receive tax breaks and good publicity by performing a service to society.* (Stellungnahme:) *This is why I believe all employers should include positive discrimination as part of their employment policy.*

Writing clearly

Listing arguments
first, second, third, etc.
next, further, furthermore, in addition

Giving examples
for example, for instance, to illustrate my point

Comparing and contrasting arguments
on the one hand / on the other hand, likewise, similarly, although, however, nevertheless, on the contrary, and yet

Showing results and consequences
as a result, consequently, for this reason, so, then, therefore, otherwise

Summarizing
in conclusion, in other words, on the whole

Überprüfen

1 Rechtschreibung und Grammatik

Überprüfen Sie Ihren Entwurf auf Rechtschreib- und Grammatikfehler. Achten Sie besonders auf mögliche Fehler bei der Wortstellung.

→ (Stellungnahme:) *~~Much persons~~ Many people think ~~so,~~ that disabled people ~~don't can~~ can't take responsibility for themselves. This is down to a lack of information~~s~~.*

2 Wortschatz

Vorsicht vor „falschen Freunden" – die sind englische Wörter, die deutschen Wörtern ähnlich sind, aber etwas anderes bedeuten.

→ (Stellungnahme:) *I ~~mean~~ think that consumers should ~~become~~ get the chance to respond to any job ~~announcement~~ advertisement.*

Überlegen Sie, ob Sie Ihren Text durch die Variation von Vokabular verbessern können.

Varying vocabulary

- **say:** mention, remark, state, express, claim.
- **good:** decent, favourable, great, outstanding, superb, excellent.
- **not good:** poor, dreadful, terrible, unpleasant, disgusting.
- **very:** really, quite, extremely, highly, remarkably.

1 Plan and write an essay on the following topic: "What advantages and disadvantages would employees with cognitive disabilities find working in ordinary jobs instead of in a sheltered workshop? What are the advantages to business and society?"

14 Mediation

In einer Mediationsaufgabe vermittelt man Inhalte von einer Sprache in die andere. Dabei geht es lediglich darum, die wesentlichen Informationen im Originaltext zu verstehen und in die andere Sprache sinngemäß und adressatenbezogen zu übertragen.

Wichtig für:

- schriftliche (und mündliche) Mediation/Sprachmittlung
- rollenbasierte Stellungnahme

BEISPIEL-AUFGABE

Sie arbeiten in einem Zentrum für gesunde Ernährung, das mit Ernährungsprogrammen Menschen unterstützt, die Probleme mit Übergewicht haben. Die Leiterin des Zentrums hat den Artikel *A healthy eating plan for people with chronic conditions* auf Seite 99 von einer Partnerorganisation in den USA erhalten und möchte ihn auch für die deutschen Klienten nutzen. Sie bittet Sie, den Artikel zu lesen und dazu eine Infobroschüre auf Deutsch zu schreiben. Erklären Sie im Detail, was der DASH-Ernährungsplan ist, warum er empfohlen wird und wem er helfen kann.

TIPPS

Analysieren

Form und Inhalt einer Mediation hängen von folgenden Faktoren ab, die in der Aufgabenstellung vorgegeben werden. Diese Faktoren geben auch den situativen Kontext vor und beeinflussen Sprachebene und Stil Ihrer Mediation, z.B. eher formell (Kunden) oder informell (Mitschüler/-innen).

Adressat – für wen?	Textsorte – wie?	Zweck – warum?	Ort – wo?
• Kunden/ Geschäftspartner • Kollegen/-innen • Mitschüler/-innen	• Brief/E-Mail • Infobroschüre • Zeitungsartikel • Telefonat	• Vermittlung von … – Informationen – Tipps/Ratschlägen – Ergebnissen/Argumenten	• Arbeitsplatz • Schule/Uni • Jugendclub

Suchen Sie dann die relevanten Aspekte, die Sie bearbeiten sollen, in der Aufgabenstellung.

1 Bestimmen Sie nun Form und Inhalt in der Aufgabenstellung der Beispielaufgabe.

Lesen

> *Schwierige Texte lesen, S. 154*

Lesen Sie den Text schnell durch, um sich einen Überblick zu verschaffen. Wenden Sie die Lesestile Skimming und Scanning an. Lesen Sie bei kleineren Verständnisproblemen einfach weiter und erschließen Sie den Sinn schwieriger Stellen aus dem Kontext. Notieren oder markieren Sie Punkte, die Sie in der Aufgabenstellung als relevant identifiziert haben.

Schreiben

- Lassen Sie unwichtige Details weg.
- Übernehmen Sie keine kompletten Absätze.
- Vermeiden Sie wörtliche Übersetzungen.
- Äußern Sie Ihre eigene Meinung nur, wenn Sie explizit dazu aufgefordert werden.

Das **Umformulieren** von Inhalten aus dem Text ist in einer Mediation wichtig und dient folgenden Zwecken:

1 Vereinfachung komplexer Inhalte

In einer Mediation fasst man das Wesentliche zusammen. Konzentrieren Sie sich auf die Kernaussagen und lassen Sie unnötige Ergänzungen, Einzelheiten, Daten, Zahlen oder Beispiele weg.

Originaltext:	Mediationstext:
Apart from lowering blood pressure, the diet may also improve blood glucose levels, lower the concentration of fats in the blood and help reduce weight.	Die Diät kann Blutdruck senken, Blutwerte verbessern und helfen, das Gewicht zu reduzieren.

2 Wiedergabe von Redewendungen und idiomatischen Ausdrücken

Wenn Sie den Sinn einer Redewendung nicht verstehen, raten Sie nicht, was die Bedeutung sein könnte. Nutzen Sie am besten ein einsprachiges Wörterbuch.

3 Wiedergabe von Zitaten

Falls Sie Zitate im Text nutzen wollen, geben Sie die Aussagen in indirekter Rede wieder.

> *Reported speech, p. 224*

2 Sie arbeiten in einer Reha-Klinik für junge Menschen, die seit kurzem eine Behinderung haben und lernen, mit ihrer Behinderung umzugehen. Ein großes Problem in dieser Gruppe sind Angst vor der Zukunft und Sorgen über den Verlust von Unabhängigkeit. Viele Ihrer Kollegen kommen aus anderen Ländern und sprechen Englisch. Ihr Chef bittet Sie, den Artikel *Wie Robotik Menschen mit Behinderung hilft* zu lesen und einen Aushang für Ihre Kollegen auf Englisch zu schreiben. Erklären Sie im Detail, welche Innovationen Menschen mit Behinderung helfen können und wie.

Wie Robotik Menschen mit Behinderung hilft

Robotertechnologie und digitale Innovationen helfen schon seit langem körperlich beeinträchtigten Arbeitnehmerinnen und Arbeitnehmern bei der Ausführung ihrer Tätigkeiten, z. B. bei der Montage. Die Roboter übernehmen dabei Aufgaben, die die Menschen nur mit besonderer Anstrengung oder gar nicht bewältigen können: Sie können Werkstücke festhalten und so drehen, dass ein Mensch problemlos daran arbeiten kann, der nur einen Arm hat. Aber auch Menschen mit schwerster Behinderung wird eine verbesserte Bewältigung des Alltags ermöglicht: Durch eine Art Joystick kann der Arm des Assistenzroboters bedient werden. Um den Joystick zu bedienen, braucht nur das Kinn eingesetzt zu werden, um die gewünschte Funktion z.B. bei der Bildschirmarbeit auszuwählen. Hierbei behält die Nutzerin bzw. der Nutzer die Kontrolle, während das System alles alleine macht.

Japans Gastronomie geht noch einen Schritt weiter: In einigen Teilen der Gastronomie werden humanoide Roboter eingesetzt, die von Kellnerinnen und Kellnern im Hintergrund bedient werden, denen jede Bewegung unmöglich ist. Sie steuern die Maschinen nur mit Bewegungen der Pupille.

Die Möglichkeiten sind noch lange nicht ausgeschöpft. Forschende arbeiten schon an Systemen, die auch Menschen mit geistiger Behinderung am Arbeitsplatz unterstützen sollen. Für viele Menschen bedeutet die zusehends ausgereifte Technologie Jobchancen, die sie sonst nicht hätten und damit einen großen Schritt in die Selbstständigkeit. (201 Wörter)

FILE 1 Topic 2, Section B, Page 35, Exercise 3

Partner A

Use the notes from the case file below to tell your partner about Christina, one of Outreach's clients.

Client name: Christina
Gender: female
Age: 17
Background: born in Scotland; alcoholic mother died when Christina was 13 years old; sent to live with aunt in Cardiff.
Ran away from aunt several times; put into care home.
Left care home at 16, lived on the street, drinking and taking drugs.
Stole alcohol from shops and earned money as a prostitute.
Picked up several times by the police, put on probation and given a "last chance" by a judge. Came to Outreach via probation officer.
Now in shared flat with two other girls. Training to be a hairdresser.
Comes into Outreach now and again for a cup of tea and a chat.

FILE 2 Topic 3, Section A, Page 57, Exercise 3

Step 2: A relative of a resident calls and would like to know how the afternoons are organized in the care home. Role-play the situation with a partner.

Partner A

You are the caller. Use the following prompts to make your own questions:

1 what kind of activities in the afternoon?
2 social interaction?
3 physical activities, gymnastics?
4 snack, tea or coffee?
5 walks to the park?
6 games or social activities – how often?

FILE 3 Exam skills, Page 149, Exercise 2

Partners A and B

Find out how Partners C and D have adjusted to life in Germany. Ask about their work, language course, social network, and any problems they might have encountered. Make notes on these subjects and give some recommendations about how they could integrate further into German society.

FILE 4 Topic 3, Section C, Page 67, Exercise 4

Partner A

You and your partner are going to take turns playing the role of a counsellor and the role of a caller.

1 Your first role is as the caller. Describe the situation below to the counsellor and ask for advice.
Your flatmate is being physically abused by her boyfriend. When you first got to know your flatmate, she liked to go out with you and other friends to clubs and parties. Since she met her boyfriend, she is tired and doesn't want to go out in the evenings. Once or twice, when you noticed bruises on her arms, your friend said she'd had a fall. The last time she came home with a bruise, she said her boyfriend was jealous. You've heard your flatmate's boyfriend has been in trouble with the police for fighting. You are worried about your friend.

2 When you play the role of the counsellor during the second call, listen to Partner B's problem. Remember to use skills for active listening to help the caller to talk.

So, you feel as if …

I understand.

Take your time.

FILE 5 Topic 4, Section A, Page 79, Exercise 4

Partner A

You are the caller. First, read through the role card carefully and make notes. Use the suggestions below to make an enquiry. Add your own ideas regarding the details. Remember to use polite language.

- Give your name and the name of your organization.
- Say you have some questions about catering for an event.
- Say you are planning a garden party for 50-70 people and need catering.
- Ask about their food options.
- Ask if you can have a barbecue instead of a buffet.
- Ask what the whole service will cost.
- Say you will talk to your boss and get back to them later.

FILE 6 Exam skills, Page 149, Exercise 2

Partner C

You work as a doctor in a hospital, where you speak mostly English. You have not yet found a German language course and you don't speak very much German at all. You miss your family in Greece very much and would like them to move to Germany, too. Make up any other details you need to answer the social workers' questions, and make notes on their recommendations for you.

FILE 7 Topic 4, Section B, Page 81, Exercise 4

Partner A

Before you start each call, read through the instructions carefully and make notes.

Call 1: You are looking after the phones for Kate while she is at a meeting. Follow the instructions below, adding relevant details where necessary. Remember to ask the caller to repeat or spell anything that is unclear.

- Take the call and greet the caller.
- Ask what you can do for the caller.
- Explain that the colleague they should talk to is not available at the moment.
- Ask if you can have the caller's contact details so that the colleague can phone back.
- Confirm the caller's details and say that you will pass them on.
- Thank the caller for phoning and say goodbye.

Call 2: You are the caller. Use the information below to make a phone call. Add your own ideas regarding the details. Just for fun, you can make up a difficult name which you have to spell.

- Give your name and say where you are calling from.
- You would like to cancel an appointment you have made with Frank Schultz.
- Give a reason why the date and time suggested are not suitable.
- Agree on a new date and time.
- Thank the person who took your call and say goodbye.

FILE 8 Topic 4, Section B, Page 83, Exercise 4B

Partners A and B

1 Work with your partner and use these headings in a logical order to create a form on an extra sheet of paper. Leave room for Virpi's information and any other details the hospital needs to know.

Symptoms (the condition which best accounts for the patient's admission to hospital):

Other conditions:

Regular medication:

Date of admission:

Name:
Address:

Telephone:
Mobile phone:

Date of birth:
Gender:

Allergies:

2 Take turns to explain the form to Virpi. Ask for the necessary information and help her to fill it in.

FILE 9 Topic 5, Section A, Page 97, Exercise 3

Partner A

With Partners B and C, follow the steps below to reconstruct a recipe for making pizza.

1 The ingredients

You are responsible for preparing the base of the pizza. Which of the ingredients below will you need? (You need five altogether.) Which will your partners need for the sauce and toppings? Work with your partners to distribute the ingredients.

- 50 g grated parmesan
- 1 level teaspoonful salt
- 15 g fresh yeast
- a handful of chopped basil
- some black olives
- a small piece of butter
- 100 g mozzarella cut into cubes
- 1 clove of garlic, crushed
- 400 g tin of chopped tomatoes
- a handful of cherry tomatoes, halved
- about 150 ml water
- 1 tablespoon tomato paste
- some fresh basil leaves
- 225 g flour

2 The instructions

The recipe has nine steps in all, but only three of them are below (and in the wrong order). Work with your partners to put all nine steps (a–i) into the correct order. Which steps are you responsible for?

a After the dough for the base has risen, knead it again then divide it into two balls.

b Bake for 8–10 minutes until crisp, then repeat the final step for the remaining pizza. Serve with a little more olive oil and additional basil leaves.

c Finally, smooth half of the sauce over one of the dough bases with the back of a spoon. Scatter half of the tomatoes, the olives and basil leaves over the sauce and sprinkle half of the cheese mixture over the toppings. Put one pizza, still on its baking paper, on top of the preheated baking tray.

FILE 10 Topic 5, Section A, Page 97, Exercise 4

Summarize this German description of what chicken nuggets are made of in simple English. The translations below will help you.

Chicken Nuggets – lecker oder eklig?

Wissenschaftler haben festgestellt, dass über 50 % der üblichen Chicken Nuggets, die in Fastfood-Ketten verkauft werden, aus Separatorenfleisch[1], das durch maschinelles Entbeinen von Hühnern gewonnen wird, bestehen. Wenn die teuren Fleischstücke vom Hühnchen entfernt sind, werden die übrig gelassenen Knochen durch ein Hochdrucksieb[2], das das Fleisch zu 100 % sauber abschabt, durchgedrückt. Diese Paste, die wie Erdbeereis oder Paprika-Frischkäse aussieht, ist das Ergebnis. Die Paste, die auch aus den Karkassen von Truthähnen, Schweinen und Rindern gewonnen wird, ist nicht nur ein Hauptbestandteil von Chicken Nuggets, sondern auch von Hot Dogs, Peperoniwurst, Salami etc. Die Industrie nennt diese Methode „Advanced Meat Recovery".

[1] mechanically separated meat [2] high-pressure sieve

FILE 11 Topic 5, Section A, Page 99, Exercise 4

Partner A

You will play yourself. Follow the steps to prepare for the conversation.

1 Study the illustration on page 98.
2 Think about questions that Mr Kasanidis might ask.
3 Note down some key words you will need.
4 Make sure you understand the vocabulary that is associated with eating plans and diabetes.
5 Think of a polite beginning and end to the conversation.

FILE 12 Topic 5, Section B, Page 105, Exercise 3

Partner A

Jason L. (aged 12) often comes to school with bruises or a black eye. He claims he was clumsy or that he fell off his skateboard but he is lying to cover up for his father, who physically abuses him. When the social worker called on the family, she noticed that Jason's mother had a black eye. She said this was because she had fallen down the stairs. Jason's mother says that her son often causes trouble at home, as he is rude to his father. She has been known to social services since she was taken into care after her father beat her.

FILE 13 Topic 5, Section B, Page 107, Exercise 2

Partners A and B

1 Read and discuss the information below about the prospective parents you have been asked to assess.

Julie and Tom Laurence
Mr and Mrs Laurence are in their late 30s. They have two children, aged 7 and 10. Both children are healthy and well looked after. Julie Laurence is a full-time wife and mother. Tom Laurence works in an office. Both Julie and Tom are smokers.

Passive smoking
Many children who are put up for adoption have been neglected and have health problems. Some of them have asthma. Passive smoking is a risk for every child.

Recommendations
- The agency should explain the risks of exposing children to passive smoking.
- Mr and Mrs Laurence's views on smoking and any decisions they make on smoking should be taken into account in their application.
- Refer them to a "quit smoking" programme. The agency medical adviser may be able to advise.

2 Describe the Laurences to the other members of the team. Point out any negative aspects in their application and explain the agency's recommendations.

FILE 14 Topic 5, Section C, Page 111, Exercise 2

Partner A

You are going to tell your partner about "Gastarbeiter" in West Germany.

1 First, read the text below. Use your dictionary to find out the meaning of any words you don't know.

How did "Gastarbeiter" come to be in West Germany?
During the 1950s, Germany experienced a so-called "Wirtschaftswunder" (economic miracle) and needed workers. The government signed bilateral agreements allowing recruitment of "Gastarbeiter" to work in the industrial sector in jobs that required few qualifications. The construction of the Berlin Wall in August 1961 reduced the large-scale flow of East German immigration, and so a second wave of recruitment started in the 1960s.

Where did "Gastarbeiter" come from?
The first "Gastarbeiter" came from Italy in 1955. After that, workers came from Greece, Spain, Turkey, Morocco, Portugal, Tunisia and Yugoslavia.

What was the main benefit for the home countries of the "Gastarbeiter"?
The Federal Republic saw employment of "Gastarbeiter" as a form of developmental aid. It was hoped that the "Gastarbeiter" would learn useful skills in Germany, which could help them develop their home countries after returning home.

Where are the "Gastarbeiter" now?
Some of them returned to their home countries, but many of them brought their wives and family members to Germany and became a fixed part of the German population.

2 Find out the following from your partner who has read about "Vertragsarbeiter" in the GDR.
   1 How did "Vertragsarbeiter" come to be in East Germany?
   2 Where did "Vertragsarbeiter" come from?
   3 How did the GDR government benefit from employing "Vertragsarbeiter"?
   4 Where are the "Vertragsarbeiter" now?

FILE 15 Topic 5, Section C, Page 111, Exercise 4

Partners A and B

You are the interviewers. You will take turns to interview the two carers.

1 Read the transcript of the interview with Liam Kelly together and identify the questions that he was asked. Decide which of the questions you should focus on in your interview with the carers. Write them down.
2 Brainstorm ideas for other questions that would suit your interview with the carers. Then use all your ideas to come up with five to seven questions to ask the carers.
3 Practise your interview with Partners C and D, then perform all or part of it in front of the class.

FILE 16 Topic 5, Section C, Page 113, Exercise 4

Partner A

Follow the senior social worker's instructions to call Olena Melnyk and leave a message in English.

Bitte Olena Melnyk anrufen
- *erklären/sagen Sie ihr, dass wir erfreut über ihren Anruf waren*
- *fragen Sie sie, ob sie Zeit hat, morgen um 16.30 Uhr zu einem Vorstellungsgespräch vorbeizukommen*
- *falls nicht, wäre es auch am Dienstagnachmittag nächste Woche möglich*
- *sagen Sie ihr, dass wir einige ukrainische Familien hier haben*

FILE 17 Topic 5, Section C, Page 113, Exercise 5

Partners A and B

You are going to interview two potential volunteers together in one interview. Neither of the candidates can speak German very well, so the interview will be in English.

Partner A: You are the senior social worker. **Partner B:** You are the volunteer.

1 Preparation for the interview
Prepare yourselves for the interview by making a list of questions you would like to ask the prospective volunteers. Think about what the interviewees might like to know from you, e.g. nationalities of the asylum seekers, types of activities volunteers do with them.

2 The interview
Partner A begins by introducing him/herself and Partner B. Explain that Partner B is a volunteer and say that the interviewees might like to ask him/her questions later in the interview. Make some small talk, e.g. ask if the interviewees found the home all right, then start the interview by asking the interviewees to introduce themselves and say a few words about why they are interested in volunteering in a home for asylum seekers.

FILE 18 Exam skills, Page 149, Exercise 2

Partner D

You work in the kitchen of a Greek restaurant, where all the other employees are Greek. You don't serve customers because you don't speak German yet. You haven't yet found a language course. You've been sleeping on your sibling's (Partner C's) couch because you haven't been able to find a flat of your own. Make up any other details you need to answer the social workers' questions, and make notes on their recommendations for you.

FILE 19	Topic 6, Section A, Page 125, Exercise 4

Partner A

Glen Carter

Your aim is to get your supervisor to recognize your skills.

Preparation: Re-read your stress checklist and make notes. Read the transcript of the previous meeting and make notes on that too. Remember, you feel that you are being treated unfairly by your supervisor and your colleagues and they are not keeping their promises.

Here are a few things that have been said about you:

HR Manager

You're the best candidate for the job. I can imagine that you will soon be head of the department!

You will go far, Glen. You are one of my best students.

Your professor at MIT

FILE 20	Topic 6, Section B, Page 129, Exercise 5

Partner A

Before you start each call, read the instructions carefully and make notes.

Call 1: You are working at the Jugendforum. Follow the instructions and add any relevant details where necessary.

- Take the call and greet the caller.
- Ask what exactly you can do for the caller.
- Show you understand and ask for further details.
- Summarize the details and repeat them to the caller.
- Explain what happened.
- Offer a solution.
- Ask whether the caller is happy with the solution.
- Thank the caller and say goodbye.

Call 2: You are the caller. Use the information below to make a phone call. Add your own details.

- Give your name and say that you are unhappy with the meal delivery service.
- Say that you regularly get meals delivered to your home, but delivery is now very late.
- Say that the meals are delivered between 1:30 and 2:00 p.m. – too late for your lunch.
- Tell the employee you would like your meals between 12:00 and 12:30.
- Ask the employee to do something about it.
- Say whether you are happy with the solution.
- Thank the employee and say goodbye.

FILE 21 Topic 2, Section B, Page 35, Exercise 3

Partner B

Use the notes from the case file below to tell your partner about Sean, one of Outreach's clients.

Client name: Sean (pronounced Shawn)
Gender: male
Age: 19
Background: came from Ireland looking for work three years ago. Worked illegally on a building site; was not paid any wages so could not pay his rent.
Began to sleep rough but when winter came, got ill and ended up in hospital.
When he came out of hospital, began to drink heavily and got into fights. During one fight, he stabbed another boy, who nearly died; put into a young offender institution for 18 months.
Now in council apartment, reporting to probation officer once a week. Working in factory and attending vocational school two days a week where he is studying mechatronics.

FILE 22 Topic 3, Section C, Page 67, Exercise 4

Partner B

You and your partner are going to take turns playing the role of a counsellor and the role of a caller.

1 **Your first role is as the counsellor. Listen to Partner A's problem. Remember to use skills for active listening to help the caller to talk.**

So, you feel as if …

I understand.

Take your time.

2 **When you play the role of the caller during the second call, describe the situation below to the counsellor and ask for advice.**

You are the parent of a teenage girl who is overweight. One day last week, your daughter came home from school with her clothes torn. She told you that she had been involved in a fight with some other girls at school. These girls are bullying your daughter and calling her names. You suggested that you both go to the head teacher and complain so that the teacher would stop the bullying. Your daughter, however, believes this would only make things worse. Instead, she has gone on a diet. She has not eaten for three days, and you are worried about her.

FILE 23 Topic 6, Section A, Page 125, Exercise 4

Partner B

Claudia Weber

Your task is to mediate between an employee, Glen, who is suffering from stress, and his supervisor, Janice. Your aim is to find the best solution for your client.

Preparation: Re-read the skills for active listening on page 67. Read the transcript of the previous meeting and make notes. Remember, Glen Carter feels that he is being treated unfairly by his supervisor and his colleagues.

Here are a few things that you have heard during your visits to the company:

Glen's colleague Mae: *Glen works really hard. Sometimes I think he does too much.*

Glen's colleague Klaus: *Glen is a very careful worker. He doesn't make mistakes.*

FILE 24 Topic 5, Section A, Page 97, Exercise 3

Partner C

With Partners A and B, follow the steps below to reconstruct a recipe for making pizza.

1 The ingredients

You are responsible for preparing the topping for the pizza. Which of the ingredients below will you need? (You need five altogether.) Which will your partners need for the base and sauce? Work with your partners to distribute the ingredients.

- 50 g grated parmesan
- 1 level teaspoonful salt
- 15 g fresh yeast
- a handful of chopped basil
- some black olives
- a small piece of butter
- 100 g mozzarella cut into cubes
- 1 clove of garlic, crushed
- 400 g tin of chopped tomatoes
- a handful of cherry tomatoes, halved
- about 150 ml water
- 1 tablespoon tomato paste
- some fresh basil leaves
- 225 g flour

2 The instructions

The recipe has nine steps in all, but only three of them are below (and in the wrong order). Work with your partners to put all nine steps (a–i) into the correct order. Which steps are you responsible for?

g Drain the tinned tomatoes and mix them with the tomato paste, chopped basil and crushed garlic. Leave the mixture to stand at room temperature while you shape the base.

h Cut each pizza into eight slices and serve with a fresh garden salad.

i Turn the dough onto a lightly floured surface and knead for 5 minutes until it is smooth. Put the kneaded dough back into the bowl, cover the bowl with a clean cloth and leave it in a warm place to rise.

FILE 25 Topic 5, Section B, Page 107, Exercise 2

Partners C and D

1 Read and discuss the information below about the prospective parents you have been asked to assess.

Gale and Kevin Jameson
Mr and Mrs Jameson are in their mid-30s. They have no children. Mrs Jameson has been receiving fertility treatment[1] for the last four years. As they have had no results so far, the couple are now considering adoption. Mrs Jameson still hopes to give birth to her own child and would like to continue fertility treatment for the next few years.

Infertility[2]
Experience suggests that infertile[2] couples need time to accept their situation before they are ready for adoption. If a couple continues with fertility treatment, and it is successful, their response to the adopted child might change.

Recommendations
- The agency should explain the problems attached to continuing with fertility treatment.
- Offer the couple counselling on why their approach is not in the interests of the adopted baby and ask them to consider the consequences if a child is born after a baby is placed with them.
- They should complete the fertility treatment and, if it is still not successful, apply for adoption again.

[1] fertility treatment *künstliche Befrüchtung* [2] infertility / infertile *Unfruchtbarkeit / unfruchtbar*

2 Describe the Jamesons to the other members of the team. Point out any negative aspects in their application and explain the agency's recommendations.

FILE 26 Topic 4, Section B, Page 81, Exercise 4

Partner B

Before you start each call, read through the instructions carefully and make notes.

Call 1: You are the caller. Use the information below to make a phone call. Add your own ideas regarding the details. Just for fun, you can make up a difficult name which you have to spell.
- Give your name and say where you are calling from.
- You would like to speak to someone about volunteering.
- Give details of who you are and say why you are interested in volunteering.
- If the person is not available, ask if you should call again.
- Thank the person who took your call and say goodbye.

Call 2: You are looking after the phones for Kate while she is at a meeting. Follow the instructions below, adding relevant details where necessary. Remember to ask the caller to repeat or spell anything that is unclear.
- Take the call and greet the caller.
- Ask what you can do for the caller.
- Offer the caller a new appointment.
- If the day and time are not convenient for the caller, offer an alternative.
- Confirm the new arrangements.
- Thank the caller for phoning and say goodbye.

FILE 27 Topic 4, Section B, Page 83, Exercise 4B

Partners C and D

You are Virpi. The volunteer who accompanied you to hospital helps you complete an admissions form.

1 You have already thought of some of the things the hospital will want to know. Talk about what other information you might have to give. Think about personal details, any medication you take, any accidents you have had before. Think, too, about how you feel at the moment.

Akneeta Hakala (mother)

Contraceptive pill

Aleksanterinkatu 21, 00100 Helsinki

I wish I didn't have such a terrible headache.

Riding accident, aged 10, broken arm

Right now, I feel as if I've been kicked by a horse.

Allergic to tree pollen, penicillin

2 Take turns to answer the questions the volunteer asks. Spell any words or names that are difficult.

FILE 28 Topic 5, Section A, Page 97, Exercise 3

Partner B

With Partners A and C, follow the steps below to reconstruct a recipe for making pizza.

1 The ingredients

You are responsible for preparing the sauce for the pizza. Which of the ingredients below will you need? (You need four altogether.) Which will your partners need for the base and toppings? Work with your partners to distribute the ingredients.

- 50 g grated parmesan
- 1 level teaspoonful salt
- 15 g fresh yeast
- a handful of chopped basil
- some black olives
- a small piece of butter
- 100 g mozzarella cut into cubes
- 1 clove of garlic, crushed
- 400 g tin of chopped tomatoes
- a handful of cherry tomatoes, halved
- about 150 ml water
- 1 tablespoon tomato paste
- some fresh basil leaves
- 225 g flour

2 The instructions

The recipe has nine steps in all, but only three of them are below (and in the wrong order). Work with your partners to put all nine steps (a–i) into the correct order. Which steps are you responsible for?

d First, prepare the base. Blend the yeast with the water. Then, mix the flour and salt together and rub in the butter. After that, pour the yeast and water mixture into the flour and mix well to make a soft dough.

e Before you put the sauce and toppings on the base of the first pizza, place a large baking tray on the top shelf of the oven and preheat the oven to 220 °C.

f On a floured surface, roll out the dough into two large discs, each about 25 cm across. The dough needs to be very thin as it will rise in the oven. Lift the discs onto two floured sheets of baking paper.

FILE 29 Topic 5, Section A, Page 99, Exercise 4

Partner B

You are Mr Kasanidis, a patient with prediabetes. Follow these steps to prepare for the conversation.

1 Think about questions that you want to ask, for example: Why do I need to follow a special diet? What kind of diet is that? Can I still eat …?
2 Note down some key words you will need.
3 Make sure you understand the vocabulary that is associated with eating plans and diabetes.
4 Think of a polite beginning and end to the conversation.

FILE 30 Topic 5, Section B, Page 105, Exercise 3

Partner B

Sylvia M. has three children: a ten-year-old daughter, Alice, and twins aged four. Her husband, who was a bank manager, was killed during a robbery in the bank. Since then, Sylvia M. has been unable to cope. She has become dependent on sleeping pills and neglects the children, her home and herself. Alice has been looking after the twins. During the current school term, she has played truant on 46 days.

FILE 31 Topic 5, Section B, Page 107, Exercise 2

Partners E and F

1 Read and discuss the information below about the prospective parents you have been asked to assess.

Helen and Evan Fletcher
Mr and Mrs Fletcher are in their late 20s. Both work for social services. They have decided not to have children of their own as Mrs Fletcher has an auto-immune disease which may be passed on genetically.

Offences
Mr Fletcher was convicted for vandalism and stealing cars when he was 17. He did community service[1] at the time. He has no other convictions. Mr Fletcher told the agency himself about these offences.

Recommendations
- The agency feels that Mr Fletcher's criminal record[2] should not affect the couple's application to adopt.
- Mrs Fletcher should give us copies of her medical records.
- A medical check-up should be carried out on Mrs Fletcher by the agency medical adviser.

[1] to do community service *Sozialstunden ableisten* [2] criminal record *Vorstrafen(register)*

2 Describe the Fletchers to the other members of the team. Point out any negative aspects in their application and explain the agency's recommendations.

FILE 32 Topic 5, Section C, Page 111, Exercise 2

Partner B

You are going to tell your partner about "Vertragsarbeiter" in East Germany.

1 First, read the text below.

How did "Vertragsarbeiter" come to be in East Germany?
After the division of Germany into East and West in 1949, there was a shortage of labour in East Germany. When the Berlin Wall was built in 1961, the labour shortage got even worse, and the GDR (German Democratic Republic) began to recruit workers from other countries.

Where did "Vertragsarbeiter" come from?
In 1965, the GDR signed its first "guest worker" contract with Poland, followed by other Eastern Bloc countries. Later, workers from Mozambique, Vietnam, North Korea, Angola and Cuba began to work in the GDR.

How did the GDR government benefit from employing "Vertragsarbeiter"?
The GDR used its "Vertragsarbeiter" programme to build international solidarity among fellow communist countries.

Where are the "Vertragsarbeiter" now?
Following the fall of the Berlin Wall in November 1989 and German reunification in 1990, the population of guest workers still remaining in the former East Germany faced deportation, premature discontinuation of residence and work permits as well as open discrimination in the workplace. Of the 100,000 guest workers remaining in East Germany after reunification, about 75% left because of an increase in xenophobia in former East German states.

2 Find out the following from your partner who has read about "Gastarbeiter" in West Germany.
   1 How did "Gastarbeiter" come to be in West Germany?
   2 Where did "Gastarbeiter" come from?
   3 How did the home countries of "Gastarbeiter" benefit?
   4 Where are the "Gastarbeiter" now?

FILE 33 Topic 5, Section C, Page 111, Exercise 4

Partners C and D

You are the carers. You will take turns to answer the interviewers' questions.

1 Read the transcript of the interview with Liam Kelly and identify the answers he gave to the questions he was asked. Decide how you as carers can use and possibly adapt these answers. Make notes.
2 Brainstorm ideas for other questions that might be asked. Remember, you are carers being asked about how you do your work, so you should focus on practical aspects like taking care that every client's religious practices are respected. Add your ideas to your notes above.
3 Practise your interview with Partners A and B, then perform all or part of it in front of the class.

FILE 34 Topic 5, Section C, Page 113, Exercise 4

Partner B

Follow the senior social worker's instructions to call Daniel Mills and leave a message in English.

> *Bitte Daniel Mills anrufen*
> - *fragen Sie ihn, ob er Interesse hat, zweimal pro Woche Computerkenntnisse zu vermitteln*
> - *wenn ja, bitten Sie ihn, entweder am Montag um 10.30 Uhr oder 15.30 Uhr zu einem Vorstellungsgespräch zu kommen*
> - *erklären Sie ihm, dass wir gerne hätten, dass er möglichst bald beginnt, falls er geeignet ist*
> - *er würde eine Gruppe von sechs jungen Männern aus verschiedenen Ländern unterrichten*

FILE 35 Topic 5, Section C, Page 113, Exercise 5

Partners C and D

You have both been invited to an interview by the senior social worker and will be interviewed together. The interview is going to be conducted in English.

1 Preparation for the interview
Prepare yourselves for the interview by deciding who you are and where you are from. Think about your reasons for volunteering for the job. Make a list of questions you would like to ask the interviewers, e.g. nationalities of the asylum seekers, how you would support them.

2 The interview
Partner A will begin by introducing him/herself and Partner B, and will make some small talk, e.g. talking about the weather. Then the interview will start.

FILE 36 Topic 6, Section A, Page 125, Exercise 4

Partner C

Janice, Glen Carter's supervisor
Your aim is to get your department running smoothly. You would like to have Glen Carter transferred to another department. During the discussion, stay polite but remain firm.

Preparation: Make notes on the following points.
- There is a high level of demotivation in the department due to Mr Carter's negative attitude.
- He is often off sick and when he is there, he is continually complaining.
- Here is an exchange you and he had a few days ago.

Glen: *I think you are harassing me.*

You: *Don't be silly. I only want my team to function properly.*

FILE 37 Topic 6, Section B, Page 129, Exercise 5

Partner B

Before you start each call, read the instructions carefully and make notes.

Call 1: You are the caller. Use the information below to make a phone call. Add your own details.

- Give your name and say that you are calling about a problem with an application form.
- Say somebody at the centre last week promised to call and help you complete the form.
- Ask who the caller spoke to and what kind of form it is.
- Say whether the details are correct.
- Ask what will happen next.
- Say whether you are happy with the solution.
- Thank the employee and say goodbye.

Call 2: You are working at the Jugendforum. Follow the instructions and add any relevant details where necessary.

- Take the call and greet the caller.
- Ask what you can do for the caller.
- Show you understand and ask for further details.
- Summarize the details and repeat them to the caller.
- Say you will check what the problem is and call back with the details.
- Ask whether the caller is happy with the solution.
- Thank the caller and say goodbye.

FILE 38 Topic 4, Section A, Page 79, Exercise 4

Partner B

You are an employee of Catering Plus, a company that offers complete catering packages. Follow the instructions below, adding relevant details where necessary. Remember to use polite language.

- Take the call and greet the caller.
- Ask what you can do for the caller.
- Say that you are happy to help.
- Tell the caller about your food options.
- Say that unfortunately you do not offer any barbecue options.
- Tell the caller about the costs.
- Say you look forward to the call and thank the caller.

FILE 39 Topic 6, Section A, Page 124, Exercise 1A

Partner B

Read Glen's comments on page 2 of the stress checklist and exchange information with your partner, who has page 1. Discuss any patterns you see.

Stress Checklist Glen Carter page 2	Statement
1	*I don't have enough responsibility, as I've frequently said!*
2	*My colleagues let me deal with all the difficult calls. I have asked my supervisor to have us take turns, but so far nothing has happened.*
3	*Only for me. My colleagues are allowed to take more breaks.*
4	*I am extremely focused!*
5	*I don't have a spouse, children or family. My boss and my co-workers ignore me.*
6	*See above.*
7	*My desk is in the worst position in the office. Nobody asked me if I wanted to sit next to the water cooler.*
8	*I get headaches and muscle tension because my colleagues always meet and chat at the water cooler and that disturbs my concentration and makes me tense.*
9	*The doctor thinks this is because I eat sandwiches at my desk at lunchtime. I prefer sandwiches to the canteen. The office is nice and quiet when the others are at lunch.*
10	*See 8 and 9.*
11	*I'm a computer geek, for heaven's sake!*
12	*It's up to me how much I drink.*

FILE 40 Topic 6, Section A, Page 124, Exercise 1B

Stress checklist	
Overall score	**Stress level and advice**
25 or under	Good – Stress level is low.
26 – 35	Average – Lowering stress level would be beneficial.
36 – 45	Bad – Employee should think seriously about changes in life to reduce stress.
46 or above	Dangerous – Having this amount of stress can lead to serious illnesses. Employee needs assistance in lowering stress levels as soon as possible.

FILE G1 Topic 1, Section A, Page 11, Exercise 2D

GUIDANCE

Follow the steps below to help you compare working conditions in different countries.

1 Re-read the texts and answer the questions below.
- What countries do these social workers work in?
- What do they say about their work, for example case loads, stress, work-life balance?
- Do they mention any support they get from their organization?
- Is their work highly valued?

2 Look at the Grammar box and Grammar summary page 231 again and think of the comparisons you want to make.
- What are you going to compare: things that are similar or different?
- What adjectives or adverbs will you need? Make sure you know the correct forms.
- What other language do you need to make your comparison interesting?

FILE G2 Topic 1, Section B, Page 13, Exercise 2F

GUIDANCE

Follow the steps below to make your notes.

1 Read the first paragraph of the completed web page *How to write your CV* on page 12 and answer the questions below.
- What is a CV?
- How can you guide a reader through your CV?
- What must you always do when you write your CV?

2 Copy the headings from the text into a table like the one below, leaving space on the right for your own notes.

Headings	Notes
Personal details	…
Profile	…
…	…

3 Carefully read the tips beside each of the headings in the text and complete the table with your details.

FILE G3 Topic 1, Section C, Page 18, Exercise 2A

GUIDANCE

Match the interview questions to possible answers.

1 What are the specific skills you would bring to this job?
2 Why should I consider you for this position?
3 Where do you see yourself five years from now?
4 What are your weaknesses?
5 What would your friends say about you?

A Because I have the right skills and qualifications for this job and I would be an asset to your team of carers.
B I would like to gain experience in this field and work as a junior manager.
C I don't have much experience in marketing, but I'm a quick learner.
D I am hardworking, flexible and I'm a team player.
E That I'm easy to work with, reliable and have a "can do" attitude.

FILE G4 Topic 2, Section A, Page 31, Exercise 2

GUIDANCE

Follow the steps below to help you compare and contrast the organizations.

1 Re-read the texts on page 30 and answer the questions below.
- What are the names of the organizations?
- When was each organization set up?
- Where/How can people get in touch with the two organizations?

2 Use your answers to **1C** on page 31 to make notes on the following:
- Who is each organization aiming to help or assist (the target group)?
- What kind of activities and help does each organization offer?

3 Use your answers and notes from Steps 1 and 2 above and the phrases below to write a short text.

The … is an organization dealing with …
In contrast, the …
One of the organizations is in …, while the other is in …
Both organizations aim to …
On the one hand, … . On the other hand, …

FILE G5 Topic 2, Section A, Page 31, Exercise 3

GUIDANCE

Match the sentences halves.

1 The organization I would like to work for
2 From the beginning, their aim has been to help
3 They provide personal and domestic
4 Their mission is to allow people to
5 The organization was set up
6 Today, they have over a 100

a in 1980 as a local charity.
b elderly people in their local communities.
c support centres across the country.
d provides support for elderly people.
e care services to elderly people.
f stay in their homes as long as possible.

FILE G6 Topic 2, Section B, Page 34, Exercise 2C

GUIDANCE

Match the expressions (1–6) that Colin and Tony used in the talks to the definitions (a–f).

1 to be entitled to sth
2 to get to grips with sth
3 to chuck sb out
4 to vandalize
5 to go right off the rails
6 to sleep rough

a to throw sb out of the house
b to cope with sth, e.g. a problem
c to destroy property deliberately and for no good reason
d to spend the night outside, usually in uncomfortable conditions
e to start behaving in a way that is unacceptable to society
f to have a right to have or do sth

FILE G7 Topic 2, Section B, Page 35, Exercise 4

GUIDANCE

Complete these sentences to produce your English summary.

The article is about …
What these young people have in common is …
Some of them come from …
Many of these young people believe that …
However, their situation is …
Some of the problems are …
Girls in particular are …
Other difficulties like illness, hygiene …

FILE G8 Topic 2, Section B, Page 39, Exercise 3

GUIDANCE

Match a–j to the functions 1–5 to say what these sentences are used for in a debate.

1 say you are for something
2 say you are against something
3 agree with someone
4 disagree with someone
5 interrupt someone

a I'm pro legalization of soft drugs because criminalizing drugs does not help.
b I don't agree with you.
c I'm against it. A "no tolerance" policy is the only way to deal with the problem.
d Absolutely. I think so too.
e Sorry, I'd like to ask you something.
f I'm in favour of legalizing drugs. It would help to decriminalize drug consumption.
g Legalizing cannabis would be a good thing because the police could focus on hard drugs.
h If I may interrupt you, I'd like to raise a new point.
i Legalizing drugs could have a negative effect on our children.
j Yes, you're right.

FILE G9 Topic 2, Section C, Page 41, Exercise 3

GUIDANCE

Work with a partner and follow the instructions below.

1 Read the advice about writing a comment on page 162 so that you know exactly what to do.
2 Read the material on pages 40 and 41 to get an overview of the information you have to work with.
3 Decide together how you are going to organize this information into notes. Would you like to make a mind map, a list or use sticky notes or cards so you can move the points around?
4 Once you have decided on the structure for your comment, write it down. This is your writing plan.
5 Follow your plan and use your notes to write your comment.

FILE G10 Topic 2, Section C, Page 43, Exercise 1E

GUIDANCE

Copy the mind map into your notebook and add words from page 42 or any other words you know.

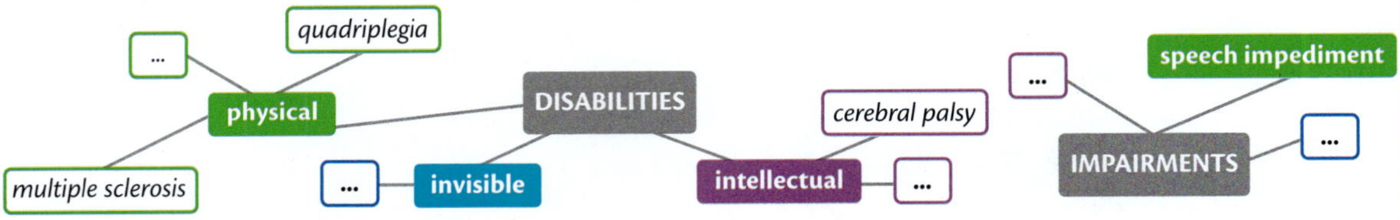

FILE G11 Topic 2, Section C, Page 44, Exercise 1C

GUIDANCE

Before you start, look up any words you don't know. When you write your summary, focus on the highlighted information. Rewrite these sentences in English first to use as the main points of the summary.

Wer sind wir?
In der Eider Werkstatten GmbH arbeiten Kolleginnen und Kollegen mit und ohne Behinderung zusammen, die sich mit vielfaltigen Problemen auseinandersetzen, welche ihre gemeinsame Arbeit aufwirft.

Was wollen wir?
Wir gestalten im Rahmen der Eingliederungshilfe den Alltag von Produktion und die Produktion von Alltag. Der ideologische Gegensatz von individueller Forderung und betrieblicher Produktivität wird durch die Praxis von Kollegialität und Leistung aufgehoben.
Im Arbeitsbereich arbeiten ca. 12 Kolleginnen und Kollegen mit dem Gruppenleiter / der Gruppenleiterin in einer Produktionsgruppe zusammen. Als Werkstatt für Menschen mit Behinderung bieten wir ein breites Angebot an verschiedenen Arbeitsplatzen in unterschiedlichen handwerklichen und industriellen Bereichen an (u. a. Metallbearbeitung, Autopflege, Gartenbau, Montage usw.), um den Interessen, Neigungen und Fähigkeiten aller Mitarbeitenden mit Behinderung gerecht zu werden. Darüber hinaus ist jeder Bereich in Tätigkeiten mit unterschiedlichen Schwierigkeitsgraden gegliedert. Nicht alle unsere Angestellten stellen neue Produkte her; manche packen lediglich z. B. Süßigkeiten um, deren Verpackung während des Transports beschädigt worden ist, und befüllen neue Tuten mit der richtigen Menge. Dies ermöglicht jeder Kollegin und jedem Kollegen, an dem Arbeitsplatz zu arbeiten, der ihrem bzw. seinem Leistungsvermögen entspricht.

FILE G12 Topic 2, Section C, Page 45, Exercise 4

GUIDANCE

Here are some questions the boss asked you. Use your answers to the questions to structure your oral report.

1 Who works there?
2 What are the aims of the workshop?
3 How does the workshop achieve its aims?
4 What goes on in the workshop?
5 How is it set up? Can you talk me through the floor plan?
6 Where can the employees relax?
7 What is the general feeling among the employees, both abled and differently abled?
8 What are the benefits that the employees get from working in this environment?
9 How much (if at all) are disabled employees involved in decision-making?

FILE G13 Topic 3, Section A, Page 57, Exercise 2B

GUIDANCE

Sort the activities in the box under the correct headings.

serving breakfast • day trip to the animal park • water gymnastics • guided walk through the town • administering medication • music session • having coffee and cake with visitors • watching a film together • helping residents with meals • playing card games • yoga

Physical activities	Social activities	Activities for active residents	Tasks for staff
…	…	…	…

FILE G14 Topic 3, Section B, Page 61, Exercise 4

GUIDANCE

Complete the email with the words from the box.

all year round • are included • highly qualified staff • main meal • many thanks • our nursery costs • pleased to hear • stay longer • welcoming you • would like to

Dear Ms Miller

___ (1) for your email.
I am ___ (2) that you are interested in our nursery and ___ (3) give you more details about our services.
We offer professional and efficient child care and work with experienced and ___ (4). Our nursery is open Monday to Friday between 8:00 a.m. and 6:00 p.m. We are open ___ (5), except on bank holidays.
A complete day at ___ (6) £29.00 and a half session costs £17.50. If your son needs to ___ (7) than a half session, we charge £3.85 per hour. Two meals ___ (8) in our package: a hot ___ (9) is offered at lunch time and a snack at tea time. Your child can also bring their own packed lunch.
We look forward to ___ (10) to KIDSPACE DAYCARE soon!

Best regards

FILE G15 Topic 3, Section C, Page 65, Exercise 3

GUIDANCE

Match these English words and phrases with their German equivalents to help you prepare for writing your German summary.

1 Understanding unspoken signs

warnings signs • domestic violence • physical violence • injuries • bruises • to keep sb away • to be restricted by sb • limited access • low self-esteem

Anzeichen • Blutergüsse • eingeschränkter Zugang • geringes Selbstwertgefühl • häusliche Gewalt • jdn fernhalten • körperliche Gewalt • Verletzungen • von jdm eingeschränkt werden

2 The cycle of violence in domestic abuse

cycle of violence • abuser • victim • punching • kicking • to make excuses • to put the blame on sb • to provoke abuse • violent • addicted

die Schuld auf jdn schieben • gewalttätig • Faustschläge • Fußtritte • Missbrauch auslösen • Opfer • sich herausreden • Spirale/Kreislauf der Gewalt • süchtig • Täter

FILE G16 Topic 3, Section C, Page 66, Exercise 2B

GUIDANCE

Find somebody else who has chosen "Guidance", then follow the steps below.

25

1 Listen to the call again and, with your partner, complete the sentences with words and phrases from the box to reconstruct what the counsellor says.

behave • behaving • close • counselling • counsellor • get better soon • lost • never have the chance • part of the problem • self-help group • talking • worried • you called

1 I can understand that you're … .
2 Have you tried … to your son?
3 Is there anything you know of that might have caused your son to … like this?
4 When did your son start … like this?
5 Was he … to his grandmother?
6 Perhaps that's … . Your son has … his grandmother.
7 He knows that he'll … to have that closeness again.
8 Do you think you could talk to your family doctor about …?
9 There is a youth grief … at the local hospital, or a school … might be of help.
10 I'm glad that … . I hope your son will … .

2 Sort the completed sentences into the categories below.
a making suggestions
b showing empathy
c asking for more information

FILE G17 Topic 4, Section A, Page 77, Exercise 5

GUIDANCE

Here are some helpful phrases:

- I am … and I work for …
- We / I saw your advert on / in …
- Could you give me some more information about …?
- Do you also offer support / help with …?
- Could you please …?
- We look forward to …

FILE G18 Topic 4, Section B, Page 81, Exercise 2B

GUIDANCE

Match a–j to the functions 1–10 to show what Kate says to:

1 indicate how she will deal with the caller's request
2 ask for the caller's name
3 check the caller's name
4 indicate that the caller should wait
5 confirm that the caller is still on the line
6 explain that someone is not available
7 make a suggestion
8 ask for contact details
9 confirm details
10 close the call

a Are you still there?
b Can I ask who's calling, please?
c Can I have your phone number, please?
d Can I take a message?
e Could you repeat your name, please?
f I'll just read that back to you.
g I'll pass on your message. Mr Schultz will phone you as soon as he can. Thank you for your call.
h I'll put you through to Frank Schulz.
i I'm afraid Mr Schultz isn't in his office at the moment.
j Just hold on one moment and I'll try to connect you.

FILE G19 Topic 4, Section B, Page 83, Exercise 4A

GUIDANCE

Follow the steps below to prepare your dialogue.

1 Look at the nurse's questions (1–5). Then complete the answers (a–e) with the correct form of the verbs in brackets and match them to the questions.

1 Can you describe what happened?
2 Was she wearing a helmet?
3 What had she been doing before the accident?
4 Did she lose consciousness at any time?
5 Have you given her any medication?

a Yes, she ___ (lose) consciousness for about five minutes.
b Yes, she ___ (be). We always ___ (wear) ski helmets on these trips.
c No. I ___ (not give) her any medication.
d Ms Hakala ___ (ski) at a normal pace when she ___ (hit) a rock and ___ (injure) her leg.
e She ___ (ski) normally with the others before she ___ (fall).

2 Now add other questions and answers to make a realistic dialogue.

FILE G20 Topic 4, Section C, Page 85, Exercise 4

GUIDANCE

Here you can see the beginning of a mind map. Add more ideas or aspects that you would like to look at when deciding on the best offer.

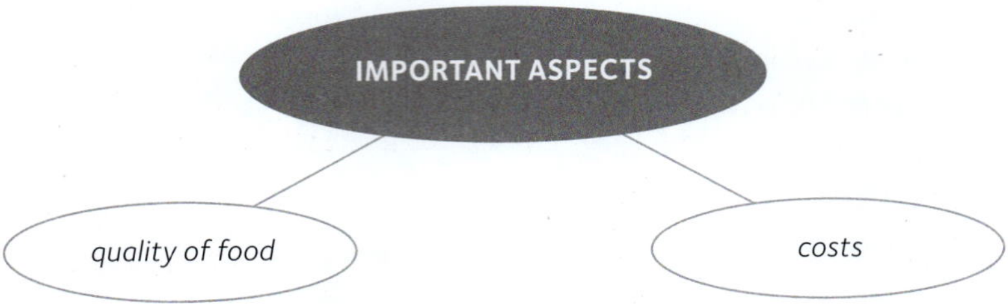

FILE G21 Topic 4, Section C, Page 87, Exercise 3

GUIDANCE

Follow these steps:

1 Find a good heading.
2 Briefly state what the report deals with (topic).
3 Then say what your task and purpose was (what you had to do and why).
4 Report your findings.
5 Make a recommendation and give reasons for it.

FILE G22 Topic 4, Practice, Page 88, Exercise 1

GUIDANCE

There are six mistakes in this email. To spot the mistakes, think of the following points:

1 salutation
2 beginning of the email (body)
3 short forms/ contractions
4 politeness
5 complimentary close
6 contact details

FILE G23 Topic 5, Section A, Page 97, Exercise 2B

GUIDANCE

Complete the sentences with the correct forms of the verbs in brackets.

1 If you ___ (eat) less sugar, your diet would be a lot healthier.
2 You would lose weight if you ___ (not drink) so many sugary drinks.
3 If you had home-cooked meals more often, you ___ (not spend) so much money on fast food.
4 If you ___ (know) more about processed food, you wouldn't buy it.
5 You would eat more organic food if you ___ (can afford) it.
6 You would feel a lot better if you ___ (eat) less fatty meat and cheese.

FILE G24 Topic 5, Section A, Page 97, Exercise 5B

GUIDANCE

Listen to the interview and complete the tasks.

1 List all the unnatural ingredients that go into a chicken burger. Choose from the list below.

AMR meat • bones • growth hormones • pesticides • pharmaceuticals • sugars • vaccines

2 Complete the definition of the word "derivative". What two examples are mentioned in the interview?
A derivative is something that …
The two examples of derivatives mentioned in the interview are: … and …
3 Describe what TBHQ and PDMS are. Which one is a petroleum derivative and which one is a silicone?
4 Explain what Andrew means by: "Nothing is wasted". Note down the parts of the carcasses that are used in the AMR process.
5 Point out what can be found in factory-farmed meat. Focus on things like medical treatment and food that the livestock has been given.
6 Explain what Fran means when she asks: "What are the costs to our health?" Mention the unhealthy things Andrew has described in the interview.

FILE G25 Topic 5, Section A, Page 99, Exercise 4

GUIDANCE

Complete the sentences with words and phrases from the box to prepare for your conversation with Mr Kasanides.

blood pressure • diagnosed • eating habits • healthy diet • in check • limiting • low-fat meat • recommend trying • reduce your risk • salt intake • should eat

1 Your doctor has ___ you with prediabetes.
2 As a risk patient, you need to think about a ___.
3 If you want to keep your blood sugar ___, you need to change your ___.
4 I would ___ DASH.
5 It's a diet that was originally developed for people with high ___.
6 This diet can help ___ of getting diabetes.
7 We recommend ___ sugary foods and reducing your ___.
8 You ___ more fruits, vegetables and ___.

FILE G26 Topic 5, Section B, Page 103, Exercise 4

GUIDANCE

Complete the sentence below with words from the box. Then use the sentences to write your text.

breadwinner • cultures • discrimination • divorce • dysfunctional • grandparents • nuclear • patriarchal • racism • same-sex • smaller • tolerance

1 Nowadays families are usually much ___ than they used to be, and there are fewer cases of ___ and other relatives living with younger members of the family.
2 The ___ family is no longer the only family set-up considered respectable. In many cases, the woman is now the "___" and families are less ___.
3 Despite this, women still face ___ when trying to balance a career with family life.
4 Adoption processes are less discriminatory than they used to be and it is easier for ___ couples to adopt.
5 It is also more common to adopt across ___. Unfortunately, ___ can still be a problem for such families.
6 Social workers might have to deal with more ___ families in the future, as there has been an increase in ___ rates and the number of single-parent families.
7 However, on the positive side, there also seems to be more ___ of difference in modern families than in previous generations.

FILE G27 Topic 5, Section B, Page 105, Exercise 2A

GUIDANCE

Match the phrases from the interview (1–7) to the explanations (a–g).

1 to cope with the situation alone
2 afraid to go to a women's refuge or seek assistance
3 to break out of the pattern
4 lack of empathy
5 marginalized
6 denial
7 to stand by and do nothing

a an example of denial
b to decide not to carry over your experience into your own adult relationships
c to get on with things without any help from anyone else
d pushed to one side and ignored
e the inability to understand another person's feelings
f the refusal to accept that something painful or unpleasant is true
g too scared to leave and get help

FILE G28 Topic 5, Section B, Page 107, Exercise 3

GUIDANCE

Follow the steps below to write your text.

1 Copy this table and complete it with the sentences below.

Termination		Adoption	
pros	cons	pro	cons
…	…	…	…

a Gives couples who can't have children of their own the chance to be parents.
b Many people are against this for religious reasons.
c May be a good option for mothers who feel they would not be able to cope with a baby.
d Not all adoptive families will be able to offer the child a 'perfect' upbringing.
e Some women find the experience traumatic.
f The baby has a chance of going to a good family and having a happy life.
g The biological mother might find it difficult to let the baby go and could suffer for a long time afterwards.
h The mother might be a young girl and feel unable to tell people about the pregnancy.
i The pregnancy might be the result of sexual abuse. Keeping the baby could cause mental health issues.
j When they find out about their situation, many of these children are told that they were "chosen" by their parents. This gives the child a feeling of being special.

2 Use words and phrases from above to complete the text below.

Termination or adoption: pros and cons

A termination may be an option in some cases, for example, in the case of a young girl ___[1], when a mother feels ___[2] or when the mother's life ___[3]. Similarly, a termination may be an option for a pregnancy which has come about as the result of ___[4], as in this case, keeping the baby could ___[5]. In some cases, these kinds of issues might also surface after a termination has been performed as some women ___[6]. Finally, many people are against termination for ___[7].

Adoption may be a difficult choice for a mother, as ___[8] and ___[9]. However, it may be a good option for mothers who feel ___[10]. While not all adoptive families will be able to ___[11], the baby has the chance of ___[12]. Many adoptive parents tell the children ___[13]. This makes the children feel ___[14]. Last but not least, adoption helps ___[15].

If you need more help, you can use these phrases.

- cause mental health issues
- couples who can't have children of their own
- find the experience traumatic
- having a happy life
- is at risk
- offer the child a "perfect" upbringing
- religious reasons
- sexual abuse
- she may find it difficult to let the baby go
- special
- suffer for a long time afterwards
- they were "chosen"
- unable to cope with a baby
- unable to give up the baby
- who has been abused

FILE G29 Topic 5, Section C, Page 111, Exercise 3A

GUIDANCE

Before you listen to the talk, match the words (1– 8) with the dictionary definitions (a–h).

1 ethnic
2 diverse
3 encounters
4 to differ
5 prejudice
6 to impose sth upon sb
7 agnostic
8 atheist

a a person who does not believe in the existence of God
b a person who believes that it is not possible to know whether God exists or not
c an unreasonable dislike or preference for a person or group, especially when it is based on their race, religion, etc.
d connected with or belonging to a nation, race or people that share a cultural tradition
e casual meetings (with people)
f to be clearly different (from one another)
g to make sb accept the same opinions, values, etc. as your own
h showing a great deal of variety or difference

FILE G30 Topic 6, Section A, Page 123, Exercise 2B

GUIDANCE

42 **Complete the sentences with words and phrases from the box. Then listen and check.**

jokes • difficult • disgusting • figure • frightened • hell • hung up • image • love • sexy • remarks

The men I work with are making my life ___[1].
First, they just made ___[2] about my clothes and my ___[3].
They made ___[4] about women who ___[5] each other.
I was really ___[6].
They made my life ___[7].
They ___[8] a ___[9] calendar.
They sent me a ___[10] by email.
It was a ___[11] photograph.

FILE G31 Topic 6, Section A, Page 125, Exercise 3

GUIDANCE

Complete the sentences using the verbs in brackets.

1 Robert said that he ___ (miss) the meeting.
2 He asked us if we ___ (bring) our laptops to the workshop.
3 Maja reported that as a child she ___ (not live) in a nice home.
4 George thought that his boss ___ (call) him while he ___ (be) away.
5 They told us that the company ___ (take on) five new employees.
6 Danila informed the team she ___ (be) very unhappy with the situation at work.

FILE G32 Topic 6, Section B, Page 130, Exercise 2 GUIDANCE

Read the email and choose the correct answer.

1 Mr Fox is writing about a holiday he booked for his ___
   a children. b son. c daughter.
2 The summer camp will last for ___ in August.
   a 10 days b two weeks c three weeks
3 Mr Fox ___ half of what the summer camp costs.
   a must pay b will now pay c has paid
4 Jugendforum promised to send a document to confirm the ___
   a agenda. b payment. c booking.
5 Mr Fox is getting a little nervous because he hasn't received a/an ___
   a deposit. b response. c invitation.
6 Mr Fox wants to ___ the booking.
   a ask about b confirm c cancel
7 He asks Mr Schmidt to ___ the matter and contact him.
   a discuss b check c prove

FILE C1 Topic 1, Section A, Page 9, Exercise 5C

CHALLENGE!

Partner A

Here are three words that describe qualities you may need in a job. Add two more words you find useful.

1 reliable
2 flexible
3 hard-working

Describe them to Partner B so that he or she can guess what the word is.
Don't say the word itself or parts of the word when you describe it!
If you are not sure what the word means, look it up in a dictionary.

FILE C2 Topic 1, Section C, Page 17, Exercise 3

CHALLENGE!

Partner B

You are the interviewer. Follow the steps below to prepare for and then do a telephone role-play.

1 First work with Partner A (the candidate) to choose a job that he/she is interviewing for. You might want to study a job advert together before working on your own.
2 Re-read the section *Understand the questions* in the tips text on page 16. Make up three more questions you might like to ask the applicant.
   - Explain why …
   - Tell me about …
   - Why did you …?
3 When you and your partner are ready, role-play the telephone interview.

FILE C3 Topic 1, Section B, Page 15, Exercise 2D

CHALLENGE!

Work with a partner.

Step 1: Identify things you liked and didn't like about Leonie's video cover letter.

Step 2: Sort these things under different headings, for example:

- message / content
- delivery / performance / body language
- language / pronunciation
- quality of video / sound

Step 3: Explain why you liked or disliked certain things.

Step 4: Suggest how she could improve her video cover letter.

Step 5: Explain exactly what effect this improvement would have. Use some of the following adjectives to explain the effect of the improvement.

impressive • memorable • clear • effective • interesting • eye-catching • appealing • distracting

FILE C4 Topic 1, Section C, Page 17, Exercise 3

CHALLENGE!

Partner A

You are the candidate. Follow the steps below to prepare for and then do a telephone role-play.

1 First work with Partner B (the interviewer) to choose a job that you are interviewing for. You might want to study a job advert together before working on your own.
2 Re-read the section *Understand the questions* in the tips text on page 16. Make up three more questions you might like to ask if the interviewer asks if you have any questions.
   - I was wondering if …
   - Could you possibly tell me a bit more about …?
   - Why does the company …?
3 When you and your partner are ready, role-play the telephone interview.

FILE C5 Topic 1, Section A, Page 9, Exercise 5C

CHALLENGE!

Partner B

Here are three words that describe qualities you may need in a job. Add two more words you find useful.

1 cheerful
2 motivated
3 pro-active

Describe them to Partner B so that he or she can guess what the word is.
Don't say the word itself or parts of the word when you describe it!
If you are not sure what the word means, look it up in a dictionary.

FILE C6 Topic 2, Section C, Page 41, Exercise 2C

CHALLENGE!

Post your own opinion by responding to one or more of the posts on page 41. Say if you agree or disagree with the writer(s) of the original post(s) and explain your thinking. These phrases may help you:

I'd like to add something to (*name*)'s statement.
As far as I am concerned, …
I completely agree/disagree with (*name*)'s point of view.
(*Name*) is right. I also think/feel/believe that …
Sorry, I disagree with what (*name*) wrote.

FILE C7 Topic 2, Section C, Page 45, Exercise 3 CHALLENGE!

Analyse Olli's use of language in order to reveal the atmosphere of the department.

- Listen out for words which express his personal feelings.
- Pay attention to how Olli describes the articles which are being packed. What might the employees feel while handling these goods?
- Note down words that Olli uses to describe the benefits of the work for his team.
- Describe how the team copes with challenges.

FILE C8 Topic 3, Section C, Page 66, Exercise 2B CHALLENGE!

25 **Listen to the telephone call again and make a note of phrases and sentences that the counsellor uses to:**

a make suggestions
b show empathy
c ask for more information

FILE C9 Topic 4, Section A, Page 78, Exercise 1A CHALLENGE!

Complete the email with the missing words.

Dear …

Thank you ___ our kids party packages.

___ to give you more details about our two most popular formats. We ___ our current price list and latest catalogue.

In our Nature Treasure Hunt, the kids go on a special adventure through woodlands with the help of a treasure map, while they fill their own treasure bag as they go.

This ___ €55.00 per child and includes the treasures (bracelets, bouncy balls, small toys) as well as transport, soft drinks, maps, a snack and an experienced guide.

Our Mini Artist package offers a range of activities that encourage your kids to be creative. ___ €21.00 per child if you arrange for a venue for the event yourself.

___ to call me if you have any further questions or ideas you would like to suggest. I am sure we can create an unforgettable experience for your children and their families!

We look forward ___ from you.

Best regards

Writing formal letters

1 Leonie Kuhn
Domkloster 6 • 50667 Cologne
Germany

Tel. +49 17764813780
Fax +49 30 6976860
Email leo_ni.kuhn@gmail.de

•
04 October 2014 **2**
•
CONFIDENTIAL **3**
•
Care Disability **4**
62 Calder Street
GLASGOW
G42 7NQ
GREAT BRITAIN
•
Attn. Ann Haslam **5**
•
Dear Ms Haslam **6**
•
Work placement **7**
•
I would like to apply for a work placement at your organization as advertised in the March edition of the magazine *Caring for People*.
•
I am very interested in gaining experience with disabled people and their families as I feel sure this will give me the opportunity to develop both personally and professionally. I am particularly keen to work in an English-speaking country where I can apply my knowledge of English on a daily basis. **8**
•
As you can see from the enclosed CV, I am currently studying at a German vocational college. My studies include Health Studies, Biology, Social Science, Home Economics and English.
•
Through the experience I gained working as an au pair, I know that I enjoy helping people and can fit in well with families. My language abilities will also make me an asset to your team. My English is excellent, I am a native German speaker and, because of family ties, I also have conversational Polish.
•
I hope that you will consider my application and grant me an interview.
•
I look forward to hearing from you soon.
•
Yours sincerely **9**
Leonie Kuhn **10**
•
Leonie Kuhn
•
•
Enc: curriculum vitae **11**

1 Letterhead
2 Date
3 Special marking
4 Inside address
5 Attention line
6 Salutation
7 Subject line
8 Body of the letter
9 Complimentary close
10 Signature
11 Enclosure (Enc), Enclosures (Encs)

Leave a free line for each dot (•).

Formal letter layout

There is no standard layout for a formal letter in the English-speaking world, so a typical block form layout used in Europe is shown here. After the letterhead all the sentences are left aligned (*linksbündig*).

1 Letterhead

There are no fixed rules for the letterhead but it should include the sender's name, postal address, telephone and fax numbers, email address and website address (if there is one).

2 Date

An all-figure date can be misunderstood. In American English 04/10/14 (or 04-10-14) means April 10, 2014 but in British English it means 04 October, 2014. For this reason the month should always be written out and the year should be a four-figure number. The usual order in which a date is written in formal letters and forms is: day (in figures) – month (as a word) – year (in figures). The example in this letter is pronounced 'the fourth of October two thousand and fourteen' (or 'twenty fourteen').

3 Special marking

These include URGENT, CONFIDENTIAL, PRIVATE AND CONFIDENTIAL, PERSONAL, AIR MAIL, REGISTERED, RECORDED DELIVERY. This line can be seen over the address in a window envelope.

4 Inside address

This is the recipient's address. Always include the country because the same city names can be found in different countries. When writing to a UK address write the town or city in capital letters and the postcode on a separate line under it.

5 Attention (Attn.)

The attention line is under the inside address and close enough to it to be seen in a window envelope. If there is an attention line, the letter may be opened by the company's post department and given to the person named. However, if the inside address starts with someone's name it may only be opened by that person or their secretary.

6/9 Salutation / Complimentary close

In most cases the salutation and complimentary close can be written **without** punctuation and they are linked as shown in the table below. In general, it is always better to write to a named person than a company but if this is not possible, start the letter 'Dear Sir or Madam' and use 'Yours faithfully' as the complimentary close.

Salutation	Complimentary close	Formality	Notes
Dear Mrs Brown	Yours sincerely	Formal	The most commonly used form
Dear Sir or Madam	Yours faithfully	Formal	Only used if the name is unknown
Dear Kim Dear Kim and Jim Jim	Regards Best regards Best wishes Yours	Friendly	Used in business if the writers know each other

7 Subject line

This is written in **bold** letters or <u>underlined</u>.

8 Body of the letter

The first word always starts with a capital letter. The paragraphs are separated by an empty line.

10 Signature
Signatures are often hard to read, so write the signatory's name and position under the signature. As there is no real English equivalent to *Sachbearbeiter/-in,* it is best to name the department where the signatory works (e.g. Sales Department for *Verkaufssachbearbeiter).*

11 Enclosure
It is sometimes enough just to write Enc or Encs but if necessary, details of the enclosure(s) can be listed like this:
Enc: Ticket or Encs: Tickets

Writing emails

More than 90% of organizations use email because it is quick, convenient and cheap. Here are some important things to remember before you hit 'send'.

To:
Subject:
Cc:
Attachment(s):

Salutation
Body
Complimentary close

Subject (Betreff):
This is the same as for a formal letter. Begin with a capital letter and keep it short.

Cc: 'carbon copy' (Kopie)

Writing the email
Most mistakes are made here: *Emails are not always informal.* Like formal letters they can be formal or informal but unlike formal letters they can be sent to thousands of recipients by mistake.

Salutation / Complimentary close
If you do not know the recipient, use one of the polite forms below. If the relationship becomes more friendly, your partner will start using informal forms and you should then do the same. Let your partner take the initiative.

	Salutation	**Complimentary close**
Polite	Dear Ms Brown Dear Mrs Brown Dear Miss Brown Dear Mr Brown	Regards Best regards Best wishes Yours sincerely
Friendly	Good morning James Dear Kim Dear Kim and Jim	Regards Best regards Best wishes
Informal	Hello Kim Hi Kim Kim	All the best (Atb) Best Cheers Must rush

Body of the email
Tips for better communication:
- Start the email with a capital letter.
- Never use text message short forms (CUL8R, etc.).
- Write in paragraphs separated by a free line.

- If you write back in the spaces between the lines of the original email and/or in a different colour,
  - do not use red
  - do not underline words
  - do not write in **bold letters**
  - do not write in CAPITALS
  - do not use exclamation marks!

  because it sounds as if you are angry or think the reader is stupid.

Most emails are read on-screen, so keep yours as short as possible.

Points of style

Use short forms to be friendly (I've, we'll, he'd, etc.) and long forms to be more formal.

Finishing the email

If you know the recipient well, it is enough to sign off with your first name. If you do not, add your position and the name of your company under it.

Writing emails	
Starting an email	
How are things?	Wie läuft's? / Wie geht's?
I hope you're well.	Hoffentlich geht es dir/Ihnen gut.
I hope you had a good trip to …	Hoffentlich hattest du / hatten Sie eine gute Reise nach …
I am writing to … (ask for information on … / book a room for … / confirm that …).	Ich schreibe … (mit der Bitte um Informationen über … / um ein Zimmer für … zu reservieren / um zu bestätigen, dass …).
Answering or forwarding an email	
I was delighted to receive your mail.	Ich habe mich sehr über deine/Ihre E-Mail gefreut.
Many thanks for your mail … (about … / inviting me to …).	Vielen Dank für deine/Ihre E-Mail (über … / mit einer Einladung zu …).
I've just got … (your email / an email from … / a phone call from …).	Eben habe ich … (deine/Ihre E-Mail / eine E-Mail von … / einen Anruf von …) erhalten.
Getting to the point	
I'd/We'd/They'd like to know … (if/what/…, e.g. if you'll be arriving after midnight).	Ich/Wir/Sie möchte(n) wissen, (ob/was/…, z. B. ob Sie nach Mitternacht eintreffen werden).
I'm pleased/delighted to accept (your invitation / your offer).	(Sehr) gerne nehme ich (deine/Ihre Einladung / dein/Ihr Angebot) an.
Request	
Please let me have some information on …	Bitte schicken Sie mir Informationen zu …
Could you tell me if/what/…?	Würden Sie mir bitte mitteilen, ob/was/…?
Could someone … (e.g. pick me/us up at the airport)?	Könnte jemand … (z. B. mich/uns am Flughafen abholen)?
Would you send us …, please?	Würden Sie uns bitte … schicken?

PHRASE BANK

INTRODUCTIONS	
Introducing people	
I would like to introduce … / This is …	Ich würde gern … vorstellen. / Das ist …
He/She decided to be a carer because …	Er/Sie entschied sich für den Beruf des Betreuers / der Betreuerin, weil …
He/She hopes to work as a/an …	Er/Sie hofft, als … arbeiten zu können.
He/She would like to work with adults.	Er/Sie würde gern mit Erwachsenen arbeiten.
Introductions and greetings	
Hi, I'm … / my name is … I'm the …	Hallo, ich bin … / mein Name ist … Ich bin der/die …
Nice to meet you.	Es freut mich, Sie kennen zu lernen.
Nice to meet you, too. / You too.	Mich auch. / Ebenso.
Hello. How are you?	Hallo. Wie geht es Ihnen?
Very well, thanks. And you?	Sehr gut, danke. Und Ihnen?
Small talk	
Do you come from around here?	Kommen Sie hier aus der Gegend?
As a matter of fact, I …	In der Tat … ich …
What about you? Where do you live?	Was ist mit Ihnen? Wo wohnen Sie?
Nice weather today.	Schönes Wetter heute.
Yes. It's great. I hope it stays like this.	Ja, es ist großartig. Ich hoffe, es bleibt so.
It's nice weather for a walk, isn't it?	Es ist gutes Wetter, um einen Spaziergang zu machen, finden Sie nicht auch?
Did you find us all right?	Haben Sie gut zu uns gefunden?
So, you had no trouble finding us, then?	Also hatten Sie keine Schwierigkeiten, zu uns zu finden?
No, no trouble at all.	Nein, überhaupt nicht.
Talking about your workplace	
My name is …	Mein Name ist … / Ich heiße …
I'm a/an *(job title)* at *(name of organization)*.	Ich bin *(Berufsbezeichnung)* bei *(Name des Unternehmens)*.
It's located in …	Es befindet sich / ist ansässig in …
I work for … *(e.g. the city council)*	Ich arbeite für … *(z. B. Stadtrat)*
(Name of organization) was set up in *(year)* by … to …	*(Name des Unternehmens)* wurde *(im Jahr)* von … gegründet, mit dem Ziel, …
We look after …	Wir kümmern uns um …

PHRASE BANK

INTRODUCTIONS	
We have a staff of … (*number*).	Wir beschäftigen … (*Anzahl)* Personen.
I'm responsible for …	Ich bin für … verantwortlich.
My responsibilities include …	Meine Verantwortlichkeiten beinhalten …
Describing yourself and your job	
I am responsible for …	Ich bin für … verantwortlich.
I report to …	Ich unterstehe …
… often/sometimes/never …	… oft/manchmal/nie …
… like/love/enjoy (…+ *ing* …)	… mag/liebe/genieße es, … zu …
… hate/dislike (…+ *ing* …)	… hasse/mag es gar nicht, … zu …
… joined the company … years ago / in (*year*) …	… habe vor … Jahren / (*Jahr)* … im Unternehmen angefangen.
… have been with the company since (*year*) …	… arbeite seit (*Jahr)* im Unternehmen.
Showing someone around	
If you look over here, you'll see …	Wenn Sie hierhin schauen, sehen Sie …
This is where the employees …	Dort … die Angestellten.
This area is used for …	Dieser Bereich wird für … verwendet.
The kitchen is opposite / next to / on the right/ left of …	Die Küche befindet sich gegenüber / neben / rechts/ links von …

JOB TITLES	
care assistant	Pfleger/in (in einem Heim)
case worker	Sozialarbeiter/in
childminder	Kinderbetreuer/in
classroom assistant	Assistent/in im Unterricht
community support worker	Sozialarbeiter/in (in einer Gemeinde)
counsellor	Berater/in
day care centre assistant	Pfleger/in in einer Tagesstätte (für Kinder, ältere Menschen oder Kranke)
geriatric assistant / care worker	Altenpfleger/in
healthcare assistant	Gesundheits(pflege)assistent/in
home care worker	Hauspflegekraft / Hauspflegedienstleister/in
kindergarten assistant/teacher	pädagogische/r Assistent/in / Kindergärtner/in

JOB TITLES	
maternity support worker	Mutterschaftshilfe
midwife	Hebamme
nursery/kindergarten nurse	Erzieher/in, Kinderpfleger/in
nutritionist	Ernährungsberater/in
occupational therapist	Beschäftigungstherapeut/in, Ergotherapeut/in
paediatric assistant/nurse	pädiatrische/r Assistent/in
personal assistant	persönliche/r Assistent/in
physiotherapist	Physiotherapeut/in, Krankengymnast/in
school nurse	Krankenpfleger/-schwester in einer Schule
social administrator	Verwalter/in für soziale Angelegenheiten
social worker	Sozialarbeiter/in
speech and language therapy assistant	Sprachtherapeut/in
substance abuse counsellor	Berater/in in der Suchtkrankenhilfe
teaching assistant for children with special needs	Unterrichtshilfskraft für Schüler/innen mit Behinderung
telephone counsellor	Telefonberater/in
youth and community worker	Jugend- und Sozialarbeiter/in

TELEPHONING	
Introducing yourself	
Hello, this is … (speaking).	Hallo, hier spricht …
I'm calling from …	Ich rufe im Namen von (*Name des Unternehmens*) an.
Can I speak to …, please? / Is this …?	Kann ich bitte … sprechen? / Spreche ich mit …?
I was wondering if …	Ich wollte fragen, ob …
Is … available at the moment?	Ist … gerade zu sprechen?
Speaking. / This is …	Am Apparat. / Hier spricht …
How can I help you?	Wie kann ich Ihnen helfen?
Putting the caller through	
Could you put me through to …, please?	Können Sie mich bitte zu … durchstellen?
Just hold on one moment and I'll try to connect you.	Bitte warten Sie einen Moment. Ich versuche, Sie zu verbinden.
I'll put you through to (*name*).	Ich stelle Sie zu (*Name*) durch.

TELEPHONING	
Asking for more information/clarification	
Can I ask who's calling, please?	Wer spricht, bitte?
Could you repeat your name / that, please?	Können Sie Ihren Namen / das bitte wiederholen?
I'm sorry. How do you spell that?	Entschuldigung, könnten Sie mir das bitte buchstabieren?
I'm sorry, I didn't understand that.	Entschuldigung, ich habe das nicht verstanden.
Can I have your phone number, please?	Können Sie mir bitte Ihre Telefonnummer geben?
Are you still there?	Sind Sie noch da?
Saying that the call isn't possible	
I'm afraid (*name*) isn't in his/her office / at his/her desk at the moment.	Leider ist (*Name*) gerade nicht im Büro / nicht erreichbar.
I'm sorry, but Mr/Ms ...'s line is engaged at the moment. Would you like to try again later?	Es tut mir leid, aber der Anschluss von Herrn/Frau ... ist gerade besetzt. Möchten Sie es später noch mal versuchen?
Can I take a message?	Kann ich etwas ausrichten?
No, thanks. I'll try again later.	Nein, danke. Ich versuche es später noch mal.
Leaving/Taking a message	
Do you have a pen and paper?	Haben Sie einen Stift und Papier?
Do you want me to spell that?	Wollen Sie, dass ich das buchstabiere?
Shall I repeat that?	Soll ich das noch einmal sagen?
I'll just read that back to you.	Ich wiederhole noch mal.
Thanks, I think I've got all that / everything.	Danke, ich glaube, ich habe alles verstanden.
I'll pass on your message.	Ich leite Ihre Nachricht weiter.
(*Name*) will phone you as soon as he/she can.	(*Name*) ruft Sie an, sobald er/sie Zeit hat.
Arranging and changing appointments	
I'd like to arrange an appointment, please.	Ich möchte bitte einen Termin vereinbaren.
When would be convenient for you?	Wann würde es Ihnen passen?
Would late afternoon on the second of April suit you?	Wäre es Ihnen am Spätnachmittag des 2. April recht?
How about Wednesday the twenty-first at 10:30?	Wie wäre es mit Mittwoch, dem 21. um 10:30 Uhr?
How about Friday afternoon instead?	Wie wäre es stattdessen mit Freitagnachmittag?
I'm afraid I've had to change my plans.	Leider haben sich meine Pläne verändert.
I'm going to have to cancel the appointment.	Ich muss den Termin absagen.

TELEPHONING	
I'm sorry but I've already got an appointment then.	Es tut mir leid, aber da habe ich schon einen Termin.
That works fine by me.	Das passt mir gut.
Making complaints	
It's about … / There seems to be a problem with …	Es geht um … / Es gibt anscheinend ein Problem mit …
The problem is (that) …	Das Problem ist, (dass) …
There's no point in … (+ *-ing)*	Es macht keinen Sinn, … zu …
Thanks for solving the problem so quickly.	Danke, dass Sie das Problem so schnell gelöst haben.
Could you send me an email confirming this (so we have a record)?	Könnten Sie mir das per E-Mail bestätigen (damit wir es dokumentiert haben)?
Answering complaints	
I'm very sorry to hear that. / I do apologize for this.	Es tut mir leid, das zu hören. / Ich bitte dafür um Entschuldigung.
Oh, no. That sounds like someone has …	Oh nein. Das klingt, als hätte jemand …
These things can happen, I'm afraid.	Leider kann so etwas passieren.
Let me talk to my boss / sort this out and I'll get back to you straight away.	Lassen Sie mich das mit meinem Chef besprechen / die Sache in Ordnung bringen. Ich melde mich dann gleich noch mal bei Ihnen.
We'll double-check to make sure that this sort of mix-up doesn't happen again.	Wir werden genau nachprüfen, um sicher zu sein, dass ein solches Durcheinander nicht mehr vorkommt.
Ending the call	
Is there anything else that I can do for you?	Kann ich noch etwas für Sie tun?
Thank you for calling / for your call.	Danke für Ihren Anruf.
Have a nice day.	Ich wünsche Ihnen noch einen schönen Tag.

INTERNATIONAL SPELLING ALPHABET							
A	Alpha	H	Hotel	O	Oscar	U	Uniform
B	Bravo	I	India	P	Papa	V	Victor
C	Charlie	J	Juliet	Q	Quebec	W	Whiskey
D	Delta	K	Kilo	R	Romeo	X	X-ray
E	Echo	L	Lima	S	Sierra	Y	Yankee
F	Foxtrot	M	Mike	T	Tango	Z	Zulu
G	Golf	N	November				

JOB INTERVIEWS	
Why you want the job	
I'm particularly interested in / keen to …	Ich interessiere mich besonders für / möchte unbedingt …
I always keep up to date with …	Ich halte mich immer bezüglich … auf dem neuesten Stand.
I have always wanted to work in this field.	Ich wollte schon immer in diesem Gebiet arbeiten.
I was able to get some good experience in/with …	Ich konnte hilfreiche Erfahrungen in/mit … sammeln.
I would like to develop my … skills.	Ich würde gerne meine …-fähigkeiten weiterentwickeln.
I really enjoyed that job / working in a team.	Ich mochte die Arbeit wirklich sehr / mochte es, in einem Team zu arbeiten.
I enjoy the challenges of my job.	Ich mag die Herausforderungen meiner Arbeit.
I am really interested in this job because I want to gain experience in this area / it sounds really interesting.	Ich bin sehr interessiert an dieser Stelle, weil ich in diesem Bereich Erfahrung sammeln möchte / es sehr interessant klingt.
I am honest and hard-working.	Ich bin ehrlich und fleißig.
Strengths and weaknesses	
My language skills are very good: I can speak …	Meine Sprachkenntnisse sind sehr gut: Ich kann … sprechen.
I am a team player / I am good at working as part of a team.	Ich bin teamfähig / arbeite gut als Teil eines Teams.
I am very personable and empathetic.	Ich bin sehr umgänglich und einfühlsam.
My strengths include working independently / good organization skills / taking responsibility …	Meine Stärken sind das selbstständige Arbeiten / gute organisatorische Fähigkeiten / die Übernahme von Verantwortung …
I think my greatest weakness is probably setting my own standards too high / my lack of experience.	Ich denke, meine größte Schwäche ist (es) wahrscheinlich, zu hohe Anforderungen an mich selbst zu stellen / das Fehlen an Erfahrung.

JOB INTERVIEWS	
Expectations of the job	
I hope that the job will be challenging and that I will be able to take on some responsibility.	Ich hoffe, dass die Arbeit herausfordernd sein wird und ich etwas Verantwortung übernehmen kann.
I hope to gain my first experiences of …	Ich hoffe, erste Erfahrungen im Bereich … zu sammeln / sammeln zu können.
I expect the job to provide me with a good insight into … (*field or work / specific place of work*).	Ich erwarte von dem Job, dass ich einen guten Einblick in … (*Arbeitsbereich / bestimmten Arbeitsplatz*) bekomme.
Future plans	
In the future, I would like to be promoted to Senior Social Worker.	Ich würde später gerne zum/zur leitenden Sozialarbeiter/in befördert werden.
In ten years' time, I see myself …	Ich sehe mich in zehn Jahren …
I am very ambitious and I hope to gain as much experience and knowledge as I can.	Ich bin sehr ehrgeizig und hoffe, möglichst viel Erfahrung zu sammeln und viel neues Wissen zu erlangen.
Further questions	
Would there be further opportunities available at the end of the internship?	Gibt es weitere zur Verfügung stehende Möglichkeiten am Ende des Praktikums?
I was wondering what/if …	Ich wollte fragen, was/ob …
What would my typical tasks be?	Was wären typische Aufgaben für mich?

PRESENTATIONS	
Introducing yourself / the topic	
Welcome to …	Willkommen in/bei …
My name is … and I'm here to tell you about …	Mein Name ist … und ich möchte Ihnen heute über … berichten.
Thank you for coming today.	Danke, dass Sie heute gekommen sind.
Today I'd like to talk about …	Ich würde heute gerne über … sprechen.
The purpose of my presentation is to …	Meine Präsentation soll dazu dienen, … zu …
Explaining the structure of the talk	
I've divided my presentation into three/four main parts: …	Ich habe meine Präsentation in drei/vier Hauptteile untergliedert: …
I've planned in time to answer any questions you might have at the end of my presentation.	Ich habe genügend Zeit eingeplant, sodass ich Ihre Fragen, die möglicherweise aufkommen, am Ende meiner Präsentation beantworten werden/kann.

PRESENTATIONS	
If you have any questions, just shout them out / feel free to interrupt.	Falls Sie irgendwelche Fragen haben (sollten), rufen Sie einfach dazwischen / können Sie mich gerne (kurz) unterbrechen.
In the first part of my talk …	Im ersten Teil meines Vortrags …
Then I will go on to …	Dann werde ich mich … zuwenden.
Putting things in sequence	
First, …	Als Erstes / Zuerst …
Second, …	Zweitens …
Then, …	Dann …
After that, …	Danach …
Next, …	Als Nächstes …
Finally, …	Zum Schluss …
Moving from one point to the next	
Moving on, …	Kommen wir zum nächsten Thema, …
Now I would like to move on to the next point: …	Ich würde jetzt gerne zum nächsten Punkt kommen/übergehen: …
The next topic I'm going to talk about is …	Das nächste Thema, über das ich sprechen werde, ist …
Presenting a website	
We've divided the website into the following pages: …	Wir haben die Website in folgende Seiten unterteilt: …
On our home page we have …	Auf unserer Homepage haben wir …
As you can see, most of the jobs are in the … sector.	Wie Sie sehen, sind die meisten der Arbeitsstellen im …-bereich.
If you click on …, you can see a list of …	Wenn Sie … anklicken, können Sie eine Liste von … sehen.
So, that's our website. Does anyone have any questions?	Das ist also unsere Website. Haben Sie (noch) Fragen?
Dealing with questions	
Are there any questions?	Gibt es (noch) Fragen?
If you have any questions, I'd be happy to answer them now.	Falls Sie (noch) Fragen haben (sollten), bin ich jetzt gerne bereit, sie zu beantworten.
Summarizing/Concluding	
So to sum up, my main points were …	Um alles zusammenzufassen, meine Hauptpunkte waren …

PRESENTATIONS	
In conclusion, I would like to say …	Zum Schluss würde ich gerne sagen …
In summary, I think it is clear that …	Zusammenfassend denke ich, dass es klar/verständlich ist, dass …
Finally, I would like to point out that …	Zu guter Letzt würde ich gerne darauf hinweisen / erwähnen, dass …
Finishing the presentation	
Thank you very much for your attention. / Thank you for listening.	Vielen Dank für Ihre Aufmerksamkeit.

DISCUSSIONS	
Asking for and giving opinions	
I think that … . What about you?	Ich denke, dass … . Was meinen Sie?
I don't agree. How do you feel about …?	Ich stimme dem nicht zu. Was halten Sie von …?
Don't you agree that …?	Sind Sie nicht der Meinung, dass …?
Yes, you're probably right.	Ja, vermutlich haben Sie Recht.
What do you think of …?	Was halten Sie von …?
I'm not sure. How about … instead?	Ich weiß nicht so recht. Wie wäre es stattdessen mit …?
Why don't we do it this way?	Warum machen wir es nicht einfach so?
We shouldn't forget that …	Wir sollten nicht vergessen, dass …
Active listening	
What's the problem?	Was ist das Problem?
Shall we talk about it?	Sollen wir uns darüber unterhalten?
I understand.	Ich verstehe.
Take your time.	Nehmen Sie sich Zeit.
So, you feel as if …?	Haben Sie also das Gefühl, als ob …?
If I understand you correctly, …	Wenn ich Sie richtig verstehe, …
I'm sorry, but I don't understand what you mean by …	Entschuldigen Sie, aber ich verstehe nicht (ganz), was Sie mit … sagen wollen.
Is it true that …?	Stimmt es, dass …?
I hear what you're saying.	Ich verstehe, was Sie sagen.
Could you give me an example / explain that, please?	Könnten Sie bitte ein Beispiel nennen / das bitte erklären?

DISCUSSIONS

Giving advice

It's a good idea to …	Es ist eine gute Idee, … zu …
If you can, you should …	Wenn Sie können, sollten Sie …
Try not to …	Versuchen Sie, … nicht zu …
Perhaps you could think about …	Vielleicht können Sie über … nachdenken.
It might not be a bad idea to …	Es ist vielleicht keine schlechte Idee, … zu …
Have you ever considered talking to …?	Haben Sie sich jemals überlegt, mit … zu sprechen?
Why don't you try speaking to …?	Warum versuchen Sie nicht, mit … zu sprechen?

THE LANGUAGE OF MEETINGS

Starting and making introductions

Good morning. Everyone seems to be here, so let's get started straight away, shall we?	Guten Morgen. Da alle anwesend zu sein scheinen, können wir gleich anfangen, oder?
I'd like to begin by welcoming … to … . Thank you for coming.	Ich würde zuerst gerne … bei … willkommen heißen. Vielen Dank, dass Sie gekommen sind.
Just to make sure that we all know who's who, my name is … and I'm the …	Damit wir alle Bescheid wissen, wer wer ist: Mein Name ist … und ich bin der/die …
Perhaps the two of you would like to introduce yourselves as well?	Vielleicht könnten Sie beide sich auch kurz persönlich vorstellen?

Introducing items on the agenda

As you can see on the agenda, the first point is …	Wie Sie auf der Tagesordnung sehen können, ist der erste Punkt …
So, if we move on quickly to the second point on the agenda: …	Lassen Sie uns jetzt rasch zum zweiten Punkt auf der Tagesordnung kommen/übergehen: …
Could we look at the third/next point on our agenda: …	Widmen wir uns nun dem dritten/nächsten Tagesordnungspunkt: …
That brings us on to the next item on today's agenda: …	Das führt uns zum nächsten Punkt der heutigen Tagesordnung: …
OK, that clearly belongs under the next point on the agenda: …	Gut, das gehört eindeutig zum nächsten Punkt auf der Tagesordnung: …
The final item on the agenda is …	Der letzte Punkt auf der Tagesordnung ist …

Inviting someone to speak

(Name), is there anything you would like to add to that?	*(Name)*, gibt es irgendetwas, was Sie dem gerne hinzufügen würden?

THE LANGUAGE OF MEETINGS	
Perhaps I can bring … in now.	Vielleicht kann ich jetzt … zur Sprache bringen / einbringen.
(*Name*), how do you see the situation?	(*Name*), wie beurteilen/sehen Sie die Situation/Lage?
Closing the meeting	
I think we've covered all the main points on the agenda, so I suggest that we bring the meeting to a close.	Ich denke, wir haben alle Hauptpunkte auf der Tagesordnung abgehandelt, daher schlage ich vor, dass wir das Meeting beenden.
OK, I think we've covered all we can on that point.	Okay, ich denke, wir haben alles angesprochen, was es zu diesem Punkt zu sagen gibt.
We'll write up the minutes of what we've discussed and will email them to you tomorrow, just for the record.	Wir werden all das, was heute besprochen wurde, zu Protokoll bringen und Ihnen dann morgen mailen, nur um das festzuhalten.
Thank you all for coming and we'll see you again on Friday.	Vielen Dank fürs Kommen und wir sehen uns dann wieder am Freitag.
Writing a record of a meeting	
(*Name*) explained/suggested/recommended that …	(*Name*) erklärte/schlug vor/empfahl, dass …
It was decided/agreed that …	Es wurde entschieden/vereinbart, dass …
(*Name*) is to talk to / meet with …	(*Name*) wird mit … sprechen / wird sich mit … treffen.

WORKING WITH CLIENTS	
Describing a case	
The client	
The client's name is …	Der Name des Klienten/der Klientin ist …
He/She is … years old.	Er/Sie ist … Jahre alt.
He/She lives …	Er/Sie lebt …
The family background	
The client's family is …	Die Familie des Klienten/der Klientin ist …
He/She was looked after by his/her …	Sein(e)/Ihr(e) … kümmerte(n) sich um ihn/sie.
When he/she was … years old, …	Als er/sie … Jahre alt war, …
Client's assessment of the situation	
The client is (not) able to understand his/her situation.	Der Klient/Die Klientin kann seine/ihre Situation (nicht) verstehen.
He/She would (not) like to …	Er/Sie würde (nicht) gerne …

WORKING WITH CLIENTS	
The current situation	
We are looking into …	Wir untersuchen gerade …
We have spoken to … and are currently …	Wir haben (bereits) mit … gesprochen und sind gerade dabei, …
Making referrals	
I would recommend that the person call …	Ich würde vorschlagen, dass die Person … anruft.
I'd suggest that the client get in touch with …	Ich schlage vor, dass sich der/die Klient/in mit … in Verbindung setzt.
I think he/she should call …	Ich denke, er/sie sollte … anrufen.
I would contact …	Ich würde … kontaktieren.
the police	die Polizei
a counsellor	einen/eine Berater/in
the youth protection service	die Jugendschutzbehörde
a doctor	einen Arzt/eine Ärztin
his/her therapist	seine/n / ihre/n Therapeuten/Therapeutin
his/her general practitioner (GP)	seine/n / ihre/n Arzt/Ärztin für Allgemeinmedizin
Giving reassurance	
There's nothing to worry about.	Es gibt keinen Grund zur Beunruhigung.
Everything will be fine.	Alles wird gut.
Don't worry, it's just a/an …	Machen Sie sich keine Sorgen, das ist nur ein/e …
It's just a routine operation/test.	Es ist nur eine Routineoperation / eine Routineuntersu-chung.
It's perfectly normal to feel like that.	Es ist ganz normal, dass Sie sich so fühlen.
Asking delicate questions	
Could you tell me / explain …?	Können Sie mir sagen/erklären, …?
Do you happen to remember when …?	Erinnern Sie sich (zufällig) daran, wann …?
Would you mind telling me how …?	Können Sie mir erzählen, wie …?
…, if you don't mind me asking.	…, wenn ich fragen darf.

WRITING ENQUIRIES

Giving the source of the address	
We saw your advertisement in … / your stand/ catalogue at the … trade fair.	Wir haben Ihre Anzeige in/im … / Ihren Stand/Katalog auf der …-messe gesehen.
I was most impressed by the products/services you showed me on your stand at the … trade fair.	Die Produkte/Dienstleistungen, die Sie mir an Ihrem Stand auf der …-messe gezeigt haben, haben mich sehr beeindruckt.
When we visited your website, we were interested to see that you …	Als wir uns Ihre Webseite angeschaut haben, haben wir mit Interesse zur Kenntnis genommen, dass Sie …
We have your address from (*business partner/ organization*)	Wir haben Ihre Adresse von (*Geschäftspartner/in / Organisation*)
Stating the purpose of your enquiry	
I am writing on behalf of (*name of organization*) where I'm a/an (*job title*).	Ich schreibe Ihnen im Auftrag/Namen von (*Name des Unternehmens*). Dort arbeite ich als (*Jobbezeichnung*).
We are putting together kits for …	Wir stellen Pakete für … zusammen.
Our aim is to …	Unser Ziel ist es, … zu …
As a well-known manufacturer of (*product*), we are sure you would like to contribute …	Als ein gutbekannter Hersteller von (*Produkt*) möchten Sie sicherlich gern … beisteuern.
We are looking specifically for (*items*).	Wir suchen insbesondere nach (*Waren*).
We are looking for a supplier of … .	Wir sind auf der Suche nach einem Lieferanten von … .
We are interested in your new range of … .	Wir haben Interesse an Ihrer neuen Auswahl an … .
Making requests	
Please send us samples of … / your latest catalogue and price list.	Senden Sie uns bitte Muster/Warenproben / Ihren neuesten Katalog und Ihre Preisliste zu.
Please give us a quotation for … .	Legen Sie uns bitte ein Angebot an … vor.
Could you please let us have details of all discounts available?	Könnten Sie uns bitte Details all Ihrer verfügbaren Preisnachlässe/Rabatte mitteilen?
Full details of your terms of payment and delivery would also be appreciated.	Vollständige Angaben Ihrer Zahlungsbedingungen und der Lieferung wären ebenfalls wünschenswert.
We would be grateful if you could send us your current export price list.	Wir wären Ihnen verbunden, wenn Sie uns Ihre aktuelle Export-Preisliste zukommen lassen könnten.
Delivery would be required within … days/weeks/ months.	Die Lieferung wäre innerhalb von … Tagen/Wochen/ Monaten erforderlich.

WRITING ENQUIRIES

Closing the letter	
We look forward to hearing from you soon / in the next few days.	Wir freuen uns, bald / in den nächsten Tagen von Ihnen zu hören.
We look forward to receiving your offer/quotation/ reply in due course.	Wir freuen uns auf den Erhalt Ihres Angebots / Ihrer Antwort zu gegebener Zeit.

WRITING OFFERS

Referring to an enquiry	
We refer to / With reference to your enquiry of … .	Wir verweisen auf / Mit Bezug auf Ihre Anfrage des/von … .
Thank you for your letter/email / telephone call of … enquiring about … .	Vielen Dank für Ihren Brief/Ihre E-Mail / Ihren Telefon-anruf vom … bezüglich/über … .
We were delighted to receive your enquiry dated … about our … .	Wir waren erfreut darüber, Ihre Anfrage vom … bezüglich/ über unser/e … zu erhalten.
I am pleased to let you have details of our offer in writing.	Ich freue mich, Ihnen Details über unser Angebot in schriftlicher Form zukommen zu lassen.
Referring to information/samples (for general enquiry)	
We are enclosing our latest brochure/flyer and current price list.	Wir fügen unsere aktuelle Broschüre/unseren aktuellen Flyer und die aktuelle Preisliste bei.
We would like to draw your attention to our latest special offer / new range of … .	Wir würden Ihre Aufmerksamkeit gerne auf unser aktuelles Sonderangebot / neues Sortiment/Angebot an … richten.
Giving details (for specific enquiry)	
We are pleased to send you / submit the following offer/quotation: …	Gerne schicken/unterbreiten wir Ihnen das folgende Angebot: …
Giving further information	
Our delivery date is approximately … days/weeks after receipt of order.	Unser Liefertermin ist ungefähr … Tage/Wochen nach Auftragseingang.
We can guarantee delivery within … days/weeks of receipt of order.	Wir können eine Lieferung innerhalb von … Tagen/ Wochen nach Auftragseingang garantieren.
Closing the letter	
If you have any questions, please get in contact with me.	Falls Sie Fragen haben (sollten), setzen Sie sich bitte mit mir in Verbindung.
We feel sure that a trial order will convince you of the quality of our products.	Wir sind überzeugt davon, dass ein Probeauftrag Sie von der Qualität unserer Produkte überzeugen wird.

WRITING OFFERS

Thank you for your interest. We look forward to receiving your order in due course.	Vielen Dank für Ihr Interesse. Wir sehen dem Erhalt Ihrer Bestellung zu gegebener Zeit entgegen.
We look forward to doing business with you in the future / to hearing from you soon.	Wir freuen uns, in Zukunft mit Ihnen Geschäfte zu machen / bald von Ihnen zu hören.

PLACING AND ACKNOWLEDGING ORDERS

Placing orders	
Thank you for your offer/quotation of … for … .	Vielen Dank für Ihr Angebot von/vom … für … .
With reference to your offer of … .	Unter Bezugnahme auf Ihr Angebot von/vom … .
We are pleased to place an order / a trial order for …	Gerne geben wir eine Bestellung / einen Probeauftrag für …
Payment is to be made by (*date*).	Zahlung soll bis zum (*Datum*) geleistet werden.
Please acknowledge receipt of this order by fax/email.	Bitte bestätigen Sie den Erhalt dieser Bestellung per Fax/E-Mail.
Could you please also let us know exactly when we can expect delivery?	Könnten Sie uns bitte ebenfalls den genauen Termin mitteilen, wann wir mit der Lieferung rechnen können?
We look forward to receiving the consignment in due course / soon.	Wir freuen uns auf den (baldigen) Erhalt der Sendung/ Lieferung / in angemessener Zeit.
We trust that you will give this order careful / your prompt attention.	Wir vertrauen darauf / gehen davon aus, dass Sie der Bestellung Sorgfalt entgegenbringen / Ihre unverzügliche Aufmerksamkeit widmen.
We look forward to receiving your confirmation of order and advice of dispatch soon.	Wir freuen uns auf den baldigen Erhalt Ihrer Auftragsbestätigung und Versandanzeige.
Acknowledging orders	
Thank you / Many thanks for your order of … for … .	Vielen/Herzlichen Dank für Ihre Bestellung vom … über … .
We acknowledge receipt of your order of (*date*) for …	Wir nehmen den Eingang Ihrer Bestellung vom (*Datum*) über …
We note that we can expect payment by (*method of payment*) on receipt of our invoice / within 30 days of delivery.	Wir stellen fest, dass wir die Zahlung per (*Zahlungsmethode*) bei Erhalt unserer Rechnung / innerhalb von 30 Tagen nach Lieferung erwarten können.
The consignment will be dispatched on (*date*) by … .	Die Sendung wird am (*Datum*) durch/per … verschickt.
We expect to complete your order within approximately … days and will inform you as soon as the goods are ready.	Wir gehen davon aus, Ihre Bestellung innerhalb von etwa … Tagen vervollständigen zu können, und werden Sie dann sofort darüber informieren, wenn die Waren auslieferbereit sind.

PLACING AND ACKNOWLEDGING ORDERS	
We are sure that you will be satisfied with the goods/ consignment.	Wir sind zuversichtlich, dass Sie mit den Waren/der Lieferung zufrieden sein werden.
If you have any questions about your order, please do not hesitate to contact us.	Falls Sie Fragen bezüglich Ihrer Bestellung haben (sollten), zögern Sie bitte nicht, uns zu kontaktieren.
We look forward to hearing from you again.	Wir freuen uns darauf, noch einmal von Ihnen zu hören.

The simple present

1 I **go** to meetings twice a week.
2 We **live** in Bavaria.
3 Mr Brown **teaches** us English every day.
4 I **don't like** team meetings.
5 **Does** he **like** travelling?

- Man gebraucht das **simple present** für regelmäßige, sich wiederholende Ereignisse oder Handlungen (1, 3) und für Dauerzustände (2, 4, 5).
- Mit Ausnahme der 3. Person Singular (*he, she, it*) hat das **simple present** dieselbe Form wie der Infinitiv (1, 2).
  ! Die **3. Person Singular** endet auf -(*e*)*s* (3).
- Die **Verneinung** und **Fragen** werden mit der entsprechenden Form von *to do* gebildet (4, 5).

Das **simple present** wird häufig mit den folgenden **Zeitangaben** benutzt:

- *always, never, often, rarely, seldom, sometimes*
- *generally, mostly, normally, regularly, usually*
- *every day/week/month/..., every morning/afternoon/...*
- *on Mondays/Tuesdays/..., on weekdays*
- *in (the) summer/winter/...*
- *at Christmas/Easter, at weekends*

The present progressive

1 I**'m calling** to say that Ben is ill.
2 He**'s working** from home today.
3 The computer **isn't working**.
4 **Are** you **eating** lunch?

- Man benutzt das **present progressive** (auch **present continuous** genannt) für Vorgänge oder Handlungen, die im Moment des Sprechens oder Schreibens passieren und noch nicht abgeschlossen sind (1, 3, 4).
- Es wird auch für vorübergehende Situationen gebraucht (2).
- Das **present progressive** wird mit dem Präsens von *to be* und der *-ing*-Form des Vollverbs gebildet.
- Die **Verneinung** wird mit *not/n't* gebildet (3).
- Fragen werden durch Umstellung gebildet (4).

Das **present progressive** wird oft mit den folgenden **Zeitangaben** benutzt:

at the moment, at present, now, this week/month, currently

! Diese Verben bilden normalerweise **keine progressive form:**

be, believe, doubt, feel (meinen), *hate, hear, imagine, know, like/dislike, love, mean, notice, prefer, realize, recognize, remember, see* (begreifen), *seem, suppose, think* (meinen), *understand, want, wish*

The simple past

1 We **wanted** to go to the USA last year.
2 She **went** on a training course in London.
3 Jasmin **did not enjoy** her holiday in Rimini last summer.
4 Where **did** you **go** last year?

- Man benutzt das **simple past**, um über Vergangenes zu berichten.
- Das **simple past** wird auch gebraucht, wenn man sagen will, **wann** etwas geschehen ist (1, 3, 4).
- Bei **regelmäßigen** Verben wird das **simple past** durch das Anhängen von *-ed* an den Infinitiv gebildet (1).
  ! Die unregelmäßigen Verben haben eine Sonderform (2), die man sich merken – auswendig lernen! – muss.
  > *Irregular verbs, p. 302*
- Man bildet die **Verneinung** und **Fragen** mit *did/didn't* (3, 4).

Das **simple past** wird häufig mit den folgenden **Zeitangaben** benutzt:

- *yesterday, the day before yesterday, the week/month/... before last*
- *last night/week/month/summer/December/Easter/...*
- *two/three/... hours/days/years/... ago*
- *in 2005 / in the 20th century ...*
- *at that time, in those days*

The past progressive

1 The boss **was talking** to Heather **throughout the presentation**.
2 The carers **were starting** their shifts when a fire alarm (suddenly) **rang**.
3 I **wasn't doing** anything particular when he **arrived**.
4 **Were** you **having** breakfast when I **phoned**?

- Wenn man ausdrücken möchte, dass eine Handlung zu einem bestimmten Zeitpunkt oder während eines bestimmten Zeitraumes in der Vergangenheit **im Gange** war, benutzt man das **past progressive** (auch **past continuous** genannt) (1).
- Das **past progressive** wird auch benutzt, um zu verdeutlichen, dass eine Handlung im Gange war, als ein neues Ereignis (plötzlich) eintrat (2–4).
- Man bildet das **past progressive** mit *was/were* und der *-ing*-Form des Vollverbs (1).
- Die **Verneinung** wird mit *was not / wasn't* bzw. *were not / weren't* gebildet (3).
- **Fragen** bildet man durch Umstellung (4).
  ! Einige Verben haben normalerweise keine progressive form (siehe die Liste unter **present progressive**, S. 219).

The present perfect

1 **I've bought** a new computer.
2 I **haven't seen** the new care home yet.
3 How long **have** you **owned** a laptop?
4 We**'ve had** snow **for** two weeks.
5 She**'s been** ill since December.

- Wenn man ausdrücken will, dass etwas geschehen ist, ohne dass der genaue Zeitpunkt des Ereignisses wichtig ist, wird das **present perfect** benutzt (1, 2).
- Man gebraucht das **present perfect** auch, um zu sagen, seit wann oder wie lange ein Zustand oder eine Handlung schon andauert (3–5). Dafür wird sehr oft *for* bzw. *since* verwendet. (Im Deutschen steht dafür oft „seit" plus Gegenwart.)
- Das **present perfect** wird mit *have/has* und der 3. Form des Vollverbs gebildet (1, 4, 5).
  ! Die unregelmäßigen Verben haben eine Sonderform (1, 2, 4, 5), die man auswendig lernen muss.
  > *Irregular verbs, p. 302*
- Die **Verneinung** wird durch das Einfügen von *not/n't* nach *have/has* gebildet (2).
- **Fragen** bildet man durch Umstellung (3).

Das **present perfect** wird oft mit den folgenden Zeitangaben benutzt:

- *already, still (not), (not) yet*
- *(not) ever, just, lately, never, recently*
- *so far this week/month/..., till/until now*

The present perfect progressive

1 **I've been learning** English since I was ten.
2 They **haven't been speaking** to each other lately.
3 **Has** he **been planning** the meeting for long?

- Das **present perfect progressive** (auch **present perfect continuous** genannt) benutzt man für Handlungen und Vorgänge, die in der Vergangenheit begonnen haben und zum Zeitpunkt des Sprechens bzw. Schreibens noch nicht beendet sind.
- Das **present perfect progressive** wird mit *have/has been* und der *-ing*-Form des Vollverbs gebildet (1).
- Die **Verneinung** bildet man durch das Einfügen von *not/n't* unmittelbar nach *have/has* (2).
- Fragen werden durch Umstellung gebildet (3).
  ! Einige Verben haben normalerweise **keine progressive form (**siehe die Liste unter **present progressive,** S. 219).

The past perfect

1 Laura couldn't pay. She **had forgotten** her purse.
2 Nina **had** already **left** the coffee bar by the time I arrived.
3 When I visited John in hospital, he **had been** there for ten days.

- Mit Hilfe des **past perfect** drückt man aus, dass zwei Handlungen oder Vorgänge in der Vergangenheit aufeinander folgten (1, 2). Die Handlung, die zeitlich voranging, steht im **past perfect**.
- Das **past perfect** wird auch verwendet, um auszudrücken, dass ein Zustand vor einem Zeitpunkt der Vergangenheit begann und zu diesem Zeitpunkt noch andauerte (3).
  ! Wenn zwei oder mehrere kurze Handlungen in der Vergangenheit direkt aufeinander folgen, wird für alle Handlungen das **simple past** verwendet:
  *The cat **ran** out when Joanne **opened** the door.*

The past perfect progressive

1 Rod **had been preparing** for his interview for three weeks when he got another job offer.
2 When I found Mary, I could see that she **had been crying**.

- Das **past perfect progressive** (auch **past perfect continuous** genannt) wird verwendet, wenn man ausdrücken will, dass eine Handlung oder ein Vorgang vor einem Zeitpunkt in der Vergangenheit begonnen hatte und bis (oder fast bis) zu diesem Zeitpunkt andauerte.

The future

A will-future

1 In the future people **will use** public transport more often.
2 We can only hope that everyone **will accept** this shift in attitudes.
3 You've forgotten your purse? Don't worry. I**'ll lend** you some money.
4 Ms Smith **will not be** at the meeting this afternoon.
5 I **won't come** either.
6 **Will** he **get** the job?

- Das **will-future** benutzt man, um Vorhersagen zu machen (1) oder Vermutungen über die Zukunft zu äußern (2).
- Man benutzt es auch, wenn man sich spontan zu etwas entschließt, Angebote oder Versprechen macht (3).
- Das **will-future** wird mit *will* + Infinitiv des Vollverbs gebildet. Es hat für alle Personen die gleiche Form (1–3).
- Die **Verneinung** bildet man durch das Einfügen von not unmittelbar nach *will* (4). Im gesprochenen Englisch sagt man häufig won't (5).
- **Fragen** werden durch Umstellung gebildet (6).

Das **will-future** kommt häufig mit den folgenden einleitenden Verben und Ausdrücken vor:

- *believe, expect, forecast, hope, imagine, suppose, think*
- *It's clear/obvious that …, There's no doubt that …*

B going to-future

1 Look at these clouds. It**'s going to rain** soon.
2 This time I**'m going to get** good marks in the class test.
3 Tom **isn't going to work** at the club any more.
4 When **are** you **going to take** your driving test?

- Das **going to-future** benutzt man für Ereignisse und Situationen, die nach Meinung des Sprechers bald eintreten werden (weil es bereits Anzeichen dafür gibt) (1).
- Es wird auch für Pläne und Absichten gebraucht (2).
- Das **going to-future** wird mit *am/is/are* + *going to* + Infinitiv gebildet (1, 2).
- Die **Verneinung** bildet man durch das Einfügen von *not/n't* unmittelbar nach *am /is/are* (3).
- **Fragen** werden durch Umstellung gebildet (4).

  ! Auch wenn in vielen Situationen sowohl das **will-future** als auch das **going to-future** ohne Unterschiede in der Bedeutung verwendet werden kann, ist es für Lernende ratsam, sich nach den oben angegebenen Gebrauchsmöglichkeiten zu richten.

C The present progressive / The simple present

1 We**'re leaving** the house at 10.30.
2 The bus **goes** at 11 o'clock.

- Man kann das **present progressive** auch **mit einer Zeitbestimmung der Zukunft** (*at 10.30, this afternoon, on Sunday)* für bereits feststehende Pläne und Verabredungen verwenden (1).
- Genau wie im Deutschen wird auch im Englischen das **simple present mit einer Zeitangabe** benutzt, um fest terminierte Vorgänge (Fahrpläne, Stundenpläne, Programme usw.) anzugeben (2).

Modal auxiliary verbs

1 He **can speak** several languages.
2 You **must accept** your new situation.
3 We **can't go** to work today.
4 **May** I **interrupt** you?

- Um zu sagen, was geschehen kann, muss, darf, soll usw., benutzt man ein modales Hilfsverb in Verbindung mit einem Vollverb (1–4).
- Modale Hilfsverben – nicht jedoch die Ersatzverben (siehe unten) – haben bei allen Personen immer die gleiche Form, einschließlich der 3. Person Singular (keine -s-Endung) (1, 2).

  ! Wenn man *must* verneint, ändert sich die Bedeutung.

  – *I mustn't miss that film* ⟶ Ich darf den Film nicht verpassen.

  "Nicht müssen" heißt *not have to*, z. B. *I don't habe to go to school today. It's Sunday.*

- Die **Verneinung** wird durch das Einfügen von *not/n't* unmittelbar nach dem Hilfsverb gebildet (3).
- **Fragen** bildet man durch Umstellung (4).
- Abgesehen von *could* kann man modale Hilfsverben nur im Präsens und – mit einer geeigneten Zeitangabe – mit zukünftiger Bedeutung benutzen, zum Beispiel:
  - *You **can go** home now.* (Präsens)
    *You **can go** home an hour early tomorrow.* (Futur)
  - *I **must write** these letters now.* (Präsens)
    *I **must write** a long report next week.* (Futur)

! Um andere Zeitformen bei modalen Hilfsverben zu bilden oder um u. a. die Bedeutung (auch im Präsens) deutlich zu machen, werden Ersatzwerben eingesetzt.

must *The provider **had to block** access to the internet last December.*
*I really **must write** to Jill. I'll do it now.* (Zwang konnt vom Sprecher)
*I **have to go** to work now.* (Zwang kommt von außen)

can *I **couldn't drive** my boyfriend's car yesterday. The battery was flat.* (Fähigkeit)
*We **couldn't leave** work early yesterday. There was too much to do.* (Erlaubnis).
*I **wasn't able to drive** my boyfriend's car yesterday.* (Fähigkeit)
*We **weren't allowed to leave** work early yesterday.* (Erlaubnis)

Übersicht der modalen Hilfsverben nach Funktion

Funktion	Modale(s) Hilfsverb(en)	
Fähigkeit	*He **can** speak several languages.* *The first satellites **could** only transmit sound.*	
Möglichkeit	*With your qualifications you **could** work abroad.* *The boss **may** come in at any moment.* *He **might** ask you what you are doing.*	
Bitte	***Can** I have a word with Ms Sims, please?* ***Could** I speak to Ms Sims, please?* ***May** I interrupt you?* ***Might** I ask you a personal question?*	(neutral) (höflich) (betont höflich) (äußerst höflich)
Erlaubnis	*You **can** go in now.* *The boss is free. You **may** go in now.*	(neutral) (gefällig)
Verbot	*We **mustn't** be late for work tomorrow.*	
Pflicht	*You **must** wear a white tunic when working in the hospital.*	
Fehlen eines Zwangs	*Most therapists **needn't** work on Sundays.* *You **don't have to** eat the food if you don't like it.*	
Empfehlung	*You **should** get better qualifications.* *You **ought to** get better qualifications.* *You **must** get better qualifications.*	(neutral) (betont) (streng)

Reported speech

A Aussagesätze

1 Some people **claim** that 'servant' robots **are putting** people out of work.
2 The speaker **reminded** his audience that there **were** some jobs robots **couldn't do**.

- Wenn man einem Dritten berichten möchte, was während eines Gespräches gesagt wurde, benutzt man die **indirekte Rede**.
- Bei Verwendung der indirekten Rede benutzt man ein einleitendes Verb wie *claim, say, remind, answer, think, mention* usw., um zu verdeutlichen, dass eine Äußerung wiedergegeben wird. Steht das einleitende Verb in der Vergangenheit – also *said, answered, mentioned* usw. –, dann verschieben sich die Zeiten wie folgt:

direkte Rede		indirekte Rede
simple present *she works hard*	→	**simple past** *she worked hard*
present progressive *she is working hard*	→	**past progressive** *she was working hard*
simple past *she worked hard*	→	**past perfect** *she had worked hard*
past progressive *she was working hard*	→	**past perfect progressive** *she had been working hard*
present perfect *she has worked hard*	→	**past perfect** *she had worked hard*
present perfect progressive *she has been working hard*	→	**past perfect progressive** *she had been working hard*
past perfect *she had worked hard*		(keine Verschiebung) –
past perfect progressive *she had been working hard*		(keine Verschiebung) –
will *she will work hard*	→	**would** *she would work hard*
am/is/are going to *she is going to work hard*	→	**was/were going to** *she was going to work hard*
would/might etc. *she would work hard*		(keine Verschiebung) –
would have/might have etc. *she had been working hard*		(keine Verschiebung) –

! Die modalen Hilfsverben werden folgendermaßen verschoben:

Modalverb	Bedeutung	indirekte Rede
can	Fähigkeit	*could, was/were able to*
can	Erlaubnis	*was/were allowed to*
may	Möglichkeit	*might*
may	Erlaubnis	*was/were allowed to*
must	Pflicht	*had to*
mustn't	Verbot	*was/were not allowed to*
needn't	freie Wahl	*did not/didn't have to*

- Außer wenn man über ein Gespräch berichtet, das am selben Tag stattgefunden hat, müssen fast alle **Zeit**- und einige **Ortsangaben** entsprechend der folgenden Tabelle geändert werden. (Angaben, die nicht aufgeführt sind, bleiben unverändert.)

direkte Rede		indirekte Rede
today	→	*on that day*
tomorrow	→	*the next day*
yesterday	→	*the day before*
the day after tomorrow	→	*two days later*
the day before yesterday	→	*two days before*
next day/Friday/week/Christmas/...	→	*the following day/Friday/week/Christmas/...*
last Friday/week/summer/...	→	*the Friday/week/summer/... before*
two years/months/weeks/... ago	→	*two years/months/weeks/... before*
now, at present	→	*then*
at the moment	→	*at that moment*
at this time	→	*at that time*
here	→	*there*
in this place	→	*in that place*
this	→	*that*
these	→	*those*

B Fragesätze

1 A member of the audience **asked what had led** to the widespread use of robots in hospitals.
2 She **wanted to know if/whether** her job **was endangered**.

- Bei indirekten **Fragen** unterscheidet man zwischen Fragen mit Fragewort (1) und Fragen ohne Fragewort (2).
- Bei Fragen **mit Fragewort** wird das Fragewort übernommen (1).
- Bei Fragen **ohne Fragewort** benutzt man *if* bzw. *whether* (= ob), um zu verdeutlichen, dass es sich um eine Frage handelt (2).
- Alle anderen Änderungen erfolgen wie bei den Aussagesätzen (siehe **Aussagesätze** S. 224).

C Bitten, Aufforderungen und Befehle

1 Lucy **asked the engineer to show her** the robot. (Direkte Rede: "Show me the robot, please.")
2 He **told her not to go** too close to it. (Direkte Rede: "Don't go too close to it.")

- **Bitten** werden meist durch *asked* (= bitten) (1), **Aufforderungen** und **Befehle** durch *told* (= sagen) (2) eingeleitet.
- Bei **positiven Sätzen** erscheint das Verb als *to* + Infinitiv (1).
- Bei **negativen Sätzen** wird *not* unmittelbar vor *to* gesetzt (2).

  ! Die beiden Verben *to tell* und *to ask* stehen immer mit einem Objekt, das die angesprochene Person erwähnt (1, 2). Ist dies vom Kontext her nicht erkennbar, wird einfach ein passender Begriff eingesetzt:
  - *Ben said, 'Don't enter the studio when the red light is on.'*
    *Ben **told everybody** not to enter the studio when the red light was on.*

The passive

1 Measures **are being introduced** to reduce traffic pollution.
2 Pollution **is caused by** some thoughtless people.

- Ist der Verursacher einer Handlung unbekannt oder zweitrangig, benutzt man das Passiv. Im Vordergrund steht also das Ergebnis des Vorgangs (1).
- Möchte man den Verursacher doch angeben, benutzt man einen *by agent* (2).
  ! Der Verursacher wird mit *by* – auf keinen Fall mit *from* – eingeleitet.
- Das Passiv wird mit einer Zeitform von *to be* und der 3. Form des Vollverbs gebildet:

Zeit	Zeitform von *to be*	3. Form
simple present	*am/is/are*	*caused*
present progressive	*am/is/are being*	*introduced*
simple past	*was/were*	*buried*
past progressive	*was/were being*	*built*
present perfect	*has/have been*	*installed*
will-future	*will be*	*blocked*
going to-future	*am/is/are going to be*	*sacked*

- Beim Gebrauch von modalen Hilfsverben wird nach folgendem Muster verfahren:

bei Aussagen	Hilfsverb + *to be* + 3. Form	*must be displayed*
bei Fragen	Hilfsverb + Subjekt + *to be* + 3. Form	*Can … be persuaded?*

Other passive forms

A

1 **I was told/advised** to be there early.
2 **I was allowed** to go on the trip.
3 **We were asked** to leave.

- Einige englische Verben können ein "persönliches Passiv" (*personal passive*) bilden. Bei den entsprechenden deutschen Verben geht dies nicht, z. B. Mir wurde gesagt…/Man sagte mir … und NICHT ~~Ich wurde gesagt~~ …

B

1 They gave her a book. **She was given a CD** too.
2 They promised him two months' holiday. **A pay rise was offered to him** too.

- Verben wie *give*, *promise*, *offer*, *show* haben im Aktiv gewöhnlich zwei Objekte nach sich: ein indirektes und ein direktes Objekt.
- Meist wird als Subjekt das persönliche Passiv verwendet (1).
- Seltener verwendet man ein Sachsubjekt (2).

C

1 People say that he is ill. **He is said to be ill.**
2 Everybody thinks he has cancer. **It is thought that he has cancer.**

- Von den Verben des Sagens und Denkens (z. B. *believe, say, think*) können im Englischen zwei Passivkonstruktionen gebildet werden.
- Das persönliche Passiv besteht aus Subjekt + Passivform + *to*-Infinitiv (1).
- Das unpersönliche Passiv besteht aus *it* + Passivform + *that*-Satz (2).

If-sentences

1 If I **go** by bus, I**'ll (= I will) be** late.
2 If I **had** a car, I**'d (= I would) be** on time.
3 If I **had won** the lottery, I **would have bought** a car.
4 I **would have been** very happy if I **had won** the lottery.
5 If we **knew** how to cook, we **would have invited** our friends to dinner last week.
6 If people **drink** too much, they **have** a headache the next day.

- Ein **Konditionalsatz** besteht aus zwei Teilen; dem ***if*-Teil** und dem **Hauptteil**. Der ***if*-Teil** drückt eine **Bedingung** aus, der **Hauptteil** eine **Folge**.
- Bei Konditionalsätzen kommen folgende Zeitmuster am häufigsten vor:

Typ I	*If* + simple present	+ *will*-Futur (1)
Typ II	*If* + simple past	+ *would* + Infinitiv (2)
Typ III	*If* + past perfect	+ *would have* + 3. Form des Verbs (3)

- Der *if*-Teil kann hinter dem Hauptteil stehen. In diesem Fall steht kein Komma dazwischen (4).
- Es gibt auch Mischformen wie z. B. Typ II + Typ III (5).
- Wenn man ausdrücken will, dass auf eine bestimmte Handlung immer ein bestimmtes Ergebnis folgt, benutzt man in beiden Satzteilen das *simple present* (Typ 0) (6).
- *if*-Sätze werden gemäß der **Wahrscheinlichkeit** der zu erwartenden Folge eingesetzt:

  Typ I: Folge (fast) sicher.
  *If we **invest in** new technology, a lot of people **will lose** their jobs.*
  D. h. viele Leute werden (vermutlich) ihre Stellen verlieren, da wir (sehr wahrscheinlich) in die neue Technologie investieren werden.

  Typ II: Folge theoretisch möglich, aber kaum unwahrscheinlich.
  *If we **invested in** new technology, a lot of people **would lose** their jobs.*
  D. h. es ist nicht zu erwarten, dass viele Leute ihre Stellen verlieren werden, da wir (wahrscheinlich) nicht in die neue Technologie investieren werden.

  Typ III: Folge unmöglich, da die Bedingung nicht erfüllt wurde und bereits in der Vergangenheit liegt.
  *If we **had invested in** new technology, a lot of people **would have lost** their jobs.*
  D. h. der Sprecher weiß schon, dass keiner den Job verloren hat, da wir in die neue Technologie nicht investiert haben.

Gerund/Infinitive

1 Max **enjoys visiting** his customers.
2 Can you **afford to buy** that new physiotherapy equipment?
3 Cem and Julie **continued to meet** even though they were no longer colleagues.
4 Cem and Julie **continued meeting** even though they were no longer colleagues.
5 Alison **normally likes meeting** clients, but **today** she would **prefer to stay** in the office.

- Nach einigen Verben folgt immer die *-ing*-Form **(gerund)** (1).
  Am wichtigsten sind:

admit, avoid, consider, deny, enjoy, finish, give up, imagine, mention, (not) mind (etwas/ nichts dagegen haben), *miss, practise, recommend, risk, stop, suggest*

- **Nach einigen Verben** folgt immer der Infinitiv **(infinitive)** (2).
  Die **wichtigsten** Verben dieser Gruppe sind:

afford, choose, decide, expect, hope, manage, mean, plan, promise, refuse, want

! Nach den Verben *begin, continue, intend* und *start* kann der **Infinitiv** oder die ***-ing* -Form beliebig benutzt werden (**3, 4).

- Einige Verben werden **je nach Bedeutung** entweder mit dem **Infinitiv** oder mit der ***-ing* -Form** benutzt. Die **wichtigsten** Verben dieser Gruppe sind:

like, love, hate, prefer

- Nach *would like, would hate, would love, would prefer* steht **nur** der Infinitiv (5).

forget/remember

Die Struktur ***forget/remember*** + ***-ing*-Form** bezieht sich auf die Vergangenheit. Sie drückt etwa die Idee „Ich werde nie vergessen …" aus.

! „Vergangenheit" bezieht sich hier nicht auf forget/remember, sondern auf das nachfolgende Verb.

*I still **remember getting** my first job.*
*I'll never **forget going** to Japan last year.*

Die Struktur ***forget/remember*** + **Infinitiv** dagegen bezieht sich auf die Zukunft. Sie drückt etwa die Idee aus „Ich darf nicht vergessen, etwas zu tun" bzw. „Ich habe noch etwas zu tun, weil ich es bis jetzt vergessen habe".

*Dad, please **remember / don't forget to pick me up** from the station.*
*Oh dear. I **forgot / didn't remember to pick Sally up** from the station.*

regret

Die Struktur ***regret*** + ***-ing* -Form** drückt Bedauern über eine vergangene Situation bzw. einen vergangenen Vorfall aus. Häufig geht es dabei um verpasste Chancen.

*I really **regret leaving** school without any qualifications.*
*I know they will **regret buying** such a big, expensive car.*

Die Struktur ***regret*** + **Infinitiv** – fast immer mit einem Verb des Mitteilens wie *inform, say, tell* kombiniert – drückt eine schlechte Nachricht aus.

*I **regret to say** that I can't attend the meeting tomorrow.*
*We **regret to inform** you that the vacancy has now been filled.*

stop

Bedeutet ***stop*** „aufhören, etwas zu tun", steht das nachfolgende Verb in der ***-ing*** **-Form.**
Bedeutet ***stop*** aber „kurz anhalten, um etwas anderes zu tun", folgt ein Verb im **Infinitiv.**

*For heaven's sake **stop shouting** at me.*
*I'm a little late because I **stopped to give** somebody a lift.*

try

Bedeutet ***try*** „etwas ausprobieren", steht das nachfolgende Verb in der ***-ing*** **-Form.**
Bedeutet ***try*** aber „sich anstrengen, etwas zu tun", folgt ein Verb im **Infinitiv.**

*I **tried phoning** Ellie, but she wasn't at home.*
*We**'ll try to repair** your computer by the weekend.*

Adjectives and adverbs

1 John has a **new** printer.
2 He always buys **expensive** equipment.
3 My computer often crashes and is **usually very slow**.
4 We can make printouts **quickly** and **cheaply**.
5 That CD sounds **terrible**.
6 I **used to** go skiing but I **kept** falling over. I didn't **enjoy** it.

- Um **Personen** oder **Sachen** näher zu beschreiben, benutzt man **Adjektive** (1–4).
- Adjektive stehen **unmittelbar** vor Substantiven oder **unmittelbar nach** einer Form von *be* (bzw. *become* oder *seem*, die *be* ersetzen können) (3). Dies gilt auch für Adverbien der inbestimmten Häufigkeit wie *always, often, usually, sometimes, never.*
- Adjektive statt Adverbien werden bei folgenden Bedeutungen von *feel* (sich fühlen), *look* (aussehen), *sound* (sich anhören), *smell* (riechen, duften) und *taste (*schmecken) verwendet (5).
- Um einen **Tätigkeitsverb** näher zu beschreiben, setzt man ein Adverb **unmittelbar hinter das Verb** bzw. Verb + Objekt (5).
  ! Im Englischen können ein Verb und sein Objekt – anders als im Deutschen – nicht durch ein Adverb getrennt werden. Also NICHT: ~~We can make quickly printouts~~. (siehe **Word order** S. 231)
- Adverbien werden auch benutzt, um **Adjektive**, **andere Adverbien** und **ganze Sätze** näher zu bestimmen:
  *MP3 players have become **surprisingly cheap**.* (Adverb + Adjektiv)
  *My fax machine prints out **terribly slowly**.* (Adverb + Adverb)
  ***Luckily** Gerd left a message on my mailbox.* (Satzadverb)
- Die meisten Adverbien werden durch Anhängen von *-ly* an das Adjektiv gebildet (4). Eine kleine Anzahl von Adverbien hat dieselbe Form wie Adjektive; die häufigsten sind *fast, hard, early late, long.* Deutsche Adverbien, z. B. „früher", „immer", „gern" werden häufig durch Verbkonstruktionen wiedergegeben (6).

Comparison of adjectives and adverbs

1 A hundred years ago life was **slower** and people may have been **happier**.
2 Which technological innovation is the **most/least important**?
3 Today elderly people can get about **more easily than** ever before.

- **Einsilbige** und **zweisilbige Adjektive**, die auf *-y* enden – zum Beispiel *easy*, *happy* und *lucky* –, werden mit *-(i)er*/*-(i)est* gesteigert (1).
- **Mehrsilbige Adjektive** und **Adverbien**, die auf *-ly* enden, werden mit *more*/*most* gesteigert (2, 3).
  ! Die Adverbien, die dieselbe Form wie das entsprechende Adjektiv haben (*fast, hard, early* usw.), werden mit *-er*/*-est* gesteigert.
- Um Personen oder Sachen im Satz miteinander zu vergleichen, gibt es folgende Möglichkeiten:

Kein Unterschied	***as*** *good* ***as***	genau so gut wie
Unterschied	***not as*** *good* ***as***	nicht so gut wie
Unterschied	*better* ***than***	besser als

Word order – positions of adverbs of time, place and frequency

1 She does home visits **every week**.
2 The care home is situated in a small town **outside of Frankfurt**.
3 **Last year** we went to an Italian restaurant for our team Christmas party.
4 Paul and Emily went to **the USA last year**.
5 She **always finishes** work early on Fridays.
6 He **is never** in the office when I call.
7 I like to work at home **now and then**.
8 Gina acted **strangely at the health care fair last week**.

- Zeitangaben (Wann?) und Ortsangaben (Wo?, Wohin?) stehen in der Regel am Satzende (1, 2).
- Um die Zeit eines bestimmten Ereignisses hervorzuheben, kann man die Zeitangabe an die erste Stelle setzen (3).
- Stehen eine Zeitangabe und eine Ortsangabe zusammen am Satzende, dann gilt die Reihenfolge Ort vor Zeit (alphabetisch merken: O vor Z!) (4).
- Besteht eine Häufigkeitsangabe aus einem Wort, z. B. *always, often, sometimes*, steht sie unmittelbar vor dem Vollverb (5).
- Lautet das Vollverb *to be*, steht das Adverb direkt dahinter (6).
- Besteht die Häufigkeitsangabe aus mehreren Wörtern, z. B. *every day, now and then*, steht sie wie eine Zeitangabe am Satzende (7).
- Adverbien der Art und Weise stehen in der Regel am Satzende. Kommen noch Zeit oder Ortsadverbien hinzu, lautet die Reihenfolge: Art und Weise – Ort – Zeit (AOZ) (8).

Relative clauses and contact clauses

1 Computer scientists are designing 'smart homes' **which/that** use data gathered from inhabitants.
2 East Asia is welcoming health tourists **who/that** are looking for a better quality of life in old age.
3 Tony filled in a job satisfaction questionnaire **(which/that)** he found on the internet.
4 Fred Foley is a is a young carer **whose** job involves helping the bereaved.
5 Care home employees, most **of whom** are quite young, work long hours.
6 Antibiotics are being incorrectly used for conditions **against which** they have no resistance.

- Relativsätze werden benutzt, um den Hauptsatz durch zusätzliche Informationen genauer zu bestimmen.
- Für **Sachen** benutzt man das Relativpronomen *which* bzw. *that* (1) und für Personen *who* bzw. *that* (2).
- Ist das Relativpronomen das **Objekt des Relativsatzes**, dann kann man es weglassen (3). Solche Relativsätze heißen **contact clauses**.
- Um **Besitz** bzw. **Zugehörigkeit** anzuzeigen, gebraucht man *whose* unmittelbar vor dem **Substantiv** bei Personen und Sachen (4).
- Steht eine **Präposition** vor dem **Relativpronomen**, wird *whom* für Personen und *which* für Sachen benutzt (5, 6). In solchen Fällen ist der Gebrauch von *that* nicht möglich.

Defining and non-defining relative clauses

1 The first Europeans **who** settled in Australia came from Britain.
2 Sydney, **which** is famous for its unusually designed opera house, is situated on the south-eastern coast of Australia.

- Im **ersten Beispielsatz** ist der Sinn des Hauptsatzes *The first Europeans came from Britain* ohne den Relativsatz *who settled in Australia* offensichtlich falsch bzw. unvollständig. Relativsätze dieser Art – die wesentlich für das Verständnis des gesamten Satzes sind – nennt man **defining relative clauses** (notwendige oder bestimmende Relativsätze).
- Im **zweiten Beispielsatz** ist die Aussage des Hauptsatzes *Sydney is situated on the south-eastern coast of Australia* ohne den Relativsatz völlig verständlich, weil der Relativsatz *which is famous for its unusually designed opera house* eine zusätzliche, also nebensächliche, Information enthält. Daher werden solche Relativsätze ***non-defining relative clauses*** (nicht notwendige oder nicht bestimmende Relativsätze) genannt.
  ! Notwendige Relativsätze werden immer **ohne** trennende **Kommas** benutzt. Dies signalisiert, dass sie fester Bestandteil der Hauptaussage sind.

Participle constructions

1 A meal **costing** two pounds is very cheap.
2 The work **involved** with cooking a simple meal is minimal.
3 **Weakened** by disease, many children die young.
4 **Having lost** so many people to AIDS, Africa needs our help more than ever.
5 **Despite facing** extreme poverty, many people haven't given up hope.
6 Donors should invest in projects that help local inhabitants become self-supporting, thereby **making** sure that the money isn't wasted.
7 AIDS represents a major challenge to sub-Saharan Africa, currently **killing** more than two million people every year.

Die englische Sprache ist geprägt durch die häufige Verwendung von Partizipialkonstruktionen. Diese ermöglichen einen eleganteren Sprachfluss.

- Ein **present participle** kann Relativsätze verkürzen (*A meal that costs* …) (1).
- Auch ein **past participle** kann zur Verkürzung von Relativsätzen verwendet werden (*The work that is involved* …) (2).
- Participles werden auch verwendet, um adverbial Nebensätze zu verkürzen (3).
- Auch das **perfect participle** wird verwendet (4).
- Manchmal sind Konjunktionen unerlässlich, um den logischen Zusammenhang herauszustellen (5, 6).
- Schließlich verknüpft man mit einer Partizipialkonstruktion zwei Hauptsätze zu einem einzigen Satz, und zwar ausnahmslos mittels **present participle** (7).

Countable and uncountable nouns

1 Visit our website for more **information** on our care services. NICHT ~~informations~~

2 Have you read the paper today? The political **news** is interesting. NICHT ~~news are~~

3 Where can I get some **advice**? NICHT ~~an advice~~

4 **Fewer people** learn French nowadays. **More people** learn Spanish than French. **Most people** learn English. **The fewest** students in Germany learn Russian.

5 We have **more bread** than butter and **less cola** than orange juice. We have brought **the least cola** and **the most bread** to the party.

- Einige wichtige **Substantive** sind **zählbar im Deutschen, nicht jedoch im Englischen**. Diese Substantive können also nicht ohne weiteres mit dem unbestimmten Artikel *a / an* oder mit einem Zahlwort benutzt werden.
  Hier ist eine Liste solcher Wörter, die Sie auswendig lernen sollten:

advice, baggage, damage, data, equipment, evidence, furniture, information, knowledge, luck, luggage, machinery, news, progress, research, rubbish, work (housework, homework)

- Um diese Substantive im Plural zu verwenden, muss *some, a bit of* bzw. *a piece of* hinzugefügt werden (3).
  ! Wenn *most* die Mehrheit allgemein bedeutet, benutzt man keinen Artikel *the*. (*Most dogs like bones*). *Most* (und auch *fewest*) kann mit oder ohne Artikel stehen, wenn es superlative Bedeutung (höchste Steigerungsstufe) hat. (*I have* (*the*) *most computer games of anybody in my class.*)

Some and *any*

1 **Some** teams prefer to hold regular weekly meetings.
2 They haven't got **any** women working in their organization.
3 Have you got **any** information about arrival times?
4 Can I have **some** more coffee, please?
5 Would you like **some** mineral water?
6 There's **something** I need to do but I can't remember what it is.
7 He can't find that letter **anywhere**. Maybe **somebody** took it.

- Wir verwenden *some* in **bejahten Aussagen** (1) und *any* in **verneinten Aussagen** (2) und **„echten" Fragen** (3).
- Drückt die Frage eine höfliche **Bitte** (4) bzw. ein **Angebot** (5) aus, worauf eine positive Antwort erwartet wird, verwenden wir ebenfalls *some*.
- Wir verwenden die Zusammensetzungen von *some* and *any* – also *somebody/someone, something, somewhere, anybody/anyone, anything* und *anywhere* – in genau derselben Art und Weise (6–7).

The definite article

1 **Sociologists** say that **violence** is increasing among young people.
2 Is **the violence** they see in **modern films** the cause of this?
3 **Most sentences** are not tough enough.
4 Nearly **half the prisoners** in **British prisons** are under 25.
5 We had **breakfast** late this morning so we came to work **by car** instead of **by bus**.

- Hat ein Substantiv eine allgemeine, uneingeschränkte Bedeutung – also „alle ohne Ausnahme" – dann steht es ohne Artikel (1, 2, 5).
- Ist die Bedeutung eines Substantives auf bestimmte Fälle eingeschränkt, benutzt man den Artikel (2, 5).
- Ferner wird der Artikel in den folgenden Fällen und Wendungen im Englischen – z. T. anders als im Deutschen – nicht gebraucht:
  - bei *most* in der Bedeutung „die meisten" (3),
  - bei öffentlichen Gebäuden im allgemeinen Sinn (4),
  - bei Mahlzeiten (6),
  - bei Verkehrsmitteln (6),
  - bei Straßennamen.
- Der Artikel wird verwendet nach *all* und *half* (4).

The indefinite article

1 Yesterday I met **a woman** who works for **a friend** of my father's.
2 We'll have to buy **a** new **computer**.
3 That's **an** interesting **idea**.
4 Jane's **an occupational therapist**? I thought she was **a nurse**.
5 My father has been **a non-smoker** all his life.
6 How much does petrol cost **a liter**?
7 We have planning meetings four times **a month**.

- Der unbestimmten Artikel a/an steht bei einer einzelnen, nicht näher bestimmten Person (1), einer Sache (2), oder einem Begriff (3).
- Anders als im Deutschen verwenden wir im Englischen den unbestimmten Artikel in folgenden Fällen:
  - bei Berufsangaben (4),
  - bei Angaben über Nationalität, Religion, Politik oder Gruppenzugehörigkeit (5)
  - bei Maß (6), Verpackungs, und Zeitangaben (7)
  - bei den folgenden Wendungen:

to be in a hurry	in Eile sein, es eilig haben
to come to an end	enden
to have a bath/shower/...	sich baden/duschen/...
to have a go	es ausprobieren
to have a turn at (+ -ing-Form)	an der Reihe sein, etwas zu tun
to make a noise	Lärm machen
to take a seat	Platz nehmen
for a change	zur Abwechslung
for a long/short time	lange/kurze Zeit
in a loud/quiet voice	mit lauter/ruhiger Stimme
What a pity!	Wie schade!
without a break	ohne Pause

! Bei *half, quite, rather* und *such* wird der unbestimmte Artikel nachgestellt:

- The meeting starts in half **an** hour.
- We had quite **a** successful year in 2005.
- Jack can be rather **an** idiot sometimes.
- We've never had such **a** busy period.

UNIT WORD LIST

Dieses Wörterverzeichnis enthält die Wörter in **Social Pulse** in der Reihenfolge ihres Auftretens. Wörter aus den Audio- und Video-Transkripte sind mit einem gelben Balken, Wörter aus den *Partner Files* mit einem grünen Balken und Wörter aus den *Guidance* und *Challenge Files* sind mit einem türkisen Balken gekennzeichnet.

TOPIC 1

page 6/7

job advert(isement) [ˈdʒɒb ædvɜːt/ədvɜːtɪsmnt]	Stellenanzeige, Stellenangebot
carer [ˈkeərə]	Pflegefachkraft, Fachkraft im Sozial- und Gesundheitswesen
to **apply for sth** [əˈplaɪ fə]	sich um/auf/für etw bewerben
curriculum vitae (CV) *BE* [kəˌrɪkjələm ˈviːtaɪ, ˌsiː ˈviː]	Lebenslauf
cover letter [ˈkʌvə letə]	Anschreiben, Begleitschreiben
work placement [ˈwɜːk pleɪsmənt]	Praktikum
organization [ˌɔːgənaɪˈzeɪʃn]	Unternehmen, Organisation
to **advertise a job** [ˌædvətaɪz ə ˈdʒɒb]	eine Stelle ausschreiben
to **care for sb** [ˈkeə fə]	jdn pflegen, jdn betreuen, jdn versorgen, sich um jdn kümmern
to **interview sb** [ˈɪntəvjuː]	ein Vorstellungsgespräch mit jdm führen
(job) interview [ˈɪntəvjuː]	Vorstellungsgespräch
personal [ˈpɜːsənl]	persönlich, privat
to **create sth** [kriˈeɪt]	etw erstellen
diagram [ˈdaɪəgræm]	Schaubild, Diagramm
aspect [ˈæspekt]	Gesichtspunkt, Aspekt, Seite
experience [ɪkˈspɪəriəns]	Erlebnis(se), Erfahrung(en)
application [ˌæplɪˈkeɪʃn]	Bewerbung
Same here. [ˌseɪm ˈhɪə]	Ich auch. Geht mir genauso.
training [ˈtreɪnɪŋ]	Ausbildung
to **collect sth** [kəˈlekt]	etw sammeln
to **pick sth** [pɪk]	sich etw aussuchen
skill [skɪl]	Fähigkeit, Kompetenz
quality [ˈkwɒləti]	Eigenschaft
candidate [ˈkændɪdət]	Bewerber/in, Kandidat/in
to **compare sth** [kəmˈpeə]	etw (miteinander) vergleichen
to **add sth to sth** [æd]	etw einer Sache hinzufügen
heading [ˈhedɪŋ]	Überschrift, Rubrik
What's to come [ˌwɒts tə ˈkʌm]	Und so geht's weiter
to **think about sth** [ˈθɪŋk əbaʊt]	über etw nachdenken, sich über etw Gedanken machen
kind [kaɪnd]	Art
abroad [əˈbrɔːd]	im Ausland
to **gain sth** [geɪn]	etw erwerben, etw erlangen, etw gewinnen, etw erreichen
care [keə]	Pflege, Betreuung, Fürsorge, Versorgung, Zuwendung, Obhut
care job [ˈkeə dʒɒb]	Pflege-/Sozialberuf, Beruf im Gesundheitswesen
to **practise (sth)** [ˈpræktɪs]	(etw) üben, (etw) trainieren
practical [ˈpræktɪkl]	praktisch
to **get started** [get ˈstɑːtɪd]	loslegen, anfangen
caring professions [ˈkeərɪŋ prəfeʃnz]	Berufe im Pflege-, Sozial- und Gesundheitsbereich
alternative [ɔːlˈtɜːnətɪv]	Alternative, Ausweichmöglichkeit

page 8

career [kəˈrɪə]	Beruf, berufliche Laufbahn, Karriere
opportunity [ˌɒpəˈtjuːnəti]	Chance, Möglichkeit
preference [ˈprefrəns]	Vorliebe, Neigung, Präferenz
to **express sth** [ɪkˈspres]	etw äußern, etw ausdrücken
health [helθ]	Gesundheit
sector [ˈsektə]	Bereich, Branche, Sektor
to **match sth to sth** [ˈmætʃ tə]	etw einer Sache zuordnen
equivalent [ɪˈkwɪvələnt]	Entsprechung
to **scan sth** [skæn]	etw *(Text)* überfliegen
type [taɪp]	Art
duty [ˈdjuːti]	Aufgabe, Pflicht
employer [ɪmˈplɔɪə]	Arbeitgeber/in
to **offer sth** [ˈɒfə]	etw bieten, etw anbieten
career perspectives *pl* [kəˌrɪə pəˈspektɪvz]	berufliche Perspektiven, Aufstiegschancen
to **share (sth) with sb** [ˈʃeə wɪð]	mit jdm (über etw) sprechen, jdm von etw erzählen
(job) applicant [ˈæplɪkənt]	Bewerber/in
trainee [treɪˈniː]	Auszubildende/r
disability [ˌdɪsəˈbɪləti]	Behinderung
to **support sb** [səˈpɔːt]	jdm helfen, jdn unterstützen, jdn fördern
disabled person [dɪsˈeɪbld pɜːsn]	Behinderte/r
physical(ly) [ˈfɪzɪkl]	körperlich
impairment [ɪmˈpeəmənt]	Beeinträchtigung, Behinderung
learning difficulties *pl* [ˈlɜːnɪŋ dɪfɪkəltiz]	Lernschwierigkeiten
long-term [ˌlɒŋˈtɜːm]	langfristig, chronisch

(health) condition [kən'dɪʃn]	Erkrankung
reliable [rɪ'laɪəbl]	zuverlässig, verantwortungsbewusst
motivated ['məʊtɪveɪtɪd]	motiviert
at least [ət 'li:st]	mindestens
social and health care [ˌsəʊʃl ənd 'helθ keə]	Gesundheit und Soziales, Sozial- und Gesundheitswesen
driving licence ['draɪvɪŋ laɪsns]	Führerschein
advantage [əd'vɑ:ntɪdʒ]	Vorteil
responsibility [rɪˌspɒnsə'bɪləti]	Aufgabe, Zuständigkeit
to **accompany sb** [ə'kʌmpəni]	jdn begleiten
to **take part in sth** [ˌteɪk 'pɑ:t ɪn]	an etw teilnehmen
leisure ['leʒə]	Freizeit
social ['səʊʃl]	gesellig, sozial
daily routine [ˌdeɪli ru:'ti:n]	Tagesablauf
support [sə'pɔ:t]	Hilfe, Unterstützung, Förderung
supervision [ˌsu:pə'vɪʒn]	Betreuung, Supervision
to **carry out sth** [ˌkæri 'aʊt]	etw ausführen, etw durchführen
task [tɑ:sk]	Aufgabe
payment ['peɪmənt]	Zahlung
day-to-day [ˌdeɪ tə 'deɪ]	täglich, tagtäglich
expenses *pl* [ɪk'spensɪz]	Ausgaben, Aufwendungen

page 9

childcare ['tʃaɪldkeə]	Kinderbetreuung
school leaver ['sku:l li:və]	Schulabgänger/in
work experience ['wɜ:k ɪkspɪəriəns]	Praktikum, Berufserfahrung
early childhood education [ɜ:li ˌtʃaɪldhʊd edʒu'keɪʃn]	frühkindliche Erziehung, Kleinkindpädagogik
on-the-job training [ɒn ðə ˌdʒɒb 'treɪnɪŋ]	Ausbildung am Arbeitsplatz
official(ly) [ə'fɪʃl]	offiziell
to **recognize sb/sth** ['rekəgnaɪz]	jdn/etw anerkennen
certificate [sə'tɪfɪkət]	Zeugnis, Nachweis, Diplom
aged … [eɪdʒd]	im Alter von …
cheerful ['tʃɪəfl]	gut gelaunt
individual [ˌɪndɪ'vɪdʒuəl]	(eigenständige) Persönlichkeit, Einzelperson, Individuum
interpersonal skills *pl* [ˌɪntə'pɜ:sənl skɪlz]	soziale Kompetenz
to **provide sth** [prə'vaɪd]	etw bieten, etw zur Verfügung stellen, etw liefern
development [dɪ'veləpmənt]	Entwicklung
as well as [əz 'wel əz]	sowie, und
ongoing ['ɒngəʊɪŋ]	laufend
mentoring ['mentɔ:rɪŋ]	Begleitung, Betreuung *(durch eine/n Mentor/in)*
to **join a company** [dʒɔɪn]	bei einer Firma anfangen, zu einer Firma kommen
to **earn sth** [ɜ:n]	etw verdienen
financial [faɪ'nænʃl]	finanziell
diploma [dɪ'pləʊmə]	Diplom
degree [dɪ'gri:]	(Universitäts-)Abschluss
to **sound** [saʊnd]	klingen
career path [kə'rɪə pɑ:θ]	Karriere, Berufsweg
form [fɔ:m]	Formular
midwife (*pl* **midwives**) ['mɪdwaɪf]	Hebamme
healthcare ['helθkeə]	medizinische Versorgung
community [kə'mju:nəti]	Gemeinde, Gemeinschaft
developing country [dɪˌveləpɪŋ 'kʌntri]	Entwicklungsland
attitude ['ætɪtju:d]	Einstellung, Haltung
to **join sb/sth** [dʒɔɪn]	sich jdm/etw anschließen, bei jdm/etw mitmachen, bei etw dabei sein
volunteer [ˌvɒlən'tɪə]	Freiwillige/r, ehrenamtliche/r Mitarbeiter/in
midwifery [ˌmɪd'wɪfəri]	Geburtshilfe
maternity ward [mə'tɜ:nəti wɔ:d]	Entbindungsstation *(im Krankenhaus)*
newborn ['nju:bɔ:n]	Neugeborenes
trained [treɪnd]	ausgebildet, geschult, qualifiziert
professional [prə'feʃənl]	Fachkraft
accommodation [əˌkɒmə'deɪʃn]	Unterkunft
location [ləʊ'keɪʃn]	Standort, Ort
to **suit sb/sth** [su:t]	für jdn/etw geeignet sein, (zu) jdm/etw passen
to **prefer sth** [prɪ'fɜ:]	etw vorziehen, etw gern/lieber tun
position [pə'zɪʃn]	Stelle, Stellung, Position
definitely ['defɪnətli]	(ganz) bestimmt
suitable ['su:təbl]	geeignet, passend
requirements *pl* [rɪ'kwaɪəmənts]	Anforderungen
category ['kætəgəri]	Kategorie
to **be a good communicator** [bi ə ˌgʊd kə'mju:nɪkeɪtə]	kommunikativ sein
to **be willing to do sth** [bi 'wɪlɪŋ tə]	bereit/willens sein, etw zu tun
a proactive individual [ə prəʊˌæktɪv ɪndɪ'vɪdʒuəl]	jd mit Eigeninitiative
to **deal with sth** ['di:l wɪð]	mit etw umgehen, mit etw zurechtkommen, etw bewältigen
hard-working [ˌhɑ:d 'wɜ:kɪŋ]	fleißig
pressure ['preʃə]	Druck
to **mention sth** ['menʃn]	etw erwähnen, etw nennen
to **summarize sth** ['sʌməraɪz]	etw zusammenfassen
key [ki:]	wichtigste/r/s, Haupt-
to **present sth to sb** [prɪ'zent]	jdm etw vorstellen, jdm etw präsentieren
to **take turns** [ˌteɪk 'tɜ:nz]	sich abwechseln

UNIT WORD LIST

page 10

working conditions *pl* ['wɜːkɪŋ kəndɪʃnz]	Arbeitsbedingungen
to **increase sth** [ɪn'kriːs]	etw erhöhen, etw steigern
option ['ɒpʃn]	(Wahl-)Möglichkeit, Option
social work ['səʊʃl wɜːk]	Sozialarbeit
social worker ['səʊʃl wɜːkə]	Sozialarbeiter/in
to **solve sth** [sɒlv]	etw *(Problem usw.)* lösen
to **take advantage of sb/sth** [ˌteɪk əd'vɑːntɪdʒ əv]	etw/jdn ausnutzen, einen Vorteil aus etw ziehen
unfair(ly) [ˌʌn'feə]	ungerecht, unlauter
to **treat sb/sth** [triːt]	jdn/etw behandeln
repeated(ly) [rɪ'piːtɪd]	wiederholt, mehrfach
cruel [kruːəl]	brutal, grausam, gemein
violent ['vaɪələnt]	gewalttätig, brutal
to **require sth** [rɪ'kwaɪə]	etw erfordern, etw verlangen
attention [ə'tenʃn]	Aufmerksamkeit
effort ['efət]	Anstrengung, Mühe
available [ə'veɪləbl]	verfügbar
physical force [ˌfɪzɪkl 'fɔːs]	körperliche Gewalt
to **be intended to do sth** [bi ɪnˌtendɪd tə 'duː]	dafür/dazu gedacht sein, etw zu tun
to **hurt sb/sth** [hɜːt]	jdn/etw verletzen, jdm wehtun
to **kill sb** [kɪl]	jdn töten
comment ['kɒment]	Kommentar, Bemerkung
true [truː]	zutreffend, wahr
false [fɔːls]	unzutreffend, falsch
statement ['steɪtmənt]	Aussage, Stellungnahme
usually ['juːʒuəli]	normalerweise, gewöhnlich
to **recruit sb** [rɪ'kruːt]	jdn einstellen, jdn *(Personal)* anwerben
staff [stɑːf]	Personal, Belegschaft, Mitarbeiter/innen
violence ['vaɪələns]	Gewalt
connected with [kə'nektɪd wɪð]	in Zusammenhang mit
gun [gʌn]	Schusswaffe
further ['fɜːðə]	weitere/r/s
Russia ['rʌʃə]	Russland
to **attend sth** [ə'tend]	etw *(Veranstaltung, Schule usw.)* besuchen, an etw teilnehmen
healthy ['helθi]	gesund
professional [prə'feʃənl]	professionell
both … and [bəʊθ ənd]	sowohl … als auch
well-qualified [ˌwel 'kwɒlɪfaɪd]	gut ausgebildet
highly ['haɪli]	sehr, in hohem Maß
to **be highly respected** [bi ˌhaɪli rɪ'spektɪd]	großes Ansehen genießen, hoch angesehen sein
demanding [dɪ'mɑːndɪŋ]	anspruchsvoll
pretty ['prɪti]	ziemlich
formal ['fɔːml]	formell
to **look after sb/sth** ['lʊk ɑːftə]	sich um jdn/etw kümmern
well-being ['wel biːɪŋ]	Wohl, Wohlbefinden, Gesundheit
(job) vacancy ['veɪkənsi]	freie/offene Stelle
challenge ['tʃælɪndʒ]	Herausforderung, (schwierige) Aufgabe
serious ['sɪəriəs]	ernst, ernsthaft
though [ðəʊ]	aber, jedoch, allerdings, doch

page 11

qualified ['kwɒlɪfaɪd]	ausgebildet, qualifiziert, examiniert
degree programme [dɪ'griː prəʊgræm]	Studiengang
sb lacks sth [læks]	jdm fehlt etw
practice ['præktɪs]	Praxis
studies *pl* ['stʌdiz]	Studium
to **focus on sth** ['fəʊkəs ɒn]	sich auf etw konzentrieren, den Schwerpunkt auf etw legen
psychology [saɪ'kɒlədʒi]	Psychologie
theory ['θɪəri]	Theorie
level ['levl]	Niveau, Pegel
caseload ['keɪsləʊd]	Fallbelastung, Arbeitsbelastung
budget ['bʌdʒɪt]	Budget, Etat
mainly ['meɪnli]	hauptsächlich
to **prevent sth** [prɪ'vent]	etw verhindern, einer Sache vorbeugen
burnout ['bɜːnaʊt]	Ausgebranntsein, Burnout
balance ['bæləns]	Gleichgewicht, Ausgewogenheit
free [friː]	kostenlos
medical ['medɪkl]	ärztlich, medizinisch, Medizin-
check [tʃek]	(ärztliche) Untersuchung
feedback ['fiːdbæk]	Meinungen, Rückmeldung, Feedback
on a peer-group level [ɒn ə ˌpɪə gruːp 'levl]	unter Kollegen und Kolleginnen
challenging ['tʃælɪndʒɪŋ]	schwierig, anspruchsvoll, fordernd
line of work [ˌlaɪn əv 'wɜːk]	Beruf, Branche
victim ['vɪktɪm]	Opfer
poverty ['pɒvəti]	Armut
mental ['mentl]	psychisch, mental, geistig
illness ['ɪlnəs]	Krankheit, Erkrankung
to **protect sb/sth (from sth)** [prə'tekt]	jdn/etw (vor etw) schützen
to **be at risk** [bi ət 'rɪsk]	gefährdet sein
to **abuse sb/sth** [ə'bjuːz]	jdn/etw missbrauchen
to **exploit sb** [ɪk'splɔɪt]	jdn ausbeuten
adult ['ædʌlt]	Erwachsene/r; erwachsen
benefit ['benɪfɪt]	Nutzen, Vorteil
professional standards *pl* [prəˌfeʃənl 'stændədz]	berufliche Anforderungen, (einheitliche) Berufsnormen
academic standard [ækəˌdemɪk 'stændəd]	Ausbildungsniveau
probably ['prɒbəbli]	wahrscheinlich
that's why ['ðæts waɪ]	daher, deshalb
to **attract sb/sth** [ə'trækt]	jdn/etw anziehen, jdn/etw anlocken

similarity [ˌsɪməˈlærəti]	Ähnlichkeit, Übereinstimmung
comparison (to sth) [kəmˈpærɪsn]	Vergleich (mit etw)
compared to sb/sth [kəmˈpeəd tə]	im Vergleich zu jdm/etw, verglichen mit jdm/etw
similar (to sb/sth) [ˈsɪmələ]	(jdm/einer Sache) ähnlich
past [pɑːst]	Vergangenheit
view (on sth) [vjuː]	Ansicht (über etw), Meinung (zu etw)
in my view/opinion [ɪn ˈmaɪ vjuː/əpɪniən]	meiner Ansicht/Meinung nach
to **give a talk (on sth)** [gɪv ə ˈtɔːk]	einen Vortrag (über etw / zum Thema …) halten
above [əˈbʌv]	oben
findings *pl* [ˈfaɪndɪŋz]	Ergebnis(se)
guidance [ˈgaɪdəns]	Orientierung, Hilfe
to **turn to page X** [ˌtɜːn tə ˈpeɪdʒ]	Seite X aufschlagen
overview [ˈəʊvəvjuː]	Überblick
to **be based on sth** [bi ˈbeɪst ɒn]	auf etw basieren, sich auf etw stützen
to **face sth** [feɪs]	mit etw konfrontiert sein/werden, einer Sache gegenüberstehen
to **sum up** [tə ˌsʌm ˈʌp]	zusammenfassend

page 12

to **make sth** [meɪk]	etw ausmachen
to **belong** [bɪˈlɒŋ]	gehören
advice [ədˈvaɪs]	Ratschläge, (guter) Rat, Beratung
paragraph [ˈpærəgrɑːf]	*(Text:)* Absatz
education [ˌedʒuˈkeɪʃn]	Bildung, Schulbildung
personal details *pl* [ˌpɜːsənl ˈdiːteɪlz]	persönliche Angaben, Angaben zur Person
reference [ˈrefrəns]	Referenz
profile [ˈprəʊfaɪl]	Porträt, Profil
summary [ˈsʌməri]	Zusammenfassung
ability [əˈbɪləti]	Fähigkeit
qualification [ˌkwɒlɪfɪˈkeɪʃn]	Qualifikation, Abschluss, Ausbildung
set [set]	fest, festgelegt, starr
to **vary** [ˈveəri]	sich unterscheiden, variieren
specific [spəˈsɪfɪk]	bestimmt, speziell
rule [ruːl]	Regel, Vorschrift
structure [ˈstrʌktʃə]	Aufbau, Konstruktion, Struktur
layout [ˈleɪaʊt]	Gestaltung, Aufmachung, Layout
honest(ly) [ˈɒnɪst]	ehrlich, aufrichtig
factual [ˈfæktʃuəl]	auf Tatsachen beruhend
to **make sure** [ˌmeɪk ˈʃʊə]	dafür sorgen(, dass …); sicherstellen(, dass …)
to **include sth** [ɪnˈkluːd]	etw einbeziehen, etw aufnehmen
however [haʊˈevə]	allerdings, aber, doch, jedoch
to **be common practice** [bi ˌkɒmən ˈpræktɪs]	allgemein üblich sein
to **outline sth** [ˈaʊtlaɪn]	etw umreißen, etw skizzieren
relevant (to sth) [ˈreləvənt]	wichtig, nötig, relevant (für etw)
to **grab sb's attention** [ˌgræb əˈtenʃn]	jds Aufmerksamkeit fesseln
reader [ˈriːdə]	Leser/in
reverse [rɪˈvɜːs]	umgekehrt
chronological [ˌkrɒnəˈlɒdʒɪkl]	chronologisch
order [ˈɔːdə]	Reihenfolge
most recent [ˌməʊst ˈriːsnt]	jüngste/r/s, neueste/r/s
employment [ɪmˈplɔɪmənt]	Beschäftigung, Anstellung
job title [ˈdʒɒb taɪtl]	Stellenbezeichnung
achievement [əˈtʃiːvmənt]	Leistung, Errungenschaft, Erfolg
brief(ly) [briːf]	knapp, kurz
educational institution [edʒuˌkeɪʃənl ɪnstɪˈtjuːʃn]	Bildungseinrichtung
e.g. [ˌiː ˈdʒiː]	z. B.
to **be equivalent to sth** [bi ɪˈkwɪvələnt tə]	einer Sache entsprechen
vocational college [vəʊˌkeɪʃənl ˈkɒlɪdʒ]	Fachoberschule
energetic [ˌenəˈdʒetɪk]	dynamisch, tatkräftig
section [ˈsekʃn]	Teil, Abschnitt
optional [ˈɒpʃənl]	fakultativ
to **consider sth** [kənˈsɪdə]	etw betrachten, über etw nachdenken
future [ˈfjuːtʃə]	künftig
personality [pɜːsəˈnæləti]	Persönlichkeit
voluntary [ˈvɒləntri]	ehrenamtlich, freiwillig
charity [ˈtʃærəti]	Hilfsorganisation
to **be careful** [bi ˈkeəfl]	aufpassen, vorsichtig sein
contact details *pl* [ˈkɒntækt diːteɪlz]	Kontaktdaten
data protection [ˈdeɪtə prətekʃn]	Datenschutz
law [lɔː]	Gesetz
instead [ɪnˈsted]	stattdessen
on request [ɒn rɪˈkwest]	auf Anfrage
permission [pəˈmɪʃn]	Erlaubnis, Genehmigung

page 13

reason [ˈriːzn]	Grund, Anlass
especially [ɪˈspeʃəli]	besonders
helpful [ˈhelpfl]	nützlich
to **guide sb** [gaɪd]	jdn führen, jdn leiten
careful(ly) [ˈkeəfl]	aufmerksam, sorgfältig, gewissenhaft
beside [bɪˈsaɪd]	neben
to **prepare sth** [prɪˈpeə]	etw erstellen, etw vorbereiten
to **seek sth** [siːk]	etw suchen
fluent [ˈfluːənt]	*(Sprache:)* fließend
main subject [ˌmeɪn ˈsʌbdʒɪkt]	Hauptfach
temporary [ˈtemprəri]	befristet
primary school [ˈpraɪməri skuːl]	Grundschule

visiting professor [ˌvɪzɪtɪŋ prəˈfesə]	Gastprofessor/in
health studies *pl* [ˈhelθ stʌdɪz]	Gesundheitswissenschaften (mit Pflege)
social studies *pl* [ˌsəʊʃl ˈstʌdiz]	Sozial- und Erziehungswissenschaften
home economics [ˌhəʊm iːkəˈnɒmɪks]	Hauswirtschaftslehre
secondary school [ˈsekəndri skuːl]	weiterführende Schule
grade [greɪd]	Note
native speaker [ˌneɪtɪv ˈspiːkə]	Muttersprachler/in
independent(ly) [ˌɪndɪˈpendənt]	selbstständig, unabhängig
oral [ˈɔːrəl]	mündlich
written [ˈrɪtn]	schriftlich
Polish [ˈpɒlɪʃ]	Polnisch
conversational [ˌkɒnvəˈseɪʃənl]	Konversations-, Umgangs-
first aid [ˌfɜːst ˈeɪd]	Erste Hilfe
refugee [ˌrefjuˈdʒiː]	Flüchtling, Geflüchtete/r
referee [ˌrefəˈriː]	Referenzgeber/in
appropriate(ly) [əˈprəʊpriət]	angemessen, passend

page 14

to **analyse sth** [ˈænəlaɪz]	etw analysieren
to **consider sb/sth** [kənˈsɪdə]	jdn/etw in Betracht ziehen
to **refer to sth** [rɪˈfɜː tə]	sich auf etw beziehen, auf etw verweisen
to **state sth** [steɪt]	etw angeben, etw sagen, etw feststellen
contact [ˈkɒntækt]	Ansprechpartner/in
Dear Sir or Madam [dɪə ˌsɜːr ɔː ˈmædəm]	*(Brief, E-Mail:)* Sehr geehrte Damen und Herren
capital letter [ˌkæpɪtl ˈletə]	Großbuchstabe
closing sentence [ˌkləʊzɪŋ ˈsentəns]	Schlusssatz
Yours sincerely [ˌjɔːz sɪnˈsɪəli]	*(Brief, E-Mail:)* Mit freundlichen Grüßen
Yours faithfully [jɔːz ˈfeɪθfəli]	*(Brief, E-Mail:)* Mit freundlichen Grüßen
Attn (= for the attention of) [əˈtenʃn]	*(Brief:)* z. Hd. (= zu Händen von)
with reference to [wɪð ˈrefrəns tə]	bezugnehmend auf, bezüglich
to **develop** [dɪˈveləp]	(sich) entwickeln
professional(ly) [prəˈfeʃənl]	beruflich
particularly [pəˈtɪkjələli]	insbesondere, besonders
to **be keen to do sth** [bɪ ˈkiːn tə]	etw (unbedingt) tun wollen, sehr an etw interessiert sein
to **apply sth** [əˈplaɪ]	etw anwenden
knowledge [ˈnɒlɪdʒ]	Wissen, Kenntnisse
on a daily basis [ɒn ə ˌdeɪli ˈbeɪsɪs]	jeden Tag, tagtäglich
sb enjoys sth [ɪnˈdʒɔɪz]	jdm gefällt etw, jdm macht etw Spaß
to **fit in with sth** [ˌfɪt ˈɪn wɪð]	sich in etw einfügen
to **be an asset to sth** [bi ən ˈæset tə]	eine Bereicherung für etw sein
excellent [ˈeksələnt]	ausgezeichnet, hervorragend
to **consider sth** [kənˈsɪdə]	sich mit etw befassen, etw prüfen
to **grant sb sth** [grɑːnt]	jdm etw gewähren
to **look forward to sth** [ˌlʊk ˈfɔːwəd tə]	sich auf etw freuen
Enc (= enclosure[s]) [ɪnˈkləʊʒə]	*(Brief:)* Anlage(n)

page 15

creative [kriˈeɪtɪv]	kreativ
effective(ly) [ɪˈfektɪv]	wirkungsvoll, effektiv
excited [ɪkˈsaɪtɪd]	begeistert, gespannt, aufgeregt
regarding [rɪˈgɑːdɪŋ]	hinsichtlich, betreffend, bezüglich
to **take the opportunity** [ˌteɪk ði ɒpəˈtjuːnəti]	die Gelegenheit ergreifen
to **take sb on** [ˌteɪk ˈɒn]	jdn einstellen
to **benefit sb** [ˈbenɪfɪt]	jdm nutzen, für jdm von Nutzen sein
field [fiːld]	Bereich, Gebiet
listener [ˈlɪsnə]	Zuhörer/in
gym [dʒɪm]	Fitnessstudio
element [ˈelɪmənt]	Bestandteil, Element
body language [ˈbɒdi læŋgwɪdʒ]	Körpersprache
visual [ˈvɪʒuəl]	visuell, optisch
to **improve sth** [ɪmˈpruːv]	etw verbessern
content [ˈkɒntent]	Inhalt(e), Content
delivery [dɪˈlɪvəri]	Vortragsweise
performance [pəˈfɔːməns]	Darbietung

page 16

step [step]	Schritt, Stufe
process [ˈprəʊses]	Verfahren, Ablauf, Prozess
mediation [ˌmiːdiˈeɪʃn]	Vermittlung, Mediation, Moderation
No sweat! [ˌnəʊ ˈswet]	Kein Ding! Kein Problem!
scary [ˈskeəri]	furchteinflößend
interviewer [ˈɪntəvjuːə]	*jd, der ein Vorstellungsgespräch führt*
meaningful [ˈmiːnɪŋfl]	wichtig, bedeutsam
face-to-face [ˌfeɪs tə ˈfeɪs]	persönlich, direkt, unter vier Augen
to **dress** [dres]	sich kleiden
even though [ˈiːvn ðəʊ]	obwohl
confident(ly) [ˈkɒnfɪdənt]	selbstsicher, selbstbewusst
impression [ɪmˈpreʃn]	Eindruck
likely [ˈlaɪkli]	wahrscheinlich, aussichtsreich
strength [streŋθ]	Stärke
weakness [ˈwiːknəs]	Schwäche
to **be aware of sth** [bi əˈweər əv]	sich einer Sache bewusst sein, etw wissen
to **work on sth** [ˈwɜːk ɒn]	sich mit etw befassen, sich mit etw auseinandersetzen
investment [ɪnˈvestmənt]	Investition

research [rɪˈsɜːtʃ]	Recherche(n), Nachforschungen
prepared [prɪˈpeəd]	vorbereitet, gerüstet
to **have sth ready** [həv ˈredi]	etw bereithalten
copy [ˈkɒpi]	Exemplar, Kopie
job description [ˈdʒɒb dɪskrɪpʃn]	Stellenbeschreibung, Tätigkeitsbeschreibung
notepad [ˈnəʊtpæd]	Notizblock
to **remind sb to do sth** [rɪˈmaɪnd]	jdn daran erinnern, etw zu tun
Practice makes perfect. [ˌpræktɪs meɪks ˈpɜːfɪkt]	Übung macht den Meister.

page 17

to **arrange sth** [əˈreɪndʒ]	etw *(Termin usw.)* ausmachen
You're welcome. [jɔː ˈwelkəm]	Bitte (sehr). Gern geschehen.
Go ahead. [ˌgəʊ əˈhed]	Legen Sie los!
to **set sth up** [ˌset ˈʌp]	etw gründen, etw einrichten
food bank [ˈfuːd bæŋk]	Tafel
I see. [aɪ ˈsiː]	Verstehe. Aha.
to **make sb do sth** [ˌmeɪk ˈduː]	jdn (dazu) veranlassen, etw zu tun
to **match sth** [mætʃ]	zu etw passen, einer Sache entsprechen
necessary [ˈnesəsəri]	nötig, notwendig
training [ˈtreɪnɪŋ]	Schulung
to **operate** [ˈɒpəreɪt]	geschäftlich tätig sein, operieren
normally [ˈnɔːməli]	normalerweise
to **be/get in touch** [bi/get ɪn ˈtʌtʃ]	sich (bei jdm) melden
background [ˈbækgraʊnd]	Werdegang, Herkunft, Hintergrund
flow chart [ˈfləʊ tʃɑːt]	Flussdiagramm
to **greet sb** [griːt]	jdn begrüßen
to **answer the phone** [ˌɑːnsə ðə ˈfəʊn]	ans Telefon gehen
to **be happy to do sth** [bi ˈhæpi tə duː]	etw gern tun
to **respond to sth** [rɪˈspɒnd tə]	auf etw reagieren, auf etw antworten
reply (to sth) [rɪˈplaɪ]	Antwort (auf etw)
... speaking. [ˈspiːkɪŋ]	*(Telefon:)* Sie sprechen mit ..., ... am Apparat
to **catch sth** [kætʃ]	etw verstehen, etw mitbekommen
You're breaking up. [jɔː ˌbreɪkɪŋ ˈʌp]	Das Signal ist schlecht.

page 18

in person [ɪn ˈpɜːsn]	persönlich, unter vier Augen
conference call [ˈkɒnfərəns kɔːl]	Video-/Telefonkonferenz
to **get sth right** [ˌget ˈraɪt]	etw (gut) hinbekommen, etw richtig machen
to **prepare for sth** [prɪˈpeə fə]	sich auf etw vorbereiten
Absolutely. [ˈæbsəluːtli]	Stimmt. Da haben Sie völlig recht. Natürlich!
comprehensive school [kɒmprɪˈhensɪv skuːl]	Gesamtschule
GCSEs *pl* [ˌdʒiː siː es ˈiːz]	Mittlere Reife
punctual [ˈpʌŋktʃuəl]	pünktlich
obviously [ˈɒbviəsli]	offenbar, natürlich
quite [kwaɪt]	ziemlich
anyway [ˈeniweɪ]	jedenfalls, wie dem auch sei
I suppose ... [aɪ səˈpəʊz]	wohl, vermutlich
to **volunteer** [ˌvɒlənˈtɪə]	ehrenamtlich tätig sein, (freiwillig) arbeiten/helfen
Red Cross [ˌred ˈkrɒs]	Rotes Kreuz
seriously [ˈsɪəriəsli]	ernsthaft, im Ernst
to **react to sth** [riˈækt tə]	auf etw reagieren
criticism [ˈkrɪtɪsɪzəm]	Kritik
shift [ʃɪft]	Schicht
to **contact sb** [ˈkɒntækt]	sich mit jdm in Verbindung setzen, sich bei jdm melden
nightmare [ˈnaɪtmeə]	Albtraum
alarm [əˈlɑːm]	Wecker
to **get a move on** [get ə ˈmuːv ɒn]	sich beeilen
to **take a seat** [ˌteɪk ə ˈsiːt]	Platz nehmen
on time [ɒn ˈtaɪm]	pünktlich
to **avoid sth** [əˈvɔɪd]	etw vermeiden
to **push oneself to do sth** [ˌpʊʃ wʌnself tə ˈduː]	sich dazu zwingen, etw zu tun
mate *BE* [meɪt]	Kumpel
brilliant [ˈbrɪliənt]	genial, super, toll
to **be glad** [bi ˈglæd]	sich freuen, froh sein
individual(ly) [ˌɪndɪˈvɪdʒʊəli]	einzeln, individuell

page 19

required [rɪˈkwaɪəd]	erforderlich, nötig
member [ˈmembə]	Mitglied, Angehörige/r *(einer Gruppe)*
observer [əbˈzɜːvə]	Beobachter/in
Pleased/Nice to meet you. [ˌpliːzd/ˌnʌɪs tə ˈmiːt ju]	Schön, dich/Sie/euch kennenzulernen.
follow-up question [ˌfɒləʊ ʌp ˈkwestʃən]	Anschlußfrage
goal [gəʊl]	Ziel
to **achieve sth** [əˈtʃiːv]	etw erreichen, etw erzielen
polite(ly) [pəˈlaɪt]	höflich
within [wɪˈðɪn]	innerhalb (von), binnen
appearance [əˈpɪərəns]	Erscheinung(sbild), Aussehen
confidence [ˈkɒnfɪdəns]	Selbstsicherheit, Selbstbewusstsein
to **perform** [pəˈfɔːm]	(leistungsmäßig) abschneiden, gut/schlecht sein

page 20

elderly people [ˌeldəli ˈpiːpl]	ältere Menschen, Senioren
response [rɪˈspɒns]	Reaktion, Antwort

to **convince sb of sth** [kənˈvɪns əv]	jdn von etw überzeugen
valuable [ˈvæljuəbl]	wertvoll
assistant nurse [əˌsɪstənt ˈnɜːs]	Schwesternhelferin, Pflegediensthelfer/in

page 21

preparation [ˌprepəˈreɪʃn]	Vorbereitung
whether [ˈweðə]	ob
key (to sth) [kiː]	Schlüssel (zu etw)
to **check sth out** [ˌtʃek ˈaʊt]	sich etw genauer ansehen
absolutely [ˈæbsəluːtli]	völlig, unbedingt
technology [tekˈnɒlədʒi]	Technik
to **improve** [ɪmˈpruːv]	sich verbessern, besser werden
extract [ˈekstrækt]	Auszug, Ausschnitt
to **attach sth** [əˈtætʃ]	*(Brief:)* etw beifügen, *(E-Mail:)* etw anhängen
to **involve sth** [ɪnˈvɒlv]	etw umfassen, etw einbeziehen
nursery [ˈnɜːsəri]	Kita, Kindergarten
insurance [ɪnˈʃʊərəns]	Versicherung
to **receive sth** [rɪˈsiːv]	etw erhalten, etw bekommen
details *pl* [ˈdiːteɪlz]	Einzelheiten, (genauere) Angaben
to **add value to sth** [ˌæd ˈvæljuː tə]	eine Bereicherung für etw sein

page 22

request (for sth) [rɪˈkwest]	Bitte (um etw), Wunsch (nach etw)
to **proofread sth** [ˈpruːfriːd]	etw Korrektur lesen
role [rəʊl]	Funktion, Stellung
open day [ˈəʊpən deɪ]	Tag der offenen Tür
to **deal with sb/sth** [ˈdiːl wɪð]	mit jdm/etw zu tun haben, sich um jdn/etw kümmern
appointment [əˈpɔɪntmənt]	Termin
doctor [ˈdɒktə]	Arzt/Ärztin
to **observe** [əbˈzɜːv]	beobachten
strong [strɒŋ]	gut, stark
general [ˈdʒenrəl]	allgemein
to **introduce sb to sb** [ˌɪntrəˈdjuːs]	jdn jdm vorstellen
viewer [ˈvjuːə]	Zuschauer/in

page 23

script [ˈskrɪpt]	Manuskript, Drehbuch
to **notice sth** [ˈnəʊtɪs]	etw bemerken
to **maintain sth** [meɪnˈteɪn]	etw aufrechterhalten
eye contact [ˈaɪ kɒntækt]	Blickkontakt
relaxed [rɪˈlækst]	locker, entspannt
untidy [ʌnˈtaɪdi]	unordentlich, unaufgeräumt
unclean [ˌʌnˈkliːn]	schmutzig
background noise [ˌbækgraʊnd ˈnɔɪz]	Hintergrundgeräusche
pet [pet]	Haustier
to **enter sth** [ˈentə]	etw betreten
constructive [kənˈstrʌktɪv]	konstruktiv
to **do a good/great job** [duː ə ˌgʊd/ˌgreɪt ˈdʒɒb]	etw gut/super machen
to **suggest sth** [səˈdʒest]	etw vorschlagen
progress [ˈprəʊgres]	Verlauf, Fortgang
to **browse** [braʊz]	stöbern, blättern
paperwork [ˈpeɪpəwɜːk]	Formulare, Unterlagen
simulated [ˈsɪmjuleɪtɪd]	gespielt, simuliert
to **formulate sth** [ˈfɔːmjuleɪt]	etw formulieren

page 24

to **gather sth** [ˈgæðə]	etw sammeln, etw einsammeln
the following [ˈðə ˈfɒləʊɪŋ]	Folgendes
benefits *pl* [ˈbenɪfɪts]	Zusatzleistungen
career development opportunities *pl* [kəˌrɪə dɪveləpmənt ɒpəˈtjuːnətiz]	berufliche Entwicklungsmöglichkeiten
length [leŋθ]	Länge
gap [gæp]	Lücke
to **match** [mætʃ]	zueinanderpassen, übereinstimmen
spelling [ˈspelɪŋ]	Rechtschreibung
in response to [ɪn rɪˈspɒns tə]	als Antwort auf
job listing [ˈdʒɒb lɪstɪŋ]	Stellenanzeige
to **train to be sth** [ˈtreɪn tə bi]	eine Ausbildung zu etw machen
to **further sth** [ˈfɜːðə]	etw fördern, etw voranbringen
to **extend sth** [ɪkˈstend]	etw ausweiten, etw erweitern

page 25

remote(ly) [rɪˈməʊt]	von zu Hause, nicht vor Ort
equipment [ɪˈkwɪpmənt]	Ausrüstung, Ausstattung, Geräte
nervousness [ˈnɜːvəsnəs]	Aufregung, Lampenfieber
to **handle sth** [ˈhændl]	etw bewältigen, etw erledigen
to **communicate** [kəˈmjuːnɪkeɪt]	sich verständigen, kommunizieren

TOPIC 2

page 26/27

workplace [ˈwɜːkpleɪs]	Arbeitsplatz, Arbeitsstätte
to **reach out to sb** [ˌriːtʃ ˈaʊt tə]	jdn zu erreichen versuchen, sich an jdn wenden
to **be in trouble** [bi ɪn ˈtrʌbl]	in Schwierigkeiten sein
the homeless [ˈhəʊmləs]	Obdachlose *pl*
strategy [ˈstrætədʒi]	Strategie
special needs *pl* [ˌspeʃl ˈniːdz]	Förderbedarf, Behinderung
inclusion [ɪnˈkluːʒn]	Integration, Inklusion
equal opportunities *pl* [ˌiːkwəl ɒpəˈtjuːnətiz]	Gleichstellung, Gleichbehandlung, Chancengleichheit
event [ɪˈvent]	Veranstaltung

figure [ˈfɪgəz]	Zahl
inclusive [ɪnˈkluːsɪv]	inklusiv, integrativ, ganzheitlich
in need [ɪn ˈniːd]	bedürftig
non-profit [ˌnɒnˈprɒfɪt]	gemeinnützig
guess [ges]	Vermutung
to **take a guess** [ˌteɪk ə ˈges]	raten, eine Vermutung anstellen
severe(ly) [sɪˈvɪə]	*(Krankheit usw.:)* schwer, stark, heftig
to **integrate sb in sth** [ˈɪntɪgreɪt]	jdn in etw eingliedern, jdn in etw integrieren
labour market [ˈleɪbə mɑːkɪt]	Arbeitsmarkt
context [ˈkɒntekst]	Zusammenhang, Kontext
outreach centre [ˈaʊtriːtʃ sentə]	Sozialzentrum, Begegnungsstätte, Bürgerbüro
care professional [ˈkeə prəfeʃənl]	Pflegefachkraft, Fachkraft im Sozial- und Gesundheitswesen
service [ˈsɜːvɪs]	Dienstleistung, Dienst, Hilfe, Service
family background [ˈfæməli bækgraʊnd]	Familienverhältnisse
homeless [ˈhəʊmləs]	obdachlos
to **run sth** [rʌn]	*(Firma usw.:)* etw führen, etw leiten, etw betreiben
fundraising [ˈfʌndreɪzɪŋ]	Einwerben von Spenden, Fundraising
purpose [ˈpɜːpəs]	Absicht, Ziel, Zweck
to **promote sth** [prəˈməʊt]	für etw werben, etw fördern
media attention [ˌmiːdiə əˈtenʃn]	Medieninteresse, Berichterstattung in den Medien
funding [ˈfʌndɪŋ]	(finanzielle) Mittel, Finanzierung
competition [ˌkɒmpəˈtɪʃn]	Wettbewerb, Wettkampf
to **get to know sb/sth** [get tə ˈnəʊ]	jdn/etw kennenlernen
workshop [ˈwɜːkʃɒp]	Kurs, Schulung, Workshop
statistics *pl* [stəˈtɪstɪks]	Statistik(en)
right (to sth) [ˈraɪt]	Recht (auf etw)
concerns *pl* [kənˈsɜːnz]	Anliegen *pl*, Belange

page 28

area [ˈeəriə]	Bereich, Gebiet
several [ˈsevrəl]	mehrere
magazine [ˌmægəˈziːn]	Zeitschrift
to **become (sth)** [bɪˈkʌm]	(zu etw / etw) werden
committed [kəˈmɪtɪd]	engagiert
to **be in demand** [bi ɪn dɪˈmɑːnd]	nachgefragt werden, gesucht werden
social support service [ˌsəʊʃl səˈpɔːt sɜːvɪs]	Sozialdienst, soziale Einrichtung
social care [ˌsəʊʃl ˈkeə]	Sozialhilfe, Sozialleistungen
to **range from … to …** [reɪndʒ frəm, tə]	von … bis … reichen, sich von … bis … erstrecken
demand (on sb/sth) [dɪˈmɑːnd]	Anforderung (an jdn/etw), Anspruch (an jdn/etw)
immense [ɪˈmens]	enorm, gewaltig
continually [kənˈtɪnjuəli]	ständig, fortwährend
to **draw** [drɔː]	zeichnen
child welfare [ˌtʃaɪld ˈwelfeə]	Kindeswohl, Kinder- und Jugendschutz
child welfare worker [ˌtʃaɪld ˈwelfeə wɜːkə]	Jugendamtsmitarbeiter/in, Kinderschutzfachkraft
community support worker [kəˌmjuːnəti səˈpɔːt wɜːkə]	Sozialarbeiter/in
day care centre [ˈdeɪ keə sentə]	Kita, Tagespflege
day care centre assistant [ˈdeɪ keə sentər əsɪstənt]	Kinderpfleger/in, Erzieher/in, Tagespflegehelfer/in
geriatric carer [dʒerɪˌætrɪk ˈkeərə]	Altenpfleger/in
nursery nurse [ˈnɜːsəri nɜːs]	Kinderpfleger/in
nursery school [ˈnɜːsəri skuːl]	Kindergarten, Kita
nursery school teacher [ˈnɜːsəri skuːl tiːtʃə]	Erzieher/in
occupational therapist [ˌɒkjuˌpeɪʃənl ˈθerəpɪst]	Ergotherapeut/in, Beschäftigungstherapeut/in
paediatric assistant [piːdiˌætrɪk əˈsɪstənt]	Pflegefachkraft mit Vertiefung Pädiatrie
physiotherapist [ˌfɪziəʊˈθerəpɪst]	Physiotherapeut/in
psychiatric assistant [piːdiˌætrɪk əˈsɪstənt]	medizinische/r Mitarbeiter/in, Assistent/in in der Psychiatrie
nurse [nɜːs]	Krankenpfleger/-schwester, Pfleger/in
social administrator [ˌsəʊʃl ədˈmɪnɪstreɪtə]	Sachbearbeiter/in, Beamte/r in der Sozialverwaltung
telephone counsellor [ˈtelɪfəʊn kaʊnsələ]	Telefonseelsorger/in
mental problems *pl* [ˈmentl prɒbləmz]	psychische Probleme
to **manage sth** [ˈmænɪdʒ]	etw verwalten, etw leiten, etw organisieren
to **assist sb (with sth)** [əˈsɪst]	jdm (bei etw) helfen, jdm (bei etw) zur Hand gehen
the elderly [ði ˈeldəli]	ältere Menschen, Senioren
needs *pl* [ˈniːdz]	Bedürfnisse
pregnant [ˈpregnənt]	schwanger
mobility problems *pl* [məʊˈbɪləti prɒbləmz]	Mobilitätseinschränkungen
regular(ly) [ˈregjələli]	regelmäßig
everyday [ˈevrideɪ]	Alltags-

page 29

sunflower [ˈsʌnflaʊə]	Sonnenblume
residence [ˈrezɪdəns]	Wohnstätte
adolescent psychiatry [ædəˌlesnt saɪˈkaɪətri]	Jugendpsychiatrie
National Health Service (NHS) [ˌnæʃnəl ˈhelθ sɜːvɪs]	*staatlicher Gesundheitsdienst in Großbritannien*
social education worker [ˌsəʊʃl edʒʊˈkeɪʃn wɜːkə]	Sozialpädagoge/-in
city council [ˈsɪti kaʊnsl]	Stadtverwaltung, Stadtrat

UNIT WORD LIST

eldest [ˈeldɪst]	älteste/r/s
original(ly) [əˈrɪdʒənəl]	ursprünglich
even if [ˈi:vn ɪf]	selbst wenn
calling [ˈkɔ:lɪŋ]	Berufung
client [ˈklaɪənt]	Kunde/Kundin, Klient/in
to **get dressed** [get ˈdrest]	sich anziehen
mealtime [ˈmi:ltaɪm]	Essenszeit, Mahlzeit
respect (for sb) [rɪˈspekt]	Achtung (vor jdm), Respekt (vor jdm)
patience [ˈpeɪʃns]	Geduld
worthwhile [ˌwɜ:θˈwaɪl]	lohnenswert, wertvoll, interessant
pragmatic [prægˈmætɪk]	pragmatisch
no matter [ˌnəʊ ˈmætə]	egal, ganz gleich, unabhängig davon
single parent [ˌsɪŋgl ˈpeərənt]	Alleinerziehende/r
day nursery [ˈdeɪ nɜ:səri]	Kita
sb realizes sth [ˈrɪəlaɪzɪz]	jdm wird/ist etw klar, jdm wird/ist etw bewusst
local authority [ˌləʊkl ɔ:ˈθɒrəti]	Kommune, Gemeinde(verwaltung)
preschool children *pl* [ˌpri:sku:l ˈtʃɪldrən]	Kinder im Vorschulalter
to **be attached to sth** [bi əˈtætʃt tə]	einer Sache angegliedert sein
apart from [əˈpɑ:t frəm]	abgesehen von, außer
to **supervise sb/sth** [ˈsu:pəvaɪz]	jdn/etw beaufsichtigen, jdn/etw betreuen
meal [mi:l]	Mahlzeit, Essen
rest time [ˈrest taɪm]	Ruhezeit, Pausenzeit
to **paint** [peɪnt]	malen
enthusiastic [ɪnˌθju:ziˈæstɪk]	begeisterungsfähig
easy-going [ˌi:zi ˈgəʊɪŋ]	locker, unkompliziert
strict(ly) [strɪkt]	streng, strikt
to **be fun** [bi ˈfʌn]	Spaß machen
to **take sth seriously** [teɪk ˈsɪəriəsli]	etw ernst nehmen
per cent [pə ˈsent]	Prozent
counsellor [ˈkaʊnsələ]	Therapeut/in, Berater/in
eating disorder [ˌi:tɪŋ dɪsˈɔ:də]	Essstörung
unit [ˈju:nɪt]	Spezialabteilung, Station *(im Krankenhaus usw.)*
psychiatric unit [saɪkiˌætrɪk ˈju:nɪt]	Psychiatrie, psychiatrische Abteilung
state-run [ˈsteɪtrʌn]	staatlich
basically [ˈbeɪsɪkli]	im Prinzip, grundsätzlich, eigentlich
to **structure sth** [ˈstrʌktʃə]	etw strukturieren, etw aufbauen
to **guide sb** [gaɪd]	jdn anleiten
sensitive (to sth**)** [ˈsensətɪv]	verständnisvoll, taktvoll, feinfühlig, sensibel (für/bezüglich etw)
point of view [ˌpɔɪnt əv ˈvju:]	Perspektive, Blickwinkel, Standpunkt
to **make a decision** [ˌmeɪk ə dɪˈsɪʒn]	eine Entscheidung treffen
to **stick to sth** [ˈstɪk tə]	sich an etw halten
at the end of the day [ət ði end əv ðə ˈdeɪ]	unterm Strich, im Endeffekt

to **reconstruct sth** [ˌri:kənˈstrʌkt]	etw rekonstruieren
to **work long hours** [wɜ:k ˌlɒŋ ˈaʊəz]	lange arbeiten, Überstunden machen
full-time [ˌfʊl ˈtaɪm]	Vollzeit(-)
introductions *pl* [ˌɪntrəˈdʌkʃnz]	Vorstellung, Bekanntmachen

page 30

senior [ˈsi:niə]	leitend, vorgesetzt
vision [ˈvɪʒn]	Vorstellung(en), Vision
to **study sth** [ˈstʌdi]	sich etw genau durchlesen/ansehen
to **predict sth** [prɪˈdɪkt]	etw voraussagen, etw vorhersagen
to **skim a text** [ˌskɪm ə ˈtekst]	einen Text überfliegen
to **cover sth** [ˈkʌvə]	etw *(Thema usw.)* behandeln, sich mit etw befassen
relationship [rɪˈleɪʃnʃɪp]	Beziehung
relationship support [rɪˈleɪʃnʃɪp səpɔ:t]	Partner- und Familienberatung
(married) couple [ˈkʌpl]	(Ehe-)Paar
thriving [ˈθraɪvɪŋ]	florierend, lebendig
society [səˈsaɪəti]	Gesellschaft
highly skilled [ˌhaɪli ˈskɪld]	hochqualifiziert
at times of crisis [ət ˌtaɪmz əf ˈkraɪsɪs]	in Krisen(zeiten)
impact [ˈɪmpækt]	Einfluss, Auswirkung(en), Folge(n)
stable [ˈsteɪbl]	stabil
to **get involved in sth** [ˌget ɪnˈvɒlvd ɪn]	sich in etw einbringen
mission [ˈmɪʃn]	Aufgabe, Auftrag, Ziel
to **work** [wɜ:k]	funktionieren
culturally sensitive [ˌkʌltʃərəli ˈsensətɪv]	kulturell angepasst, kultursensibel
caring [ˈkeərɪŋ]	fürsorglich, sozial
multicultural [ˌmʌltiˈkʌltʃərəl]	multikulturell
elderly care [ˌeldəli ˈkeə]	Seniorenbetreuung, Altenfürsorge
assistance [əˈsɪstəns]	Hilfe, Unterstützung
home support [ˌhəʊm səˈpɔ:t]	häusliche Unterstützung
to **undertake sth** [ˌʌndəˈteɪk]	etw übernehmen, etw durchführen
crisis management [ˌkraɪsɪs ˈmænɪdʒmənt]	Krisenmanagement
isolated [ˈaɪsəleɪtɪd]	alleinstehend, einsam
aim [eɪm]	Ziel
to **establish sth** [ɪˈstæblɪʃ]	etw schaffen, etw einrichten
minority [maɪˈnɒrəti]	Minderheit
ethnic [ˈeθnɪk]	ethnisch
personal care [ˌpɜ:sənl ˈkeə]	Körperpflege, Unterstützung der Selbstversorgung
domestic care [dəˌmestɪk ˈkeə]	häusliche Pflege
carer support [ˈkeərə səpɔ:t]	Unterstützung für pflegende Angehörige

crisis care [ˈkraɪsɪs keə]	Notfallpflege, Kurzzeitpflege
bureaucracy [bjʊəˈrɒkrəsi]	Bürokratie
facility [fəˈsɪləti]	Einrichtung
to **be aimed at sb** [bi ˈeɪmd ət]	sich an jdn richten
hand-picked [ˌhænd ˈpɪkt]	handverlesen
elder [ˈeldə]	Ältere/r
home carer [ˌhəʊm ˈkeərə]	häusliche/ambulante Pflegekraft

page 31

target group [ˈtɑːɡɪt ɡruːp]	Zielgruppe
evidence [ˈevɪdəns]	Indizien, Hinweise
competent [ˈkɒmpɪtənt]	kompetent
to **fund sth** [fʌnd]	etw finanzieren
gift of money [ˌɡɪft əv ˈmʌni]	Geldgeschenk
private individual [ˌpraɪvət ɪndɪˈvɪdʒuəl]	Privatperson
to **earn sth** [ɜːn]	etw verdienen
to **give advice** [ɡɪv ədˈvaɪs]	beraten, Rat erteilen
employee [ɪmˈplɔɪiː]	Angestellte/r, Beschäftigte/r, Mitarbeiter/in
to **respect sb** [rɪˈspekt]	jdn achten, jdn respektieren
each other [iːtʃ ˈʌðə]	einander, gegenseitig
effect [ɪˈfekt]	Auswirkung, Wirkung
to **aim to do sth** [eɪm]	etw tun wollen; sich vornehmen, etw zu tun
particular [pəˈtɪkjələ]	bestimmte/r/s, besondere/r/s, speziell
to **found sth** [faʊnd]	etw gründen
in order to [ɪn ˈɔːdə tə]	um … zu
main purpose [ˌmeɪn ˈpɜːpəs]	Hauptanliegen, Hauptziel
to **contrast sth** [kənˈtrɑːst]	etw (einander) gegenüberstellen, etw (miteinander) vergleichen
in contrast [ɪn ˈkɒntrɑːst]	im Gegensatz dazu
on the one hand [ɒn ðə ˈwʌn hænd]	einerseits
on the other hand [ɒn ði ˈʌðə hænd]	andererseits
to **serve sb** [sɜːv]	jdm dienen
support centre [səˈpɔːt sentə]	Hilfsstelle, Hilfszentrum

page 32

greeting(s) [ˈɡriːtɪŋ]	Begrüßung
conversation [ˌkɒnvəˈseɪʃn]	Gespräch, Unterhaltung
in a minute [ɪn ə ˈmɪnɪt]	gleich, sofort
actual(ly) [ˈæktʃuəl]	eigentlich
as a matter of fact [əz ə ˌmætər əv ˈfækt]	tatsächlich, sogar
excuse [ɪkˈskjuːs]	Ausrede
to **drive sb over** [ˌdraɪv ˈəʊvə]	jdm (mit dem Auto) fahren/bringen
accident [ˈæksɪdənt]	Unfall
motorway *BE* [ˈməʊtəweɪ]	Autobahn
to **be happy to do sth** [bi ˈhæpi tə duː]	sich freuen, etw zu tun
to **give sb a lift** [ˌɡɪv ə ˈlɪft]	jdm (mit dem Auto) fahren/bringen, jdm mitnehmen
satnav [ˈsætnæv]	Navi
latecomer [ˈleɪtkʌmə]	Nachzügler/in

page 33

community outreach worker [kəˌmjuːnəti ˈaʊtriːtʃ wɜːkə]	Sozialarbeiter/in für gesellschaftliche Randgruppen
tough [tʌf]	hart
outdoors [aʊtˈdɔːz]	draußen
conference [ˈkɒnfərəns]	Tagung, Konferenz
health education [ˈhelθ edʒukeɪʃn]	gesundheitliche Aufklärung
administrative [ədˈmɪnɪstrətɪv]	Verwaltungs-
paperwork [ˈpeɪpəwɜːk]	Schreibarbeit, Formalitäten
filing [ˈfaɪlɪŋ]	Ablage
office manager [ˌɒfɪs ˈmænɪdʒə]	Büroleiter/in
records *pl* [ˈrekɔːdz]	Datensätze, Unterlagen, Akten
to **compile sth** [kəmˈpaɪl]	etw erstellen, etw zusammenstellen
to **maintain sth** [meɪnˈteɪn]	etw *(Daten usw.)* pflegen, etw instandhalten
report (on sth) [rɪˈpɔːt]	Bericht (über etw), Protokoll
statistical [stəˈtɪstɪkl]	statistisch
information [ɪnfəˈmeɪʃn]	Daten, Angaben, Informationen
customer [ˈkʌstəmə]	Kunde/Kundin
counter [ˈkaʊntə]	Tresen, Schalter
education programme [ˌedʒuˈkeɪʃn prəʊɡræm]	Bildungsangebot, -programm
lifestyle [ˈlaɪfstaɪl]	Lebensweise
on assigned topics [ɒn əˌsaɪnd ˈtɒpɪks]	zu bestimmten Themen
to **imagine sth** [ɪˈmædʒɪn]	sich etw vorstellen
to **invent sth** [ɪnˈvent]	etw erfinden, sich etw ausdenken
therapist [ˈθerəpɪst]	Therapeut/in

page 34

participant [pɑːˈtɪsɪpənt]	Teilnehmer/in
percentage [pəˈsentɪdʒ]	Anteil, Prozentsatz
progress [ˈprəʊɡres]	Fortschritt(e)
anger management [ˈæŋɡə mænɪdʒmənt]	Agressionsbewältigung
self-harm [ˌself ˈhɑːm]	Selbstverletzung
abuse [əˈbjuːs]	Missbrauch, Gewalt, Beschimpfungen
offending [əˈfendɪŋ]	Begehen von Straftaten, Kriminalität
all over … [ɔːl ˈəʊvə]	in ganz …
sort [sɔːt]	Art
majority [məˈdʒɒrəti]	Mehrheit, Großteil
to **be in care** [bi ˌɪn ˈkeə]	betreut / in Pflegefamilien / im Heim wohnen
domestic abuse [dəˌmestɪk əˈbjuːs]	häusliche Gewalt
sexual abuse [ˌsekʃuəl əˈbjuːs]	sexueller Missbrauch

UNIT WORD LIST

to **drop out of sth** [ˌdrɒp ˈaʊt əv]	aus etw herausfallen
education system [ˌedʒuˈkeɪʃn sɪstəm]	Bildungssystem
as far as sb/sth is concerned [əz fɑːr əz ɪz kənˈsɜːnd]	was jdn/etw angeht
broad [brɔːd]	breit
range [reɪndʒ]	Spektrum, Angebot
to **meet sb's needs** [miːt ˈniːdz]	jds Bedürfnisse erfüllen, jds Bedürfnissen entsprechen
to **be sb's priority** [bi ˌsʌmbədiz praɪˈɒrəti]	für jdn an erster Stelle stehen
homelessness [ˈhəʊmləsnəs]	Obdachlosigkeit
to **be entitled to sth** [bi ɪnˈtaɪtld tə]	Anspruch auf etw haben, ein Recht auf etw haben
to **cause sth** [kɔːz]	etw verursachen
in the first place [ɪn ðə ˈfɜːst pleɪs]	eigentlich (erst)
for the same reason [fə ðə ˌseɪm ˈriːzn]	aus demselben Grund
to **throw sb out** [ˌθrəʊ ˈaʊt]	jdn hinauswerfen, jdn rauswerfen
behaviour [bɪˈheɪvjə]	Benehmen, Verhalten
to **cope with sth** [ˈkəʊp wɪð]	mit etw zurechtkommen, etw bewältigen
to **act** [ækt]	sich verhalten, sich benehmen
to **re-establish contact** [riːɪˌstæblɪʃ ˈkɒntækt]	den Kontakt wiederherstellen
focus of concern [ˌfəʊkəs əf kənˈsɜːn]	Aufmerksamkeitsschwerpunkt
life skills *pl* [ˈlaɪf skɪlz]	lebenspraktische Fertigkeiten, Lebenskompetenz
to **reunite sb with sb** [ˌriːjuːˈnaɪt wɪð]	jd mit jdm zusammenbringen/-führen
to **encourage sb** [ɪnˈkʌrɪdʒ]	jdn ermutigen, jdn ermuntern
to **motivate sb** [ˈməʊtɪveɪt]	jdn motivieren
to **take sth up** [ˌteɪk ˈʌp]	etw anfangen
proud (of sb/sth) [praʊd]	stolz (auf jdn/etw)
to **overcome sth** [ˌəʊvəˈkʌm]	etw überwinden, etw bewältigen
success rate [səkˈses reɪt]	Erfolgsquote
improvement [ɪmˈpruːvmənt]	Verbesserung
in terms of [ɪn ˈtɜːmz əv]	hinsichtlich
to **manage sth** [ˈmænɪdʒ]	etw steuern, etw beherrschen
anger [ˈæŋgə]	Ärger, Wut, Aggression
to **harm sb** [hɑːm]	jdn verletzen
cutting [ˈkʌtɪŋ]	Ritzen
burning [ˈbɜːnɪŋ]	Verbrennung
poisoning [ˈpɔɪzənɪŋ]	Vergiftung
substance abuse [ˈsʌbstəns əbjuːs]	Drogenmissbrauch
to **get to grips with** [get tu grɪps wɪð]	etw in den Griff bekommen
to **sort sth out** [ˌsɔːt ˈaʊt]	etw klären, etw regeln
criminal [ˈkrɪmɪnl]	kriminell
to **offend** [əˈfend]	straffällig werden
to **commit a crime** [kəˌmɪt ə ˈkraɪm]	eine Straftat begehen
to **agree** [əˈgriː]	zustimmen
It's me. [ɪts ˈmiː]	Ich bin's.
to **chuck sb out** [ˌtʃʌk ˈaʊt]	jdn rausschmeißen
to **drink heavily** [ˌdrɪŋk ˈhevɪli]	stark trinken
constant(ly) [ˈkɒnstənt]	ständig, andauernd
warning [ˈwɔːnɪŋ]	Verwarnung, Ermahnung
to **vandalize sth** [ˈvændəlaɪz]	etw mutwillig beschädigen
a couple of [ə ˈkʌpl əv]	ein paar
youth court [ˈjuːθ kɔːt]	Jugendgericht
stepdad [ˈstepdæd]	Stiefvater
to **experiment** [ɪkˈsperɪmənt]	experimentieren
to **go along with sb** [ˌgəʊ əˈlɒŋ wɪð]	mit jdm mitziehen/-machen
crowd [kraʊd]	Clique, (breite) Masse
to **go binge-drinking** [ˌgəʊ ˈbɪndʒ drɪŋkɪŋ]	auf Sauftour gehen
on weekdays [ˌɒn ˈwiːkdeɪz]	werktags, unter der Woche
to **fail** [feɪl]	durchfallen
instead of [ɪnˈsted əv]	anstatt
to **go off the rails** [gəʊ ˌɒf ðə ˈreɪlz]	auf die schiefe Bahn geraten
result [rɪˈzʌlt]	Ergebnis, Resultat
either ... or [ˌaɪðə ˈɔː]	entweder ... oder
with a hangover [wɪð ə ˈhæŋgəʊvə]	verkatert
to **hang out** [ˌhæŋ ˈaʊt]	abhängen, rumhängen
alcohol-dependent [ˈælkəhɒl dɪpendənt]	alkoholabhängig
to **sleep rough** [ˌsliːp ˈrʌf]	auf der Straße schlafen
to **end up somewhere** [ˌend ˈʌp]	irgendwo landen
to **put sb in touch with sb** [ˌpʊt ɪn ˈtʌtʃ wɪð]	jdm einen Kontakt zu jdm vermitteln
sheltered accommodation [ˌʃeltəd əˌkɒməˈdeɪʃn]	betreutes Wohnen
one-to-one therapy [wʌn tə ˌwʌn ˈθerəpi]	Einzeltherapie
addiction [əˈdɪkʃn]	Sucht
mark [mɑːk]	Note
to **pass an exam** [ˌpɑːs ən ɪgˈzæm]	eine Prüfung bestehen
hairdresser [ˈheədresə]	Friseur/in
salon [ˈsælɒn]	(Kosmetik-, Friseur-)Salon
issue [ˈɪʃuː]	Problem, Streitpunkt, Frage
circumstances *pl* [ˈsɜːkəmstənsɪz]	Umstände
to **damage sth** [ˈdæmɪdʒ]	etw beschädigen, etw schädigen
on purpose [ɒn ˈpɜːpəs]	absichtlich, vorsätzlich
to **get rid of sb/sth** [get ˈrɪd əv]	jdn/etw loswerden
in a strange way [ɪn ə ˌstreɪndʒ ˈweɪ]	seltsam
to **spend** [spend]	*(Zeit:)* verbringen

to **destroy sth** [dɪˈstrɔɪ]	etw zerstören
property [ˈprɒpəti]	Eigentum, (Grund-)Besitz, Immobilie(n)
deliberately [dɪˈlɪbərətli]	absichtlich, vorsätzlich, mutwillig
uncomfortable [ʌnˈkʌmftəbl]	ungemützlich, unangenehm
unacceptable [ˌʌnəkˈseptəbl]	inakzeptabel

page 35

case file [keɪs]	Patientenakte, Vorgang
sex [seks]	Geschlecht
female [ˈfiːmeɪl]	weiblich
alcoholic [ˌælkəˈhɒlɪk]	alkoholsüchtig; Alkoholiker/in
to **die** [daɪ]	sterben
care home [ˈkeə həʊm]	Jugendheim, betreutes Wohnen
to **steal** [stiːl]	stehlen, rauben
prostitute [ˈprɒstɪtjuːt]	Prostituierte/r
to **pick sb up** [ˌpɪk ˈʌp]	jdn aufgreifen
to **put sb on probation** [ˌpʊt ɒn prəˈbeɪʃn]	jdn auf Bewährung verurteilen
judge [dʒʌdʒ]	Richter/in
via [ˈvaɪə]	über, mittels
shared flat *BE* [ˌʃeəd ˈflæt]	Wohngemeinschaft
chat [tʃæt]	Unterhaltung, Schwätzchen
male [meɪl]	männlich
illegal(ly) [ɪˈliːgl]	illegal
building site [ˈbɪldɪŋ saɪt]	Baustelle
wages *pl* [ˈweɪdʒɪz]	Lohn
rent [rent]	Miete
ill [ɪl]	krank
fight [faɪt]	Schlägerei, Prügelei
to **stab sb** [stæb]	auf jdn einstechen
nearly [ˈnɪəli]	fast, beinah
young offender institution [ˌjʌŋ əˌfendə ˌɪnstɪˈtjuːʃn]	Jugendstrafanstalt
council apartment [ˈkaʊnsl əpɑːtmənt]	Sozialwohnung
to **report to sb/sth** [rɪˈpɔːt tə]	sich bei jdm/etw melden
probation officer [prəˈbeɪʃn ɒfɪsə]	Bewährungshelfer/in
factory [ˈfæktəri]	Fabrik
mechatronics [mekəˈtrɒnɪks]	Mechatronik
locker [ˈlɒkə]	Schließfach, Spind
to **lighten the load for sb** [ˌlaɪtn ðə ˈləʊd fə]	jdn entlasten
to **own sth** [əʊn]	etw besitzen
to **fit** [fɪt]	passen
jumper *BE* [ˈdʒʌmpə]	Pullover
presentable [prɪˈzentəbl]	ansehnlich, vorzeigbar
to **be designed to do sth** [bi dɪˈzaɪnd tə]	dazu/dafür gedacht sein, etw zu tun
to **get sth back on track** [get ˌbæk ɒn ˈtræk]	etw wieder auf Kurs bringen
to **assign sth to sb** [əˈsaɪn tə]	jdm etw zuteilen, jdm etw zuweisen
a small measure [ə ˌsmɔːl ˈmeʒə]	ein geringes Maß
security [sɪˈkjʊərəti]	Sicherheit
uncertain [ʌnˈsɜːtn]	unsicher, ungewiss
solution (to sth) [səˈluːʃn]	Lösung (für etw)
belongings *pl* [bɪˈlɒŋɪŋz]	Habe, Hab und Gut
to **start from scratch** [stɑːt frəm ˈskrætʃ]	ganz von vorn / bei Null anfangen
local government [ˌləʊkl ˈgʌvənmənt]	Kommunalverwaltung
to **obtain sth** [əbˈteɪn]	etw erhalten, etw bekommen
treatment [ˈtriːtmənt]	Behandlung
state pension [ˌsteɪt ˈpenʃn]	staatliche Rente
housing [ˈhaʊzɪŋ]	Wohnungen, Unterkunft
in return [ɪn rɪˈtɜːn]	als Gegenleistung, im Gegenzug
to **stay in touch** [ˌsteɪ ɪn ˈtʌtʃ]	in Verbindung bleiben
scale [skeɪl]	Skala
to **adapt sth (to sb/sth)** [əˈdæpt]	etw (an jdn/etw) anpassen
to **be missing** [bi ˈmɪsɪŋ]	fehlen
lounge *BE* [laʊndʒ]	Wohnzimmer
cupboard [ˈkʌbəd]	Schrank
financial crisis [faɪˌnænʃl ˈkraɪsɪs]	Finanzkrise
to **hit sb/sth** [hɪt]	jdn etw treffen
stepping stones *pl* [ˈstepɪŋ stəʊnz]	Sprungbrett, (wichtige) Schritte
prospect (of sth) [ˈprɒspekt]	Aussicht (auf etw)
above all [əˌbʌv ˈɔːl]	vor allen Dingen
to **install sth** [ɪnˈstɔːl]	etw aufstellen, etw installieren
additional [əˈdɪʃənl]	zusätzlich
in so doing [ɪn ˌsəʊ ˈduːɪŋ]	auf diese Weise
to **open a door of opportunity for sb** [ˌəʊpən ə ˌdɔːr əv ɒpəˈtjuːnəti fə]	jdm eine (einmalige) Möglichkeit eröffnen
to **have sth in common** [həv ɪn ˈkɒmən]	etw gemeinsam haben
to **believe sth** [bɪˈliːv]	etw glauben, von etw überzeugt sein
in particular [ɪn pəˈtɪkjələ]	insbesondere, besonders
personal hygiene [ˌpɜːsənl ˈhaɪdʒiːn]	Körperpflege

page 36

insight [ˈɪnsaɪt]	Einblick
chart [tʃɑːt]	Diagramm, Grafik, Schaubild
to **persuade sb to do sth** [pəˈsweɪd]	jdn von etw überzeugen, etw zu tun; jdn dazu überreden, etw zu tun
trust [trʌst]	Vertrauen
dignity [ˈdɪgnəti]	Würde
to **define sth** [dɪˈfaɪn]	etw definieren
term [tɜːm]	Begriff
shelter [ˈʃeltə]	Unterkunft, Unterstand, Quartier
to **trust sb** [trʌst]	jdm vertrauen

to **live rough** [lɪv ˈrʌf]	auf der Straße leben
as a result [əz ə rɪˈzʌlt]	daher, infolgedessen
to **be unwilling to do sth** [bi ʌnˌwɪlɪŋ tə ˈduː]	nicht bereit sein, etw zu tun
in case [ɪn ˈkeɪs]	für den Fall, dass …
moreover [mɔːrˈəʊvə]	außerdem, darüber hinaus
to **be suspicious of sb** [bi səˈspɪʃəs əv]	jdm misstrauen
to **take sth** [teɪk]	etw benötigen, etw erfordern
persuasion [pəˈsweɪʒn]	gutes Zureden
to **force sth on sb** [fɔːs]	jdm etw aufzwingen
youth [juːθ]	Jugendliche/r
to **view sb as sth** [ˈvjuː əz]	jdn als etw betrachten
case number [ˈkeɪs nʌmbə]	Vorgangsnummer
to **deserve sth** [dɪˈzɜːv]	etw verdienen
to **retain sth** [rɪˈteɪn]	etw bewahren, etw behalten
thus [ðʌs]	folglich
privately [ˈpraɪvətli]	nicht öffentlich, diskret, vertraulich
qualified nurse [ˌkwɒlɪfaɪd ˈnɜːs]	examinierte/r Kranken-schwester/-pfleger
to **travel** [trævl]	fahren
medical problem [ˌmedɪkl ˈprɒbləm]	Gesundheitsproblem
to **examine sb/sth** [ɪɡˈzæmɪn]	jdn/etw untersuchen
in privacy [ɪn ˈprɪvəsi]	diskret, vertraulich
medication [ˌmedɪˈkeɪʃn]	Arzneimittel, Medikamente
to **be in the process of doing sth** [bi ɪn ðə ˈprəʊses əv]	dabei sein, etw zu tun
kit [kɪt]	Set
hygiene [ˈhaɪdʒiːn]	Hygiene
item [ˈaɪtəm]	Artikel, Ware
to **distribute sth (to sb)** [dɪˈstrɪbjuːt]	etw (an jdn) verteilen
to **stay** [steɪ]	bleiben
rehabilitation clinic [ˌriːəbɪlɪˈteɪʃn klɪnɪk]	Reha-Klinik
unfortunately [ʌnˈfɔːtʃənətli]	leider, unglücklicherweise
habit [ˈhæbɪt]	Gewohnheit
once [wʌns]	sobald
rehab [ˈriːhæb]	Reha, Entzug(skur)
to **tackle sth** [ˈtækl]	etw *(Problem usw.)* angehen, etw bekämpfen
to **make up one's mind** [ˌmeɪk ˈʌp wʌnz maɪnd]	sich entscheiden, sich entschließen

page 37

current(ly) [ˈkʌrənt]	aktuell
schedule [ˈʃedjuːl]	Zeitplan, Stundenplan, Dienstplan
case manager [ˈkeɪs mænɪdʒə]	Fallbearbeiter/in, Case Manager/in
case report [ˈkeɪs rɪpɔːt]	Fallbericht
prison [ˈprɪzn]	Gefängnis
to **be on duty** [bi ˌɒn ˈdjuːti]	Dienst haben, eingeteilt sein
on a regular basis [ɒn ə ˌregjələ ˈbeɪsɪs]	regelmäßig
therapy session [ˈθerəpi seʃn]	Therapiesitzung
working schedule [ˈwɜːkɪŋ ʃedjuːl]	Dienstplan, Arbeitsplan
update [ˈʌpdeɪt]	Aktualisierung
to **make sth up** [ˌmeɪk ˈʌp]	sich etw ausdenken

page 38

drug-related [ˈdrʌg rɪleɪtɪd]	in Zusammenhang mit Drogen
stay [steɪ]	Aufenthalt
case worker [ˈkeɪs wɜːkə]	Sozialarbeiter/in
bar chart [ˈbɑː tʃɑːt]	Säulendiagramm
to **depict sth** [dɪˈpɪkt]	etw abbilden, etw darstellen
hospital admission [ˈhɒspɪtl ədmɪʃn]	Einlieferung/Einweisung ins Krankenhaus
in bold [ɪn ˈbəʊld]	in Fettdruck, fett gedruckt
trend [trend]	Tendenz, Trend
to **admit sb to hospital** [ədˈmɪt]	jdn ins Krankenhaus einliefern/einweisen
mental disorder [ˌmentl dɪsˈɔːdə]	psychische Erkrankung
behavioural disorder [bɪˌheɪvjərl dɪsˈɔːdə]	Verhaltensstörung
to **rise** [raɪz]	steigen, ansteigen
drastic(ally) [ˈdræstɪk]	drastisch
decrease (in sth) [ˈdiːkriːs]	Abnahme (von etw), Rückgang (von etw)
increase (in sth) [ˈɪŋkriːs]	Anstieg (von etw), Zunahme (von etw)
to **remain** [rɪˈmeɪn]	bleiben
level [ˈlevl]	Niveau, Stand
to **decrease** [dɪˈkriːs]	abnehmen, sinken
to **increase** [ɪnˈkriːs]	zunehmen, steigen
bar [bɑː]	Balken
to **represent sth** [ˌreprɪˈzent]	etw darstellen
misuse [mɪsˈjuːs]	Missbrauch
to **look at / study sth closely** [ˌlʊk ət / ˌstʌdi ˈkləʊsli]	sich etw näher/genau ansehen
to **peak** [piːk]	den Höchststand erreichen
total [ˈtəʊtl]	Gesamt-
slight(ly) [slaɪt]	leicht, geringfügig, ein wenig

page 39

drug policies *pl* [ˈdrʌg pɒləsiz]	Drogenpolitik
to **implement sth** [ˈɪmplɪmənt]	etw umsetzen
the Netherlands *pl* [ðə ˈneðələndz]	die Niederlande
consumption [kənˈsʌmpʃn]	Konsum
Dutch [dʌtʃ]	niederländisch
drug crime [ˈdrʌg kraɪm]	Drogenkriminalität
drug addict [ˈdrʌg ædɪkt]	Drogensüchtige/r, Drogenabhängige/r
across … [əˈkrɒs]	in ganz …
border [ˈbɔːdə]	Grenze
goods *pl* [gʊdz]	Waren
freely [ˈfriːli]	ungehindert, freizügig

to **be true for sb/sth** [bi ˈtruː fə]	auf etw zutreffen, für jdn/ etw gelten
common [ˈkɒmən]	gemeinsam
approach [əˈprəʊtʃ]	Herangehensweise, Ansatz
to **criminalize sb/sth** [ˈkrɪmɪnəlaɪz]	jdn/etw kriminalisieren
possession [pəˈzeʃn]	Besitz
distribution [ˌdɪstrɪˈbjuːʃn]	Vertrieb, Handel
to **decriminalize sth** [diːˈkrɪmɪnəlaɪz]	etw legalisieren
to **regard sth** [rɪˈɡɑːd]	etw betrachten
(criminal) offence [əˈfens]	Straftat
to **punish sb/sth** [ˈpʌnɪʃ]	jdn/etw bestrafen
public health [ˌpʌblɪk ˈhelθ]	Gesundheitswesen, Volksgesundheit
tolerance (of sth) [ˈtɒlərəns]	Duldung (von etw)
legal [ˈliːɡl]	legal
to **be the case** [bi ðə ˈkeɪs]	der Fall sein
policy [ˈpɒləsi]	Strategie, Vorgehen, Linie, Politik
substance [ˈsʌbstəns]	Droge
heroin [ˈherəʊɪn]	Heroin
cocaine [kəʊˈkeɪn]	Kokain
crime [kraɪm]	Verbrechen, Kriminalität
drug use [ˈdrʌɡ juːs]	Drogenkonsum
to **report sth** [rɪˈpɔːt]	etw melden, etw anzeigen
urgent(ly) [ˈɜːdʒənt]	dringend
offender [əˈfendə]	Straftäter/in
patient [ˈpeɪʃnt]	Patient/in
criminal [ˈkrɪmɪnl]	Verbrecher/in, Kriminelle/r
prevention [prɪˈvenʃn]	Prävention
massive [ˈmæsɪv]	groß, gewaltig, massiv
drug user [ˈdrʌɡ juːzə]	Drogenkonsument/in
restrictive [rɪˈstrɪktɪv]	restriktiv
zero tolerance [ˌzɪərəʊ ˈtɒlərəns]	null Toleranz
to **invest in sth** [ɪnˈvest]	in etw investieren
strict [strɪkt]	rigoros, strikt
law enforcement [ˌlɔː ɪnˈfɔːsmənt]	Rechtsdurchsetzung
to **praise sb/sth** [preɪz]	jdn/etw loben
hard-line [ˈhɑːd laɪn]	unnachgiebig, kompromisslos
considerably [kənˈsɪdərəbli]	beträchtlich, erheblich
death rate [ˈdeθ reɪt]	Zahl der Todesfälle
as a result of [əz ə rɪˈzʌlt əv]	als Folge von
overdose [ˈəʊvədəʊs]	Überdosis
to **rewrite sth** [ˌriːˈraɪt]	etw umformulieren, etw ändern
bracket [ˈbrækɪt]	Klammer
extra [ˈekstrə]	zusätzlich, Zusatz-
to **register sth** [ˈredʒɪstə]	etw registrieren
to **aim at sth** [ˈeɪm ət]	auf etw hinarbeiten
to **join sth** [dʒɔɪn]	etw verbinden, etw zusammenfügen
in place of [ɪn ˈpleɪs əv]	anstelle von
to **introduce sth** [ˌɪntrəˈdjuːs]	etw einführen
debate [dɪˈbeɪt]	Diskussion, Debatte
to **legalize sth** [ˈliːɡəlaɪz]	etw legalisieren
legalization [ˌliːɡəlaɪˈzeɪʃn]	Legalisierung

to **agree with sb** [əˈɡriː wɪð]	jdm zustimmen, der gleichen Meinung wie jd sein
to **disagree with sb** [ˌdɪsəˈɡriː wɪð]	jdm widersprechen, anderer Meinung als jd sein
to **interrupt sb/sth** [ˌɪntəˈrʌpt]	jdn/etw unterbrechen, jdm ins Wort fallen
to **be in favour of sth** [bi ɪn ˈfeɪvər əv]	etw befürworten, für etw sein

page 40

convention [kənˈvenʃn]	Konvention, Abkommen
principle [ˈprɪnsəpl]	Grundsatz, Prinzip
inherent [ɪnˈhɪərənt]	innewohnend, angeboren
autonomy [ɔːˈtɒnəmi]	Eigenständigkeit, Autonomie
freedom [ˈfriːdəm]	Freiheit
choice [tʃɔɪs]	Wahl, Entscheidung
independence [ˌɪndɪˈpendəns]	Unabhängigkeit, Selbständigkeit
non-discrimination [ˌnɒn dɪskrɪmɪˈneɪʃn]	Nichtdiskriminierung
participation [ˌpɑːtɪsɪˈpeɪʃn]	Teilhabe, Teilnahme
acceptance [əkˈseptəns]	Anerkennung, Akzeptanz
human [ˈhjuːmən]	menschlich
diversity [daɪˈvɜːsəti]	Vielfalt, Diversität
humanity [hjuːˈmænəti]	Menschheit
equality of opportunity [ɪˌkwɒləti əv ɒpəˈtjuːnəti]	Chancengleichheit
accessibility [əkˌsesəˈbɪləti]	Barrierefreiheit
equality [ɪˈkwɒləti]	Gleichheit, Gleichberechtigung, Gleichbehandlung
to **evolve** [ɪˈvɒlv]	sich entwickeln
capacity [kəˈpæsəti]	Fähigkeit
to **preserve sth** [prɪˈzɜːv]	etw bewahren, etw schützen
identity [aɪˈdentəti]	Identität
according to [əˈkɔːdɪŋ tə]	laut, gemäß, nach
latest [ˈleɪtɪst]	jüngste/r/s, aktuell
to **correspond to sth** [ˌkɒrɪˈspɒnd tə]	einer Sache entsprechen
population [ˌpɒpjuˈleɪʃn]	Bevölkerung
global(ly) [ˈɡləʊbl]	weltweit
significant(ly) [sɪɡˈnɪfɪkənt]	erheblich, bedeutend
employment age [ɪmˈplɔɪmənt eɪdʒ]	Erwerbsalter
to **be likely to do sth** [bi ˌlaɪkli tə ˈduː]	etw wahrscheinlich tun (werden)
unemployed [ˌʌnɪmˈplɔɪd]	arbeitslos
non-disabled [ˌnɒn dɪsˈeɪbld]	nichtbehindert
economic [iːkəˈnɒmɪk]	wirtschaftlich
cooperation [kəʊˌɒpəˈreɪʃn]	Zusammenarbeit
employment rate [ɪmˈplɔɪmənt reɪt]	Beschäftigungsquote, Erwerbsquote
despite [dɪˈspaɪt]	trotz
discrimination [dɪˌskrɪmɪˈneɪʃn]	Diskriminierung

page 41

topic [ˈtɒpɪk]	Thema
trisomy 21 [ˌtrɪsəmi ˌtwenti ˈwʌn]	Trisomie 21
Down's syndrome [ˌdaʊnz ˈsɪndrəʊm]	Down-Syndrom
mainstream [ˈmeɪnstriːm]	regulär
to **suffer** [ˈsʌfə]	leiden, Schaden nehmen
academic expectations *pl* [ækəˌdemɪk ekspekˈteɪʃnz]	schulische (Leistungs-) Erwartungen
differently abled [ˌdɪfrənt-li ˈeɪbld]	eingeschränkt, behindert
able [ˈeɪbl]	fähig, ohne Einschränkung, nichtbehindert
developmental [dɪˌveləpˈməntəl]	Entwicklungs-
bright [braɪt]	aufgeweckt, intelligent
to **agree with sth** [əˈgriː wɪð]	etw befürworten, etw *(Meinung usw.)* teilen
cerebral palsy [ˌserəbrəl ˈpɔːlzi]	Zerebralparese
to **grow up** [ˌgrəʊ ˈʌp]	aufwachsen
sleepover [ˈsliːpəʊvə]	Pyjamaparty
to **adapt to sb/sth** [əˈdæpt tə]	sich an jdn/etw anpassen, sich auf jdn/etw einstellen
specialist teacher [ˌspeʃəlɪst ˈtiːtʃə]	Fachlehrer/in
to **allocate sth to sb/sth** [ˈæləkeɪt]	etw jdm / einer Sache zuteilen
resources *pl* [rɪˈsɔːsɪz]	Mittel, Ressourcen
limited [ˈlɪmɪtɪd]	begrenzt, eingeschränkt
to **cater for sb/sth** [ˈkeɪtə fə]	sich um jdn/etw kümmern
convincing [kənˈvɪnsɪŋ]	überzeugend
all parties concerned [ɔːl ˌpɑːtiz kənˈsɜːnd]	alle Beteiligten, alle Betroffenen
hands-on [ˌhændz ˈɒn]	praktisch, manuell
sticky note [ˈstɪki nəʊt]	Haftnotiz, Klebezettel
to **justify sth** [ˈdʒʌstɪfaɪ]	etw begründen, etw rechtfertigen
to **illustrate sth** [ˈɪləstreɪt]	etw veranschaulichen, etw illustrieren

page 42

terminology [ˌtɜːmɪˈnɒlədʒi]	Begriffe, Terminologie
impaired [ɪmˈpeəd]	beeinträchtigt, behindert
common [ˈkɒmən]	üblich, häufig, verbreitet
rather [ˈrɑːðə]	eher, lieber
to **refer to sb/sth (as sth)** [rɪˈfɜː tə]	jdn/etw (als etw) bezeichnen
handicapped [ˈhændikæpt]	behindert, benachteiligt
meaning [ˈmiːnɪŋ]	Bedeutung
absence [ˈæbsəns]	Abwesenheit
race [reɪs]	Rasse
gender [ˈdʒendə]	Geschlecht
sexual orientation [ˌsekʃuəl ɔːriənˈteɪʃn]	sexuelle Orientierung
national origin [ˌnæʃnəl ˈɒrɪdʒɪn]	nationale Herkunft
expression [ɪkˈspreʃn]	Ausdruck
to **be widely used** [bi ˌwaɪdli ˈjuːzd]	weit verbreitet sein, häufig verwendet werden
visual/vision impairment [ˌvɪʒuəl ɪmˈpeəmənt / ˈvɪʒn ɪmpeəmənt]	Sehbehinderung, Sehschwäche
intellectual disability [ɪntəˌlektʃuəl ˌdɪsəˈbɪləti]	geistige Behinderung
to **characterize sth** [ˈkærəktəraɪz]	etw charakterisieren
mental capacity [ˌmentl kəˈpæsəti]	geistige Leistungsfähigkeit
social interaction [ˌsəʊʃl ɪntərˈækʃn]	Umgang mit anderen, soziale Interaktion
to **originate** [əˈrɪdʒɪneɪt]	entstehen
to **result from sth** [rɪˈzʌlt frəm]	auf etw zurückzuführen sein
cause (of sth) [kɔːz]	Ursache (für/von etw), Grund (für/von etw)
autism [ˈɔːtɪzm]	Autismus
lack (of sth) [læk]	Mangel (an etw)
stimulation [ˌstɪmjəˈleɪʃn]	Reiz(e), Anregung(en), Stimulation
responsiveness (towards sb) [rɪˈspɒnsɪvnəs]	(feinfühliges) Eingehen (auf jdn)
to **lead to sth** [ˈliːd tə]	zu etw führen
inability [ˌɪnəˈbɪləti]	Unfähigkeit, Unvermögen
injury [ˈɪndʒəri]	Verletzung
motor neuron disease [ˌməʊtə ˈnjʊərɒn dɪziːz]	Motoneuron-Krankheit
multiple sclerosis [ˌmʌltɪpl skləˈrəʊsɪs]	Multiple Sklerose
paraplegia [ˌpærəˈpliːdʒə]	Querschnittslähmung
quadriplegia [ˌkwɒdrɪˈpliːdʒə]	Tetraplegie
amputated [ˈæmpjuteɪtɪd]	amputiert, abgetrennt
limb [lɪm]	Gliedmaß, Extremität
total [ˈtəʊtl]	völlige/r/s, vollständig
deafness [ˈdefnəs]	Taubheit
blindness [ˈblaɪndnəs]	Blindheit
to **limit sth** [ˈlɪmɪt]	etw beschränken, etw einschränken
motor ability [ˈməʊtər əbɪləti]	motorische Fähigkeit
speech impairment [ˈspiːtʃ ɪmpeəmənt]	Sprachbehinderung, Sprechbehinderung
speech impediment [ˈspiːtʃ ɪmpedɪmənt]	Sprachfehler, Sprachbehin-derung
hearing impairment [ˈhɪərɪŋ ɪmpeəmənt]	Schwerhörigkeit, Hörbehinderung, Hörschaden
mild [maɪld]	*(Krankheit usw.:)* leicht
hearing loss [ˈhɪərɪŋ lɒs]	Hörverlust, Hörschädigung
to **be considered sth** [bi kənˈsɪdəd]	als etw gelten, als etw angesehen werden
invisible [ɪnˈvɪzəbl]	unsichtbar
chronic disorder [ˌkrɒnɪk dɪsˈɔːdə]	chronische Krankheit
diabetes [ˌdaɪəˈbiːtiːz]	Diabetes
asthma [ˈæsmə]	Asthma
chronic inflammatory bowel disease [ˌkrɒnɪk ɪnˌflæmətri ˈbaʊəl dɪziːz]	chronisch-entzündliche Darmerkrankung
epilepsy [ˈepɪlepsi]	Epilepsie

to **be counted as sth** [bi ˈkaʊntɪd əz]	zu etw gezählt werden
as opposed to [əz əˈpəʊzd tə]	im Gegensatz zu
visible [ˈvɪzəbl]	sichtbar, erkennbar
use [juːs]	Verwendung, Gebrauch, Nutzung
wheelchair [ˈwiːltʃeə]	Rollstuhl

page 43

long-lasting [ˌlɒŋ ˈlɑːstɪŋ]	langanhaltend, dauerhaft
to **cure sth** [sɪˈkjʊə]	etw heilen
to **point sth out** [ˌpɔɪnt ˈaʊt]	etw darlegen, auf etw hinweisen
to **what extent** [tu ˌwɒt ɪkˈstent]	inwieweit, inwiefern
to **enter the workplace** [ˌentə ðə ˈwɜːkpleɪs]	in die Arbeitswelt einsteigen
adviser [ədˈvaɪzə]	Berater/in
prejudice [ˈpredʒudɪs]	Vorurteil(e)
to **hire sb** [ˈhaɪə]	jdn einstellen
to **search for sth** [ˈsɜːtʃ fə]	etw suchen
to **fill sth in** [ˌfɪl ˈɪn]	etw *(Formular usw.)* ausfüllen
to **advise sb on sth** [ədˈvaɪz ɒn]	jdn in/zu etw beraten, jdm etw zeigen
questionnaire [ˌkwestʃəˈneə]	Fragebogen
to **go one step further** [gəʊ ˌwʌn step ˈfɜːðə]	einen Schritt weiter gehen
to **display sth** [dɪˈspleɪ]	etw zeigen
as long as [əz ˈlɒŋ əz]	solange
to **meet requirements** [miːt rɪˈkwaɪəmənts]	Anforderungen erfüllen
to **guarantee sb sth** [ˌgærənˈtiː]	jdm etw garantieren
to **be committed to doing sth** [bi kəˈmɪtɪd tə duːɪŋ]	fest vorhaben, etw zu tun
to **favour sb/sth** [ˈfeɪvə]	jdn/etw bevorzugen, jdn/etw favorisieren
chain [tʃeɪn]	Kette
opening [ˈəʊpnɪŋ]	freie Stelle
autism spectrum disorder [ˌɔːtɪzm spektrəm dɪsˈɔːdə]	Autismusspektrumstörung
software testing [ˈsɒftweə testɪŋ]	Softwareprüfung, Softwaretests
data entry [ˈdeɪtə entri]	Dateneingabe
characteristic [ˌkærəktəˈrɪstɪk]	Merkmal, Eigenschaft
to **be common to sb** [bi ˈkɒmən tə]	jdm gemeinsam sein
perfectionism [pəˈfekʃənɪzm]	Perfektionismus
eye for detail [ˌaɪ fə ˈdiːteɪl]	Blick für Details
repetition [ˌrepəˈtɪʃn]	Wiederholung
potential [pəˈtenʃl]	potenziell
competitive advantage [kəmˌpetətɪv ədˈvɑːntɪdʒ]	Wettbewerbsvorteil
so-called [ˌsəʊˈkɔːld]	sogenannt
on an individual basis [ɒn ən ɪndɪˌvɪdʒuəl ˈbeɪsɪs]	auf den Einzelfall bezogen, individuell
to **be hesitant to do sth** [bi ˌhezɪtənt tə ˈduː]	etw nur zögerlich tun; zögern, etw zu tun
proper(ly) [ˈprɒpə]	richtig, sachgerecht, ordentlich
to **create sth** [kriˈeɪt]	etw schaffen
I'm afraid [ˌaɪm əˈfreɪd]	leider
to **come up** [ˌkʌm ˈʌp]	aufkommen, genannt werden
to **be off sick** [bi ˌɒf ˈsɪk]	krankgeschrieben sein, *(am Arbeitsplatz)* fehlen
prejudiced [ˈpredʒudɪst]	voreingenommen, vorurteilsbehaftet
stereotype [ˈsteriətaɪp]	Rollenklischee, Vorurteil, Stereotyp
unreliable [ˌʌnrɪˈlaɪəbl]	unzuverlässig
recent [ˈriːsnt]	aktuell, aus jüngster Zeit
to **stick in sb's mind** [ˌstɪk ɪn ˈmaɪnd]	bei jdm hängen/haften bleiben
moderate [ˈmɒdərət]	gemäßigt, leicht
learning disability [ˈlɜːnɪŋ dɪsəbɪləti]	Lernbehinderung
catering [ˈkeɪtərɪŋ]	Gastronomie
to **prove sth** [pruːv]	etw nachweisen, etw belegen
food hygiene [ˈfuːd haɪdʒiːn]	Lebensmittelhygiene
cognitive [ˈkɒgnɪtɪv]	kognitiv
especially [ɪˈspeʃəli]	eigens, speziell
to **pool sth** [puːl]	etw zusammenlegen

page 44

invitation [ˌɪnvɪˈteɪʃn]	Einladung
tour [tʊə]	Rundgang, Besichtigung
self-esteem [ˌself ɪˈstiːm]	Selbstwertgefühl
empowerment [ɪmˈpaʊəmənt]	Stärkung der Selbständigkeit
to **put sth into action** [ˌpʊt ɪntu ˈækʃn]	etw in die Tat umsetzen
printout [ˈprɪntaʊt]	Ausdruck
to **highlight sth** [ˈhaɪlaɪt]	etw hervorheben

page 45

workshop [ˈwɜːkʃɒp]	Werkstatt
senior supervisor [ˌsiːniə ˈsuːpəvaɪzə]	Leiter/in
reception [rɪˈsepʃn]	Empfang
floor plan [ˈflɔː plæn]	Grundriss, Lageplan
trip to the countryside [ˌtrɪp tə ðə ˈkʌntrisaɪd]	Fahrt/Ausflug aufs Land
corridor [ˈkɒrɪdɔː]	Flur, Korridor
to **design sth** [dɪˈzaɪn]	etw entwerfen, etw gestalten, etw anlegen
wheelchair accesss [ˈwiːltʃeə ækses]	rollstuh-/behinderten-gerechter Zugang
painting [ˈpeɪntɪŋ]	Gemälde, Bild
plant [plɑːnt]	Pflanze
cube [kjuːb]	Würfel, Kubus
opposite [ˈɒpəzɪt]	gegenüber (von)
meeting [ˈmiːtɪŋ]	Sitzung, Besprechung
fire exit [ˈfaɪər eksɪt]	Notausgang
to **reach sb/sth** [riːtʃ]	jdn/etw erreichen
entrance [ˈentrəns]	Eingang
to **evacuate sth** [ɪˈvækjueɪt]	etw räumen, etw evakuieren
fire drill [ˈfaɪə drɪl]	Brandschutzübung

medical room [ˈmedɪkl ruːm]	Sanitätsraum, Erste-Hilfe-Raum
seating area [ˈsiːtɪŋ eəriə]	Sitzgelegenheiten
to **hang sth** [hæŋ]	etw aufhängen
sb is keen on sth [ɪz ˈkiːn ɒn]	jdm ist sehr an etw gelegen
storage [ˈstɔːrɪdʒ]	Aufbewahrung, Lagerung
can [kæn]	Dose
far corner [ˌfɑː ˈkɔːnə]	hintere Ecke
soft toy [sɒft ˈtɔɪ]	Stofftier, Kuscheltier
packaging [ˈpækɪdʒɪŋ]	Verpackung
to **pack sth** [pæk]	etw verpacken
see-through [ˈsiːθruː]	durchsichtig, Klarsicht-
discounter [dɪsˈkaʊntə]	Billigsupermarkt, Discounter
storeroom [ˈstɔːruːm]	Lagerraum, Lager
team leader [ˈtiːm liːdə]	Gruppenleiter/in
to **provoke sth** [prəˈvəʊk]	etw hervorrufen
to **encourage sth** [ɪnˈkʌrɪdʒ]	etw unterstützen, etw fördern
assistant carer [əˌsɪstənt ˈkeərə]	Sozialassistent/in mit Schwerpunkt Heilerziehungspflege
coat [kəʊt]	Kittel
hairnet [ˈheənet]	Haarnetz
Santa [ˈsæntə]	Nikolaus, Weihnachtsmann
chocolates *pl* [ˈtʃɒkləts]	Pralinen
outside firm [autˌsaɪd ˈfɜːm]	externe Firma, Fremdfirma
order [ˈɔːdə]	Auftrag, Bestellung
confectionery [kənˈfekʃənəri]	Süßwaren
Easter bunny [ˌiːstə ˈbʌni]	Osterhase
night shift [ˈnaɪtʃɪft]	Nachtschicht
to **have a sense of purpose (in sth)** [həv ə ˌsens əf ˈpɜːpəs]	einen Sinn in etw sehen, Tatkraft spüren
self-confidence [ˌself ˈkɒnfɪdəns]	Selbstvertrauen
to **benefit (from sth)** [ˈbenɪfɪt]	(von etw) profitieren
to **tend to do sth** [ˈtend tə]	dazu neigen, etw zu tun
on sb's own initiative [ɒn sʌmbədiz ˌəʊn ɪˈnɪʃətɪv]	aus eigenem Antrieb
even then [ˌiːvn ˈθen]	selbst dann
to **have an argument** [həv ən ˈɑːgjumənt]	sich streiten
feeling of togetherness [ˌfiːlɪŋ əf təˈgeðənəs]	Zusammengehörigkeitsgefühl
to **handle sth** [ˈhændl]	mit etw umgehen, etw handhaben
to **give a report** [ˌgɪv ə rɪˈpɔːt]	Bericht erstatten, berichten
enterprise [ˈentəpraɪz]	Unternehmen
to **show sb around** [ˌʃəʊ əˈraʊnd]	jdn herumführen
next to [ˈnekst tə]	neben
to **be involved (in sth)** [bi ɪnˈvɒlvd ɪn]	(an etw) beteiligt sein
decision-making [dɪˈsɪʒn meɪkɪŋ]	Entscheidungsfindung, Entscheidungsprozess(e)

page 46

once [wʌns]	einmal
geriatric nurse [ˌdʒeriˈætrɪk nɜːs]	(examinierte/r) Altenpfleger/in
clinic [ˈklɪnɪk]	Klinik
to **serve sth** [sɜːv]	etw servieren
patient(ly) [ˈpeɪʃnt]	geduldig
to **meditate** [ˈmedɪteɪt]	meditieren
to **fit with sth** [ˈfɪt wɪð]	zu etw passen
sociable [ˈsəʊʃəbl]	gesellig, umgänglich
gentle [ˈdʒentl]	sanft, behutsam
kind [kaɪnd]	liebenswürdig, freundlich, gütig
balanced [ˈbælənst]	ausgeglichen
talkative [ˈtɔːkətɪv]	geschwätzig
supportive [səˈpɔːtɪv]	unterstützend, hilfsbereit
internship [ˈɪntɜːnʃɪp]	Praktikum

page 47

arrangement [əˈreɪndʒmənt]	Planungen, Termine, Vereinbarungen
prompt [prɒmpt]	Stichwort
to **sit in on sth** [ˌsɪt ˈɪn ɒn]	bei etw dabei sein, an etw teilnehmen
counselling [ˈkaʊnsəlɪŋ]	Therapie, Beratung
shelter [ˈʃeltə]	Obdachlosenunterkunft
to **bother sb** [ˈbɒðə]	jdn stören, jdn belästigen
infographic [ˈɪnfəʊgræfɪk]	Infografik
quota [ˈkwəʊtə]	Anteil, Quote

page 48

to **divide sth** [dɪˈvaɪd]	etw aufteilen
related to sth [rɪˈleɪtɪd tə]	im Zusammenhang mit etw, bezogen auf etw
to **be affected by sth** [bi əˈfektɪd baɪ]	von etw betroffen sein
relevant [ˈreləvənt]	entsprechend, einschlägig
graph [grɑːf]	Diagramm, Kurve
to **refer to page X** [rɪˈfɜː tə]	auf Seite X nachsehen/nachschlagen
to **upload sth** [ˌʌpˈləʊd]	etw hochladen
visuals *pl* [ˈvɪʒuəlz]	Bildmaterial, Bilder
to **support sth** [səˈpɔːt]	etw *(Argument usw.)* untermauern, etw stützen
handout [ˈhændaʊt]	Arbeitsblatt, Handzettel
audience [ˈɔːdiəns]	Publikum, Zuschauer/innen, Zuhörer/innen
to **give sb an idea of sth** [ˌgɪv ən aɪˈdɪə əv]	jdm eine Vorstellung von etw vermitteln
source [sɔːs]	Quelle
Moving on, … [ˌmuːvɪŋ ˈɒn]	Zum nächsten Punkt. Als nächstes …
That's a good point. [ðəts ə ˌgʊd ˈpɔɪnt]	Das ist ein interessanter Punkt. Da ist was dran.

page 49

concept [ˈkɒnsept]	Konzept
after-school care centre [ɑːftə ˌskuːl ˈkeə sentə]	Schulhort, Nachmittagsbetreuung
amongst [əˈmʌŋst]	unter, untereinander

mission statement [ˈmɪʃn steɪtmənt]	Leitbild
value [ˈvæljuː]	Wert
to **brainstorm** [ˈbreɪnstɔːm]	(Ideen) sammeln
final [ˈfaɪnl]	endgültig
smooth(ly) [smuːð]	reibungslos
intention [ɪnˈtenʃn]	Absicht
environment [ɪnˈvaɪrənmənt]	Umfeld
to **strive to do sth** [ˈstraɪv tə]	sich bemühen, etw zu tun; danach streben, etw zu tun
to **mediate** [ˈmiːdieɪt]	vermitteln
controversial [ˌkɒntrəˈvɜːʃl]	umstritten

page 50

to **divide into sth** [dɪˈvaɪd ɪntə]	sich in etw aufteilen
suggestion [səˈdʒestʃən]	Vorschlag
to **order sth** [ˈɔːdə]	etw bestellen
baking [ˈbeɪkɪŋ]	Backen
venue [ˈvenjuː]	Veranstaltungsort
to **inform sb** [ɪnˈfɔːm]	jdn benachrichtigen, jdn informieren
theme [θiːm]	Thema
slogan [ˈsləʊgən]	Motto, Werbespruch, Slogan
maximum [ˈmæksɪməm]	höchstens, maximal
speech [spiːtʃ]	Rede, Ansprache
agenda [əˈdʒendə]	Tagesordnung

page 51

to **advertise sth** [ˈædvətaɪz]	für etw Werbung machen, etw bewerben
essential [ɪˈsenʃl]	wesentlich
eye-catching [ˈaɪkætʃɪŋ]	auffällig, prägnant
advertising [ˈædvətaɪzɪŋ]	Werbung, Werbe-
to **invite sth from sb** [ɪnˈvaɪt frəm]	jdn um etw bitten
generally [ˈdʒenrəli]	im Allgemeinen
charitable [ˈtʃærətəbl]	wohltätig
cause [kɔːz]	Anliegen, Zweck, (gute) Sache
to **generate money** [ˌdʒenəreɪt ˈmʌni]	Geld erwirtschaften, Einnahmen erzielen
to **raise money** [ˌreɪz ˈmʌni]	Geld beschaffen
donor [ˈdəʊnə]	Spender/in
boardgame [ˈbɔːdgeɪm]	Brettspiel
contest [ˈkɒntest]	Wettbewerb
art auction [ˈɑːt ɔːkʃn]	Kunstauktion
costumed race [ˌkɒstjuːmd ˈreɪs]	Kostümwettlauf

TOPIC 3

page 52/53

on the job [ɒn ðə dʒɒb]	bei der Arbeit
to **identify sth** [aɪˈdentɪfaɪ]	etw herausfinden, etw feststellen, etw bestimmen
helpline [ˈhelplaɪn]	Hotline, Beratungstelefon
helpline advice [ˈhelplaɪn ədvaɪs]	Telefonberatung, Telefonseelsorge
to **act sth out** [ˌækt ˈaʊt]	etw (mit verteilten Rollen) spielen
care services *pl* [ˈkeə sɜːvɪsɪz]	Pflegeleistungen, Pflegedienste
care facility [ˈkeə fəsɪləti]	Pflegeeinrichtung
quote [kwəʊt]	Zitat
to **relate to sth** [rɪˈleɪt tə]	mit etw zu tun haben, in einem Verhältnis zu etw stehen
to **practise sth** [ˈpræktɪs]	etw praktizieren, etw ausüben
compassion [kəmˈpæʃn]	Mitgefühl, Barmherzigkeit
state [steɪt]	Zustand
to **matter** [ˈmætə]	wichtig sein, von Belang sein
tenderness [ˈtendənəs]	Güte, Wärme, Zärtlichkeit
psychologist [saɪˈkɒlədʒɪst]	Psychologe/-in
to **launch sth** [lɔːntʃ]	etw *(Aktion usw.)* starten, etw *(Unternehmen usw.)* gründen
initiative [ɪˈnɪʃətɪv]	Initiative
campaign [kæmˈpeɪn]	Kampagne, Aktion
promotional [prəˈməʊʃənl]	Werbe-
upcoming [ˈʌpkʌmɪŋ]	bevorstehend, demächst stattfindend
fair [feə]	(Branchen-/Handels-) Messe
to **highlight sth** [ˈhaɪlaɪt]	etw in den Mittelpunkt stellen, etw herausstellen
to **involve sb (in sth)** [ɪnˈvɒlv]	jdn (an etw) beteiligen
recently [ˈriːsntli]	in letzter Zeit, neulich
segment [ˈsegmənt]	Teil(stück), Abschnitt, Segment
to **combine sth** [kəmˈbaɪn]	etw (miteinander) verbinden, etw kombinieren
to **document sth** [ˈdɒkjumənt]	etw dokumentieren
scheduling [ˈʃedjuːlɪŋ]	Planung, Terminplanung
work processes *pl* [ˈwɜːk prəʊsesɪz]	Arbeitsabläufe
print ads *pl* [ˈprɪnt ædz]	Anzeigen in Printmedien
to **shoot** [ʃuːt]	*(Film usw.)* drehen

page 54

entry [ˈentri]	Eintrag, Beitrag
stroke [strəʊk]	Schlaganfall
to **print sth off** [ˌprɪnt ˈɒf]	etw ausdrucken
handover [ˈhændəʊvə]	Übergabe
integrated [ˈɪntɪgreɪtɪd]	*(Therapie usw.:)* multimodal, ganzheitlich, integriert
assessment [əˈsesmənt]	Beurteilung, Bewertung, Einschätzung
that way [ˌðæt ˈweɪ]	auf diese Weise
consultant [kənˈsʌltənt]	Facharzt/-ärztin
speech therapist [ˈspiːtʃ θerəpɪst]	Logopäde/-in
to **check on sb** [ˈtʃek ɒn]	nach jdm sehen

UNIT WORD LIST

twice [twaɪs]	zweimal
to **review sth** [rɪ'vjuː]	etw (erneut) prüfen, etw nochmals durchgehen
CT scan [ˌsiː 'tiː skæn]	Computertomographie
condition [kən'dɪʃn]	Zustand
cognition [kɒg'nɪʃn]	Wahrnehmung
mood [muːd]	Stimmung, Laune
rarely ['reəli]	selten, kaum
straight [streɪt]	direkt, sofort
to **refer sb to sth** [rɪ'fɜː tə]	jdn an etw verweisen, *(Medizin:)* jdn an etw überweisen
to **carry on with sth** [ˌkæri 'ɒn wɪð]	mit etw weitermachen
to **speed sth up** [ˌspiːd 'ʌp]	etw beschleunigen
recovery process [rɪ'kʌvəri prəʊses]	Genesung, Genesungsprozess
to **keep a record of sth** [ˌkiːp ə 'rekɔːd əv]	etw protokollieren
treatment plan ['triːtmənt plæn]	Behandlungsplan, Therapiekonzept
multidisciplinary [ˌmʌltɪdɪsə'plɪnəri]	fachübergreifend, inter-/multidisziplinär
to **manage to do sth** ['mænɪdʒ]	es schaffen, etw zu tun
to **record sth** [rɪ'kɔːd]	etw protokollieren, etw aufzeichnen

page 55

frequency ['friːkwənsi]	Häufigkeit, Frequenz
frequent(ly) ['friːkwənt]	häufig
women's refuge [ˌwɪmɪnz 'refjuːdʒ]	Frauenhaus
co-ordinator [kəʊ'ɔːdɪneɪtə]	Koordinator/in
domestic violence [dəˌmestɪk 'vaɪələns]	häusliche Gewalt
emergency accommodation [ɪˌmɜːdʒənsi əkɒmə'deɪʃn]	Notunterkunft
permanent ['pɜːmənənt]	dauerhaft
emotional(ly) [ɪ'məʊʃənl]	emotional
resident ['rezɪdənt]	Bewohner/in
move [muːv]	Umzug
on-call [ɒn 'kɔːl]	Bereitschafts-
to **take over (from sb)** [ˌteɪk 'əʊvə]	(von jdm) übernehmen
to **update sth** [ˌʌp'deɪt]	etw aktualisieren, etw auf den neuesten Stand bringen
to **divert sth** [daɪ'vɜːt]	etw umleiten, etw umstellen
external [ɪk'stɜːnl]	extern, Außen-
rewarding [rɪ'wɔːdɪŋ]	lohnend, bereichernd
tiring ['taɪərɪŋ]	anstrengend, ermüdend
frustrating [frʌ'streɪtɪŋ]	frustrierend
uninteresting [ʌn'ɪntrəstɪŋ]	uninteressant
weekly ['wiːkli]	wöchentlich

page 56

head nurse [ˌhed 'nɜːs]	Pflegeleiter/in, Oberschwester
long-term care home [lɒŋ ˌtɜːm 'keə həʊm]	Langzeitpflegeeinrichtung
long-term care [lɒŋ ˌtɜːm 'keə]	Langzeitpflege
chronic disease [ˌkrɒnɪk dɪ'ziːz]	chronische Erkrankung
age-related ['eɪdʒ rɪleɪtɪd]	altersbedingt
medical condition [ˌmedɪkl kən'dɪʃn]	Krankheit
loss of hearing [ˌlɒs əv 'hɪərɪŋ]	Schwerhörigkeit, Hörverlust
loss of sight [ˌlɒs əf 'saɪt]	Erblindung, Erblindungserscheinungen
loss of movement [ˌlɒs əv 'muːvmənt]	Bewegungseinschränkungen, Mobilitätsverlust
dementia [dɪ'menʃə]	Demenz
Alzheimer's disease ['æltshaɪməz dɪdiːz]	Alzheimer-Krankheit
fall [fɔːl]	Sturz
need (for sth) [niːd]	Bedarf (an etw)
to **estimate** ['estɪmeɪt]	schätzen
to **be estimated to do sth** [bi ˌestɪmeɪtɪd tə 'duː]	etw schätzungsweise tun
care setting ['keə setɪŋ]	Pflegeumfeld, Pflegesituation, Pflegeeinrichtung
info sheet ['ɪnfəʊ ʃiːt]	Informationsblatt
nursing home ['nɜːsɪŋ həʊm]	Pflegeheim
residential home [rezɪˌdenʃl 'həʊm]	Wohnheim, Seniorenheim
adult day care [ˌædʌlt 'deɪ keə]	Tagespflege, Tagesbetreuung
assisted living facility [əsɪstɪd ˌlɪvɪŋ fə'sɪləti]	(Einrichtung für) betreutes Wohnen
home care [ˌhəʊm 'keə]	häusliche Pflege
music session ['mjuːzɪk seʃn]	Konzert, gemeinsames Musizieren
outing ['aʊtɪŋ]	Ausflug
living arrangement ['lɪvɪŋ əreɪndʒmənt]	Form des Wohnens, Wohnkonzept
medical care ['medɪkl keə]	medizinische Versorgung
support service [sə'pɔːt sɜːvɪs]	Betreuungsdienst(leistung)
supervised professional care [ˌsuːpəvaɪzd prəˌfeʃənl 'keə]	Pflege/Betreuung unter fachkundiger Leitung
health challenges *pl* ['helθ tʃælɪndʒɪz]	gesundheitliche Probleme
care assistance ['keər əsɪstəns]	Pflegeleistung, Betreuungshilfe
to **experience sth** [ɪk'spɪəriəns]	etw erleben

page 57

basic body care [ˌbeɪsɪk 'bodi keə]	Grundpflege
to **administer sth** [əd'mɪnɪstə]	etw verabreichen
laundry ['lɔːndri]	Wäsche
medicine ['medsn]	Medikament
to **escort sb** [ɪ'skɔːt]	jdn begleiten, jdn sicher geleiten
nap time ['næp taɪm]	Mittagsschlaf
social interaction [ˌsəʊʃl ɪntər'ækʃn]	Geselligkeit, geselliges Miteinander

period [ˈpɪəriəd]	Zeitraum, Zeitspanne
relative [ˈrelətɪv]	Verwandte/r
caller [ˈkɔːlə]	Anrufer/in

page 58

to **come across sb/sth** [ˌkʌm əˈkrɒs]	auf jdn/etw stoßen, jdn/etw (zufällig) finden
activities *pl* **of daily living** [ækˌtɪvətiz əv ˌdeɪli ˈlɪvɪŋ]	Aktivitäten/Verrichtungen des täglichen Lebens
to **bathe** [beɪð]	baden, ein Bad nehmen
fundamental [ˌfʌndəˈmentl]	grundlegend
normalcy [ˈnɔːməlsi]	Normalität
blood circulation [ˈblʌd sɜːkjəleɪʃn]	Blutkreislauf
infection [ɪnˈfekʃn]	Infektion, Entzündung
practice [ˈpræktɪs]	Gewohnheit, Sitte
religious [rɪˈlɪdʒəs]	religiös, Religions-
to **distract sb** [dɪˈstrækt]	jdn ablenken
dry [draɪ]	trocken
sponge [spʌndʒ]	Schwamm
washcloth [ˈwɒʃklɒθ]	Waschlappen
well lit [ˌwel ˈlɪt]	gut beleuchtet
to **be about to happen** [bi əˌbaʊt tə ˈhæpən]	gleich geschehen, unmittelbar bevorstehen
to **have a bath** [həv ə ˈbɑːθ]	ein Bad nehmen
comfortable [ˈkʌmftəbl]	angenehm
lap [læp]	Schoß
to **be/get upset** [bi/get ʌpˈset]	sich aufregen
to **pat** [pæt]	tupfen, abtupfen
skin [skɪn]	Haut
rash [ræʃ]	Hautausschlag
to **do a sponge bath** [duː ə ˈspʌndʒ bɑːθ]	(jdn) mit dem Schwamm (im Bett) waschen
to **apply sth** [əˈplaɪ]	etw *(Creme usw.)* auftragen
cream [kriːm]	Creme
to **feel in control** [ˌfiːl ɪn kənˈtrəʊl]	das Gefühl haben, Herr/in des eigenen Handelns zu sein
matter-of-fact [ˌmætərəvˈfækt]	sachlich, nüchtern, direkt
respectful [rɪˈspektfl]	respektvoll, pietätvoll
slippery [ˈslɪpəri]	rutschig
to **step into sth** [ˈstep ɪntə]	in etw gehen, in etw steigen
procedure [prəˈsiːdʒə]	Vorgang, Prozedur
to **give the impression that ...** [ˌgɪv ði impression ðət]	den Eindruck erwecken, dass ...
complicated [ˈkɒmplɪkeɪtɪd]	kompliziert
soft [sɒft]	*(Musik usw.:)* leise, sanft
at all times [ət ˌɔːl ˈtaɪmz]	stets, immer

page 59

on one's own [ɒn ˌwʌnz ˈəʊn]	allein, selbst
action [ˈækʃn]	Handlung
privacy [ˈprɪvəsi]	Privatsphäre
to **feed oneself** [ˈfiːd wʌnself]	(selbst) essen
due to [ˈdjuː tə]	aufgrund von
poor vision [ˌpʊə ˈvɪʒn]	Sehschwäche
to **keep sth in mind** [ˌkiːp ɪn ˈmaɪnd]	etw beachten, an etw denken
private setting [ˌpraɪvət ˈsetɪŋ]	ungestörter/vertraulicher Rahmen
to **feed sb** [fiːd]	jdm zu essen geben, jdn füttern
eyeglasses *pl* [ˈaɪglɑːsɪz]	Brille
if required [ɪf rɪˈkwaɪəd]	falls erforderlich, falls nötig
to **place sb/sth** [pleɪs]	jdn/etw platzieren
comfortable [ˈkʌmftəbl]	bequem
wide-grip utensils *pl* [waɪd ˌgrɪp juˈtenslz]	Besteck mit breitem Griff
straw [strɔː]	Strohhalm
to **chew** [tʃuː]	kauen
to **swallow** [ˈswɒləʊ]	schlucken
to **feel embarrassed** [ˌfiːl ɪmˈbærəst]	sich genieren, sich schämen
to **spill sth** [spɪl]	etw verschütten, kleckern
plate [pleɪt]	Teller

page 60

day care nursery [ˌdeɪkeə ˈnɜːsəri]	Kita
to **rank sth** [ræŋk]	etw einstufen, etw (der Rangfolge nach) ordnen
to **compare with sth** [kəmˈpeə wɪð]	sich mit etw vergleichen lassen, Gemeinsamkeiten/Unterschiede zu etw haben
outstanding [aʊtˈstændɪŋ]	hervorragend, herausragend
homely [ˈhəʊmli]	behaglich, gemütlich
wide [waɪd]	breit
affordable [əˈfɔːdəbl]	erschwinglich, günstig
session [ˈseʃn]	*(Betreuung, Unterricht usw.:)* Stunde, Tag

page 61

to **establish sth** [ɪˈstæblɪʃ]	etw *(Unternehmen usw.)* gründen
opening hours *pl* [ˈəʊpənɪŋ aʊəz]	Öffnungszeiten
through [θruː]	bis
bank holiday [ˌbæŋk ˈhɒlədeɪ]	gesetzlicher Feiertag
fee [fiː]	Gebühr, Honorar, Preis
to **charge sth** [tʃɑːdʒ]	etw *(Preis usw.)* in Rechnung stellen, etw berechnen
on top of sth [ɒn ˈtɒp əv]	über etw hinaus(gehend), zusätzlich zu etw
dessert [dɪˈzɜːt]	Nachspeise, Nachtisch
delicious [dɪˈlɪʃəs]	lecker, köstlich
dish [dɪʃ]	Gericht, Speise, Essen
jam [dʒæm]	Marmelade
to **be welcome to do sth** [bi ˌwelkəm tə ˈduː]	gern etw tun können
packed lunch [ˌpækt ˈlʌntʃ]	Lunchpaket
cosy [ˈkəʊzi]	gemütlich, wohnlich
taste [teɪst]	Geschmack
feature [ˈfiːtʃə]	Merkmal, Kennzeichen
to **swap** [swɒp]	tauschen, vertauschen
trial session [ˈtraɪəl seʃn]	Probestunde, Probetag
query [ˈkwɪəri]	Frage, Rückfrage, Anfrage

page 62

to **schedule sth** [ˈʃedjuːl]	etw *(Termin usw.)* ansetzen, etw vereinbaren
to **communicate sth** [kəˈmjuːnɪkeɪt]	etw vermitteln, etw kommunizieren
instantly [ˈɪnstəntli]	sofort, auf Anhieb
memorable [ˈmemərəbl]	einprägsam
skillful [ˈskɪlfl]	geschickt, gekonnt
technique [tekˈniːk]	Technik, Praktik, Methode
Thanks for having me. [ˌθæŋks fə ˈhævɪŋ mi]	Vielen Dank für die Einladung.
public [ˈpʌblɪk]	öffentlich
to **get vaccinated** [ˌget ˈvæksɪneɪtɪd]	sich impfen lassen
commercial [kəˈmɜːʃl]	gewerblich, kommerziell
to **get sth across** [ˌget əˈkrɒs]	etw klarmachen, etw verständlich machen
catchy [ˈkætʃi]	eingängig, prägnant, griffig
artwork [ˈɑːtwɜːk]	Illustrationen, Bildmaterial
to **believe in sth** [bɪˈliːv ɪn]	an etw glauben, von etw überzeugt sein
worth [wɜːθ]	wert
call to action [ˌkɔːl tu ˈækʃn]	Handlungsaufforderung
et cetera [ˌet ˈsetərə]	und so weiter
importance [ɪmˈpɔːtns]	Bedeutung, Wichtigkeit
suicide [ˈsuːɪsaɪd]	Selbstmord
quitter [ˈkwɪtə]	*jd, der leicht aufgibt*
loved ones *pl* [ˈlʌvd wʌnz]	Angehörige, Nahestehende
to **reflect sth** [rɪˈflekt]	etw widerspiegeln, etw wiedergeben

page 63

to **educate sb** [ˈedʒukeɪt]	jdn unterrichten, jdn (über etw) aufklären
to **inspire sb** [ɪnˈspaɪə]	jdn anregen, jdn inspirieren
competitor [kəmˈpetɪtə]	Konkurrent/in
to **stand out from the crowd** [ˌstænd ˈaʊt frəm ðə ˈkraʊd]	sich von der Masse abheben
to **talk highly of sb/sth** [ˌtɔːk ˈhaɪli əv]	sich anerkennend über jdn/etw äußern
prospective [prəˈspektɪv]	potenziell, interessiert
demo(nstration) [ˈdeməʊ, ˌdemənˈstreɪʃn]	Vorführung
review [rɪˈvjuː]	Kritik, Rezension, Besprechung
to **feature sb** [ˈfiːtʃə]	jdn in der Hauptrolle zeigen
reviewer [rɪˈvjuːə]	Rezensent/in
excitement [ɪkˈsaɪtmənt]	Spannung, Nervenkitzel
injection [ɪnˈdʒekʃn]	Injektion, Spritze
to **monitor sth** [ˈmɒnɪtə]	etw beobachten, etw überwachen
unstable [ʌnˈsteɪbl]	instabil
health status [ˈhelθ steɪtəs]	Gesundheitszustand
blood pressure [ˈblʌd preʃə]	Blutdruck
heart rate [ˈhɑːt reɪt]	Herzfrequenz, Puls
breathing [ˈbriːðɪŋ]	Atmung
caregiver [ˈkeəgɪvə]	Pflegeperson, Bezugsperson
coordinated [kəʊˈɔːdɪneɪtɪd]	koordiniert
to **manage sth** [ˈmænɪdʒ]	etw bewältigen
close(ly) [kləʊs]	eng, nah
family doctor [ˌfæməli ˈdɒktə]	Hausarzt/-ärztin
to **coordinate sth** [kəʊˈɔːdɪneɪt]	etw aufeinander abstimmen, etw koordinieren
medical supplies *pl* [ˌmedɪkl səˈplaɪz]	Sanitätsartikel, Medizinbedarf
medical devices/equipment *pl* [ˌmeɪkl dɪˈvaɪsɪz/ɪˈkwɪpmənt]	Medizingeräte, Medizintechnik
rating [ˈreɪtɪŋ]	Bewertung, Einstufung
service package [ˈsɜːvɪs pækɪdʒ]	Leistungspaket

page 64

to **recognize sth** [ˈrekəgnaɪz]	etw erkennen
warning sign [ˈwɔːnɪŋ saɪn]	Anzeichen, Hinweis
unspoken [ʌnˈspəʊkən]	unausgesprochen
depressed [dɪˈprest]	depressiv, deprimiert
anxious [ˈæŋkʃəs]	besorgt, ängstlich
to **be suicidal** [bi ˌsuːiˈsaɪdl]	Selbstmordgedanken haben, selbstmordgefährdet sein
accessories *pl* [əkˈsesəriz]	*(Kleidung usw.:)* Accessoires
to **hide sth** [haɪd]	etw verbergen
bruise [bruːz]	blauer Fleck, Bluterguss
scar [skɑː]	Narbe
indoors [ɪnˈdɔːz]	drinnen
in public [ɪn ˈpʌblɪk]	in der Öffentlichkeit, unter Leuten
access (to sth) [ˈækses]	Zugang (zu etw), Zugriff (auf etw)
social occasion [ˌsəʊʃl əˈkeɪʒn]	geselliges Treffen, private Zusammenkunft
major [ˈmeɪdʒə]	groß, wichtig, bedeutend
personality changes *pl* [ˌpɜːsəˈnæləti tʃeɪndʒɪz]	Persönlichkeitsveränderung(en)
withdrawn [wɪðˈdrɔːn]	verschlossen, introvertiert
to **be afraid** [bi əˈfreɪd]	Angst haben
to **be anxious to do sth** [bi ˌæŋkʃəs tə ˈduː]	darauf bedacht sein, etw zu tun
to **please sb** [pliːz]	es jdm recht machen, jdn zufriedenstellen
to **check in with sb** [ˌtʃek ˈɪn wɪð]	sich (kurz) bei jdm melden
to **go along with sth** [ˌgəʊ əˈlɒŋ wɪð]	einer Sache zustimmen, bei etw mitspielen
to **miss sth** [mɪs]	etw verpassen
isolation [ˌaɪsəˈleɪʃn]	(soziale) Isolation, Vereinsamung
to **restrict sb/sth** [rɪˈstrɪkt]	jdn/etw einschränken, jdn/etw einengen
abuser [əˈbjuːzə]	*jd, der jdn missbraucht;* Täter/in
to **appear** [əˈpɪə]	auftreten, sich zeigen
psychological [ˌsaɪkəˈlɒdʒɪkl]	psychologisch
to **exhibit sth** [ɪgˈzɪbɪt]	etw aufweisen, etw an den Tag legen

to **behave** [bɪˈheɪv]	sich verhalten, sich benehmen
to **appear** [əˈpɪə]	scheinen
unhappy [ʌnˈhæpi]	unzufrieden, unglücklich

page 65

cycle [ˈsaɪkl]	Kreislauf, Spirale, Zyklus
stage [steɪdʒ]	Phase, Stadium, Schritt
to **decide on sth** [dɪˈsaɪd ɒn]	etw festlegen, sich für etw entscheiden
to **fantasize about sth** [ˈfæntəsaɪz əbaʊt]	sich etw vorstellen, von etw fantasieren
to **make excuses** [meɪk ɪkˈskjuːsɪz]	sich herausreden, Ausreden suchen
to **provoke sb/sth** [prəˈvəʊk]	jdn/etw provozieren
physical abuse [ˌfɪzɪkl əˈbjuːs]	(körperliche) Misshandlungen, Schläge, Übergriffe
to **hit** [hɪt]	schlagen
to **punch** [pʌntʃ]	(mit der Faust) schlagen
to **kick** [kɪk]	treten
to **set a trap** [ˌset ə ˈtræp]	eine Falle stellen
all over again [ɔːl ˌəʊvər əˈgen]	von neuem, von vorn
pattern [ˈpætn]	Muster
abusive behaviour [əˌbjuːsɪv bɪˈheɪvjə]	Missbrauchsverhalten, Missbrauch
to **misunderstand sth** [ˌmɪsʌndəˈstænd]	etw missverstehen, etw falsch verstehen
spouse [spaʊz]	Ehepartner/in, Ehegatte/-gattin
so far [ˌsəʊ ˈfɑː]	bisher, bislang
to **be scared** [bi ˈskeəd]	Angst haben
immediate [ɪˈmiːdiət]	sofortig, direkt
to **put the blame on sb** [ˌpʊt ðə ˈbleɪm ɒn]	jdm die Schuld geben
jealous (of sb) [ˈdʒeləs]	eifersüchtig (auf jdn)
to **cheat on sb** [ˈtʃiːt ɒn]	jdn betrügen
to **shift the blame** [ˌʃɪft ðə ˈbleɪm]	die Schuld jd anderem zuschieben
to **admit sth** [ədˈmɪt]	etw zugeben, etw eingestehen
surge of energy [ˌsɜːdʒ əv ˈenədʒi]	Energieschub
to **wear off** [ˌweər ˈɒf]	abklingen, nachlassen
fix [fɪks]	*(Drogen:)* Schuss, Ladung
to **present an opportunity** [prɪˌzent ən ɒpəˈtjuːnəti]	eine Gelegenheit bieten
rush hour [ˈrʌʃaʊə]	Hauptverkehrszeit
to **crave sth** [kreɪv]	Gier auf etw haben, etw unbedingt (und sofort) brauchen
to **break the cycle** [ˌbreɪk ðə ˈsaɪkl]	die Spirale durchbrechen
to **remove sb/sth** [rɪˈmuːv]	jdn/etw entfernen, jdn/etw aus etw nehmen
usefulness [ˈjuːsfəlnəs]	Nutzen
to **blame sb** [bleɪm]	jdm die Schuld geben
to **advise sb to do sth** [ədˈvaɪz]	jdm raten/empfehlen, etw zu tun

page 66

referral [rɪˈfɜːrəl]	(ärztliche) Überweisung, Verweis, Weitervermittlung
to **call sb in** [ˌkɔːl ˈɪn]	jdn hinzuziehen, jdn rufen
emergency service [ɪˈmɜːdʒənsi sɜːvɪs]	Notdienst, Rettungsdienst
immediately [ɪˈmiːdiətli]	sofort, unverzüglich
to **rape sb** [reɪp]	jdn vergewaltigen
baby brother [ˌbeɪbi ˈbrʌðə]	kleines Brüderchen
cyber-bullying [ˈsaɪbə bʊliŋ]	Cyber-Mobbing
sleeping pill [ˈsliːpɪŋ pɪl]	Schlaftablette
to **get off drugs** [get ˌɒf ˈdrʌgz]	von Drogen loskommen
to **refer sb to sb/sth** [rɪˈfɜː tə]	jdn an jdn/etw überweisen, jdn an jdn/etw verweisen
youth protection service(s) [ˌjuːθ prəˈtekʃn sɜːvɪs]	Jugendamt
general practitioner (GP) [ˌdʒenrəl prækˈtɪʃənə]	Hausarzt/-ärztin
to **recommend** [ˌrekəˈmend]	empfehlen
to **get in touch with sth** [get ɪn ˈtʌtʃ wɪð]	mit etw in Kontakt kommen
recording [rɪˈkɔːdɪŋ]	Aufnahme
curtains *pl* [ˈkɜːtnz]	Vorhänge
over and over again [ˌəʊvər ənd ˌəʊvər əˈgen]	(immer und) immer wieder
to **cause sb/sth to do sth** [kɔːz]	jdn/etw dazu veranlassen, etw zu tun; dazu führen, dass jd/etw etw tut
to **be close to sb** [bi ˈkləʊs tə]	jdm (sehr) nahestehen
closeness [ˈkləʊsnəs]	Nähe, enge Verbundenheit
grief [griːf]	Trauer
self-help group [self ˌhelp ˈgruːp]	Selbsthilfegruppe
to **be of help (to sb)** [bi əv ˈhelp]	(jdm) helfen
to **pay attention to sth** [ˌpeɪ əˈtenʃn tə]	auf etw achten
instruction [ɪnˈstrʌkʃn]	Anweisung, Anleitung
empathy [ˈempəθi]	Mitgefühl, Einfühlung(svermögen)

page 67

present [ˈpreznt]	anwesend
a matter of life and death [ə ˌmætər əv ˌlaɪf ən ˈdeθ]	lebensbedrohliche Situation, Frage von Leben oder Tod
to **reassure sb** [ˌriːəˈʃʊə]	jdn beruhigen, jdm etw versichern
to **feel at ease** [fiːl ət ˈiːz]	sich wohlfühlen, sich entspannen
to **enable sb to do sth** [ɪˈneɪbl]	jdm ermöglichen, etw zu tun
to **master sth** [ˈmɑːstə]	etw beherrschen
silence [ˈsaɪləns]	Stille
to **explore sth** [ɪkˈsplɔː]	etw erkunden, etw erforschen
to **jump in** [ˌdʒʌmp ˈɪn]	dazwischenreden, etw sagen

to **judge sth** [dʒʌdʒ]	etw bewerten, etw beurteilen
non-threatening [ˌnɒn ˈθretnɪŋ]	harmlos, nicht bedrohlich
to **nod one's head** [ˌnɒd wʌnz ˈhed]	(mit dem Kopf) nicken
to **indicate sth** [ˈɪndɪkeɪt]	etw erkennen lassen, etw signalisieren
neutral [ˈnjuːtrəl]	neutral
non-judgemental [ˌnɒn dʒʌdʒˈmentl]	unvoreingenommen, wertfrei, nicht wertend
to **take sides** [teɪk ˈsaɪdz]	Partei ergreifen
guideline [ˈgaɪdlaɪn]	Richtlinie, Empfehlung
introductory [ɪntrəˈdʌktəri]	einleitend
trainer [ˈtreɪnə]	Dozent/in, Ausbilder/in
flatmate [ˈflætmeɪt]	Mitbewohner/in
to **have a fall** [həv ə ˈfɔːl]	stürzen, hinfallen
fighting [ˈfaɪtɪŋ]	Beteiligung an einer Schlägerei / an Schlägereien
parent [ˈpeərənt]	Elternteil
overweight [ˌəʊvəˈweɪt]	übergewichtig
torn [tɔːn]	zerrissen, zerfetzt
to **bully sb** [ˈbʊli]	jdn mobben, jdn tyrannisieren
to **call sb names** [ˌkɔːl ˈneɪmz]	jdn beschimpfen
head teacher [ˌhed ˈtiːtʃə]	Schuldirektor/in
to **complain (to sb about sth)** [kəmˈpleɪn]	sich (bei jdm über etw) beschweren
to **go on a diet** [gəʊ ɒn ə ˈdaɪət]	eine Diät machen

page 68

to **be situated** [bi ˈsɪtʃueɪtɪd]	liegen

page 69

to **be abusive to sb** [bi əˈbjuːsɪv tə]	jdn misshandeln
to **apologize (to sb)** [əˈpɒlədʒaɪz]	sich (bei jdm) entschuldigen
apology [əˈpɒlədʒi]	Entschuldigung
to **get back to normal** [get ˌbæk tə ˈnɔːməl]	zur Normalität zurückkehren, sich normalisieren
to **be married to sb** [bi ˈmærid tə]	mit jdm verheiratet sein
previous [ˈpriːviəs]	vorherig, vorig
marriage [ˈmærɪdʒ]	Ehe
affair [əˈfeə]	Affäre
to **think sth up** [ˌθɪŋk ˈʌp]	sich etw ausdenken, etw erfinden
household [ˈhaʊshəʊld]	Haushalt
jumbled [ˈdʒʌmbld]	durcheinandergeworfen, ungeordnet
to **argue (with sb)** [ˈɑːgjuː]	sich (mit jdm) streiten
marriage guidance [ˌmærɪdʒ ˈgaɪdəns]	Eheberatung

page 70

to **revise sth** [rɪˈvaɪz]	etw überarbeiten, etw revidieren
sketch [sketʃ]	Skizze
desire (for sth) [dɪˈzaɪə]	Verlangen (nach etw), Wunsch (nach etw)
powerful [ˈpaʊəfl]	stark
bullet point [ˈbʊlɪt pɔɪnt]	Stichpunkt
subheading [ˈsʌbhedɪŋ]	Zwischenüberschrift
to **appeal to sth** [əˈpiːl tə]	etw ansprechen
to **be connected** [bi kəˈnektɪd]	zusammenhängen

page 71

to **put yourself in sb's shoes** [ˌpʊt jəself ɪn ˌsʌmbədiz ˈʃuːz]	sich in jds Lage versetzen
speech [spiːtʃ]	(Art zu) Sprechen, Redestil
correction [kəˈrekʃn]	Korrektur
to **perform sth** [pəˈfɔːm]	etw aufführen, etw spielen
to **pick sth out** [ˌpɪk ˈaʊt]	etw hervorheben
performance [pəˈfɔːməns]	Darbietung, Aufführung

page 72

age group [ˈeɪdʒ gruːp]	Altersgruppe
to **target sb/sth** [ˈtɑːgɪt]	jdn/etw ins Visier nehmen, jdn ansprechen
to **appear in a video** [əˌpɪər ɪn ə ˈvɪdiəʊ]	in einem Video mitspielen
to **be designed for sb/sth** [bi dɪˈzaɪnd fə]	für jdn/etw gedacht sein
editing [ˈedɪtɪŋ]	*(Film usw.:)* Schnitt
tone [təʊn]	Ton, Tonfall, Unterton

page 73

storyboard [ˈstɔːribɔːd]	*(Film usw.:)* Szenenbuch, Storyboard
shot [ʃɒt]	*(Film usw.:)* Einstellung
shot list [ˈʃɒt lɪst]	Liste der Einstellungen, Shotlist
exterior shot [ɪkˈstɪəriə ʃɒt]	Außenaufnahme
interior shot [ɪnˈtɪəriə ʃɒt]	Innenaufnahme
seated [ˈsiːtɪd]	sitzend
to **rehearse** [rɪˈhɜːs]	proben
footage [ˈfʊtɪdʒ]	Aufnahme(n), Filmmaterial
to **edit** [ˈedɪt]	*(Film usw.:)* schneiden
in writing [ɪn ˈraɪtɪŋ]	schriftlich, in Schriftform
privacy rights *pl* [ˈprɪvəsi raɪts]	Persönlichkeitsrechte
shooting [ˈʃuːtɪŋ]	*(Film usw.:)* Dreh, Drehen
model release [ˌmɒdl rɪˈliːs]	Modelvertrag, Model Release
to **sign** [saɪn]	unterzeichnen, unterschreiben
underage person [ʌndərˌeɪdʒ ˈpɜːsn]	Minderjährige/r
legal problem [ˌliːgl ˈprɒbləm]	juristisches Problem
to **compose** [kəmˈpəʊz]	komponieren
composer [kəmˈpəʊzə]	Komponist/in
record company [ˈrekɔːd kʌmpəni]	Schallplattenfirma
musician [mjuːˈzɪʃn]	Musiker/in
rights-free [ˌraɪts ˈfriː]	lizenzfrei, *(D:)* GEMA-frei

TOPIC 4

page 74/75

work-related [ˈwɜːk rɪleɪtɪd]	arbeitsbezogen, berufsbezogen
to **enquire about sth** [ɪnˈkwaɪər əbaʊt]	sich nach etw erkundigen
enquiry [ɪnˈkwaɪəri]	Anfrage, Erkundigung
to **make enquiries** [ˌmeɪk ɪnˈkwaɪəriz]	sich erkundigen, Nachforschungen anstellen
emergency [ɪˈmɜːdʒənsi]	Notfall
catering [ˈkeɪtərɪŋ]	Verpflegung, (Versorgung mit) Essen, Catering
means of communication [ˌmiːnz əf kəmjuːnɪˈkeɪʃn]	Kommunikationsmittel
business letter [ˈbɪznəs letə]	Geschäftsbrief
text message [ˈtekst mesɪdʒ]	SMS, Textnachricht
landline [ˈlændlaɪn]	Festnetzanschluss
informal [ɪnˈfɔːml]	zwanglos, informell
business organization [ˈbɪznəs ɔːgənaɪzeɪʃn]	Wirtschaftsunternehmen, Unternehmensform
service provider [ˈsɜːvɪs prəvaɪdə]	Dienstleister/in
supplier [səˈplaɪə]	Lieferant/in, Zulieferer
little rascal [ˌlɪtl ˈræskəl]	Bengel
to **research sth** [rɪˈsɜːtʃ]	etw recherchieren, Nachforschungen über etw anstellen
to **place an order** [ˌpleɪs ən ˈɔːdə]	eine Bestellung aufgeben, einen Auftrag erteilen
lastly [ˈlɑːstli]	zuletzt, als Letztes
business communication [ˈbɪznəs kəmjuːnɪkeɪʃn]	Geschäftskorrespondenz, Unternehmenskommunikation
setting [ˈsetɪŋ]	Situation, Rahmen, Umfeld
to **assess sth** [əˈses]	etw beurteilen, etw einschätzen
request [rɪˈkwest]	Anfrage
offer [ˈɒfə]	Angebot
to **take a message** [ˌteɪk ə ˈmesɪdʒ]	*(Telefon:)* jdm etw ausrichten
accident report [ˈæksɪdənt rɪpɔːt]	Unfallbericht
recommendation [ˌrekəmenˈdeɪʃn]	Empfehlung
Good luck! [ˌgʊd ˈlʌk]	Viel Erfolg! Viel Glück!

page 76

bilingual [ˌbaɪˈlɪŋgwəl]	zweisprachig
package [ˈpækɪdʒ]	Paket
bouncy castle [ˌbaʊnsi ˈkɑːsl]	Hüpfburg
face painting (for children) [ˈfeɪs peɪntɪŋ]	Kinderschminken
to **integrate sth in sth** [ˈɪntɪgreɪt]	etw in etw einbinden, etw in etw integrieren
entertainment [ˌentəˈteɪnmənt]	Unterhaltung
to **be committed to sth** [bi kəˈmɪtɪd tə]	sich (voll und ganz) für etw engagieren
hassle-free package [ˌhæsl friː ˈpækɪdʒ]	Rundum-sorglos-Paket
to **run an event** [ˌrʌn ɪn ɪˈvent]	eine Veranstaltung durchführen
from start to finish [frəm ˌstɑːt tə ˈfɪnɪʃ]	von Anfang bis Ende
to **take sth on board** [ˌteɪk ɒn ˈbɔːd]	etw annehmen, etw übernehmen
to **personalize sth** [ˈpɜːsnəlaɪz]	etw individuell anpassen/gestalten
treasure hunt [ˈtreʒə hʌnt]	Schatzsuche, Schnitzeljagd
unforgettable [ˌʌnfəˈgetəbl]	unvergesslich
artist [ˈɑːtɪst]	Künstler/in
to **discover sth** [dɪˈskʌvə]	etw entdecken
inner [ˈɪnə]	innere/r/s

page 77

slide [slaɪd]	Rutsche, Rutschbahn
to **have sth for hire** [həv fə ˈhaɪə]	etw vermieten
conditions *pl* [kənˈdɪʃnz]	Bedingungen, Konditionen
to **celebrate (sth)** [ˈselɪbreɪt]	(etw) feiern
inflatable [ɪnˈfleɪtəbl]	aufblasbar
water slide [ˈwɔːtə slaɪd]	Wasserrutsche
price list [ˈpraɪs lɪst]	Preisliste
catalogue [ˈkætəlɒg]	Katalog
(Best) regards *pl* [rɪˈgɑːdz]	*(Brief, E-Mail:)* Viele Grüße
unsure [ˌʌnˈʃʊə]	unsicher
basics *pl* [ˈbeɪsɪks]	Grundlagen, Grundsätzliches
mail [meɪl]	Post
subject line [ˈsʌbdʒɪkt laɪn]	Betreffzeile
specific [spəˈsɪfɪk]	konkret
subject matter [ˈsʌbdʒɪkt mætə]	Thema, Thematik, Inhalt
salutation [ˌsæljuˈteɪʃn]	*(Brief, E-Mail:)* Anrede
greeting [ˈgriːtɪŋ]	Gruß, Begrüßung
closing [ˈkləʊzɪŋ]	Abschieds-, Schluss-
whichever [wɪtʃˈevə]	welche/r/s (auch immer)
consistent [kənˈsɪstənt]	einheitlich, konsequent
complimentary close [ˌkɒmplɪˌmentri ˈkləʊz]	*(Brief, E-Mail:)* Schlussformel
to **sign off** [ˌsaɪn ˈɒf]	sich verabschieden, Schluss machen
recipient [rɪˈsɪpiənt]	Empfänger/in
Best wishes *pl* [ˌbest ˈwɪʃɪz]	*(Brief, E-Mail:)* Viele Grüße
contraction [kənˈtrækʃn]	zusammengezogene Form, Kontraktion
introduction [ˌɪntrəˈdʌkʃn]	*(Text:)* Einleitung
body [ˈbɒdi]	*(Text:)* Hauptteil
close [kləʊs]	Schluss
subject [ˈsʌbdʒɪkt]	Thema, *(Brief, E-Mail:)* Betreff
to **consist of sth** [kənˈsɪst əv]	aus etw bestehen
to **request sth** [rɪˈkwest]	um etw bitten

page 78

follow-up [ˈfɒləʊ ʌp]	Folge-, Anschluss-, Nachfass-
to **be pleased** [bi ˈpliːzd]	sich freuen
adventure [ədˈventʃə]	Abenteuer

woodlands *pl* ['wʊdləndz]	Wälder
treasure ['treʒə]	Schatz
as sb **goes** [əz gəʊz]	unterwegs
bracelet ['breɪslət]	Armband
bouncy ball [ˌbaʊnsi 'bɔːl]	Flummi
transport ['trænspɔːt]	Beförderung, Transport
guide [gaɪd]	Führer/in, Reiseleiter/in
rate [reɪt]	Preis, Tarif
celebration [ˌselɪ'breɪʃn]	Feier, Fest
balloon modelling [bə'luːn mɒdəlɪŋ]	Ballonkunst, Ballonmodellieren
obstacle course ['ɒbstəkl kɔːs]	Hindernislauf, Hindernisparcours
to **get back to** sb [ˌget 'bæk tə]	sich wieder bei jdm melden
grounds *pl* [graʊndz]	Gelände, Außenanlage

page 79

directness [də'rektnəs]	Direktheit
politeness [pə'laɪtnəs]	Höflichkeit
barbecue ['bɑːbɪkjuː]	Grillparty
buffet ['bʊfeɪ]	Büfett

page 80

to **mail** sth **to** sb [meɪl]	jdm etw (mit der Post) schicken
grant proposal ['grɑːnt prəpəʊzl]	Zuschussantrag, Förderantrag
to **participate in** sth [pɑː'tɪsɪpeɪt ɪn]	an etw teilnehmen
instructor [ɪn'strʌktə]	Lehrer/in
hiking ['haɪkɪŋ]	Wandern
white-water rafting [ˌwaɪt wɔːtə 'rɑːftɪŋ]	Rafting, Wildwasserfahren
cross-country skiing [ˌkrɒs'kʌntri]	Skilanglauf
facilitating [fə'sɪlɪteɪtɪŋ]	Moderation, Vermittlung
debriefing [dɪ'briːfɪŋ]	Nachbesprechung, Auswertung, Reflexion
training session ['treɪnɪŋ seʃn]	Schulung
to **attain** sth [ə'teɪn]	etw erreichen, etw erlangen
accredited [ə'kredɪtɪd]	anerkannt, zugelassen, akkreditiert
accreditation [əkredɪ'teɪʃn]	Anerkennung, Zulassung, Akkreditierung

page 81

alongside [əˌlɒŋ'saɪd]	an der Seite von
head [hed]	Leiter/in
vocational school [vəʊˌkeɪʃənl 'skuːl]	Berufsschule
to **put** sb **through to** sb [ˌpʊt 'θruː tə]	*(Telefon:)* jdn mit jdm verbinden
to **be in charge (of** sth**)** [bi ɪn 'tʃɑːdʒ]	(für etw) verantwortlich sein, für etw zuständig sein
to **hold on** [ˌhəʊld 'ɒn]	warten
country code ['kʌntri kəʊd]	*(Telefon:)* Ländervorwahl
to **pass** sth **on** [ˌpɑːs 'ɒn]	etw weitergeben
My pleasure. [maɪ 'pleʒə]	Gern geschehen.
to **confirm** sth [kən'fɜːm]	etw bestätigen
on the line [ɒn ðə 'laɪn]	*(Telefon:)* in der Leitung, am Telefon
to **close** sth [kləʊz]	etw beenden, etw abschließen
to **connect** sb [kə'nekt]	*(Telefon:)* jdn durchstellen
to **postpone** sth [pə'spəʊn]	etw *(Termin usw.)* verschieben
to **cancel** sth ['kænsl]	etw absagen, etw stornieren
to **reschedule** sth [ˌriː'ʃedjuːl]	etw *(Termin usw.)* verlegen
to **bring** sth **forward** [ˌbrɪŋ 'fɔːwəd]	etw *(Termin usw.)* vorziehen, etw vorverlegen
to **call** sth **off** [ˌkɔːl 'ɒf]	etw absagen
to **fix** sth [fɪks]	etw *(Termin usw.)* festlegen
to **put** sth **off** [ˌpʊt 'ɒf]	etw *(Termin usw.)* verschieben
to **spell** sth [spel]	etw buchstabieren
to **be available** [bi ə'veɪləbl]	*(Telefon:)* zu sprechen sein
to **agree on** sth [ə'griː ɒn]	sich auf etw einigen
convenient [kən'viːniənt]	günstig, passend

page 82

to **host** sth [həʊst]	etw *(Veranstaltung usw.)* ausrichten
to **pack** [pæk]	packen
medical officer [ˌmedɪkl 'ɒfɪsə]	Betriebssanitäter/in
in charge [ɪn 'tʃɑːdʒ]	zuständig, amtierend
first-aid kit [ˌfɜːst'eɪd kɪt]	Verbandskasten, Erste-Hilfe-Ausrüstung
wound [wuːnd]	Wunde
wound care ['wuːnd keə]	Wundversorgung
antibiotic [ˌæntibaɪ'ɒtɪk]	antibiotisch
ointment ['ɔɪntmənt]	Salbe
blanket ['blæŋkɪt]	Decke
gauze [gɔːz]	Gaze
antihistamine [ˌænti'hɪstəmiːn]	Antihistamin
safety pin ['seɪfti pɪn]	Sicherheitsnadel
bandage ['bændɪdʒ]	Verband, Bandage
iodine ['aɪədiːn]	Jod
scissors *pl* ['sɪzəz]	Schere
adhesive tape [əd'hiːsɪv teɪp]	Heftpflaster
tweezers *pl* ['twiːzəz]	Pinzette
needle ['niːdl]	Nadel
gloves *pl* [glʌvz]	Handschuhe
SAM splint ['sæm splɪnt]	Alu-Polsterschiene, SAM-Schiene
to **relieve** sth [rɪ'liːv]	etw lindern, etw mildern
symptom ['sɪmptəm]	Anzeichen, Erscheinung, Symptom
bite [baɪt]	(Insekten-)Biss
sting [stɪŋ]	(Insekten-)Stich
to **save** sb/sth [seɪv]	jdn/etw retten
allergic reaction (to sth**)** [əˌlɜːdʒɪk ri'ækʃn]	allergische Reaktion (auf etw)
to **stabilize** sth ['steɪbəlaɪz]	etw stabilisieren
break [breɪk]	(Knochen-)Bruch

sprain [spreɪn]	Verstauchung, Verrenkung
fever ['fiːvə]	Fieber
inflammation [ˌɪnflə'meɪʃn]	Entzündung
anticoagulant [ˌæntikəʊ'ægjələnt]	Gerinnungshemmer
to **clot** [klɒt]	gerinnen
to **bleed** [bliːd]	bluten
bleeding ['bliːdɪŋ]	Blutung
painkiller ['peɪnkɪlə]	Schmerzmittel
to **fit sth in sth** ['fɪt ɪn]	etw in etw einbauen, etw in etw einpassen
tube [tjuːb]	Rohr, Röhre
nut [nʌt]	Nuss
to **have sb along** [həv ə'lɒŋ]	jdn dabei haben
excursion [ɪk'skɜːʃn]	Wanderung
heat [hiːt]	Erwärmung, Wärme, Hitze
to **scratch** ['skrætʃ]	sich kratzen
to **attend to sb** [ə'tend tə]	sich um jdn kümmern, jdn versorgen
whoever [huː'evə]	wer auch immer
dirt [dɜːt]	Schmutz, Dreck
to **become infected** [bɪˌkʌm ɪn'fektɪd]	*(Wunde:)* sich entzünden
last but not least [ˌlɑːst bʌt nɒt 'liːst]	zu guter Letzt
to **wonder** ['wʌndə]	sich fragen
to **be made up of sth** [bi ˌmeɪd 'ʌp əv]	aus etw bestehen
strip [strɪp]	Streifen
polythene foam ['pɒliθiːn fəʊm]	Polyethylen-Schaumstoff
coating ['kəʊtɪŋ]	Beschichtung
to **unroll sth** [ˌʌn'rəʊl]	etw entrollen, etw aufrollen
to **fold** [fəʊld]	falten
shape [ʃeɪp]	Form, Gestalt
rigid ['rɪdʒɪd]	steif, fest
to **immobilize sth** [ɪ'məʊbəlaɪz]	etw ruhigstellen
to **look sth up** [ˌlʊk 'ʌp]	etw *(in einem Wörterbuch)* nachschlagen

page 83

to **hit sth** [hɪt]	gegen etw stoßen
rock [rɒk]	Stein, Fels
to **injure sth** ['ɪndʒə]	sich etw verletzen
to **make sb comfortable** [ˌmeɪk 'kʌmftəbl]	sich um jdn kümmern
ambulance ['æmbjələns]	Rettungswagen
admissions [əd'mɪʃnz]	*(Krankenhaus:)* Aufnahme(station)
measure ['meʒə]	Maßnahme
to **take measures** [ˌteɪk 'meʒəz]	Maßnahmen ergreifen
consciousness ['kɒnʃəsnəs]	Bewusstsein
helmet ['helmɪt]	Helm
to **ski** [skiː]	(Ski) fahren
pace [peɪs]	Geschwindigkeit
logical ['lɒdʒɪkl]	logisch
principal diagnosis [ˌprɪnsəpl daɪəg'nəʊsɪs]	Erstdiagnose
to **account for sth** [ə'kaʊnt fə]	etw erklären
admission [əd'mɪʃn]	*(Krankenhaus:)* Einlieferung, Aufnahme
allergy ['ælədʒi]	Allergie
contraceptive pill [ˌkɒntrə'septɪv pɪl]	Verhütungspille, Antibabypille
headache(s) ['hedeɪk]	Kopfschmerzen
riding accident ['raɪdɪŋ æksɪdənt]	Reitunfall
to **be allergic to sth** [bi ə'lɜːdʒɪk tə]	auf etw allergisch sein
pollen ['pɒlən]	Pollen
penicillin [ˌpenɪ'sɪlɪn]	Penicillin
to **submit sth to sb** [səb'mɪt tə]	etw bei jdm einreichen
outcome ['aʊtkʌm]	Ergebnis, Resultat

page 84

admin(istration) ['ædmɪn, ədˌmɪnɪ'streɪʃn]	Verwaltung
caterer ['keɪtərə]	Speiselieferant/in, Cateringservice
handling (of sth) ['hændlɪŋ]	Umgang (mit etw)
environmental impact [ɪn!vaɪrən!mentl ɪmpækt]	Umweltbelastung, Umweltfolgen
quantity ['kwɒntəti]	Menge
dietary ['daɪətri]	Ernährungs-, diätetisch
unhealthy [ʌn'helθi]	ungesund
to **die tragically** [ˌdaɪ 'trædʒɪkli]	auf tragische Weise ums Leben kommen
contaminated [kən'tæmɪneɪtɪd]	kontaminiert
bacteria *pl* [bæk'tɪəriə]	Bakterien
allergen ['ælədʒn]	Allergen
food intolerance ['fuːd ɪntɒlərəns]	Nahrungsmittelunverträglichkeit
plastic tub [ˌplæstɪk 'tʌb]	Kunststoffschale, -becher
inpatient ['ɪn peɪʃnt]	stationäre/r Patient/in
vending machine ['vendɪŋ məʃiːn]	(Verkaufs-)Automat
sugary ['ʃʊgəri]	zuckerhaltig
high in sth ['haɪ ɪn]	mit hohem Gehalt an etw
fat [fæt]	Fett
to **generate sth** ['dʒenəreɪt]	etw erzeugen
tonne [tʌn]	Tonne *(1000 kg)*
waste [weɪst]	Abfall, Müll
to **spend sth on sth** [ˌspend 'ɒn]	etw *(Geld usw.)* für etw ausgeben
labour costs *pl* ['leɪbə kɒsts]	Arbeitskosten, Lohnkosten
overheads *pl* ['əʊvəhedz]	Betriebskosten, Gemeinkosten
proposal [prə'pəʊzl]	Angebot
inside address [ˌɪnsaɪd ə'dres]	Innenadresse
signature ['sɪgnətʃə]	Unterschrift
letterhead ['letəhed]	Briefkopf
reference initials *pl* ['refərəns ɪnɪʃlz]	Zeichen

page 85

to **fit sb's needs** [ˌfɪt sʌmbədiz ˈniːdz]	jds Bedürfnissen entsprechen
brochure [ˈbrəʊʃə]	Prospekt, Broschüre
to **hesitate** [ˈhezɪteɪt]	zögern
sales manager [ˈseɪlz mænɪdʒə]	Vertriebsleiter/in, Verkaufsleiter/in
in detail [ɪn ˈdiːteɪl]	genau, detailliert

page 86

to **evaluate sth** [ɪˈvæljueɪt]	etw auswerten, etw bewerten
tasty [ˈteɪsti]	schmackhaft, lecker
nutritious [njuˈtrɪʃəs]	nahrhaft
to **consider sth** [kənˈsɪdə]	etw berücksichtigen
to **deliver** [dɪˈlɪvə]	liefern
organic [ɔːˈgænɪk]	Bio-
sustainable [səˈsteɪnəbl]	nachhaltig
disadvantage [ˌdɪsədˈvɑːntɪdʒ]	Nachteil
chef [ʃef]	Koch/Köchin, Küchenchef/in
first-rate [ˌfɜːst ˈreɪt]	erstklassig
ingredient [ɪnˈgriːdiənt]	Zutat
cage-free [ˈkeɪdʒ friː]	nicht aus Käfighaltung
reduction (in sth) [rɪˈdʌkʃn]	Reduzierung, Rückgang (von etw)
palm oil [ˈpɑːm ɔɪl]	Palmöl
to **prepare sth** [prɪˈpeə]	etw *(Essen usw.)* zubereiten, etw kochen
timely [ˈtaɪmli]	rechtzeitig, pünktlich
delivery [dɪˈlɪvəri]	Lieferung, Zustellung
to **range between … and …** [ˈreɪndʒ bɪtwiːn ənd]	sich zwischen … und … bewegen
pastry [ˈpeɪstri]	Gebäck
to **be priced** [bi ˈpraɪst]	kosten, (preislich) liegen
per item [ˌpər ˈaɪtəm]	pro Stück

page 87

cost-effective [ˌkɒstɪˈfektɪv]	kostengünstig
to **trial sth** [ˈtraɪəl]	etw testen, etw erproben
safe [seɪf]	ungefährlich
nutritionally balanced [njuˌtrɪʃənli ˈbælənst]	(ernährungsphysiologisch) ausgewogen
to **cater to sth** [ˈkeɪtə tə]	auf etw *(Bedürfnisse usw.)* eingehen
vegetarian [ˌvedʒəˈteəriən]	vegetarisch; Vegetarier/in
vegan [ˈviːgən]	vegan
kosher [ˈkəʊʃə]	koscher
pack [pæk]	Packung, Beutel
to **microwave sth** [ˈmaɪkrəweɪv]	etw in der Mikrowelle erhitzen
to **pressure-steam sth** [ˈpreʃə stiːm]	etw im Druckdampfgarer zubereiten
to **ensure sth** [ɪnˈʃʊə]	etw gewährleisten, für etw sorgen
retention [rɪˈtenʃn]	Erhaltung, Bewahrung
nutrients *pl* [ˈnjuːtriənts]	Nährstoffe
texture [ˈtekstʃə]	Konsistenz
refrigerator [rɪˈfrɪdʒəreɪtə]	Kühlschrank
to **store sth** [stɔː]	etw lagern, etw aufbewahren
microwave oven [ˌmaɪkrəweɪv ˈʌvn]	Mikrowelle(nherd)
to **heat sth** [hiːt]	etw erhitzen, etw erwärmen
chilled [tʃɪld]	gekühlt
to **collect sth** [kəˈlekt]	etw abholen
composting [ˈkɒmpɒstɪŋ]	Kompostierung
draft [drɑːft]	Entwurf
management [ˈmænɪdʒmənt]	Geschäftsleitung

page 88

carnival outfit [ˈkɑːnɪvl aʊtfɪt]	Karnevalskostüm
costume [ˈkɒstjuːm]	Kostüm
to **mind** [maɪnd]	etw dagegen haben

page 89

hardly [ˈhɑːdli]	kaum
to **run out of sth** [ˌrʌn ˈaʊt əv]	etw nicht mehr haben
relief organization [rɪˈliːf ɔːgənaɪzeɪʃn]	Hilfsorganisation
to **hike** [haɪk]	Wandern
to **recover (from sth)** [rɪˈkʌvə]	sich (von etw) erholen
to **take charge** [teɪk ˈtʃɑːdʒ]	etw in die Hand nehmen, das Kommando übernehmen
voicemail [ˈvɔɪsmeɪl]	Anrufbeantworter, Mailbox

page 90

Something has come up. [sʌmθɪŋ həz ˌkʌm ˈʌp]	Es ist etwas dazwischengekommen.
department [dɪˈpɑːtmənt]	Abteilung
to **set sth out** [ˌset ˈaʊt]	etw darlegen, etw aufstellen
depending on [dɪˈpendɪŋ ɒn]	je nach(dem)
etiquette [ˈetɪket]	Etikette

page 91

to **format sth** [ˈfɔːmæt]	etw formatieren

page 92

criteria *pl* [kraɪˈtɪəriə]	Kriterien
placemat [ˈpleɪsmæt]	Tischset
attendee [əˌtenˈdiː]	Teilnehmer/in
to **select sth** [sɪˈlekt]	etw auswählen
good value for money [gʊd ˌvæljuː fə ˈmʌni]	preiswert, günstig
I see your point. [aɪˌ siː jɔː ˈpɔɪnt]	Ich verstehe, was Sie meinen.

TOPIC 5

page 94/95

diet [ˈdaɪət]	Ernährung, Kost
chronic condition [ˌkrɒnɪk kənˈdɪʃn]	chronische Krankheit
changing [ˈtʃeɪndʒɪŋ]	im Wandel, sich wandelnd
dysfunctional [dɪsˈfʌŋkʃənl]	zerrüttet, gestört, Problem-, dysfunktional
awareness [əˈweənəs]	Bewusstsein, Sensibilität

migrant [ˈmaɪgrənt]	Migrant/in
scene [siːn]	Szene
reality show [riˈæləti ʃəʊ]	Reality-TV-Sendung/-Serie
immigrant [ˈɪmɪgrənt]	Einwanderer/-in
bubble [ˈbʌbl]	Blase
minimum [ˈmɪnɪməm]	Mindest-
amount [əˈmaʊnt]	Menge
exercise [ˈeksəsaɪz]	Bewegung, körperliche Betätigung, Sport
bisexual [baɪˈsekʃuəl]	bisexuell
lesbian [ˈlezbiən]	lesbisch
gay [geɪ]	schwul
to **die from sth** [ˈdaɪ frəm]	an etw sterben
nutrition [njuˈtrɪʃn]	Ernährung
to **struggle** [ˈstrʌgl]	kämpfen, zu kämpfen haben, sich abmühen
research [rɪˈsɜːtʃ]	Forschung
pregnancy [ˈpregnənsi]	Schwangerschaft
adoption [əˈdɒpʃn]	Adoption
competence [ˈkɒmpɪtəns]	Kompetenz

page 96

pre-teen [priː ˈtiːn]	*Kind im Alter von 9–12 J.*
overweight [ˈəʊvəweɪt]	Übergewicht
obesity [əʊˈbiːsəti]	Fettleibigkeit
adolescent [ˌædəˈlesnt]	Jugendliche/r, Heranwachsende/r
obese [əʊˈbiːs]	fettleibig
World Health Organization (WHO) [ˌwɜːld ˈhelθ ɔːgənaɪzeɪʃn]	Weltgesundheitsorganisation
physical activity [ˌfɪzɪkl ækˈtɪvəti]	körperliche Betätigung
projection [prəˈdʒekʃn]	Prognose
stepmum [ˈstepmʌm]	Stiefmutter
convenience food [kənˈviːniəns fuːd]	Fertiggerichte, Fertigprodukte
factory-farmed [ˈfæktəri fɑːmd]	aus Massentierhaltung
meat [miːt]	Fleisch
chemicals *pl* [ˈkemɪklz]	Chemikalien
schoolmate [ˈskuːlmeɪt]	Schulkamerad/in, Mitschüler/in
to **afford sth** [əˈfɔːd]	sich etw leisten
free-range eggs *pl* [ˌfriː reɪndʒ ˈegz]	Eier aus Freilandhaltung
processed food [ˌprəʊsest ˈfuːd]	verarbeitete Lebensmittel
farming [ˈfɑːmɪŋ]	Landwirtschaft, Tierhaltung
to **cook sth** [kʊk]	etw zubereiten, etw kochen
to **last** [lɑːst]	halten
frozen food [ˌfrəʊzn ˈfuːd]	Tiefkühlkost
canned food [kænd ˈfuːd]	Konserven
livestock [ˈlaɪvstɒk]	Vieh, Nutztiere
to **grow sth** [grəʊ]	etw *(Pflanzen usw.)* anbauen, etw ziehen
to **raise sth** [reɪz]	*(Tiere:)* etw züchten, etw aufziehen
genetic manipulation [dʒəˌnetɪk məˌnɪpjuˈleɪʃn]	Genmanipulation

page 97

fatty [ˈfæti]	fett, fetthaltig
to **lose weight** [ˌluːz ˈweɪt]	abnehmen
to **lower sth** [ˈləʊə]	etw senken
from scratch [frəm ˈskrætʃ]	ganz von vorn, komplett
recipe [ˈresɪpi]	Rezept
to **be responsible for sth** [bi rɪˈspɒnsəbl fə]	für etw zuständig/verantwortlich sein
base [beɪs]	Boden
topping [ˈtɒpɪŋ]	*(Pizza:)* Belag
grated [ˈgreɪtɪd]	gerieben
level teaspoonful [ˌlevl ˈtiːspuːnfʊl]	gestrichener Teelöffel
yeast [jiːst]	Hefe
chopped [tʃɒpt]	gehackt
basil [ˈbæzl]	Basilikum
olive [ˈɒlɪv]	Olive
to **cut** [kʌt]	schneiden, zerschneiden
clove of garlic [ˌkləʊv əv ˈgɑːlɪk]	Knoblauchzehe
tin [tɪn]	Dose
halved [hɑːvd]	halbiert
tablespoon [ˈteɪblspuːn]	Esslöffel
tomato paste [təˈmɑːtəʊ peɪst]	Tomatenmark
leaf (*pl* **leaves**) [liːf]	Blatt
flour [ˈflaʊə]	Mehl
in all [ɪn ˈɔːl]	insgesamt
dough [dəʊ]	Teig
to **rise** [raɪz]	*(Teig:)* gehen, aufgehen
to **knead** [niːd]	kneten
to **bake** [beɪk]	backen
crisp [krɪsp]	knusprig
remaining [rɪˈmeɪnɪŋ]	übrige/r/s
to **smooth sth** [smuːð]	etw glattstreichen
spoon [spuːn]	Löffel
to **scatter sth** [ˈskætə]	etw verteilen, etw verstreuen
to **sprinkle sth** [ˈsprɪŋkl]	etw streuen
baking paper [ˈbeɪkɪŋ peɪpə]	Backpapier
to **preheat sth** [ˌpriːˈhiːt]	etw vorheizen
baking tray [ˈbeɪkɪŋ treɪ]	Backblech
to **blend sth with sth** [ˈblend wɪð]	etw mit etw vermischen
to **mix sth** [mɪks]	etw mischen, etw vermengen
to **rub** [rʌb]	reiben
to **pour sth** [pɔː]	etw gießen, etw schütten
top shelf [ˌtɒp ˈʃelf]	oberste Schiene *(im Backofen)*
oven [ˈʌvn]	Ofen
floured [ˈflaʊəd]	bemehlt
surface [ˈsɜːfɪs]	Oberfläche, Arbeitsfläche
rolling pin [ˈrəʊlɪŋ pɪn]	Nudelholz
disc [dɪsk]	Scheibe
to **drain sth** [dreɪn]	etw abseihen
to **crush sth** [krʌʃ]	etw zerquetschen
to **shape sth** [ʃeɪp]	etw formen
slice [slaɪs]	*(Pizza, Kuchen usw.:)* Stück
smooth [smuːð]	glatt, geschmeidig
bowl [bəʊl]	Schüssel

to **cover** sth ['kʌvə]	etw bedecken, etw abdecken
cloth [klɒθ]	Tuch
translation [træns'leɪʃn]	Übersetzung
nutritionist [nju'trɪʃənɪst]	Ernährungsberater/in, -wissenschaftler/in
gleaming ['gli:mɪŋ]	blitzblank
stainless steel [ˌsteɪnləs 'sti:l]	(aus) Edelstahl
foodstuffs *pl* ['fu:dstʌfs]	Lebensmittel
to **chop** sth **up** [ˌtʃɒp 'ʌp]	etw kleinschneiden, etw hacken
blender ['blendə]	Mixer
flavouring ['fleɪvərɪŋ]	Aroma
corn [kɔ:n]	Getreide, Mais
derivative [dɪ'rɪvətɪv]	Derivat
petroleum [pə'trəʊliəm]	Erdöl
silicone ['sɪlɪkəʊn]	Silikon
mouthful ['maʊθfʊl]	Zungenbrecher
crude oil [ˌkru:d 'ɔɪl]	Rohöl
rather ['rɑ:ðə]	ziemlich
frightening ['fraɪtnɪŋ]	beängstigend
preferably ['prefərəbli]	vorzugsweise, am liebsten
carcass ['kɑ:kəs]	Gerippe, Tierkörper
to **waste** sth [weɪst]	etw vergeuden
bone marrow ['bəʊn mærəʊ]	Knochenmark
to **scrape** [skreɪp]	schaben, kratzen
Yuck! [jʌk]	Bäh! Igitt!
trace [treɪs]	Spur, Rückstand
growth hormone ['grəʊθ hɔ:məʊn]	Wachstumshormon
vaccine ['væksi:n]	Impfstoff
to **medicate** sb/sth ['medɪkeɪt]	jdn/etw medizinisch behandeln
pharmaceutical [ˌfɑ:mə'su:tɪkl]	Arzneimittel
pesticide ['pestɪsaɪd]	Schädlingsbekämpfungsmittel
food for thought [ˌfʊd fə 'θɔ:t]	Denkanstöße, Stoff zum Nachdenken
educator ['edʒukeɪtə]	Pädagoge/-in

page 98

diet plan ['daɪət plæn]	Diätplan, Ernährungsplan
to **do** sth **about** sth ['du: əbaʊt]	etw an etw ändern, etw an etw machen
to **gain weight** [geɪn 'weɪt]	zunehmen
calories *pl* ['kæləriz]	Kalorien
weight [weɪt]	Gewicht
grain [greɪn]	Getreide
serving ['sɜ:vɪŋ]	Portion
dairy (products) ['deəri]	Milchprodukte
legumes *pl* ['legju:mz]	Hülsenfrüchte
seeds *pl* [si:dz]	Samen, Körner
lean [li:n]	mager
protein ['prəʊti:n]	Eiweiß, Protein
cholesterol levels *pl* [kə'lestərɒl levlz]	Cholesterinwerte
dangerous ['deɪndʒərəs]	gefährlich

page 99

to **affect** sb/sth [ə'fekt]	jdn/etw betreffen, jdn/etw treffen
increased risk [ɪnˌkri:st 'rɪsk]	erhöhtes Risiko
insufficient [ˌɪnsə'fɪʃnt]	unzureichend
to **adopt** sth [ə'dɒpt]	etw übernehmen, etw annehmen
to **be key to** sth [bi 'ki: tə]	für etw entscheidend sein
to **manage** sth ['mænɪdʒ]	mit etw zurechtkommen, etw in den Griff bekommen
to **keep** sth **in check** [ˌki:p ɪn 'tʃek]	etw unter Kontrolle halten
hypertension [ˌhaɪpə'tenʃn]	erhöhter Blutdruck, Hypertonie
low-density lipoprotein [ləʊ ˌdensəti ˌlɪpəʊ'prəʊti:n]	Lipoprotein niedriger Dichte
blood glucose levels *pl* ['blʌd glu:kəʊz levlz]	Blutzuckerwerte
vital ['vaɪtl]	unerlässlich, unverzichtbar
heart damage ['hɑ:t dæmɪdʒ]	Herzschäden, Herzschädigung
throughout sb's life [θru:ˌaʊt 'laɪf]	jds ganzes Leben lang
whole grains *pl* ['həʊl greɪnz]	Vollkorngetreide
to **cut back on** sth [ˌkʌt 'bæk ɒn]	etw reduzieren
spice [spaɪs]	Gewürz
sodium ['səʊdiəm]	Natrium
intake ['ɪnteɪk]	Verzehr, Konsum, Zufuhr
prediabetes [ˌpri:daɪə'bi:ti:z]	Prädiabetes
Greece [gri:s]	Griechenland
to **diagnose** sb **with** sth ['daɪəgnəʊz]	etw bei jdm diagnostizieren
to **be associated with** sth [bi ə'səʊʃieɪt wɪð]	mit etw in Zusammenhang stehen

page 100

consequence ['kɒnsɪkwəns]	Folge, Konsequenz
life expectancy ['laɪf ɪkspektənsi]	Lebenserwartung
to **be related (to** sth**)** [bi rɪ'leɪtɪd tə]	(mit etw) zusammenhängen
device [dɪ'vaɪs]	(elektronisches) Gerät
to **measure** sth ['meʒə]	etw messen
to **turn** sb/sth **into** sth ['tɜ:n ɪntə]	etw aus jdm/etw machen, jdn/etw zu etw machen, jdn/etw in etw umwandeln
growth [grəʊθ]	Wachstum
nothing in particular [ˌnʌθɪŋ ɪn pə'tɪkjələ]	nichts Besonderes
cause of death [kɔ:z əv 'deθ]	Todesursache
to **lessen** sth [lesn]	etw verringern, etw vermindern
on average [ɒn 'ævərɪdʒ]	im Durchschnitt
to **loaf around** [ˌləʊf ə'raʊnd]	herumhängen, herumgammeln
researcher [rɪ'sɜ:tʃə]	Forscher/in, Wissenschaftler/in
Dane [deɪn]	Däne/Dänin
the key [ðə 'ki:]	die Hauptsache

pedometer [pɪˈdɒmətə]	Schrittzähler
accelerometer [əkˌseləˈrɒmɪtə]	Beschleunigungsmesser
subject [ˈsʌbdʒɪkt]	Versuchsperson
stress test [ˈstres test]	Belastungstest
to **determine sth** [dɪˈtɜːmɪn]	etw bestimmen
to **be equal to sth** [bi ˈiːkwəl tə]	einer Sache entsprechen
merely [ˈmɪəli]	lediglich, bloß, nur
typically [ˈtɪpɪkli]	normalerweise
lazy [ˈleɪzi]	träge, faul
mental state [ˌmentl ˈsteɪt]	Befindlichkeit, seelische Verfassung
somewhat [ˈsʌmwɒt]	ein wenig, irgendwie
mechanism [ˈmekənɪzəm]	Mechanismus
inactivity [ˌɪnækˈtɪvəti]	Untätigkeit, Trägheit, Inaktivität
laziness [ˈleɪzinəs]	Trägheit, Faulheit
astonishing [əˈstɒnɪʃɪŋ]	erstaunlich
endurance [ɪnˈdjʊərəns]	Ausdauer
performance [pəˈfɔːməns]	Leistung
average [ˈævərɪdʒ]	Durchschnitt; durchschnitt-lich
to **signify sth** [ˈsɪgnɪfaɪ]	etw bedeuten, für etw stehen
muscle mass [ˈmʌsl mæs]	Muskelmasse
idle [ˈaɪdl]	untätig
organism [ˈɔːgənɪzəm]	Organismus
to **metabolize sth** [məˈtæbəlaɪz]	etw verstoffwechseln
previously [ˈpriːviəsli]	vorher, zuvor
lipid counts *pl* [ˈlɪpɪd kaʊnts]	Lipidwerte
insulin resistant [ˈɪnsjʊlɪn rɪzɪstənt]	insulinresistent
meaning [ˈmiːnɪŋ]	das heißt
dosis (*pl* **doses**) [ˈdəʊsɪs (ˈdəʊsiːz)]	Dosis
cutaway image [ˈkʌtəweɪ ɪmɪdʒ]	*(Tomografie:)* Schnittbild
abdominal area [æbˌdɒmɪnl ˈeəriə]	Bauchraum
to **be suspected to do sth** [bi səˌspektɪd tə ˈduː]	im/unter Verdacht stehen, etw zu tun
idleness [ˈaɪdlnəs]	Untätigkeit
to **take its toll on sth** [ˌteɪk ɪts ˈtəʊl ɒn]	seinen Tribut von etw fordern, etw (gehörig) mitnehmen
to **transform sth** [trænsˈfɔːm]	etw verwandeln, etw umwandeln

page 101

to **reveal sth** [rɪˈviːl]	etw aufdecken, etw enthüllen, etw zeigen
moderate [ˈmɒdərət]	mäßig, gemäßigt
vigorous [ˈvɪgərəs]	energisch, kräftig
income [ˈɪnkʌm]	Einkommen
expenditure [ɪkˈspendɪtʃə]	Ausgaben, Kosten
per capita [pə ˈkæpɪtə]	pro Kopf
subtitle [ˈsʌbtaɪtl]	Untertitel

page 102

folder [ˈfəʊldə]	Mappe, Ordner
official [əˈfɪʃl]	Amtsträger/in, Beamte/r
extended [ɪkˈstendɪd]	erweitert
nuclear family [ˌnjuːkliə ˈfæməli]	Kernfamilie, Kleinfamilie
stepfamily [ˈstepfæməli]	Stieffamilie
stepparents *pl* [ˈsteppeərənts]	Stiefeltern
stepchild [ˈsteptʃaɪld]	Stiefkind
breadwinner [ˈbredwɪnə]	Ernährer/in
housewife [ˈhaʊswaɪf]	Hausfrau
traditional [trəˈdɪʃənl]	hergebracht, traditionell
set-up [ˈsetʌp]	Rahmen, Konstellation
homeland [ˈhəʊmlænd]	Heimatland
patriarchal [ˌpeɪtrɪˈɑːkl]	patriarchalisch
to **marry** [ˈmæri]	heiraten
native [ˈneɪtɪv]	einheimisch
separation [ˌsepəˈreɪʃn]	Trennung
divorce [dɪˈvɔːs]	Scheidung
statistically [stəˈtɪstɪkli]	statistisch gesehen
to **split sth** [splɪt]	etw teilen, etw aufteilen
caring [ˈkeərɪŋ]	Betreuung
to **be in need of care** [bi ɪn ˌniːd əf ˈkeə]	pflegebedürftig sein
daughter-in-law [ˈdɔːtər ɪn lɔː]	Schwiegertochter
to **adjust to sth** [əˈdʒʌst tə]	sich an etw anpassen
to **integrate into sth** [ˈɪntɪgreɪt]	sich in etw integrieren
rise (in sth) [raɪz]	Anstieg (von etw), Zunahme (von etw)
bond [bɒnd]	Bindung, Verbundenheit
to **be beneficial to sb** [bi ˌbenɪˈfɪʃl tə]	für jdn vorteilhaft/gut sein

page 103

to **come into being** [ˌkʌm ɪntə ˈbiːɪŋ]	entstehen
to **arise** [əˈraɪz]	*(Probleme usw.:)* enstehen
to **exchange sth** [ɪksˈtʃeɪndʒ]	etw austauschen
unusual [ʌnˈjuːʒʊəl]	unüblich
lately [ˈleɪtli]	in letzter Zeit
If you're just joining us … [ɪf jɔː ˌdʒʌst ˈdʒɔɪnɪŋ ʌs]	*(Radio-/TV-Sendung:)* Wenn Sie gerade erst zugeschaltet haben, …
member state [ˌmembə ˈsteɪt]	Mitgliedsstaat
to **record sth** [rɪˈkɔːd]	etw verzeichnen
huge [hjuːdʒ]	riesig, riesengroß
proportion [prəˈpɔːʃn]	Anteil
Lithuania [ˌlɪθjuˈeɪniə]	Litauen
Estonia [eˈstəuniə]	Estland
to **share sth** [ʃeə]	sich etw teilen
rate [reɪt]	Quote, Anteil
to **be in line with sth** [bɪ ˌɪn ˈlaɪn wɪð]	mit etw übereinstimmen, sich mit etw decken
worrying [ˈwʌriɪŋ]	bedenklich, beunruhigend
to **influence sb/sth** [ˈɪnfluəns]	jdn/etw beeinflussen

racism [ˈreɪsɪzəm]	Rassismus
same-sex [ˌseɪm ˈseks]	gleichgeschlechtlich
tolerance [ˈtɒlərəns]	Toleranz
nowadays [ˈnaʊədeɪz]	heute, heutzutage
respectable [rɪˈspektəbl]	respektabel, anständig, ehrbar
to **balance sth with sth** [ˈbæləns wɪð]	etw mit etw in Einklang bringen
discriminatory [dɪˈskrɪmɪnətəri]	diskriminierend
to **adopt** [əˈdɒpt]	adoptieren

page 104

crisis (*pl* **crises**) [ˈkraɪsɪs (ˈkraɪsiːz)]	Krise
of one's own [əv wʌnz ˈəʊn]	eigene/r/s
to **function** [ˈfʌŋkʃn]	funktionieren
to **be faced with sth** [bi ˈfeɪst wɪð]	mit etw konfrontiert werden
stressful [ˈstresfl]	belastend, anstrengend, stressig
to **hand sth down** [ˌhænd ˈdaʊn]	etw weitergeben, etw vererben
to **neglect sb/sth** [nɪˈglekt]	jdn/etw vernachlässigen
behaviour(al) pattern [bɪˈheɪvjə pætn]	Verhaltensmuster
adultery [əˈdʌltəri]	Ehebruch, Fremdgehen
bullying [ˈbʊliɪŋ]	Mobbing, Tyrannisieren
to **lie** [laɪ]	lügen
manipulative [məˈnɪpjələtɪv]	manipulativ
mental abuse [ˌmentl əˈbjuːs]	psychischer Missbrauch
battering [ˈbætərɪŋ]	(körperliche) Misshandlung
to **play truant** [ˌpleɪ ˈtruːənt]	die Schule schwänzen
promiscuity [ˌprɒmɪˈskjuːəti]	Promiskuität, wechselnde Sexualpartner/innen
series [ˈsɪəriːz]	Serie, Reihe
siblings *pl* [ˈsɪblɪŋz]	Geschwister
character [ˈkærəktə]	*(Roman, Film usw.:)* Figur

page 105

family support centre [ˌfæməli səˈpɔːt sentə]	Familienhilfe, Familienhilfezentrum
conflict [ˈkɒnflɪkt]	Konflikt(e), Auseinandersetzung(en), Streit
to **occur** [əˈkɜː]	vorkommen, auftreten
I'm afraid so. [aɪm əˌfreɪd ˈsəʊ]	Leider ja.
to **separate** [ˈsepəreɪt]	sich trennen
to **divorce** [dɪˈvɔːs]	sich scheiden lassen
not necessarily [nɒt ˌnesəˈserəli]	nicht unbedingt
fault [fɔːlt]	Fehler, Schwäche
to **complement each other** [ˈkɒmplɪmənt iːtʃ ʌðə]	sich gegenseitig ergänzen
district nurse [ˈdɪstrɪkt nɜːs]	Pflegekraft in der ambulanten Pflege
understanding [ˌʌndəˈstændɪŋ]	Verständnis
sensitivity [ˌsensəˈtɪvəti]	Sensibilität
to **pick on sb** [ˈpɪk ɒn]	an jdm herumnörgeln, auf jdm herumhacken
to **marginalize sb** [ˈmɑːdʒɪnlaɪz]	jdn ausgrenzen
to **ignore sb/sth** [ɪgˈnɔː]	jdn/etw ignorieren
denial [dɪˈnaɪəl]	Leugnung, Abstreiten
refusal [rɪˈfjuːzl]	Weigerung
painful [ˈpeɪnfl]	schmerzhaft
unpleasant [ʌnˈpleznt]	unangenehm, unerfreulich
incest [ˈɪnsest]	Inzest
court [kɔːt]	Gericht
to **insist** [ɪnˈsɪst]	darauf bestehen, etw mit Nachdruck behaupten
to **stand by** [ˌstænd ˈbaɪ]	zusehen, dabeistehen
possibly [ˈpɒsəbli]	womöglich
to **dislike sb/sth** [dɪsˈlaɪk]	jdn/etw nicht mögen
sexual intercourse [ˌsekʃuəl ˈɪntəkɔːs]	Geschlechtsverkehr
to **go off** [ˌgəʊ ˈɒf]	abhauen, davonlaufen
horrible [ˈhɒrəbl]	schrecklich, furchtbar
to **bring sb up** [ˌbrɪŋ ˈʌp]	jdn aufziehen, jdn großziehen
to **claim sth** [kleɪm]	etw behaupten
to **cover up for sb** [ˌkʌvər ˈʌp fə]	jdn decken
to **call on sb** [ˈkɔːl ɒn]	bei jdm vorbeischauen
stairs *pl* [steəz]	Treppe
rude [ruːd]	unverschämt, unhöflich
childhood [ˈtʃaɪldhʊd]	Kindheit
to **beat sb** [biːt]	jdn schlagen
twins *pl* [twɪnz]	Zwillinge
to **be/get killed** [bi/ˌget ˈkɪld]	ums Leben kommen
robbery [ˈrɒbəri]	Überfall
to **be unable to do sth** [bi ʌnˈeɪbl tə]	nicht in der Lage sein, etw zu tun; etw nicht tun können
dependent (on sth) [dɪˈpendənt]	abhängig (von etw)
term *BE* [tɜːm]	Trimester
a total of [ə ˈtəʊtl əv]	insgesamt
to **feature sth** [ˈfiːtʃə]	über etw groß berichten

page 106

in general [ɪn ˈdʒenrəl]	allgemein
to **give sb up for adoption** [gɪv ˌʌp fər əˈdɒpʃn]	jdn zur Adoption freigeben
case notes *pl* [ˈkeɪs nəʊts]	Fallakte, Fallnotizen
to **proceed** [prəˈsiːd]	vor sich gehen, laufen
abortion [əˈbɔːʃn]	Abtreibung
termination [tɜːmɪˈneɪʃn]	Schwangerschaftsabbruch
traumatic [trɔːˈmætɪk]	traumatisch
stepfather [ˈstepfɑːðə]	Stiefvater
half-brother [ˌhɑːf ˈbrʌðə]	Halbbruder
neighbourhood [ˈneɪbəhʊd]	Nachbarschaft, Wohnviertel
to **have a chat with sb** [həv ə ˈtʃæt wɪð]	mit jdm sprechen
figure [ˈfɪgə]	Figur

verbal abuse [ˌvɜ:bl əˈbju:s]	Beschimpfungen, Beleidigungen
hostility [hɒˈstɪləti]	Feindseligkeit, ablehnende Haltung
god [gɒd]	Gott
legal(ly) [ˈli:gl]	rechtmäßig, legal
Roman Catholic [ˌrəʊmən ˈkæθəlɪk]	römisch-katholisch
antenatal clinic [ˌæntɪˈneɪtəl klɪnɪk]	Schwangerschaftsfürsorge, Pränataldiagnostik
to **give birth** [gɪv ˈbɜ:θ]	entbinden, gebären
to **liaise with sb** [liˈeɪz wɪð]	mit jdm in Kontakt sein
agency [ˈeɪdʒənsi]	Agentur
adoptive couple [əˌdɒptɪv ˈkʌpl]	Adoptivpaar

page 107

to **take sth into account** [ˌteɪk ɪntu əˈkaʊnt]	etw berücksichtigen
to **affect sb/sth** [əˈfekt]	sich auf jdn/etw auswirken, jdn/etw beeinflussen
adopter [əˈdɒptə]	Adoptierende/r
application [ˌæplɪˈkeɪʃn]	Antrag
smoker [ˈsməʊkə]	Raucher/in
to **expose sb to sth** [ɪkˈspəʊz tə]	jdn einer Sache aussetzen
to **quit sth** [kwɪt]	mit etw aufhören
medical adviser [ˌmedɪkl ədˈvaɪzə]	medizinische/r Berater/in
fertility treatment [fəˈtɪləti tri:tmənt]	Kinderwunschbehandlung, künstliche Befruchtung
infertility [ˌɪnfəˈtɪləti]	Unfruchtbarkeit
infertile [ɪnˈfɜ:taɪl]	unfruchtbar
to **suggest sth** [səˈdʒest]	auf etw hindeuten, etw nahelegen
to **place sb somewhere** [pleɪs]	jdn irgendwo unterbringen
to **apply for sth** [əˈplaɪ fə]	etw beantragen
auto-immune disease [ˌɔ:təʊ ɪˈmju:n dɪzi:z]	Autoimmunkrankheit
to **pass sth on genetically** [pɑ:s ˌɒn dʒəˈnetɪkli]	etw (genetisch) vererben
to **convict sb for sth** [kənˈvɪkt fə]	jdn wegen etw verurteilen
vandalism [ˈvændəlɪzəm]	(mutwillige) Sachbeschädigung
to **do community service** [du ˌkəˈmju:nəti sɜ:vɪs]	Sozialstunden ableisten
at the time [ət ðə ˈtaɪm]	seinerzeit
conviction [kənˈvɪkʃn]	Verurteilung
criminal record [ˈkrɪmɪnl rekɔ:d]	Vorstrafen(register)
medical records *pl* [ˌmedɪkl ˈrekɔ:dz]	Patientenakte
medical check-up [ˌmedɪkl ˈtʃekʌp]	ärztliche Untersuchung
to **counsel sb** [ˈkaʊnsəl]	jdn beraten
pros and cons *pl* [ˌprəʊz ənd ˈkɒnz]	Argumente dafür und dagegen, Vor- und Nachteile
upbringing [ˈʌpbrɪŋɪŋ]	Erziehung, Elternhaus
biological mother [baɪəˌlɒdʒɪkl ˈmʌðə]	leibliche Mutter
afterwards [ˈɑ:ftəwədz]	danach
to **feel unable to do sth** [ˌfi:l ʌnˈeɪbl tə]	sich nicht in der Lage sehen, etw zu tun; sich nicht trauen, etw zu tun
similarly [ˈsɪmələli]	ebenso, in gleicher Weise
to **come about** [ˌkʌm əˈbaʊt]	entstehen
to **surface** [ˈsɜ:fɪs]	auftauchen, auftreten
to **perform sth** [pəˈfɔ:m]	etw durchführen, etw ausführen

page 108

to **settle** [setl]	sich niederlassen
schooling [ˈsku:lɪŋ]	Schulbildung, Schulunterricht
conflict [ˈkɒnflɪkt]	militärische Auseinandersetzung(en), Kämpfe, Krieg
to **result in sth** [rɪˈzʌlt ɪn]	etw zur Folge haben, zu etw führen
to **enter school** [ˌentə ˈsku:l]	in die Schule kommen, eingeschult werden
overwhelming [ˌəʊvəˈwelmɪŋ]	überwältigend
special classes *pl* [ˌspeʃl ˈklɑ:sɪz]	Sonderklassen
sharp [ʃɑ:p]	drastisch, stark, plötzlich
immigration [ˌɪmɪˈgreɪʃn]	Einwanderung, Immigration
EU enlargement [ˌi: ˈju: ɪnlɑ:dʒmənt]	EU-Erweiterung
Bulgaria [bʌlˈgeəriə]	Bulgarien
Romania [ru:ˈmeɪniə]	Rumänien
to **flee sth** [fli:]	vor etw fliehen
Syria [ˈsɪriə]	Syrien
wave [weɪv]	Welle
war [wɔ:]	Krieg
Ukraine [ju:ˈkreɪn]	Ukraine
academic [ˌækəˈdemɪk]	Akademiker/in
working class [ˌwɜ:kɪŋ ˈklɑ:s]	Arbeiterklasse
to **put a huge burden on sb/sth** [pʊt ə ˌhju:dʒ ˈbɜ:dn ɒn]	jdn/etw stark belasten, eine starke Belastung für jdn/etw sein
newly [ˈnju:li]	gerade erst, vor kurzem
growing [ˈgrəʊɪŋ]	steigend, zunehmend
to **contract sb** [kənˈtrækt]	jdn einstellen
Hesse [hes]	Hessen
North Rhine-Westphalia [nɔ:θ ˌraɪn westˈfeɪliə]	Nordrhein-Westfalen
instruction [ɪnˈstrʌkʃn]	Unterricht
technical college [ˈteknɪkl kɒlɪdʒ]	Berufskolleg, Fachhochschule
Algerian [ælˈdʒɪəriən]	algerisch
Greek [gri:k]	griechisch; Griechisch

page 109

to **call a meeting** [ˌkɔ:l ə ˈmi:tɪŋ]	eine Sitzung einberufen, eine Besprechung ansetzen

to **hate sth** [heɪt]	etw überhaupt nicht mögen, etw hassen
self-conscious [ˌself ˈkɒnʃəs]	gehemmt, befangen, unsicher
to **stare at sb** [ˈsteər ət]	jdn anstarren
at one point [ət wʌn ˈpɔɪnt]	irgendwann
Somali [səˈmɑːli]	Somalier/in
to **fit in** [ˌfɪt ˈɪn]	dazugehören, sich einfügen
flea market [ˈfliː mɑːkɪt]	Flohmarkt
Naples [ˈneɪplz]	Neapel
to **start with** [tə ˈstɑːt wɪð]	am Anfang, anfangs
to **tease sb** [tiːz]	jdn aufziehen, jdn provozieren, jdn scharfmachen
remark [rɪˈmɑːk]	Bemerkung
to **annoy sb** [əˈnɔɪ]	jdn nerven, jdn ärgern
Russian [ˈrʌʃn]	Russe/-in; Russisch
to **survive** [səˈvaɪv]	überleben
memo [ˈmeməʊ]	(Gesprächs-)Notiz, Mitteilung
manual [ˈmænjuəl]	Handbuch, Leitfaden
to **threaten sb** [ˈθretn]	jdn bedrohen
to **enjoy doing sth** [ɪnˈdʒɔɪ]	etw gern tun
to **refuse to do sth** [rɪˌfjuːz tə ˈduː]	sich weigern, etw zu tun
revenge [rɪˈvendʒ]	Rache
luckily [ˈlʌkɪli]	zum Glück, glücklicherweise
chess [tʃes]	Schach

page 110

from the field [frəm ðə ˈfiːld]	aus der Praxis
encounter [ɪnˈkaʊntə]	Begegnung
to **mix** [mɪks]	*(Party usw.:)* sich kennenlernen, miteinander in Kontakt kommen
belief [bɪˈliːf]	Überzeugung, Glaube
heaven [ˈhevn]	Himmel
taboo [təˈbuː]	Tabu; tabu
mourner [ˈmɔːnə]	Trauernde/r
funeral [ˈfjuːnərəl]	Begräbnis, Bestattung
place of worship [pleɪs əv ˈwɜːʃɪp]	Gebetsstätte, Gotteshaus
apart from sb/sth [əˈpɑːt frəm]	von jdm/etw getrennt
mother tongue [ˈmʌðə tʌŋ]	Muttersprache
it is fortunate that [ɪt ɪz ˈfɔːtʃənət ðət]	glücklicherweise, erfreulicherweise
multilingual [ˌmʌltiˈlɪŋgwəl]	mehrsprachig
to **pair up** [ˌpeər ˈʌp]	sich paarweise zusammentun

page 111

to **migrate** [maɪˈgreɪt]	auswandern, migrieren
government [ˈgʌvənmnt]	Regierung
bilateral agreement [baɪˌlætrəl əˈgriːmənt]	bilaterales Abkommen
recruitment [rɪˈkruːtmənt]	Anwerbung *(von Personal)*, Einstellung
industrial sector [ɪnˌdʌstriəl ˈsektə]	Industrie
construction [kənˈstrʌkʃn]	Bau
large-scale flow [lɑːdʒ ˌskeɪl ˈfləʊ]	großer Zustrom
Morocco [məˈrɒkəʊ]	Marokko
Tunisia [tjuːˈnɪziə]	Tunesien
Yugoslavia [ˌjuːgəʊˈslɑːviə]	Jugoslawien
home country [ˌhəʊm ˈkʌntri]	Heimatland
federal republic [ˌfedərəl rɪˈpʌblɪk]	Bundesrepublik
developmental aid [dɪveləpˌmentl ˈeɪd]	Entwicklungshilfe
fixed [fɪkst]	fest
division [dɪˈvɪʒn]	Teilung
labour shortage [ˈleɪbə ʃɔːtɪdʒ]	Arbeitskräftemangel
contract [ˈkɒntrækt]	Vertrag
Poland [ˈpəʊlənd]	Polen
Eastern Bloc [ˌiːstən ˈblɒk]	Ostblock
Mozambique [ˌməʊzæmˈbiːk]	Mosambik
solidarity [ˌsɒlɪˈdærəti]	Solidarität
fellow communist countries *pl* [ˌfeləʊ ˌkɒmjənɪst ˈkʌntriz]	kommunistische Bruderstaaten
reunification [ˌriːjuːnɪfɪˈkeɪʃn]	Wiedervereinigung
former [ˈfɔːmə]	ehemalig, früher
deportation [dɪpɔːˈteɪʃn]	Abschiebung
premature [ˈprematjʊə]	vorzeitig
discontinuation [ˌdɪskənˌtɪnjuˈeɪʃn]	Entzug, Kündigung
(right of) residence [ˈrezɪdəns]	Aufenthaltsrecht, Bleiberecht
work permit [ˌwɜːk ˈpɜːmɪt]	Arbeitserlaubnis
xenophobia [zenəˈfəʊbɪə]	Fremdenfeindlichkeit
(federal) state [steɪt]	Bundesland
existence [ɪgˈzɪstəns]	Existenz
to **exist** [ɪgˈzɪst]	existieren
unreasonable [ʌnˈriːznəbl]	unvernünftig, abwegig
dislike [dɪsˈlaɪk]	Abneigung
belonging [bɪˈlɒŋɪŋ]	Zugehörigkeit
casual [ˈkæʒuəl]	zufällig
variety [vəˈraɪəti]	Vielfalt
to **settle down** [ˌsetl ˈdaʊn]	zur Ruhe kommen, sich beruhigen
diverse [daɪˈvɜːs]	vielfältig, unterschiedlich, divers
one by one [ˌwʌn baɪ ˈwʌn]	nacheinander, der Reihe nach
to **differ (from sb/sth)** [ˈdɪfə]	sich (von jdm/etw) unterscheiden
tendency [ˈtendənsi]	Neigung, Tendenz
to **impose sth upon sb** [ɪmˈpəuz əpɒn]	jdm etw aufzwingen, jdm etw auferlegen
That's it. [ðætsˈ ɪt]	Genau!
to **familiarize oneself with sth** [fəˈmɪliəraɪz wʌnself wɪð]	sich mit etw vertraut machen
fascinating [ˈfæsɪneɪtɪŋ]	faszinierend
to **begin with** [tə bɪˈgɪn wɪð]	zunächst (einmal)
agnostic [ægˈnɒstɪk]	agnostisch; Agnostiker/in

atheist [ˈeɪθiɪst]	atheistisch; Atheist/in
assuming (that) [əˈsjuːmɪŋ]	vorausgesetzt, angenommen
to **draw on sth** [ˈdrɔː ɒn]	auf etw zurückgreifen, an etw anknüpfen
to **come in** [ˌkʌm ˈɪn]	ins Spiel kommen
set of values [ˌset əv ˈvæljuːz]	Werte
to **stop at sth** [ˈstɒp ət]	bei/vor etw Halt machen
from the general to the specific [frəm ðə ˌdʒenrəl tə ðə spəˈsɪfɪk]	vom Allgemeinen zum Konkreten
to **make sense** [ˌmeɪk ˈsens]	vernünftig sein, einleuchten
automatically [ˌɔːtəˈmætɪkli]	automatisch
to **assume sth** [əˈsjuːm]	etw annehmen, etw unterstellen
to **conform to sth** [kənˈfɔːm tə]	mit etw übereinstimmen, einer Sache entsprechen
custom [ˈkʌstəm]	Sitte, Brauch
indeed [ɪnˈdiːd]	in der Tat, allerdings
to **interact with sb** [ˌɪntərˈækt wɪð]	sich mit jdm auseinandersetzen, mit jdm interagieren
to **close** [kləʊz]	Schluss machen, schließen
piece of advice [piːs əv ədˈvaɪs]	Ratschlag, Rat
objective [əbˈdʒektɪv]	objektiv
to **acquire sth** [əˈkwaɪə]	etw erwerben
to **come up with sth** [ˌkʌm ˈʌp wɪð]	sich etw ausdenken, sich etw einfallen lassen

page 112

asylum seeker [əˈsaɪləm siːkə]	Asylsuchende/r
nationality [ˌnæʃəˈnæləti]	Staatsangehörigkeit
human rights violations *pl* [ˌhjuːmən ˈraɪts vaɪəleɪʃnz]	Menschenrechtsverstöße
traumatized [ˈtrɔːmətaɪzd]	traumatisiert
political [pəˈlɪtɪkl]	politisch
torture [ˈtɔːtʃə]	Folter
ethnic cleansing [ˌeθnɪk ˈklenzɪŋ]	ethnische Säuberungen
harmful [ˈhɑːmfl]	schädlich
mentor [ˈmentɔː]	Mentor/in
to **convey sth** [kənˈveɪ]	etw vermitteln, etw deutlich machen

page 113

Ukrainian [juːˈkreɪmiən]	Ukrainisch
citizen [ˈsɪtɪzn]	Staatsbürger/in
computing [kəmˈpjuːtɪŋ]	Informatik
exchange [ɪksˈtʃeɪndʒ]	Austausch
assistant teacher [əˌsɪstənt ˈtiːtʃə]	(Aus-)Hilfslehrer/in, Assistenzlehrer/in
sometime [ˈsʌmtaɪm]	irgendwann (einmal)
on sb's behalf [ɒn bɪˈhɑːf]	für jdn, in jds Namen
neither [ˈnaɪðə]	keine/r *(von mehreren)*
interviewee [ˌɪntəvjuːˈiː]	*Person, mit der ein Vorstellungsgespräch geführt wird*
to **conduct sth** [kənˈdʌkt]	etw durchführen

page 114

to **start sb off** [ˌstɑːt ˈɒf]	jdm Starthilfe geben
the odd one out [ði ˌɒd wʌn ˈaʊt]	etw, was nicht dazugehört
anorexia [ˌænəˈreksɪə]	Magersucht
bulimia [bjuːˈlɪmiə]	Bulimie
respiratory problem [rɪˈspɪrətri prɒbləm]	Atemwegserkrankung
height [haɪt]	Körpergröße
sluggish [ˈslʌgɪʃ]	träge, schwerfällig
weight-reducing products *pl* [ˌweɪt rɪdjuːsɪŋ ˈprɒdʌkts]	Schlankheitsprodukte

page 115

until recently [ənˌtɪl ˈriːsntli]	bis vor kurzem
to **take leave** [ˌteɪk ˈliːv]	Urlaub nehmen
childbirth [ˈtʃaɪldbɜːθ]	Geburt, Entbindung
drunk [drʌŋk]	betrunken
in secret [ɪn ˈsiːkrɪt]	heimlich

page 116

clientele [kliːɒnˈtel]	Klientel
thorough(ly) [ˈθʌrə]	gründlich
colourful [ˈkʌləfl]	farbenfroh, bunt

page 117

scripted [ˈskrɪptɪd]	mit Drehbuch
to **shout sth at sb** [ˈʃaʊt ət]	jdn (lautstark) mit etw beschimpfen
episode [ˈepɪsəʊd]	Folge *(einer TV-Serie usw.)*

page 118

arrival [əˈraɪvl]	Ankunft, Eintreffen
to **hold a meeting** [həʊld ə ˈmiːtɪŋ]	eine Sitzung/Besprechung abhalten
action plan [ˈækʃn plæn]	Aktionsplan, Maßnahmenkatalog

page 119

concrete [ˈkɒŋkriːt]	konkret
to **take steps** [teɪk ˈsteps]	Schritte unternehmen, Maßnahmen ergreifen
contribution [kɒntrɪˈbjuːʃn]	Beitrag, Spende
newcomer [ˈnjuːkʌmə]	Neuankömmling
manufacturer [ˌmænjuˈfæktʃərə]	Hersteller/in
provider [prəˈvaɪdə]	Anbieter
to **contribute sth** [kɒnˈtrɪbjuːt]	etw beisteuern, etw spenden
language class [ˈlæŋgwɪdʒ klɑːs]	Sprachkurs
to **translate** [trænsˈleɪt]	übersetzen
out of office [ˌaʊt əv ˈɒfɪs]	nicht am Platz, außer Haus
recorded message [rɪˌkɔːdɪd ˈmesɪdʒ]	(automatische) Ansage, Bandansage
bank details *pl* [ˈbæŋk diːteɪlz]	Bankverbindung

TOPIC 6

page 120/121

harassment [ˈhærəsmənt]	Belästigung, Mobbing, Schikanieren
case assessment [ˈkeɪs əsesmənt]	Falleinschätzung
downsizing [ˈdaʊnsaɪzɪŋ]	Stellenabbau, Personalabbau
complaint [kəmˈpleɪnt]	Beschwerde, Reklamation
sexual harassment [ˌsekʃuəl ˈhærəsmənt]	sexuelle Belästigung
alcoholism [ˈælkəhɒlɪzəm]	Alkoholsucht
racial discrimination [ˌreɪʃl dɪˌskrɪmɪˈneɪʃn]	Rassendiskriminierung
legal advice [ˌliːgl ədˈvaɪs]	Rechtsberatung, juristischer Rat
intimidation [ɪnˌtɪmɪˈdeɪʃn]	Einschüchterung
inner resignation [ˌɪnə rezɪgˈneɪʃn]	innere Kündigung
match [mætʃ]	Entsprechung
to **take sth over** [ˌteɪk ˈəʊvə]	etw übernehmen
to **reduce staff** [rɪˌdjuːs ˈstɑːf]	Personal abbauen
unwelcome [ʌnˈwelkəm]	unerwünscht
hostile [ˈhɒstaɪl]	feindselig, aggressiv
to **tolerate sth** [ˈtɒləreɪt]	etw dulden, etw tolerieren
human resources (HR) [ˌhjuːmən rɪˈsɔːsɪz]	Personal(abteilung)
concerned [kənˈsɜːnd]	besorgt, beunruhigt
workplace harassment [ˌwɜːkpleɪs ˈhærəsmənt]	Mobbing am Arbeitsplatz
restructuring [ˌriːˈstrʌktʃərɪŋ]	Umstrukturierung
unresolved [ˌʌnrɪˈzɒlvd]	ungeklärt, ungelöst
disssatisfaction [dɪsˌsætɪsˈfækʃn]	Unzufriedenheit
to **work on sth** [ˈwɜːk ɒn]	etw erarbeiten, an etw arbeiten
to **assign sb to sth** [əˈsaɪn tə]	jdm mit etw betrauen, jdm etw *(Aufgabe usw.)* übertragen

page 122

electronics engineer [ˌɪlekˈtrɒnɪks endʒɪnɪə]	Elektroingenieur/in
to **harass sb** [ˈhærəs]	jdn belästigen, jdn mobben, jdn schikanieren
offensive [əˈfensɪv]	beleidigend, anstößig
(sexually) suggestive [səˈdʒestɪv]	anzüglich, aufreizend
gesture [ˈdʒestʃə]	Geste
to **stare** [steə]	starren
in a … manner [ɪn ə ˈmænə]	auf … (Art und) Weise
lewd [luːd]	anzüglich, obszön
touching [ˈtʌtʃɪŋ]	Berührung(en), Anfassen
inappropriate [ˌɪnəˈprəʊpriət]	unangemessen, unangebracht
R&D (research & development) [ˌɑːr ən ˈdiː]	Forschung(s-) und Entwicklung(sabteilung)
to **feel comfortable** [ˌfiːl ˈkʌmftəbl]	sich wohlfühlen

page 123

to **pretend** [prɪˈtend]	so tun, als ob
while [waɪl]	Weile
to **bring sb along** [ˌbrɪŋ əˈlɒŋ]	jdn mitbringen
since then [sɪns ˈðen]	seitdem
to **be frightened** [bi ˈfraɪtnd]	Angst haben
to **make sb's life hell** [meɪk ˌlaɪf ˈhel]	jdm das Leben zur Hölle machen
to **discriminate against sb** [dɪˈskrɪmɪneɪt]	jdn diskriminieren, jdn benachteiligen
to **send sb to prison** [ˌsend tə ˈprɪzn]	jdn ins Gefängnis werfen, jdn zu einer Haftstrafe verurteilen
homosexual [ˌhəʊməˈsekʃuəl]	homosexuell
calendar [ˈkælɪndə]	Kalender
to **make sounds** [ˌmeɪk ˈsaʊndz]	Laute von sich geben
disgusting [dɪsˈgʌstɪŋ]	ekelhaft
to **perceive sth** [pəˈsiːv]	etw wahrnehmen
conclusion [kənˈkluːʒn]	Schluss
to **delete sth** [dɪˈliːt]	etw löschen
witness [ˈwɪtnəs]	Zeuge/Zeugin
Oh dear! [əʊ ˈdɪə]	Oje! Du meine Güte!
evidence [ˈevɪdəns]	Beweise
to **prove sth** [pruːv]	etw beweisen
to **hurt sb** [hɜːt]	jdm schaden
between the lines [bɪˌtwiːn ðə ˈlaɪnz]	zwischen den Zeilen
observation [ˌɒbzəˈveɪʃn]	Beobachtung

page 124

company doctor [ˌkʌmpəni ˈdɒktə]	Betriebsarzt/-ärztin
to **suffer from sth** [ˈsʌfə frəm]	an/unter etw leiden
stress level [ˈstres levl]	Stressbelastung, Stressniveau
responsibility [rɪˌspɒnsəˈbɪləti]	Verantwortung
to **satisfy sb** [ˈsætɪsfaɪ]	jdn zufriedenstellen
a great deal [ə ˌgreɪt ˈdiːl]	ziemlich viel, eine Menge
co-worker [ˈkəʊwɜːkə]	Kollege/-in
to **have a say in sth** [həv ə ˈseɪ ɪn]	ein Mitspracherecht bei etw haben
muscle tension [ˈmʌsl tenʃn]	Muskelverspannung(en)
stomach pains *pl* [ˈstʌmək peɪnz]	Magenschmerzen, Bauchschmerzen
indigestion [ˌɪndɪˈdʒestʃən]	Magenverstimmung
digestive problems *pl* [daɪˈdʒestɪv prɒbləmz]	Verdauungsprobleme
tranquilizer [ˈtræŋkwəlaɪzə]	Beruhigungsmittel
caffeinated [ˈkæfiːneɪtɪd]	koffeinhaltig
beverage [ˈbevərɪdʒ]	Getränk
supervisor [ˈsuːpəvaɪzə]	Vorgesetzte/r
water cooler [ˈwɔːtə kuːlə]	Wasserspender
to **disturb sb/sth** [dɪˈstɜːb]	jdn/etw stören
tense [tens]	angespannt

canteen [kæn'ti:n]	Kantine
geek [gi:k]	Nerd, Freak
for heaven's sake [fə hevnz 'seɪk]	verdammt nochmal
to **be up to sb** [ˌbi 'ʌp tə]	jdm überlassen bleiben, jds Entscheidung sein
to **add sth up** [ˌæd 'ʌp]	etw zusammenzählen, etw addieren
overall score [əʊvərˌɔ:l 'skɔ:]	Gesamtpunktzahl
excerpt ['eksɜ:pt]	Ausschnitt, Auszug
to **force sb to do sth** [fɔ:s]	jdn (dazu) zwingen, etw zu tun
waste of time [ˌweɪst əf 'taɪm]	Zeitverschwendung
company file ['kʌmpəni faɪl]	Betriebsakte
to **contain sth** [kən'teɪn]	etw enthalten
intelligence [ɪn'telɪdʒəns]	Intelligenz
to **keep to a deadline** [ˌki:p tu ə 'dedlaɪn]	eine Frist einhalten, einen Abgabetermin einhalten
to **have time off** [həv ˌtaɪm 'ɒf]	frei haben

page 125

to **get at sth** ['get ət]	auf etw hinauswollen
graduate ['grædʒuət]	Hochschulabsolvent/in
to **quit** [kwɪt]	kündigen
appreciation [əˌpri:ʃi'eɪʃn]	Wertschätzung, Würdigung
recognition [ˌrekəg'nɪʃn]	Anerkennung
programming language ['prəʊgræmɪŋ læŋgwɪdʒ]	Programmiersprache
approval [ə'pru:vl]	Genehmigung, Zustimmung
to **get your act together** [ˌget jʊer 'ækt təgeðə]	sich zusammenreißen
talk [tɔ:k]	Gespräch
to **graduate** ['grædʒueɪt]	den (Schul-/Uni-) Abschluss machen
promotion [prə'məʊʃn]	Beförderung
promise ['prɒmɪs]	Versprechen
demotivation [ˌdi:məʊtɪ'veɪʃn]	Demotivierung
exchange [ɪks'tʃeɪndʒ]	Wortwechsel
silly ['sɪli]	albern
record ['rekɔ:d]	Aufzeichnung(en), Protokoll
accurate(ly) ['ækjərət]	richtig, präzise, korrekt
to **be to do sth** [ˌbi tə 'du:]	etw tun sollen

page 126

to **lay sb off** [ˌleɪ 'ɒf]	jdn (betriebsbedingt) entlassen
HR manager [eɪtʃ ˌɑ: 'mænɪdʒə]	Personalchef/in, Personalleiter/in
cuts *pl* [kʌts]	Kürzungen
market ['mɑ:kɪt]	Markt
severance package ['sevrəns pækɪdʒ]	Abfindung
to **calculate sth** ['kælkjuleɪt]	etw berechnen
notice ['nəʊtɪs]	Aushang, Mitteilung
bulletin board ['bʊlətɪn bɔ:d]	Schwarzes Brett
lay-off ['leɪ ɒf]	(betriebsbedingte) Kündigung
to **announce sth** [ə'naʊns]	etw ankündigen
to **break the news** [ˌbreɪk ðə 'nju:z]	die Neuigkeit(en) überbringen
to **work overtime** [ˌwɜ:k 'əʊvətaɪm]	Überstunden machen
to **be back to square one** [bi ˌbæk tə ˌskweə 'wʌn]	wieder ganz am Anfang stehen
to **stand in line** [ˌstænd ɪn 'laɪn]	Schlange stehen, anstehen
smart [smɑ:t]	intelligent, schlau
rival ['raɪvl]	Konkurrent/in
to **downsize** ['daʊnsaɪz]	Stellen abbauen
to **fire sb** ['faɪə]	jdn entlassen, jdn feuern
to **keep sb on** [ˌki:p 'ɒn]	jdn weiterbeschäftigen
to **retrain sb** [ˌri:'treɪn]	jdn umschulen
teleworker ['teliwɜ:kə]	Telearbeiter/in
to **miss sb/sth** [mɪs]	jdn/etw vermissen
atmosphere ['ætməsfɪə]	Atmosphäre
insensitive(ly) [ɪn'sensətɪv]	taktlos, instinktlos
to **go freelance** [ˌgəʊ 'fri:lɑ:ns]	sich selbständig machen
to **outsource sth** ['aʊtsɔ:s]	etw auslagern
to **be made unemployed** [bi ˌmeɪd ʌnɪm'plɔɪd]	arbeitslos werden
work contract ['wɜ:k kɒntrækt]	Arbeitsvertrag
telework ['teliwɜ:k]	Telearbeit

page 127

entire [ɪn'taɪə]	gesamte/r/s
overseas [ˌəʊvə'si:z]	im/ins Ausland, in/nach Übersee
at least [ət 'li:st]	wenigstens, zumindest
to **start a business** [ˌstɑ:t ə 'bɪznəs]	ein Unternehmen gründen
clearly ['klɪəli]	offenbar, offensichtlich
to **be mistaken** [bi mɪ'steɪkən]	sich täuschen
nor [nɔ:]	und auch nicht
CEO (Chief Executive Officer) [ˌtʃi:f ɪg'zekjətɪv ɒfɪsə]	Vorstandsvorsitzende/r, Geschäftsführer/in
freelancer ['fri:lɑ:nsə]	Selbständige/r
senior manager [ˌsi:niə 'mænɪdʒə]	leitende/r Angestellte/r
beyond sb's control [bɪˌjɒnd kən'trəʊl]	außerhalb jds Einflussbereichs
socially sensitive [ˌsəʊʃəli 'sensətɪv]	sozialverträglich
tool [tu:l]	Werkzeug
to **restructure** [ˌri:'strʌktʃə]	umstrukturieren
mobility assistance [məʊ'bɪləti əsɪstəns]	Mobilitätshilfe
work schedule ['wɜ:k ʃedju:l]	Arbeitszeit, Arbeitsplan
compensation [ˌkɒmpən'seɪʃn]	Entschädigung, Schadenersatz
survivor [sə'vaɪvə]	Überlebende/r

round table [ˌraʊnd ˈteɪbl]	Gesprächsrunde, Runder Tisch
flexitime [ˈfleksitaɪm]	Gleitzeit
teleworking [ˈteliwɜːkɪŋ]	Telearbeit
loss of earnings [ˌlɒs əv ˈɜːnɪŋz]	Verdienstausfall, Einkommenseinbußen

page 128

conflict management [ˈkɒnflɪkt mænɪdʒmənt]	Konfliktbewältigung, -bearbeitung, -management
sb cares for sth [ˈkeəz fə]	jdm ist an etw gelegen
upset [ˌʌpˈset]	verärgert, aufgebracht
noise [nɔɪz]	Geräusch
to **type** [taɪp]	tippen
to **empathize** [ˈempəθaɪz]	Mitgefühl zeigen, Verständnis zeigen
sth is sb's fault [ɪz ˌsʌmbədiz ˈfɔːlt]	jd ist schuld an etw
to **make sb happy** [ˌmeɪk ˈhæpi]	jdn zufriedenstellen
willingness [ˈwɪlɪŋnəs]	Bereitschaft
to **fix a problem** [ˌfɪks ə ˈprɒbləm]	ein Problem lösen/beheben
to **resolve sth** [rɪˈzɒlv]	etw lösen, etw (auf)klären
as we speak [əz ˌwiː ˈspiːk]	gerade, in diesem Moment
to **enter sth into sth** [ˈentər ɪntə]	etw in etw eintragen
matter [ˈmætə]	Angelegenheit, Sache
straight away [ˌstreɪt əˈweɪ]	sofort
to **bring sth to sb's attention** [ˌbrɪŋ tu əˈtenʃn]	jdn auf etw aufmerksam machen

page 129

cancellation policy [ˌkænsəˈleɪʃn pɒləsi]	Stornierungsbedingungen
to **get hold of sb** [get ˈhəʊld əv]	jdn erreichen, jdn an die Strippe kriegen
unbelievable [ˌʌnbɪˈliːvəbl]	unglaublich, unerhört
devastated [ˈdevəsteɪtɪd]	am Boden zerstört
deposit [dɪˈpɒzɪt]	Anzahlung
reference number [ˈrefərəns nʌmbə]	Kennziffer
to **be supposed to do sth** [bi səˈpəʊzd tə]	etw (eigentlich) tun sollen
travel contract [ˈtrævl kɒntrækt]	Reisevertrag
travel agency [ˈtrævl eɪdʒənsi]	Reisebüro, Reiseagentur
departure date [dɪˈpɑːtʃə deɪt]	Abreisedatum
snorkeling [ˈsnɔːkəlɪŋ]	Schnorcheln
Croatia [krəʊˈeɪʃə]	Kroatien
to **promise** [ˈprɒmɪs]	versprechen

page 130

to **address sth** [əˈdres]	etw *(Problem usw.)* ansprechen
confusion [kənˈfjuːʒn]	Verwirrung
delay [dɪˈleɪ]	Verzögerung, Verspätung
error [ˈerə]	Fehler, Irrtum
fault [fɔːlt]	Defekt, Fehler
failure [ˈfeɪljə]	Ausfall, Versagen
misunderstanding [ˌmɪsʌndəˈstændɪŋ]	Missverständnis
mix-up [ˈmɪks ʌp]	Durcheinander, Verwirrung
oversight [ˈəʊvəsaɪt]	Flüchtigkeitsfehler, Versehen
to **look into sth** [ˈlʊk ɪntə]	etw untersuchen, sich um etw kümmern
on our part [ɒn ˈaʊə pɑːt]	unsererseits
to **reject sth** [rɪˈdʒekt]	etw ablehnen, etw zurückweisen
destination [ˌdestɪˈneɪʃn]	Reiseziel
Austria [ˈɒstriə]	Österreich
booking [ˈbʊkɪŋ]	Buchung, Reservierung
confirmation [ˌkɒnfəˈmeɪʃn]	Bestätigung

page 131

to **draft sth** [drɑːft]	etw entwerfen
in italics [ɪn ɪˈtælɪks]	kursiv (gesetzt)
as if [əz ˈɪf]	als ob
Please accept my apologies. [pliːz əˌksept maɪ əˈpɒlədʒiz]	Ich bitte um Entschuldigung.
status [ˈsteɪtəs]	Stand (der Dinge), Lage, Zustand
database [ˈdeɪtəbeɪs]	Datenbank
incorrect [ˌɪnkəˈrekt]	falsch, fehlerhaft, unrichtig
to **return sth** [rɪˈtɜːn]	etw zurücksenden, etw zurückschicken
to **check sth against sth** [ˈtʃek əgenst]	etw mit etw abgleichen
inconvenience [ˌɪnkənˈviːniəns]	Unannehmlichkeiten
to **feel free to do sth** [fiːl ˌfriː tə ˈduː]	etw gern tun können

page 132

spokesperson [ˈspəʊkspɜːsn]	(offizielle/r) Sprecher/in
overworked [ˌəʊvəˈwɜːkt]	überarbeitet
rumour [ˈruːmə]	Gerücht
to **propose sth** [prəˈpəʊz]	etw vorschlagen, etw beabsichtigen
to **keep a close eye on sth** [kiːp ə ˌkləʊz ˈaɪ ɒn]	etw genau beobachten

page 133

severance pay [ˈsevrəns peɪ]	Abfindung
bank transfer [ˈbæŋk trænsfɜː]	Überweisung
account [əˈkaʊnt]	Konto
typing error [ˈtaɪpɪŋ erə]	Tippfehler
surname [ˈsɜːneɪm]	Nachname
accidentally [ˌæksɪˈdentəli]	versehentlich
understaffed [ˌʌndəˈstɑːft]	unterbesetzt
once again [wʌns əˈgen]	erneut, noch einmal

page 134

dissatisfied [dɪsˈsætɪsfaɪd]	unzufrieden
line manager [laɪn ˈmænɪdʒə]	direkte/r Vorgesetzte/r

disappointed (in sb/ sth) [ˌdɪsəˈpɔɪntɪd]	enttäuscht (von jdm/etw)
separate [ˈseprət]	separat, eigen, einzeln
to **rate sth** [reɪt]	etw einstufen, etw bewerten

page 135

sequence [ˈsiːkwəns]	Abfolge, Folge
to **peer-review sth** [ˌpɪə rɪˈvjuː]	etw (unter Kollegen und Kolleginnen) bewerten

page 137

confidential(ly) [ˌkɒnfɪˈdenʃl]	vertraulich
jigsaw [ˈdʒɪgsɔː]]	Puzzle

A–Z WORD LIST

Dieses Wörterverzeichnis enthält die Wörter in **Social Pulse** in alphabetischer Reihenfolge.

T = *Audio Transcript* P = *Partner File* C = *Challenge File*
V = *Video Transcript* G = *Guidance File*

A

abdominal area *100V* Bauchraum
ability *12* Fähigkeit; **motor ~** *42* motorische Fähigkeit
able *41* fähig, ohne Einschränkung, nichtbehindert
abled, differently ~ *41* eingeschränkt, behindert
abortion *106* Abtreibung
about, to **be ~ to happen** *58* gleich geschehen, unmittelbar bevorstehen
above *11* oben; **~ all** *35V* vor allen Dingen
abroad *7* im Ausland
absence *42* Abwesenheit
absolutely *21* völlig, unbedingt; **Absolutely.** *18V* Stimmt. Da haben Sie völlig recht. Natürlich!
to **abuse sb/sth** *11* jdn/etw missbrauchen
abuse *34* Missbrauch, Gewalt, Beschimpfungen; **domestic ~** *34T* häusliche Gewalt; **mental ~** *104* psychischer Missbrauch; **physical ~** *65* (körperliche) Misshandlungen, Schläge, Übergriffe; **sexual ~** *34T* sexueller Missbrauch; **substance ~** *34T* Drogenmissbrauch; **verbal ~** *106* Beschimpfungen, Beleidigungen
abuser *64 jd, der jdn missbraucht;* Täter/in
abusive, to **be ~ to sb** *69* jdn misshandeln; **~ behaviour** *65T* Missbrauchsverhalten, Missbrauch
academic *108* Akademiker/in; **~ expectations** *pl* *41* schulische (Leistungs-)Erwartungen; **~ standard** *11* Ausbildungsniveau
accelerometer *100V* Beschleunigungsmesser
to **accept: Please ~ my apologies.** *131* Ich bitte um Entschuldigung.
acceptance *40* Anerkennung, Akzeptanz
access: ~ (to sth) *64* Zugang (zu etw), Zugriff (auf etw); **wheelchair ~** *45T* rollstuh-/behindertengerechter Zugang
accessibility *40* Barrierefreiheit
accessories *pl* *64 (Kleidung usw.:)* Accessoires
accident *32T* Unfall; **riding ~** *83P* Reitunfall; **~ report** *75* Unfallbericht
accidentally *133* versehentlich
accommodation *9* Unterkunft; **emergency ~** *55T* Notunterkunft; **sheltered ~** *34T* betreutes Wohnen
to **accompany sb** *8* jdn begleiten
according to *40* laut, gemäß, nach
account *133* Konto; to **take sth into ~** *107* etw berücksichtigen
to **account for sth** *83P* etw erklären
accreditation *80* Anerkennung, Zulassung, Akkreditierung
accredited *80* anerkannt, zugelassen, akkreditiert
accurate(ly) *125* richtig, präzise, korrekt
to **achieve sth** *19* etw erreichen, etw erzielen
achievement *12* Leistung, Errungenschaft, Erfolg
to **acquire sth** *111* etw erwerben
across ... *39* in ganz ...
act, to **get your ~ together** *125T* sich zusammenreißen
to **act** *34T* sich verhalten, sich benehmen; **~ sth out** *53* etw (mit verteilten Rollen) spielen
action *59* Handlung; to **put sth into ~** *44* etw in die Tat umsetzen; **call to ~** *62T* Handlungsaufforderung; **~ plan** *118* Aktionsplan, Maßnahmenkatalog
activity, physical ~ *96* körperliche Betätigung; **~ies** *pl* **of daily living** *58T* Aktivitäten/Verrichtungen des täglichen Lebens
actual(ly) *32T* eigentlich
ad, print ~s *pl* *53* Anzeigen in Printmedien
to **adapt: ~ to sb/sth** *41* sich an jdn/etw anpassen, sich auf jdn/etw einstellen; **~ sth (to sb/sth)** *35V* etw an jdn/etw anpassen
to **add: ~ sth to sth** *6* etw einer Sache hinzufügen; **~ sth up** *124* etw zusammenzählen, etw addieren; **~ value to sth** *21* eine Bereicherung für etw sein
addict, drug ~ *39* Drogensüchtige/r, Drogenabhängige/r
addiction *34T* Sucht
additional *35V* zusätzlich
address, inside ~ *84* Innenadresse
to **address sth** *130* etw *(Problem usw.)* ansprechen
adhesive tape *82* Heftpflaster
to **adjust to sth** *102* sich an etw anpassen
to **administer sth** *57* etw verabreichen
admin(istration) *84* Verwaltung
administrative *33* Verwaltungs-
administrator, social ~ *28* Sachbearbeiter/in, Beamte/r in der Sozialverwaltung
admission *83P (Krankenhaus:)* Einlieferung, Aufnahme; **~s** *83 (Krankenhaus:)* Aufnahme(station); **hospital ~** *38* Einlieferung/ Einweisung ins Krankenhaus
to **admit: ~ sth** *65T* etw zugeben, etw eingestehen; **~ sb to hospital** *38* jdn ins Krankenhaus einliefern/ einweisen
adolescent *96* Jugendliche/r, Heranwachsende/r; **~ psychiatry** *29* Jugendpsychiatrie
to **adopt** *103G* adoptieren; **~ sth** *99* etw übernehmen, etw annehmen
adopter *107* Adoptierende/r
adoption *95* Adoption; to **give sb up for ~** *106* jdn zur Adoption freigeben
adoptive couple *106* Adoptivpaar
adult *11* Erwachsene/r; erwachsen; **~ day care** *56* Tagespflege, Tagesbetreuung
adultery *104* Ehebruch, Fremdgehen
advantage *8* Vorteil; **competitive ~** *43T* Wettbewerbsvorteil; to **take ~ of sb/sth** *10* etw/jdn ausnutzen, einen Vorteil aus etw ziehen
adventure *78* Abenteuer
to **advertise: ~ sth** *51* für etw Werbung machen, etw bewerben; **~ a job** *6* eine Stelle ausschreiben
advertising *51* Werbung, Werbe-
advert(isement), job ~ *6* Stellenanzeige, Stellenangebot
advice *12* Ratschläge, (guter) Rat, Beratung; **piece of ~** *111T* Ratschlag, Rat; **legal ~** *121* Rechtsberatung, juristischer Rat; to **give ~** *31* beraten, Rat erteilen
to **advise: ~ sb on sth** *43T* jdn in/zu etw beraten, jdm etw zeigen; **~ sb to do sth** *65* jdm raten/empfehlen, etw zu tun
adviser *43* Berater/in; **medical ~** *107P* medizinische/r Berater/in

affair 69 Affäre
to **affect sb/sth** 99 jdn/etw betreffen, jdn/etw treffen; 107 sich auf jdn/etw auswirken, jdn/etw beeinflussen
affected, to **be ~ by sth** 48 von etw betroffen sein
to **afford sth** 96 sich etw leisten
affordable 60 erschwinglich, günstig
afraid: I'm ~ 43T leider; **I'm ~ so.** 105T Leider ja.; to **be ~** 64 Angst haben
after-school care centre 49 Schulhort, Nachmittagsbetreuung
afterwards 107G danach
again, once ~ 133 erneut, noch einmal; **over and over ~** 66T (immer und) immer wieder
age, employment ~ 40 Erwerbsalter; **~ group** 72 Altersgruppe
age-related 56 altersbedingt
aged … 9 im Alter von …
agency 106 Agentur; **travel ~** 129T Reisebüro, Reiseagentur
agenda 50 Tagesordnung
agnostic 111T agnostisch; Agnostiker/in
to **agree** 34T zustimmen; **~ on sth** 81P sich auf etw einigen; **~ with sb** 39G jdm zustimmen, der gleichen Meinung wie jd sein; **~ with sth** 41 etw befürworten, etw *(Meinung usw.)* teilen
agreement, bilateral ~ 111P bilaterales Abkommen
aid, developmental ~ 111P Entwicklungshilfe; **first ~** 13 Erste Hilfe; **first-~ kit** 82 Verbandskasten, Erste-Hilfe-Ausrüstung
aim 30 Ziel
to **aim: ~ to do sth** 31 etw tun wollen; sich vornehmen, etw zu tun; **~ at sth** 39 auf etw hinarbeiten
aimed, to **be ~ at sb** 30 sich an jdn richten
alarm 18V Wecker
alcohol-dependent 34T alkoholabhängig
alcoholic 35P alkoholsüchtig; Alkoholiker/in
alcoholism 121 Alkoholsucht
Algerian 108 algerisch
all, above ~ 35V vor allen Dingen; **at ~ times** 58T stets, immer; **in ~** 97P insgesamt; **~ over …** 34T in ganz …; **~ over again** 65 von neuem, von vorn; **~ parties concerned** 41 alle Beteiligten, alle Betroffenen
allergen 84 Allergen
allergic, to **be ~ to sth** 83P auf etw allergisch sein; **~ reaction (to sth)** 82 allergische Reaktion (auf etw)
allergy 83P Allergie
to **allocate sth to sb/sth** 41 etw jdm / einer Sache zuteilen
along, to **have sb ~** 82T jdn dabei haben
alongside 81 an der Seite von
alternative 7 Alternative, Ausweichmöglichkeit
Alzheimer's disease 56 Alzheimer-Krankheit
ambulance 83 Rettungswagen
amongst 49 unter, untereinander
amount 94 Menge
amputated 42 amputiert, abgetrennt
to **analyse sth** 14 etw analysieren
anger 34T Ärger, Wut, Aggression; **~ management** 34 Agressionsbewältigung
to **announce sth** 126 etw ankündigen
to **annoy sb** 109T jdn nerven, jdn ärgern
anorexia 114 Magersucht
to **answer the phone** 17 ans Telefon gehen
antenatal clinic 106 Schwangerschaftsfürsorge, Pränataldiagnostik
antibiotic 82 antibiotisch
anticoagulant 82T Gerinnungshemmer
antihistamine 82 Antihistamin
anxious 64 besorgt, ängstlich; to **be ~ to do sth** 64 darauf bedacht sein, etw zu tun
anyway 18V jedenfalls, wie dem auch sei
apart from 29T abgesehen von, außer; **~ sb/sth** 110 von jdm/etw getrennt
apartment, council ~ 35P Sozialwohnung
to **apologize (to sb)** 69 sich (bei jdm) entschuldigen
apology 69 Entschuldigung; **Please accept my ~ies.** 131 Ich bitte um Entschuldigung.
to **appeal to sth** 70 etw ansprechen
to **appear** 64 auftreten, sich zeigen, scheinen; **~ in a video** 72 in einem Video mitspielen
appearance 19 Erscheinung(sbild), Aussehen
applicant 8 Bewerber/in
application 6 Bewerbung; 107 Antrag
to **apply: ~ sth** 14 etw anwenden; 58 etw *(Creme usw.)* auftragen; **~ for sth** 6 sich um/auf/für etw bewerben; 107P etw beantragen
appointment 22 Termin
appreciation 125T Wertschätzung, Würdigung
approach 39 Herangehensweise, Ansatz
appropriate(ly) 13 angemessen, passend
approval 125T Genehmigung, Zustimmung
area 28 Bereich, Gebiet; **abdominal ~** 100V Bauchraum; **seating ~** 45T Sitzgelegenheiten
to **argue (with sb)** 69 sich (mit jdm) streiten
argument, to **have an ~** 45T sich streiten
to **arise** 103 *(Probleme usw.:)* enstehen
to **arrange sth** 17T etw *(Termin usw.)* ausmachen
arrangement 47 Planungen, Termine, Vereinbarungen; **living ~** 56 Form des Wohnens, Wohnkonzept
arrival 118 Ankunft, Eintreffen
art auction 51 Kunstauktion
artist 76 Künstler/in
artwork 62T Illustrationen, Bildmaterial
as: ~ if 131 als ob; **~ long as** 43T solange; **~ well as** 9 sowie, und; **~ sb goes** 78 unterwegs; **~ we speak** 128 gerade, in diesem Moment
aspect 6 Gesichtspunkt, Aspekt, Seite
to **assess sth** 75 etw beurteilen, etw einschätzen
assessment 54 Beurteilung, Bewertung, Einschätzung; **case ~** 120 Falleinschätzung
asset, to **be an ~ to sth** 14 eine Bereicherung für etw sein
to **assign: ~ sth to sb** 35V jdm etw zuteilen, jdm etw zuweisen; **~ sb to sth** 121 jdm mit etw betrauen, jdm etw *(Aufgabe usw.)* übertragen
assigned, on ~ topics 33 zu bestimmten Themen
to **assist sb (with sth)** 28 jdm (bei etw) helfen, jdm (bei etw) zur Hand gehen
assistance 30 Hilfe, Unterstützung; **care ~** 56 Pflegeleistung, Betreuungshilfe; **mobility ~** 127 Mobilitätshilfe
assistant, day care centre ~ 28 Kinderpfleger/in, Erzieher/in, Tagespflegehelfer/in; **paediatric ~** 28 Pflegefachkraft mit Vertiefung Pädiatrie; **psychiatric ~** 28 Medizinische/r Mitarbeiter/in, Assistent/in

in der Psychiatrie; ~ **carer** 45 Sozialassistent/in mit Schwerpunkt Heilerziehungspflege; ~ **nurse** 20 Schwesternhelferin, Pflegediensthelfer/in; ~ **teacher** 113T (Aus-)Hilfslehrer/in, Assistenzlehrer/in

assisted living facility 56 (Einrichtung für) betreutes Wohnen

associated, to **be ~ with sth** 99P mit etw in Zusammenhang stehen

to **assume sth** 111T etw annehmen, etw unterstellen

assuming (that) 111T vorausgesetzt, angenommen

asthma 42 Asthma

astonishing 100V erstaunlich

asylum seeker 112 Asylsuchende/r

atheist 111T atheistisch; Atheist/in

atmosphere 126 Atmosphäre

to **attach sth** 21 *(Brief:)* etw beifügen, *(E-Mail:)* etw anhängen

attached, to **be ~ to sth** 29T einer Sache angegliedert sein

to **attain sth** 80 etw erreichen, etw erlangen

to **attend: ~ sth** 10 etw *(Veranstaltung, Schule usw.)* besuchen, an etw teilnehmen; **~ to sb** 82T sich um jdn kümmern, jdn versorgen

attendee 92 Teilnehmer/in

attention 10 Aufmerksamkeit; **media ~** 27 Medieninteresse, Berichterstattung in den Medien; to **bring sth to sb's ~** 128 jdn auf etw aufmerksam machen; to **grab sb's ~** 12 jds Aufmerksamkeit fesseln; to **pay ~ to sth** 66 auf etw achten

attitude 9 Einstellung, Haltung

Attn (= for the attention of) 14 *(Brief:)* z. Hd. (= zu Händen von)

to **attract sb/sth** 11 jdn/etw anziehen, jdn/etw anlocken

auction, art ~ 51 Kunstauktion

audience 48 Publikum, Zuschauer/innen, Zuhörer/innen

Austria 130 Österreich

authority, local ~ 29T Kommune, Gemeinde(verwaltung)

autism 42 Autismus; **~ spectrum disorder** 43T Autismusspektrumstörung

auto-immune disease 107P Autoimmunkrankheit

automatically 111T automatisch

autonomy 40 Eigenständigkeit, Autonomie

available 10 verfügbar; to **be ~** 81P *(Telefon:)* zu sprechen sein

average 100V Durchschnitt; durchschnittlich; **on ~** 100V im Durchschnitt

to **avoid sth** 18V etw vermeiden

aware, to be ~ of sth 16 sich einer Sache bewusst sein, etw wissen

awareness 95 Bewusstsein, Sensibilität

B

baby brother 66 kleines Brüderchen

back, to **be ~ to square one** 126 wieder ganz am Anfang stehen

background 17 Werdegang, Herkunft, Hintergrund; **family ~** 27 Familienverhältnisse; **~ noise** 23 Hintergrundgeräusche

bacteria *pl* 84 Bakterien

to **bake** 97P backen

baking 50 Backen; **~ paper** 97P Backpapier; **~ tray** 97P Backblech

balance 11 Gleichgewicht, Ausgewogenheit

to **balance sth with sth** 103G etw mit etw in Einklang bringen

balanced 46 ausgeglichen; **nutritionally ~** 87 (ernährungsphysiologisch) ausgewogen

balloon modelling 78T Ballonkunst, Ballonmodellieren

bandage 82 Verband, Bandage

bank, food ~ 17T Tafel; **~ details** *pl* 119 Bankverbindung; **~ holiday** 61 gesetzlicher Feiertag; **~ transfer** 133 Überweisung

bar 38T Balken; **~ chart** 38 Säulendiagramm

barbecue 79P Grillparty

base 97P Boden

based, to **be ~ on sth** 11 auf etw basieren, sich auf etw stützen

basic body care 57 Grundpflege

basically 29T im Prinzip, grundsätzlich, eigentlich

basics *pl* 77T Grundlagen, Grundsätzliches

basil 97P Basilikum

basis, on a daily ~ 14 jeden Tag, tagtäglich; **on a regular ~** 37 regelmäßig; **on an individual ~** 43T auf den Einzelfall bezogen, individuell

bath, to **have a ~** 58 ein Bad nehmen; to **do a sponge ~** 58 (jdn) mit dem Schwamm (im Bett) waschen

to **bathe** 58T baden, ein Bad nehmen

battering 104 (körperliche) Misshandlung

to **be: ~ to do sth** 125 etw tun sollen; **It's me.** 34T Ich bin's.

to **beat sb** 105P jdn schlagen

to **become (sth)** 28 (zu etw / etw) werden; **~ infected** 82T *(Wunde:)* sich entzünden

to **begin: to ~ with** 111T zunächst (einmal)

behalf, on sb's ~ 113 für jdn, in jds Namen

to **behave** 64 sich verhalten, sich benehmen

behaviour 34T Benehmen, Verhalten; **abusive ~** 65T Missbrauchsverhalten, Missbrauch; **~ pattern** 104 Verhaltensmuster

behavioural: ~ disorder 38 Verhaltensstörung; **~ pattern** 104 Verhaltensmuster

being, to **come into ~** 103 entstehen

belief 110 Überzeugung, Glaube

to **believe: ~ sth** 35G etw glauben, von etw überzeugt sein; **~ in sth** 62T an etw glauben, von etw überzeugt sein

to **belong** 12 gehören

belonging 111G Zugehörigkeit

belongings *pl* 35V Habe, Hab und Gut

beneficial, to **be ~ to sb** 102 für jdn vorteilhaft/gut sein

benefit 11 Nutzen, Vorteil; **benefits** *pl* 24 Zusatzleistungen

to **benefit: ~ sb** 15V jdm nutzen, für jdm von Nutzen sein; **~ (from sth)** 45T (von etw) profitieren

beside 13G neben

Best wishes *pl* 77T *(Brief, E-Mail:)* Viele Grüße

between the lines 123 zwischen den Zeilen

beverage 124 Getränk

beyond sb's control 127 außerhalb jds Einflussbereichs

bilateral agreement 111P bilaterales Abkommen

bilingual 76 zweisprachig

binge-drinking, to **go ~** 34T auf Sauftour gehen

biological mother 107G leibliche Mutter

birth, to **give ~** 106 entbinden, gebären

bisexual 94 bisexuell

bite 82 (Insekten-)Biss

blame, to **put the ~ on sb** 65T jdm die Schuld geben; to **shift the ~** 65T die Schuld jd anderem zuschieben

to **blame sb** 65 jdm die Schuld geben

blanket 82 Decke

to **bleed** 82T bluten

bleeding 82T Blutung

to **blend sth with sth** 97P etw mit etw vermischen

blender 97T Mixer

blindness 42 Blindheit

bloc, Eastern B~ 111P Ostblock

blood: ~ circulation *58T* Blutkreislauf; **~ glucose levels** *pl* *99* Blutzuckerwerte; **~ pressure** *63V* Blutdruck
board, bulletin ~ *126* Schwarzes Brett; to **take sth on ~** *76* etw annehmen, etw übernehmen
boardgame *51* Brettspiel
body *77T* *(Text:)* Hauptteil; **~ language** *15* Körpersprache; **basic ~ care** *57* Grundpflege
bold, in ~ *38* in Fettdruck, fett gedruckt
bond *102* Bindung, Verbundenheit
bone marrow *97T* Knochenmark
booking *130* Buchung, Reservierung
border *39* Grenze
both … and *10* sowohl … als auch
to **bother sb** *47* jdn stören, jdn belästigen
bouncy: ~ ball *78* Flummi; **~ castle** *76* Hüpfburg
bowel, chronic inflammatory ~ disease *42* chronisch-entzündliche Darmerkrankung
bowl *97P* Schüssel
bracelet *78* Armband
bracket *39* Klammer
to **brainstorm** *49* (Ideen) sammeln
breadwinner *102* Ernährer/in
break *82* (Knochen-)Bruch
to **break: ~ the cycle** *65T* die Spirale durchbrechen; **~ the news** *126* die Neuigkeit(en) überbringen; **You're ~ing up.** *17* Das Signal ist schlecht.
breathing *63V* Atmung
brief(ly) *12* knapp, kurz
bright *41* aufgeweckt, intelligent
brilliant *18V* genial, super, toll
to **bring: ~ sb along** *123T* jdn mitbringen; **~ sth forward** *81* etw *(Termin usw.)* vorziehen, etw vorverlegen; **~ sb up** *105* jdn aufziehen, jdn großziehen; **~ sth to sb's attention** *128* jdn auf etw aufmerksam machen
broad *34T* breit
brochure *85* Prospekt, Broschüre
brother, baby ~ *66* kleines Brüderchen; **half-~** *106* Halbbruder
to **browse** *23* stöbern, blättern
bruise *64* blauer Fleck, Bluterguss
bubble *94* Blase
budget *11* Budget, Etat
buffet *79P* Büfett
building site *35P* Baustelle
Bulgaria *108* Bulgarien
bulimia *114* Bulimie
bullet point *70* Stichpunkt
bulletin board *126* Schwarzes Brett
to **bully sb** *67P* jdn mobben, jdn tyrannisieren
bullying *104* Mobbing, Tyrannisieren
bunny, Easter ~ *45T* Osterhase
bureaucracy *30* Bürokratie
burden, to **put a huge ~ on sb/sth** *108* jdn/etw stark belasten, eine starke Belastung für jdn/etw sein
burning *34T* Verbrennung
burnout *11* Ausgebranntsein, Burnout
business: ~ communication *75* Geschäftskorrespondenz, Unternehmenskommunikation; **~ letter** *74* Geschäftsbrief; **~ organization** *75* Wirtschaftsunternehmen, Unternehmensform; to **start a ~** *127* ein Unternehmen gründen
by, one ~ one *111T* nacheinander, der Reihe nach

C

caffeinated *124* koffeinhaltig
cage-free *86* nicht aus Käfighaltung
to **calculate sth** *126* etw berechnen
calendar *123T* Kalender
to **call: ~ on sb** *105P* bei jdm vorbeischauen; **~ sb in** *66* jdn hinzuziehen, jdn rufen; **~ sth off** *81* etw absagen; **~ a meeting** *109* eine Sitzung einberufen, eine Besprechung ansetzen; **~ sb names** *67P* jdn beschimpfen
call to action *62T* Handlungsaufforderung
caller *57* Anrufer/in
calling *29T* Berufung
calories *pl* *98* Kalorien
campaign *53* Kampagne, Aktion
can *45T* Dose
to **cancel sth** *81* etw absagen, etw stornieren
cancellation policy *129* Stornierungsbedingungen
candidate *6* Bewerber/in, Kandidat/in
canned food *96* Konserven
canteen *124P* Kantine
capacity *40* Fähigkeit; **mental ~** *42* geistige Leistungsfähigkeit
capita, per ~ *101* pro Kopf
capital letter *14* Großbuchstabe
carcass *97T* Gerippe, Tierkörper
to **care: ~ for sb** *6* jdn pflegen, jdn betreuen, jdn versorgen, sich um jdn kümmern; **sb cares for sth** *128* jdm ist an etw gelegen
care *7* Pflege, Betreuung, Fürsorge, Versorgung, Zuwendung, Obhut; to **be in ~** *34T* betreut / in Pflegefamilien / im Heim wohnen; to **be in need of ~** *102* pflegebedürftig sein; **adult day ~** *56* Tagespflege, Tagesbetreuung; **basic body ~** *57* Grundpflege; **crisis ~** *30* Notfallpflege, Kurzzeitpflege; **domestic ~** *30* häusliche Pflege; **elderly ~** *30* Seniorenbetreuung, Altenfürsorge; **home ~** *56* häusliche Pflege; **long-term ~** *56* Langzeitpflege; **medical ~** *56* medizinische Versorgung; **personal ~** *30* Körperpflege, Unterstützung der Selbstversorgung; **social ~** *28* Sozialhilfe, Sozialleistungen; **social and health ~** *8* Gesundheit und Soziales, Sozial- und Gesundheitswesen; **supervised professional ~** *56* Pflege/Betreuung unter fachkundiger Leitung; **wound ~** *82* Wundversorgung; **~ assistance** *56* Pflegeleistung, Betreuungshilfe; **day ~ centre** *28* Kita, Tagespflege; **after-school ~ centre** *49* Schulhort, Nachmittagsbetreuung; **day ~ centre assistant** *28* Kinderpfleger/in, Erzieher/in, Tagespflegehelfer/in; **~ facility** *52* Pflegeeinrichtung; **~ home** *35P* Jugendheim, betreutes Wohnen; **long-term ~ home** *56* Langzeitpflegeeinrichtung; **~ job** *7* Pflege-/Sozialberuf, Beruf im Gesundheitswesen; **~ professional** *27* Pflegefachkraft, Fachkraft im Sozial- und Gesundheitswesen; **~ services** *pl* *52* Pflegeleistungen, Pflegedienste; **~ setting** *56* Pflegeumfeld, Pflegesituation, Pflegeeinrichtung
careful, to **be ~** *12* aufpassen, vorsichtig sein
carer, assistant ~ *45* Sozialassistent/in mit Schwerpunkt Heilerziehungspflege
carer, geriatric ~ *28* Altenpfleger/in
carer, home ~ *30* häusliche/ambulante Pflegekraft
career *8* Beruf, berufliche Laufbahn, Karriere; **~ development opportunities** *pl* *24* berufliche Entwicklungsmöglichkeiten; **~ path** *9* Karriere, Berufsweg; **~ perspectives** *pl* *8* berufliche Perspektiven, Aufstiegschancen
careful(ly) *13G* aufmerksam, sorgfältig, gewissenhaft
caregiver *63V* Pflegeperson, Bezugsperson
carer *6* Pflegefachkraft, Fachkraft im Sozial- und Gesundheitswesen; **~ support** *30* Unterstützung für pflegende Angehörige

caring *30* fürsorglich, sozial; *102* Betreuung; **~ professions** *7* Berufe im Pflege-, Sozial- und Gesundheitsbereich
carnival outfit *88* Karnevalskostüm
to **carry: ~ on with sth** *54* mit etw weitermachen; **~ out sth** *8* etw ausführen, etw durchführen
case, in ~ *36* für den Fall, dass …; to **be the ~** *39* der Fall sein; **~ assessment** *120* Falleinschätzung; **~ file** *35* Patientenakte, Vorgang; **~ manager** *37* Fallbearbeiter/in, Case Manager/in; **~ notes** *pl* *106* Fallakte, Fallnotizen; **~ number** *36* Vorgangsnummer; **~ report** *37* Fallbericht; **~ worker** *38* Sozialarbeiter/in
caseload *11* Fallbelastung, Arbeitsbelastung
castle, bouncy ~ *76* Hüpfburg
casual *111G* zufällig
catalogue *77* Katalog
to **catch sth** *17* etw verstehen, etw mitbekommen
catchy *62T* eingängig, prägnant, griffig
category *9* Kategorie
to **cater: ~ for sb/sth** *41* sich um jdn/etw kümmern; **~ to sth** *87* auf etw *(Bedürfnisse usw.)* eingehen
caterer *84* Speiselieferant/in, Cateringservice
catering *43T* Gastronomie; *75* Verpflegung, (Versorgung mit) Essen, Catering
catholic, Roman C~ *106* römisch-katholisch
cause *51* Anliegen, Zweck, (gute) Sache; **~ (of sth)** *42* Ursache (für/von etw), Grund (für/von etw); **~ of death** *100V* Todesursache
to **cause: ~ sth** *34T* etw verursachen; **~ sb/sth to do sth** *66T* jdn/etw dazu veranlassen, etw zu tun; dazu führen, dass jd/etw etw tut
to **celebrate (sth)** *77* (etw) feiern
celebration *78* Feier, Fest
centre, after-school care ~ *49* Schulhort, Nachmittagsbetreuung; **day care ~** *28* Kita, Tagespflege; **family support ~** *105* Familienhilfe, Familienhilfezentrum; **outreach ~** *27* Sozialzentrum, Begegnungsstätte, Bürgerbüro; **support ~** *31G* Hilfsstelle, Hilfszentrum; **day care ~ assistant** *28* Kinderpfleger/in, Erzieher/in, Tagespflegehelfer/in
CEO (Chief Executive Officer) *127* Vorstandsvorsitzende/r, Geschäftsführer/in
cerebral palsy *41* Zerebralparese
certificate *9* Zeugnis, Nachweis, Diplom
chain *43T* Kette
challenge *10* Herausforderung, (schwierige) Aufgabe; **health ~s** *pl* *56* gesundheitliche Probleme
challenging *11* schwierig, anspruchsvoll, fordernd
change, personality ~s *pl* *64* Persönlichkeitsveränderung(en)
changing *94* im Wandel, sich wandelnd
character *104* *(Roman, Film usw.:)* Figur
characteristic *43T* Merkmal, Eigenschaft
to **characterize sth** *42* etw charakterisieren
charge, in ~ *82* zuständig, amtierend; to **be in ~ (of sth)** *81T* (für etw) verantwortlich sein, für etw zuständig sein; to **take ~** *89* etw in die Hand nehmen, das Kommando übernehmen
to **charge sth** *61* etw *(Preis usw.)* in Rechnung stellen, etw berechnen
charitable *51* wohltätig
charity *12* Hilfsorganisation
chart *36* Diagramm, Grafik, Schaubild; **bar ~** *38* Säulendiagramm; **flow ~** *17* Flussdiagramm
chat *35P* Unterhaltung, Schwätzchen; to **have a ~ with sb** *106* mit jdm sprechen
to **cheat on sb** *65T* jdn betrügen
to **check: ~ on sb** *54* nach jdm sehen; **~ sth against sth** *131* etw mit etw abgleichen; **~ in with sb** *64* sich (kurz) bei jdm melden; **~ sth out** *21* sich etw genauer ansehen
check *11* (ärztliche) Untersuchung; to **keep sth in ~** *99* etw unter Kontrolle halten
check-up, medical ~ *107P* ärztliche Untersuchung
cheerful *9* gut gelaunt
chef *86* Koch/Köchin, Küchenchef/in
chemicals *pl* *96* Chemikalien
chess *109* Schach
to **chew** *59* kauen
child, preschool ~ren *pl* *29T* Kinder im Vorschulalter; **~ welfare** *28* Kindeswohl, Kinder- und Jugendschutz; **~ welfare worker** *28* Jugendamtsmitarbeiter/in, Kinderschutzfachkraft
childbirth *115* Geburt, Entbindung
childcare *9* Kinderbetreuung
childhood *105P* Kindheit; **early ~ education** *9* frühkindliche Erziehung, Kleinkindpädagogik
chilled *87* gekühlt
chocolates *pl* *45T* Pralinen
choice *40* Wahl, Entscheidung
cholesterol levels *pl* *98* Cholesterinwerte
to **chop sth up** *97T* etw kleinschneiden, etw hacken
chopped *97P* gehackt
chronic: ~ condition *94* chronische Krankheit; **~ disease** *56* chronische Erkrankung; **~ disorder** *42* chronische Krankheit; **~ inflammatory bowel disease** *42* chronisch-entzündliche Darmerkrankung
chronological *12* chronologische
to **chuck sb out** *34T* jdn rausschmeißen
circulation, blood ~ *58T* Blutkreislauf
circumstances *pl* *34* Umstände
citizen *113T* Staatsbürger/in
city council *29* Stadtverwaltung, Stadtrat
to **claim sth** *105P* etw behaupten
class, language ~ *119* Sprachkurs; **special ~es** *pl* *108* Sonderklassen; **working ~** *108* Arbeiterklasse
cleansing, ethnic ~ *112* ethnische Säuberungen
clearly *127* offenbar, offensichtlich
client *29T* Kunde/Kundin, Klient/in
clientele *116* Klientel
clinic *46* Klinik; **antenatal ~** *106* Schwangerschaftsfürsorge, Pränataldiagnostik; **rehabilitation ~** *36* Reha-Klinik
to **close** *111T* Schluss machen, schließen; **~ sth** *81* etw beenden, etw abschließen
close *77T* Schluss; **complimentary ~** *77T* *(Brief, E-Mail:)* Schlussformel
close(ly) *63V* eng, nah; to **be ~ to sb** *66T* jdm (sehr) nahestehen; to **keep a ~ eye on sth** *132* etw genau beobachten, to **look at / study sth ~ly** *38T* sich etw näher/genau ansehen
closeness *66T* Nähe, enge Verbundenheit
closing *77T* Abschieds-, Schluss-; **~ sentence** *14* Schlusssatz
to **clot** *82T* gerinnen
cloth *97P* Tuch
clove of garlic *97P* Knoblauchzehe
coat *45T* Kittel
coating *82T* Beschichtung
cocaine *39* Kokain
code, country ~ *81T* *(Telefon:)* Ländervorwahl
cognition *54* Wahrnehmung
cognitive *43T* kognitiv
to **collect sth** *6* etw sammeln; *87* etw abholen

college, technical ~ *108* Berufskolleg, Fachhochschule; **vocational ~** *12* Fachoberschule
colourful *116* farbenfroh, bunt
to **combine sth** *53* etw (miteinander) verbinden, etw kombinieren
to **come: ~ about** *107G* entstehen; **~ across sb/sth** *58T* auf jdn/etw stoßen, jdn/etw (zufällig) finden; **~ in** *111T* ins Spiel kommen; **~ up** *43T* aufkommen, genannt werden; **~ up with sth** *111P* sich etw ausdenken, sich etw einfallen lassen; **~ into being** *103* entstehen; **Something has come up.** *89* Es ist etwas dazwischengekommen. **What's to ~** *7* Und so geht's weiter:
comfortable *58* angenehm; *59* bequem; to **feel ~** *122* sich wohlfühlen; to **make sb ~** *83* sich um jdn kümmern
comment *10* Kommentar, Bemerkung
commercial *62T* gewerblich, kommerziell
to **commit a crime** *34T* eine Straftat begehen
committed *28* engagiert; to **be ~ to doing sth** *43T* fest vorhaben, etw zu tun; to **be ~ to sth** *76* sich (voll und ganz) für etw engagieren
common *39* gemeinsam; *42* üblich, häufig, verbreitet; to **have sth in ~** *35G* etw gemeinsam haben; to **be ~ to sb** *43T* jdm gemeinsam sein; to **be ~ practice** *12* allgemein üblich sein
to **communicate** *25* sich verständigen, kommunizieren; **~ sth** *62* etw vermitteln, etw kommunizieren
communication, business ~ *75* Geschäftskorrespondenz, Unternehmenskommunikation; **means of ~** *74* Kommunikationsmittel
communicator, to **be a good ~** *9* kommunikativ sein
communist, fellow ~ countries *pl* *111P* kommunistische Bruderstaaten
community *9* Gemeinde, Gemeinschaft; **~ outreach worker** *33* Sozialarbeiter/in für gesellschaftliche Randgruppen; **~ support worker** *28* Sozialarbeiter/in; **~ doctor** *124* Betriebsarzt/-ärztin
company, record ~ *73* Schallplattenfirma; to **join a ~** *9* bei einer Firma anfangen, zu einer Firma kommen; **~ file** *124T* Betriebsakte
to **compare: ~ with sth** *60* sich mit etw vergleichen lassen, Gemeinsamkeiten/Unterschiede zu etw haben; **~ sth** *6* etw (miteinander) vergleichen
compared to sb/sth *11* im Vergleich zu jdm/etw, verglichen mit jdm/etw
comparison (to sth) *11* Vergleich (mit etw)
compassion *52* Mitgefühl, Barmherzigkeit
compensation *127* Entschädigung, Schadenersatz
competence *95* Kompetenz
competent *31* kompetent
competition *27* Wettbewerb, Wettkampf
competitive advantage *43T* Wettbewerbsvorteil
competitor *63* Konkurrent/in
to **compile sth** *33* etw erstellen, etw zusammenstellen
to **complain (to sb about sth)** *67P* sich (bei jdm über etw) beschweren
complaint *120* Beschwerde, Reklamation
to **complement each other** *105T* sich gegenseitig ergänzen
complicated *58T* kompliziert
complimentary close *77T (Brief, E-Mail:)* Schlussformel
to **compose** *73* komponieren
composer *73* Komponist/in
composting *87* Kompostierung
comprehensive school *18V* Gesamtschule
computing *113T* Informatik
concept *49* Konzept
concern, focus of ~ *34T* Aufmerksamkeitsschwerpunkt; **concerns** *pl 27* Anliegen *pl*, Belange
concerned *121* besorgt, beunruhigt; **as far as sb/sth is ~** *34T* was jdn/etw angeht; **all parties ~** *41* alle Beteiligten, alle Betroffenen
conclusion *123* Schluss
concrete *119* konkret
condition *54* Zustand; *8* Erkrankung; **chronic ~** *94* chronische Krankheit; **medical ~** *56* Krankheit; **conditions** *pl 77* Bedingungen, Konditionen; **working ~s** *pl 10* Arbeitsbedingungen
to **conduct sth** *113P* etw durchführen
confectionery *45T* Süßwaren
conference *33* Tagung, Konferenz; **~ call** *18* Video-/Telefonkonferenz
confidence *19* Selbstsicherheit, Selbstbewusstsein
confident(ly) *16* selbstsicher, selbstbewusst
confidential(ly) *137* vertraulich
to **confirm sth** *81* etw bestätigen
confirmation *130* Bestätigung
conflict *105T* Konflikt(e), Auseinandersetzung(en), Streit; *108* militärische Auseinandersetzung(en), Kämpfe, Krieg; **~ management** *128* Konfliktbewältigung, -bearbeitung, -management
to **conform to sth** *111T* mit etw übereinstimmen, einer Sache entsprechen
confusion *130* Verwirrung
to **connect sb** *81G (Telefon:)* jdn durchstellen
connected, to **be ~** *70* zusammenhängen; **~ with** *10* in Zusammenhang mit
consciousness *83* Bewusstsein
consequence *100* Folge, Konsequenz
to **consider sb/sth** *14* jdn/etw in Betracht ziehen
to **consider sth** *12* etw betrachten, über etw nachdenken; *14* sich mit etw befassen, etw prüfen; *86* etw berücksichtigen
considerably *39* beträchtlich, erheblich
considered, to **be ~ sth** *42* als etw gelten, als etw angesehen werden
to **consist of sth** *77* aus etw bestehen
consistent *77T* einheitlich, konsequent
constant(ly) *34T* ständig, andauernd
construction *111P* Bau
constructive *23* konstruktiv
consultant *54* Facharzt/-ärztin
consumption *39* Konsum
contact *14* Ansprechpartner/in; **eye ~** *23* Blickkontakt; **~ details** *pl 12* Kontaktdaten; to **re-establish ~** *34T* den Kontakt wiederherstellen
to **contact sb** *18V* sich mit jdm in Verbindung setzen, sich bei jdm melden
to **contain sth** *124T* etw enthalten
contaminated *84* kontaminiert
content *15C* Inhalt(e), Content
contest *51* Wettbewerb
context *26* Zusammenhang, Kontext
continually *28* ständig, fortwährend
contraceptive pill *83P* Verhütungspille, Antibabypille
contract *111P* Vertrag; **travel ~** *129T* Reisevertrag; **work ~** *126* Arbeitsvertrag
to **contract sb** *108* jdn einstellen
contraction *77T* zusammengezogene Form, Kontraktion
contrast, in ~ *31G* im Gegensatz dazu

to **contrast sth** *31G* etw (einander) gegenüberstellen, etw (miteinander) vergleichen
to **contribute sth** *119* etw beisteuern, etw spenden
contribution *119* Beitrag, Spende
control, to **feel in ~** *58* das Gefühl haben, Herr/in des eigenen Handelns zu sein; **beyond sb's ~** *127* außerhalb jds Einflussbereichs
controversial *49* umstritten
convenience food *96* Fertiggerichte, Fertigprodukte
convenient *81P* günstig, passend
convention *40* Konvention, Abkommen
conversation *32* Gespräch, Unterhaltung
conversational *13* Konversations-, Umgangs-
to **convey sth** *112* etw vermitteln, etw deutlich machen
to **convict sb for sth** *107P* jdn wegen etw verurteilen
conviction *107P* Verurteilung
to **convince sb of sth** *20* jdn von etw überzeugen
convincing *41* überzeugend
to **cook sth** *96* etw zubereiten, etw kochen
cooler, water ~ *124P* Wasserspender
cooperation *40* Zusammenarbeit
to **coordinate sth** *63V* etw aufeinander abstimmen, etw koordinieren
coordinated *63V* koordiniert
co-ordinator *55T* Koordinator/in
to **cope with sth** *34T* mit etw zurechtkommen, etw bewältigen
copy *16* Exemplar, Kopie
corn *97T* Getreide, Mais
corner, far ~ *45T* hintere Ecke
correction *71* Korrektur
to **correspond to sth** *40* einer Sache entsprechen
corridor *45T* Flur, Korridor
cost, labour ~s *pl* *84* Arbeitskosten, Lohnkosten
cost-effective *87* kostengünstig
costume *88* Kostüm
costumed race *51* Kostümwettlauf
cosy *61* gemütlich, wohnlich
council, city ~ *29* Stadtverwaltung, Stadtrat; **~ apartment** *35P* Sozialwohnung
to **counsel sb** *107* jdn beraten
counselling *47* Therapie, Beratung
counsellor *29T* Therapeut/in, Berater/in; **telephone ~** *28* Telefonseelsorger/in
count, lipid ~s *pl* *100V* Lipidwerte
counted, to **be ~ as sth** *42* zu etw gezählt werden
counter *33* Tresen, Schalter
country, developing ~ *9* Entwicklungsland
country, home ~ *111P* Heimatland; **fellow communist ~ies** *pl* *111P* kommunistische Bruderstaaten; **~ code** *81T* *(Telefon:)* Ländervorwahl
countryside, trip to the ~ *45T* Fahrt/Ausflug aufs Land
couple *30* Paar; **a ~ of** *34T* ein paar; **adoptive ~** *106* Adoptivpaar
course, obstacle ~ *78T* Hindernislauf, Hindernisparcours
court *105T* Gericht; **youth ~** *34T* Jugendgericht
cover letter *6* Anschreiben, Begleitschreiben
to **cover: ~ sth** *30* etw *(Thema usw.)* behandeln, sich mit etw befassen; *97P* etw bedecken, etw abdecken; **~ up for sb** *105P* jdn decken
co-worker *124* Kollege/-in
to **crave sth** *65T* Gier auf etw haben, etw unbedingt (und sofort) brauchen
cream *58* Creme
to **create sth** *7* etw erstellen; *43T* etw schaffen
creative *15* kreativ
crime *39* Verbrechen, Kriminalität; **drug ~** *39* Drogenkriminaität; to **commit a ~** *34T* eine Straftat begehen
criminal *34T* kriminell; *39* Verbrecher/in, Kriminelle/r; **~ offence** *39* Straftat; **~ record** *107P* Vorstrafen(register)
to **criminalize sb/sth** *39* jdn/etw kriminalisieren
crisis (*pl* **crises**) *104* Krise; **financial ~** *35V* Finanzkrise; **at times of ~** *30* in Krisen(zeiten); **~ care** *30* Notfallpflege, Kurzzeitpflege; **~ management** *30* Krisenmanagement
crisp *97P* knusprig
criteria *pl* *92* Kriterien
criticism *18V* Kritik
Croatia *129T* Kroatien
cross-country skiing *80* Skilanglauf
crowd *34T* Clique, (breite) Masse; to **stand out from the ~** *63* sich von der Masse abheben
crude oil *97T* Rohöl
cruel *10* brutal, grausam, gemein
to **crush sth** *97P* etw zerquetschen
CT scan *54* Computertomographie
cube *45T* Würfel, Kubus
culturally sensitive *30* kulturell angepasst, kultursensibel
cupboard *35V* Schrank
to **cure sth** *43* etw heilen
current(ly) *37* aktuell
curriculum vitae (CV) *BE* *6* Lebenslauf
curtains *pl* *66T* Vorhänge
custom *111T* Sitte, Brauch
customer *33* Kunde/Kundin
to **cut** *97P* schneiden, zerschneiden; **~ back on sth** *99* etw reduzieren
cutaway image *100V* *(Tomografie:)* Schnittbild
cuts *pl* *126* Kürzungen
cutting *34T* Ritzen
cyber-bullying *66* Cyber-Mobbing
cycle *65* Kreislauf, Spirale, Zyklus; to **break the ~** *65T* die Spirale durchbrechen

D

daily, on a ~ basis *14* jeden Tag, tagtäglich; **~ routine** *8* Tagesablauf; **activities** *pl* **of ~ living** *58T* Aktivitäten/Verrichtungen des täglichen Lebens
dairy (products) *98* Milchprodukte
to **damage sth** *34* etw beschädigen, etw schädigen
damage, heart ~ *99* Herzschäden, Herzschädigung
Dane *100V* Däne/Dänin
dangerous *98* gefährlich
data: ~ entry *43T* Dateneingabe; **~ protection** *12* Datenschutz
database *131* Datenbank
date, departure ~ *129T* Abreisedatum
daughter-in-law *102* Schwiegertochter
day, open ~ *22* Tag der offenen Tür; **at the end of the ~** *29T* unterm Strich, im Endeffekt; **~-to-day** *8* täglich, tagtäglich; **adult ~ care** *56* Tagespflege, Tagesbetreuung; **~ care centre** *28* Kita, Tagespflege; **~ nursery** *29T* Kita; **~ care centre assistant** *28* Kinderpfleger/in, Erzieher/in, Tagespflegehelfer/in
day care nursery *60* Kita
deadline, to keep to a ~ *124T* eine Frist einhalten, einen Abgabetermin einhalten
deafness *42* Taubheit
deal, a great ~ *124* ziemlich viel, eine Menge
to **deal: ~ with sth** *9* mit etw umgehen, mit etw zurechtkommen, etw bewältigen; **~ with sb/sth**

22 mit jdm/etw zu tun haben, sich um jdn/etw kümmern

dear: Oh ~! 123T Oje! Du meine Güte! **D~ Sir or Madam** 14 *(Brief, E-Mail:)* Sehr geehrte Damen und Herren,

death, a matter of life and ~ 67 lebensbedrohliche Situation, Frage von Leben oder Tod; **cause of ~** 100V Todesursache; **~ rate** 39 Zahl der Todesfälle

debate 39 Diskussion, Debatte

debriefing 80 Nachbesprechung, Auswertung, Reflexion

to **decide on sth** 65 etw festlegen, sich für etw entscheiden

decision, to **make a ~** 29T eine Entscheidung treffen

decision-making 45G Entscheidungsfindung, Entscheidungsprozess(e)

decrease (in sth) 38 Abnahme (von etw), Rückgang (von etw)

to **decrease** 38 abnehmen, sinken

to **decriminalize sth** 39 etw legalisieren

to **define sth** 36 etw definieren

definitely 9 (ganz) bestimmt

degree 9 (Universitäts-)Abschluss; **~ programme** 11 Studiengang

delay 130 Verzögerung, Verspätung

to **delete sth** 123T etw löschen

deliberately 34G absichtlich, vorsätzlich, mutwillig

delicious 61 lecker, köstlich

to **deliver** 86 liefern

delivery 15C Vortragsweise; 86 Lieferung, Zustellung

demand: ~ (on sb/sth) 28 Anforderung (an jdn/etw), Anspruch (an jdn/etw); to **be in ~** 28 nachgefragt werden, gesucht werden

demanding 10 anspruchsvoll

dementia 56 Demenz

demo(nstration) 63 Vorführung

demotivation 125P Demotivierung

denial 105T Leugnung, Abstreiten

department 90 Abteilung

departure date 129T Abreisedatum

dependent: ~ (on sth) 105P abhängig (von etw); **alcohol-~** 34T alkoholabhängig

depending on 90 je nach(dem)

to **depict sth** 38 etw abbilden, etw darstellen

deportation 111P Abschiebung

deposit 129T Anzahlung

depressed 64 depressiv, deprimiert

derivative 97T Derivat

description, job ~ 16 Stellenbeschreibung, Tätigkeitsbeschreibung

to **deserve sth** 36 etw verdienen

to **design sth** 45T etw entwerfen, etw gestalten, etw anlegen

designed, to be ~ for sb/sth 72 für jdn/etw gedacht sein; to **be ~ to do sth** 35V dazu/dafür gedacht sein, etw zu tun

desire (for sth) 70 Verlangen (nach etw), Wunsch (nach etw)

despite 40 trotz

dessert 61 Nachspeise, Nachtisch

destination 130 Reiseziel

to **destroy sth** 34G etw zerstören

detail, in ~ 85 genau, detailliert; **eye for ~** 43T Blick für Details

details *pl* 21 Einzelheiten, (genauere) Angaben; **bank ~** 119 Bankverbindung; **contact ~** 12 Kontaktdaten; **personal ~** 12 persönliche Angaben, Angaben zur Person

to **determine sth** 100V etw bestimmen

devastated 129T am Boden zerstört

to **develop** 14 (sich) entwickeln

developing country 9 Entwicklungsland

development 9 Entwicklung; **career ~ opportunities** *pl* 24 berufliche Entwicklungsmöglichkeiten

developmental 41 Entwicklungs-; **~ aid** 111P Entwicklungshilfe

device 100 (elektronisches) Gerät; **medical ~s** *pl* 63V Medizingeräte, Medizintechnik

diabetes 42 Diabetes

to **diagnose sb with sth** 99 etw bei jdm diagnostizieren

diagnosis, principal ~ 83P Erstdiagnose

diagram 6 Schaubild, Diagramm

to **die** 35P sterben; **~ from sth** 94 an etw sterben; **~ tragically** 84 auf tragische Weise ums Leben kommen

diet 94 Ernährung, Kost; **~ plan** 98 Diätplan, Ernährungsplan; to **go on a ~** 67P eine Diät machen

dietary 84 Ernährungs-, diätetisch

to **differ (from sb/sth)** 111T sich (von jdm/etw) unterscheiden

differently abled 41 eingeschränkt, behindert

difficulty, learning ~ies *pl* 8 Lernschwierigkeiten

digestive problems *pl* 124 Verdauungsprobleme

dignity 36 Würde

diploma 9 Diplom

directness 79 Direktheit

dirt 82T Schmutz, Dreck

disability 8 Behinderung; **intellectual ~** 42 geistige Behinderung; **learning ~** 43T Lernbehinderung

disabled person 8 Behinderte/r

disadvantage 86 Nachteil

to **disagree with sb** 39G jdm widersprechen, anderer Meinung als jd sein

disappointed (in sb/sth) 134 enttäuscht (von jdm/etw)

disc 97P Scheibe

discontinuation 111P Entzug, Kündigung

discounter 45T Billigsupermarkt, Discounter

to **discover sth** 76 etw entdecken

to **discriminate against sb** 123T jdn diskriminieren, jdn benachteiligen

discrimination 40 Diskriminierung; **racial ~** 121 Rassendiskriminierung

discriminatory 103G diskriminierend

disease, Alzheimer's ~ 56 Alzheimer-Krankheit; **auto-immune ~** 107P Autoimmunkrankheit; **chronic ~** 56 chronische Erkrankung; **chronic inflammatory bowel ~** 42 chronisch-entzündliche Darmerkrankung; **motor neuron ~** 42 Motoneuron-Krankheit

disgusting 123T ekelhaft

dish 61 Gericht, Speise, Essen

dislike 111G Abneigung

to **dislike sb/sth** 105T jdn/etw nicht mögen

disorder, autism spectrum ~ 43T Autismusspektrumstörung; **behavioural ~** 38 Verhaltensstörung; **chronic ~** 42 chronische Krankheit; **eating ~** 29T Essstörung; **mental ~** 38 psychische Erkrankung

to **display sth** 43T etw zeigen

dissatisfied 134 unzufrieden

disssatisfaction 121 Unzufriedenheit

to **distract sb** 58 jdn ablenken

to **distribute sth (to sb)** 36 etw (an jdn) verteilen

distribution 39 Vertrieb, Handel

district nurse 105T Pflegekraft in der ambulanten Pflege

to **disturb sb/sth** 124P jdn/etw stören

diverse 111T vielfältig, unterschiedlich, divers

diversity 40 Vielfalt, Diversität

to **divert sth** 55T etw umleiten, etw umstellen

to **divide: ~ into sth** 50 sich in etw aufteilen; **~ sth** 48 etw aufteilen

division 111P Teilung

divorce 102 Scheidung

to **divorce** 105T sich scheiden lassen

to **do: ~ sth about sth** 98 etw an etw ändern, etw an etw machen; **in so doing** 35V auf diese Weise

doctor 22 Arzt/Ärztin; **company ~** 124 Betriebsarzt/-ärztin; **family ~** 63V Hausarzt/-ärztin
to **document sth** 53 etw dokumentieren
domestic: ~ abuse 34T häusliche Gewalt; **~ care** 30 häusliche Pflege; **~ violence** 55T häusliche Gewalt
donor 51 Spender/in
door, to **open a ~ of opportunity for sb** 35V jdm eine (einmalige) Möglichkeit eröffnen
dosis (*pl* **doses**) 100V Dosis
dough 97P Teig
Down's syndrome 41 Down-Syndrom
to **downsize** 126 Stellen abbauen
downsizing 120 Stellenabbau, Personalabbau
draft 87 Entwurf
to **draft sth** 131 etw entwerfen
to **drain sth** 97P etw abseihen
drastic(ally) 38 drastisch
to **draw** 28 zeichnen; **~ on sth** 111T auf etw zurückgreifen, an etw anknüpfen
to **dress** 16 sich kleiden
dressed, to **get ~** 29T sich anziehen
drill, fire ~ 45T Brandschutzübung
to **drink heavily** 34T stark trinken
to **drive sb over** 32T jdm (mit dem Auto) fahren/bringen
driving licence 8 Führerschein
to **drop out of sth** 34T aus etw herausfallen
drug: ~ addict 39 Drogensüchtige/r, Drogenabhängige/r; **~ crime** 39 Drogenkriminaität; **~ policies** *pl* 39 Drogenpolitik; **~ use** 39 Drogenkonsum; **~ user** 39 Drogenkonsument/in; **~-related** 38 in Zusammenhang mit Drogen; to **get off ~s** 66 von Drogen loskommen
drunk 115 betrunken
dry 58 trocken
due to 59 aufgrund von
Dutch 39 niederländisch
duty 8 Aufgabe, Pflicht; to **be on ~** 37 Dienst haben, eingeteilt sein
dysfunctional 94 zerrüttet, gestört, Problem-, dysfunktional

E

e.g. 12 z. B.
each other 31 einander, gegenseitig
early childhood education 9 frühkindliche Erziehung, Kleinkindpädagogik
to **earn sth** 9 etw verdienen
earnings, loss of ~ 127 Verdienstausfall, Einkommenseinbußen
ease, to **feel at ~** 67 sich wohlfühlen, sich entspannen
Easter bunny 45T Osterhase
Eastern Bloc 111P Ostblock
easy-going 29T locker, unkompliziert
eating disorder 29T Essstörung
economic 40 wirtschaftlich
economics, home ~ 13 Hauswirtschaftslehre
to **edit** 73 *(Film usw.:)* schneiden
editing 72 *(Film usw.:)* Schnitt
to **educate sb** 63 jdn unterrichten, jdn (über etw) aufklären
education 12 Bildung, Schulbildung; **early childhood ~** 9 frühkindliche Erziehung, Kleinkindpädagogik; **health ~** 33 gesundheitliche Aufklärung; **social ~ worker** 29 Sozialpädagoge/-in; **~ programme** 33 Bildungsangebot, -programm; **~ system** 34T Bildungssystem; **~ institution** 12 Bildungseinrichtung
educator 97 Pädagoge/-in
effect 31 Auswirkung, Wirkung, Effekt
effective(ly) 15 wirkungsvoll, effektiv
effort 10 Anstrengung, Mühe
either ... or 34T entweder ... oder
elder 30 Ältere/r
elderly: the ~ 28 ältere Menschen, Senioren; **~ care** 30 Seniorenbetreuung, Altenfürsorge; **~ people** 20 ältere Menschen, Senioren
eldest 29T älteste/r/s
electronics engineer 122 Elektroingenieur/in
element 15 Bestandteil, Element
embarrassed, to **feel ~** 59 sich genieren, sich schämen
emergency 74 Notfall; **~ accommodation** 55T Notunterkunft; **~ service** 66 Notdienst, Rettungsdienst
emotional(ly) 55T emotional
to **empathize** 128 Mitgefühl zeigen, Verständnis zeigen
empathy 66G Mitgefühl, Einfühlung(svermögen)
employee 31 Angestellte/r, Beschäftigte/r, Mitarbeiter/in
employer 8 Arbeitgeber/in
employment 12 Beschäftigung, Anstellung; **~ age** 40 Erwerbsalter; **~ rate** 40 Beschäftigungsquote, Erwerbsquote
empowerment 44 Stärkung der Selbständigkeit
to **enable sb to do sth** 67 jdm ermöglichen, etw zu tun
Enc (= enclosure[s]) 14 *(Brief:)* Anlage(n)
encounter 110 Begegnung
to **encourage: ~ sb** 34T jdn ermutigen, jdn ermuntern; **~ sth** 45 etw unterstützen, etw fördern
end, at the ~ of the day 29T unterm Strich, im Endeffekt
to **end up somewhere** 34T irgendwo landen
endurance 100V Ausdauer
energetic 12 dynamisch, tatkräftig
energy, surge of ~ 65T Energieschub
enforcement, law ~ 39 Rechtsdurchsetzung
engineer, electronics ~ 122 Elektroingenieur/in
to **enjoy: ~ doing sth** 109 etw gern tun; **sb ~s sth** 14 jdm gefällt etw, jdm macht etw Spaß
enlargement, EU ~ 108 EU-Erweiterung
to **enquire about sth** 74 sich nach etw erkundigen
enquiry 74 Anfrage, Erkundigung; to **make ~ies** 74 sich erkundigen, Nachforschungen anstellen
to **ensure sth** 87 etw gewährleisten, für etw sorgen
to **enter: ~ sth** 23 etw betreten; **~ sth into sth** 128 etw in etw eintragen; **~ school** 108 in die Schule kommen, eingeschult werden; **~ the workplace** 43 in die Arbeitswelt einsteigen
enterprise 45 Unternehmen
entertainment 76 Unterhaltung
enthusiastic 29T begeisterungsfähig
entire 127 gesamte/r/s
entitled, to be ~ to sth 34T Anspruch auf etw haben, ein Recht auf etw haben
entrance 45T Eingang
entry 54 Eintrag, Beitrag; **data ~** 43T Dateneingabe
environment 49 Umfeld
environmental impact 84 Umweltbelastung, Umweltfolgen
epilepsy 42 Epilepsie
episode 117 Folge *(einer TV-Serie usw.)*
equal, to **be ~ to sth** 100V einer Sache entsprechen; **~ opportunities** *pl* 26 Gleichstellung, Gleichbehandlung, Chancengleichheit
equality 40 Gleichheit, Gleichberechtigung, Gleichbehandlung; **~ of opportunity** 40 Chancengleichheit
equipment 25 Ausrüstung, Ausstattung, Geräte; **medical ~** 63V Medizingeräte, Medizintechnik

equivalent *8* Entsprechung; to **be ~ to sth** *12* einer Sache entsprechen
error *130* Fehler, Irrtum; **typing ~** *133* Tippfehler
to **escort sb** *57* jdn begleiten, jdn sicher geleiten
especially *13* besonders; *43T* eigens, speziell
essential *51* wesentlich
to **establish sth** *30* etw schaffen, etw einrichten; *61* etw *(Unternehmen usw.)* gründen
to **estimate** *56* schätzen
estimated, to **be ~ to do sth** *56* etw schätzungsweise tun
Estonia *103T* Estland
et cetera *62T* und so weiter
ethnic *30* ethnisch; **~ cleansing** *112* ethnische Säuberungen
etiquette *90* Etikette
EU enlargement *108* EU-Erweiterung
to **evacuate sth** *45T* etw räumen, etw evakuieren
to **evaluate sth** *86* etw auswerten, etw bewerten
even: ~ if *29T* selbst wenn; **~ then** *45T* selbst dann; **~ though** *16* obwohl
event *26* Veranstaltung; to **run an ~** *76* eine Veranstaltung durchführen
everyday *28* Alltags-
evidence *31* Indizien, Hinweise; *123T* Beweise
to **evolve** *40* sich entwickeln
exam, to **pass an ~** *34T* eine Prüfung bestehen
to **examine sb/sth** *36* jdn/etw untersuchen
excellent *14* ausgezeichnet, hervorragend
excerpt *124* Ausschnitt, Auszug
exchange *113T* Austausch; *125P* Wortwechsel
to **exchange sth** *103* etw austauschen
excited *15V* begeistert, gespannt, aufgeregt
excitement *63* Spannung, Nervenkitzel
excursion *82T* Wanderung
excuse *32T* Ausrede; to **make ~s** *65* sich herausreden, Ausreden suchen
exercise *94* Bewegung, körperliche Betätigung, Sport
to **exhibit sth** *64* etw aufweisen, etw an den Tag legen
to **exist** *111G* existieren
existence *111G* Existenz
exit, fire ~ *45T* Notausgang
expectancy, life ~ *100* Lebenserwartung
expectation, academic ~s *pl 41* schulische (Leistungs-)Erwartungen
expenditure *101* Ausgaben, Kosten
expenses *pl 8* Ausgaben, Aufwendungen
experience *6* Erlebnis(se), Erfahrung(en); **work ~** *9* Praktikum, Berufserfahrung
to **experience sth** *56* etw erleben
to **experiment** *34T* experimentieren
to **exploit sb** *11* jdn ausbeuten
to **explore sth** *67* etw erkunden, etw erforschen
to **expose sb to sth** *107P* jdn einer Sache aussetzen
to **express sth** *8* etw äußern, etw ausdrücken
expression *42* Ausdruck
to **extend sth** *24* etw ausweiten, etw erweitern
extended *102* erweitert
extent, to what ~ *43* inwieweit, inwiefern
exterior shot *73* Außenaufnahme
external *55* extern, Außen-
extra *39* zusätzlich, Zusatz-
extract *21* Auszug, Ausschnitt
eye: ~ for detail *43T* Blick für Details; **~ contact** *23* Blickkontakt; to **keep a close ~ on sth** *132* etw genau beobachten
eye-catching *51* auffällig, prägnant
eyeglasses *pl 59* Brille

F

face: ~-to-face *16* persönlich, direkt, unter vier Augen; **~ painting (for children)** *76* Kinderschminken
to **face sth** *11* mit etw konfrontiert sein/werden, einer Sache gegenüberstehen
faced, to **be ~ with sth** *104* mit etw konfrontiert werden
facilitating *80* Moderation, Vermittlung
facility *30* Einrichtung; **assisted living ~** *56* (Einrichtung für) betreutes Wohnen; **care ~** *52* Pflegeeinrichtung
factory *35P* Fabrik; **~-farmed** *96* aus Massentierhaltung
factual *12* auf Tatsachen beruhend
to **fail** *34T* durchfallen
failure *130* Ausfall, Versagen
fair *53* (Branchen-/Handels-)Messe
faithfully: Yours ~ *14 (Brief, E-Mail:)* Mit freundlichen Grüßen
fall *56* Sturz; to **have a ~** *67P* stürzen, hinfallen
false *10* unzutreffend, falsch
to **familiarize oneself with sth** *111T* sich mit etw vertraut machen
family, nuclear ~ *102* Kernfamilie, Kleinfamilie; **~ background** *27* Familienverhältnisse; **~ doctor** *63V* Hausarzt/-ärztin; **~ support centre** *105* Familienhilfe, Familienhilfezentrum
to **fantasize about sth** *65* sich etw vorstellen, von etw fantasieren
far, so ~ *65T* bisher, bislang; **~ corner** *45T* hintere Ecke
farming *96* Landwirtschaft, Tierhaltung
fascinating *111T* faszinierend
fat *84* Fett
fatty *97* fett, fetthaltig
fault *105T* Fehler, Schwäche; *130* Defekt; **sth is sb's ~** *128* jd ist schuld an etw
favour, to **be in ~ of sth** *39G* etw befürworten, für etw sein
to **favour sb/sth** *43T* jdn/etw bevorzugen, jdn/etw favorisieren
feature *61* Merkmal, Kennzeichen
to **feature: ~sb** *63* jdn in der Hauptrolle zeigen; **~ sth** *105* über etw groß berichten
federal: ~ republic *111P* Bundesrepublik; **~ state** *111P* Bundesland
fee *61* Gebühr, Honorar, Preis
to **feed: ~ sb** *59* jdm zu essen geben, jdn füttern; **~ oneself** *59* (selbst) essen
feedback *11* Meinungen, Rückmeldung, Feedback
to **feel: ~ at ease** *67* sich wohlfühlen, sich entspannen; **~ free to do sth** *131* etw gern tun können
feeling of togetherness *45T* Zusammengehörigkeitsgefühl
fellow communist countries *pl 111P* kommunistische Bruderstaaten
female *35P* weiblich
fertility treatment *107P* Kinderwunschbehandlung, künstliche Befruchtung
fever *82* Fieber
field *15V* Bereich, Gebiet; **from the ~** *110* aus der Praxis
fight *35P* Schlägerei, Prügelei
fighting *67P* Beteiligung an einer Schlägerei / an Schlägereien
figure *26* Zahl; *106* Figur
file, case ~ *35* Patientenakte, Vorgang; **company ~** *124T* Betriebsakte
filing *33* Ablage
to **fill sth in** *43T* etw *(Formular usw.)* ausfüllen
final *49* endgültig

financial 9 finanziell; **~ crisis** 35V Finanzkrise
findings *pl* 11 Ergebnis(se)
finish, from start to ~ 76 von Anfang bis Ende
fire: ~ drill 45T Brandschutzübung; **~ exit** 45T Notausgang
to **fire sb** 126 jdn entlassen, jdn feuern
firm, outside ~ 45T externe Firma, Fremdfirma
first: ~ aid 13 Erste Hilfe; **in the ~ place** 34T eigentlich (erst)
first-aid kit 82 Verbandskasten, Erste-Hilfe-Ausrüstung
first-rate 86 erstklassig
to **fit** 35V passen; **~ sth in sth** 82T etw in etw einbauen, etw in etw einpassen; **~ in** 109T dazugehören, sich einfügen; **~ in with sth** 14 sich in etw einfügen; **~ with sth** 46 zu etw passen; **~ sb's needs** 85 jds Bedürfnissen entsprechen
fix 65T *(Drogen:)* Schuss, Ladung
to **fix: ~ sth** 81 etw *(Termin usw.)* festlegen; **~ a problem** 128 ein Problem lösen/beheben
fixed 111P fest
flat, shared ~ *BE* 35P Wohngemeinschaft
flatmate 67P Mitbewohner/in
flavouring 97T Aroma
flea market 109T Flohmarkt
to **flee sth** 108 vor etw fliehen
flexitime 127 Gleitzeit
floor plan 45 Grundriss, Lageplan
flour 97P Mehl
floured 97P bemehlt
flow, large-scale ~ 111P großer Zustrom; **~ chart** 17 Flussdiagramm
fluent 13 *(Sprache:)* fließend
foam, polythene ~ 82T Polyethylen-Schaumstoff
focus of concern 34T Aufmerksamkeitsschwerpunkt
to **focus on sth** 11 sich auf etw konzentrieren, den Schwerpunkt auf etw legen
to **fold** 82T falten
folder 102 Mappe, Ordner
following, the ~ 24 Folgendes
follow-up 78 Folge-, Anschluss-, Nachfass-; **~ question** 19 Anschluß-frage
food: ~ for thought 97T Denkanstöße, Stoff zum Nachdenken; **canned ~** 96 Konserven; **convenience ~** 96 Fertiggerichte, Fertigprodukte; **frozen ~** 96 Tiefkühlkost; **processed ~** 96 verarbeitete Lebensmittel; **~ bank** 17T Tafel; **~ hygiene** 43T Lebensmittelhygiene; **~ intolerance** 84 Nahrungsmittelunverträglichkeit
foodstuffs *pl* 97T Lebensmittel
footage 73 Aufnahme(n), Filmmaterial
to **force: ~ sth on sb** 36 jdm etw aufzwingen; **~ sb** to **do sth** 124 jdn (dazu) zwingen, etw zu tun
force, physical ~ 10 körperliche Gewalt
form 9 Formular
formal 10 formell
to **format sth** 91 etw formatieren
former 111P ehemalig, früher
to **formulate sth** 23 etw formulieren
fortunate, it is ~ that 110 glücklicherweise, erfreulicherweise
to **found sth** 31 etw gründen
free 11 kostenlos; to **feel ~ to do sth** 131 etw gern tun können; **~-range eggs** *pl* 96 Eier aus Freilandhaltung
freedom 40 Freiheit
freelance, to **go ~** 126 sich selbständig machen
freelancer 127 Selbständige/r
freely 39 ungehindert, freizügig
frequency 55 Häufigkeit, Frequenz
frequent(ly) 55 häufig
frightened, to **be ~** 123T Angst haben
frightening 97T beängstigend
frozen food 96 Tiefkühlkost
frustrating 55 frustrierend
full-time 29 Vollzeit(-)
fun, to **be ~** 29T Spaß machen
to **function** 104 funktionieren
to **fund sth** 31 etw finanzieren
fundamental 58T grundlegend
funding 27 (finanzielle) Mittel, Finanzierung
fundraising 27 Einwerben von Spenden, Fundraising
funeral 110 Begräbnis, Bestattung
further 10 weitere/r/s; to **go one step ~** 43T einen Schritt weiter gehen
to **further sth** 24 etw fördern, etw voranbringen
future 12 künftig

G

to **gain: ~ sth** 7 etw erwerben, etw erlangen, etw gewinnen, etw erreichen; **~ weight** 98 zunehmen
gap 24 Lücke
garlic, clove of ~ 97P Knoblauchzehe
to **gather sth** 24 etw sammeln, etw einsammeln
gauze 82 Gaze
gay 94 schwul
GCSEs *pl* 18V Mittlere Reife
geek 124P Nerd, Freak
gender 42 Geschlecht
general 22 allgemein; **in ~** 106 allgemein; **from the ~** to **the specific** 111T vom Allgemeinen zum Konkreten; **~ practitioner (GP)** 66 Hausarzt/-ärztin
generally 51 im Allgemeinen
to **generate: ~ sth** 84 etw erzeugen; **~ money** 51 Geld erwirtschaften, Einnahmen erzielen
genetic manipulation 96 Genmanipulation
genetically, to **pass sth on ~** 107P etw (genetisch) vererben
gentle 46 sanft, behutsam
geriatric: ~ carer 28 Altenpfleger/in; **~ nurse** 46 (examinierte/r) Altenpfleger/in
gesture 122 Geste
to **get: ~ sth across** 62T etw klarmachen, etw verständlich machen; **~ at sth** 125T auf etw hinauswollen; **~ back to sb** 78T sich wieder bei jdm melden; **~ back to normal** 69 zur Normalität zurückkehren, sich normalisieren; **~ sth back on track** 35V etw wieder auf Kurs bringen; **~ sth right** 18 etw (gut) hinbekommen, etw richtig machen; **~ off drugs** 66 von Drogen loskommen; **~ your act together** 125T sich zusammenreißen
gift of money 31 Geldgeschenk
to **give: ~ sb an idea of sth** 48 jdm eine Vorstellung von etw vermitteln; **~ sb up for adoption** 106 jdn zur Adoption freigeben; **~ the impression that …** 58T den Eindruck erwecken, dass …
glad, to **be ~** 18V sich freuen, froh sein
gleaming 97T blitzblank
global(ly) 40 weltweit
gloves *pl* 82 Handschuhe
glucose, blood ~ levels *pl* 99 Blutzuckerwerte
to **go: ~ along with sb** 34T mit jdm mitziehen/-machen; **~ along with sth** 64 einer Sache zustimmen, bei etw mitspielen; **~ off** 105T abhauen, davonlaufen; **Go ahead.** 17T Legen Sie los! **~ off the rails** 34T auf die schiefe Bahn geraten; **~ on a diet** 67P eine Diät machen; **as sb goes** 78 unterwegs
goal 19 Ziel
god 106 Gott
goods *pl* 39 Waren
government 111P Regierung; **local ~** 35V Kommunalverwaltung
to **grab sb's attention** 12 jds Aufmerksamkeit fesseln

grade *13* Note
graduate *125T* Hochschulabsolvent/in
to **graduate** *125* den (Schul-/Uni-) Abschluss machen
grain *98* Getreide; **whole ~s** *pl 99* Vollkorngetreide
grant proposal *80* Zuschussantrag, Förderantrag
to **grant sb sth** *14* jdm etw gewähren
graph *48* Diagramm, Kurve
grated *97P* gerieben
Greece *99* Griechenland
Greek *108* griechisch; Griechisch
to **greet sb** *17* jdn begrüßen
greeting *77T* Gruß, Begrüßung; *32* Begrüßung
grief *66T* Trauer
grip: to get to ~ s with *34T* etw in den Griff bekommen; **wide-~ utensils** *pl 59* Besteck mit breitem Griff
grounds *pl 78T* Gelände, Außenanlage
to **grow: ~ sth** *96* etw *(Pflanzen usw.)* anbauen, etw ziehen; **~ up** *41* aufwachsen
growing *108* steigend, zunehmend
growth *100* Wachstum; **~ hormone** *97T* Wachstumshormon
to **guarantee sb sth** *43T* jdm etw garantieren
guess *26* Vermutung; to **take a ~** *26* raten, eine Vermutung anstellen
guidance *11* Orientierung, Hilfe; **marriage ~** *69* Eheberatung
guide *78* Führer/in, Reiseleiter/in
to **guide sb** *13G* jdn führen, jdn leiten; *29T* jdn anleiten
guideline *67* Richtlinie, Empfehlung
gun *10* Schusswaffe
gym *15V* Fitnessstudio

H

habit *36* Gewohnheit
hairdresser *34T* Friseur/in
hairnet *45T* Haarnetz
half-brother *106* Halbbruder
halved *97P* halbiert
hand, on the one ~ *31G* einerseits; **on the other ~** *31G* andererseits
to **hand sth down** *104* etw weitergeben, etw vererben
handicapped *42* behindert, benachteiligt
to **handle sth** *25* etw bewältigen, etw erledigen; *45C* mit etw umgehen, etw handhaben
handling (of sth) *84* Umgang (mit etw)
handout *48* Arbeitsblatt, Handzettel
handover *54* Übergabe
hand-picked *30* handverlesen
hands-on *41G* praktisch, manuell
to **hang: ~ sth** *45T* etw aufhängen; **~ out** *34T* abhängen, rumhängen
hangover, with a ~ *34T* verkatert
happen, to be about to ~ *58* gleich geschehen, unmittelbar bevorstehen
happy, to be ~ to do sth *17* etw gern tun; *32T* sich freuen, etw zu tun; to **make sb ~** *128* jdn zufriedenstellen
to **harass sb** *122* jdn belästigen, jdn mobben, jdn schikanieren
harassment *120* Belästigung, Mobbing, Schikanieren; **sexual ~** *121* sexuelle Belästigung; **workplace ~** *121* Mobbing am Arbeitsplatz
hard-line *39* unnachgiebig, kompromisslos
hardly *89* kaum
hard-working *9* fleißig
to **harm sb** *34T* jdn verletzen
harmful *112* schädlich
hassle-free package *76* Rundum-Sorglos-Paket
to **hate sth** *109T* etw überhaupt nicht mögen, etw hassen
to **have: ~ sb along** *82T* jdn dabei haben; **Thanks for ~ing me.** *62T* Vielen Dank für die Einladung.
head *81* Leiter/in; **~ nurse** *56* Pflegeleiter/in, Oberschwester; **~ teacher** *67P* Schuldirektor/in; to **nod one's ~** *67* (mit dem Kopf) nicken
headache(s) *83P* Kopfschmerzen
heading *6* Überschrift, Rubrik
health *8* Gesundheit; **public ~** *39* Gesundheitswesen, Volksgesundheit; **social and ~ care** *8* Gesundheit und Soziales, Sozial- und Gesundheitswesen; **~ challenges** *pl 56* gesundheitliche Probleme; **~ condition** *8* Erkrankung; **~ education** *33* gesundheitliche Aufklärung; **~ status** *63V* Gesundheitszustand; **~ studies** *pl 13* Gesundheitswissenschaften (mit Pflege); **National H~ Service (NHS)** *29 staatlicher Gesundheitsdienst in Großbritannien;* **World H~ Organization (WHO)** *96* Weltgesundheitsorganisation
healthcare *9* medizinische Versorgung
healthy *10* gesund
hearing, loss of ~ *56* Schwerhörigkeit, Hörverlust; **~ impairment** *42* Schwerhörigkeit, Hörbehinderung, Hörschaden; **~ loss** *42* Hörverlust, Hörschädigung
heart: ~ damage *99* Herzschäden, Herzschädigung; **~ rate** *63V* Herzfrequenz, Puls
heat *82T* Erwärmung, Wärme, Hitze
to **heat sth** *87* etw erhitzen, etw erwärmen
heaven *110* Himmel; **for ~'s sake** *124P* verdammt nochmal
height *114* Körpergröße
hell, to make sb's life ~ *123T* jdm das Leben zur Hölle machen
helmet *83* Helm
help, to be of ~ (to sb) *66T* (jdm) helfen
helpful *13* nützlich
helpline *53* Hotline, Beratungstelefon; **~ advice** *53* Telefonseelsorge, Telefonberatung
heroin *39* Heroin
hesitant, to be ~ to do sth *43T* etw nur zögerlich tun; zögern, etw zu tun
to **hesitate** *85* zögern
Hesse *108* Hessen
to **hide sth** *64* etw verbergen
high in sth *84* mit hohem Gehalt an etw
to **highlight sth** *44G* etw hervorheben; *53* etw in den Mittelpunkt stellen, etw herausstellen
highly *10* sehr, in hohem Maß; to **talk ~ of sb/sth** *63* sich anerkennend über jdn/etw äußern; to **be ~ respected** *10* großes Ansehen genießen, hoch angesehen sein; **~ skilled** *30* hochqualifiziert
to **hike** *89* Wandern
hiking *80* Wandern
hire, to have sth for ~ *77* etw vermieten
to **hire sb** *43* jdn einstellen
to **hit** *65* schlagen; **~ sb/sth** *35V* jdn etw treffen; **~ sth** *83* gegen etw stoßen
hold, to get ~ of sb *129T* jdn erreichen, jdn an die Strippe kriegen
to **hold: ~ on** *81T* warten; **~ a meeting** *118* eine Sitzung/Besprechung abhalten
holiday, bank ~ *61* gesetzlicher Feiertag
home, care ~ *35P* Jugendheim, betreutes Wohnen; **long-term care ~** *56* Langzeitpflegeeinrichtung; **nursing ~** *56* Pflegeheim; **residential ~** *56* Wohnheim, Seniorenheim; **~ care** *56* häusliche Pflege; **~ carer** *30* häusliche/ambulante Pflegekraft; **~ country** *111P* Heimatland; **~ economics** *13* Hauswirtschaftslehre; **~ support** *30* häusliche Unterstützung

homeland *102* Heimatland
homeless *27* obdachlos; **the ~** *26* Obdachlose *pl*
homelessness *34T* Obdachlosigkeit
homely *60* behaglich, gemütlich
homosexual *123T* homosexuell
honest(ly) *12* ehrlich, aufrichtig
hormone, growth ~ *97T* Wachstumshormon
horrible *105T* schrecklich, furchtbar
hospital admission *38* Einlieferung/Einweisung ins Krankenhaus
to **host sth** *82* etw *(Veranstaltung usw.)* ausrichten
hostile *120* feindselig, aggressiv
hostility *106* Feindseligkeit, ablehnende Haltung
hour, opening ~s *pl* *61* Öffnungszeiten; **rush ~** *65T* Hauptverkehrszeit; to **work long ~s** *29* lange arbeiten, Überstunden machen
household *69* Haushalt
housewife *102* Hausfrau
housing *35V* Wohnungen, Unterkunft
however *12* allerdings, aber, doch, jedoch
HR manager *126* Personalchef/in, Personalleiter/in
huge *103T* riesig, riesengroß
human *40* menschlich; **~ resources (HR)** *121* Personal(abteilung); **~ rights violations** *pl* *112* Menschenrechtsverstöße
humanity *40* Menschheit
hunt, treasure ~ *76* Schatzsuche, Schnitzeljadg
to **hurt: ~ sb/sth** *10* jdn/etw verletzen, jdm wehtun; **~ sb** *123T* jdm schaden
hygiene *36* Hygiene; **food ~** *43T* Lebensmittelhygiene; **personal ~** *35G* Körperpflege
hypertension *99* erhöhter Blutdruck, Hypertonie

I

idea, to give sb an ~ of sth *48* jdm eine Vorstellung von etw vermitteln
to **identify sth** *53* etw herausfinden, etw feststellen, etw bestimmen
identity *40* Identität
idle *100V* untätig
idleness *100V* Untätigkeit
if, as ~ *131* als ob; **even ~** *29T* selbst wenn
to **ignore sb/sth** *105T* jdn/etw ignorieren
ill *35P* krank
illegal(ly) *35P* illegal
illness *12* Krankheit, Erkrankung
to **illustrate sth** *41G* etw veranschaulichen, etw illustrieren
to **imagine sth** *33* sich etw vorstellen
image, cutaway ~ *100V* *(Tomografie:)* Schnittbild
immediate *65T* sofortig, direkt
immediately *66* sofort, unverzüglich
immense *28* enorm, gewaltig
immigrant *94* Einwanderer/-in
immigration *108* Einwanderung, Immigration
to **immobilize sth** *82T* etw ruhigstellen
impact *30* Einfluss, Auswirkung(en), Folge(n); **environmental ~** *84* Umweltbelastung, Umweltfolgen
impaired *42* beeinträchtigt, behindert
impairment *8* Beeinträchtigung, Behinderung; **hearing ~** *42* Schwerhörigkeit, Hörbehinderung, Hörschaden; **speech ~** *42* Sprachbehinderung, Sprechbehinderung; **visual/vision ~** *42* Sehbehinderung, Sehschwäche
impediment, speech ~ *42* Sprachfehler, Sprachbehinderung
to **implement sth** *39* etw umsetzen
importance *62* Bedeutung, Wichtigkeit
to **impose sth upon sb** *111T* jdm etw aufzwingen, jdm etw auferlegen
impression *16* Eindruck; to **give the ~ that …** *58T* den Eindruck erwecken, dass …
to **improve** *21* sich verbessern, besser werden; **~ sth** *15* etw verbessern
improvement *34T* Verbesserung
in so doing *35V* auf diese Weise
inability *42* Unfähigkeit, Unvermögen
inactivity *100V* Untätigkeit, Trägheit, Inaktivität
inappropriate *122* unangemessen, unangebracht
incest *105T* Inzest
to **include sth** *12* etw einbeziehen, etw aufnehmen
inclusion *26* Integration, Inklusion
inclusive *27* inklusiv, integrativ, ganzheitlich
income *101* Einkommen
inconvenience *131* Unannehmlichkeiten
incorrect *131* falsch, fehlerhaft, unrichtig
increase (in sth) *38* Anstieg (von etw), Zunahme (von etw)
to **increase** *38* zunehmen, steigen; **~ sth** *10* etw erhöhen, etw steigern
increased risk *99* erhöhtes Risiko
indeed *111T* in der Tat, allerdings
independence *40* Unabhängigkeit, Selbständigkeit
independent(ly) *13* selbstständig, unabhängig
to **indicate sth** *67* etw erkennen lassen, etw signalisieren
indigestion *124* Magenverstimmung
individual *9* (eigenständige) Persönlichkeit, Einzelperson, Individuum; **a proactive ~** *9* jd mit Eigeninitiative; **private ~** *31* Privatperson
individual(ly) *18* einzeln, individuell; **on an ~ basis** *43T* auf den Einzelfall bezogen, individuell
indoors *64* drinnen
industrial sector *111P* Industrie
infected, to become ~ *82T* *(Wunde:)* sich entzünden
infection *58T* Infektion, Entzündung
infertile *107P* unfruchtbar
infertility *107P* Unfruchtbarkeit
inflammation *82T* Entzündung
inflammatory, chronic ~ bowel disease *42* chronisch-entzündliche Darmerkrankung
inflatable *77* aufblasbar
to **influence sb/sth** *103* jdn/etw beeinflussen
info sheet *56* Informationsblatt
infographic *47* Infografik
to **inform sb** *50* jdn benachrichtigen, jdn informieren
informal *74* zwanglos, informell
information *33* Daten, Angaben, Informationen
ingredient *86* Zutat
inherent *40* innewohnend, angeboren
initials *pl*, **reference ~** *84* Zeichen
initiative *53* Initiative; **on sb's own ~** *45T* aus eigenem Antrieb
injection *63V* Injektion, Spritze
to **injure sth** *83* sich etw verletzen
injury *42* Verletzung
inner *76* innere/r/s; **~ resignation** *121* innere Kündigung
inpatient *84* stationäre/r Patient/in
insensitive(ly) *126* taktlos, instinktlos
inside address *84* Innenadresse
insight *36* Einblick
to **insist** *105T* darauf bestehen, etw mit Nachdruck behaupten
to **inspire sb** *63* jdn anregen, jdn inspirieren
to **install sth** *35V* etw aufstellen, etw installieren
instantly *62* sofort, auf Anhieb
instead *12* stattdessen; **~ of** *34T* anstatt

institution, educational ~ *12* Bildungseinrichtung; **young offender ~** *35P* Jugendstrafanstalt
instruction *66* Anweisung, Anleitung; *108* Unterricht
instructor *80* Lehrer/in
insufficient *99* unzureichend
insulin resistant *100V* insulinresistent
insurance *21* Versicherung
intake *99* Verzehr, Konsum, Zufuhr
to **integrate: ~ into sth** *102* sich in etw integrieren; **~ sb in sth** *26* jdn in etw eingliedern, jdn in etw integrieren; **~ sth in sth** *76* etw in etw einbinden, etw in etw integrieren
integrated *54 (Therapie usw.:)* multimodal, ganzheitlich, integriert
intellectual disability *42* geistige Behinderung
intelligence *124T* Intelligenz
intended, to be ~ to do sth *10* dafür/dazu gedacht sein, etw zu tun
intention *49* Absicht
to **interact with sb** *111T* sich mit jdm auseinandersetzen, mit jdm interagieren
interaction, social ~ *42* Umgang mit anderen, soziale Interaktion; *57* Geselligkeit, geselliges Miteinander
intercourse, sexual ~ *105T* Geschlechtsverkehr
interior shot *73* Innenaufnahme
internship *46* Praktikum
interpersonal skills *pl* *9* soziale Kompetenz
to **interrupt sb/sth** *39G* jdn/etw unterbrechen, jdm ins Wort fallen
to **interview sb** *7* ein Vorstellungsgespräch mit jdm führen
interview *7* Vorstellungsgespräch
interviewee *113P Person, mit der ein Vorstellungsgespräch geführt wird*
interviewer *16 jd, der ein Vorstellungsgespräch führt*
intimidation *121* Einschüchterung
intolerance, food ~ *84* Nahrungsmittelunverträglichkeit
to **introduce: ~ sb to sb** *22* jdn jdm vorstellen; **~ sth** *39* etw einführen
introduction *77T (Text:)* Einleitung
introductions *pl* *29* Vorstellung, Bekanntmachen
introductory *67* einleitend
to **invent sth** *33* etw erfinden, sich etw ausdenken
to **invest in sth** *39* in etw investieren
investment *16* Investition
invisible *42* unsichtbar
invitation *44* Einladung
to **invite sth from sb** *51* jdn um etw bitten
to **involve: ~ sb (in sth)** *53* jdn (an etw) beteiligen; **~ sth** *21* etw umfassen, etw einbeziehen
involved, to **be ~ (in sth)** *45G* (an etw) beteiligt sein; to **get ~ in sth** *30* sich in etw einbringen
iodine *82* Jod
isolated *30* alleinstehend, einsam
isolation *64* (soziale) Isolation, Vereinsamung
issue *34T* Problem, Streitpunkt, Frage
italics *pl*, **in ~** *131* kursiv (gesetzt)
item *36* Artikel, Ware; **per ~** *86* pro Stück

J

jam *61* Marmelade
jealous (of sb) *65T* eifersüchtig (auf jdn)
jigsaw *137* Puzzle
job, care ~ *7* Pflege-/Sozialberuf, Beruf im Gesundheitswesen **~ advert(isement)** *6* Stellenanzeige, Stellenangebot; **~ description** *16* Stellenbeschreibung, Tätigkeitsbeschreibung; **~ interview** *7* Vorstellungsgespräch; **~ listing** *24* Stellenanzeige; **~ title** *12* Stellenbezeichnung; **~ vacancy** *10* freie/offene Stelle; **on the ~** *52* bei der Arbeit; to **do a good/great ~** *23* etw gut/super machen
to **join: ~ sb/sth** *9* sich jdm/etw anschließen, bei jdm/etw mitmachen, bei etw dabei sein; **~ sth** *39* etw verbinden, etw zusammenfügen; **~ a company** *9* bei einer Firma anfangen, zu einer Firma kommen; **If you're just ~ing us …** *103T (Radio-/TV-Sendung:)* Wenn Sie gerade erst zugeschaltet haben, …
judge *35P* Richter/in
to **judge sth** *67* etw bewerten, etw beurteilen
jumbled *69* durcheinandergeworfen, ungeordnet
to **jump in** *67* dazwischenreden, etw sagen
jumper *BE* *35V* Pullover
to **justify sth** *41G* etw begründen, etw rechtfertigen

K

keen, to **be ~ to do sth** *14* etw (unbedingt) tun wollen, sehr an etw interessiert sein; **sb is ~ on sth** *45T* jdm ist sehr an etw gelegen
to **keep: ~ sb on** *126* jdn weiterbeschäftigen; **~ sth in mind** *59* etw beachten, an etw denken
key *9* wichtigste/r/s, Haupt-; **the ~** *100V* die Hauptsache; **~ (to sth)** *21* Schlüssel (zu etw); to **be ~ to sth** *99* für etw entscheidend sein
to **kick** *65* treten
to **kill sb** *10* jdn töten
killed, to **be/get ~** *105P* ums Leben kommen
kind *7* Art; *46* liebenswürdig, freundlich, gütig
kit *36* Set; **first-aid ~** *82* Verbandskasten, Erste-Hilfe-Ausrüstung
to **knead** *97P* kneten
to **know:** to **get to ~ sb/sth** *27* jdn/etw kennenlernen
knowledge *14* Wissen, Kenntnisse
kosher *87* koscher

L

labour: ~ costs *pl* *84* Arbeitskosten, Lohnkosten; **~ market** *26* Arbeitsmarkt; **~ shortage** *111P* Arbeitskräftemangel
lack (of sth) *42* Mangel (an etw)
to **lack: sb ~s sth** *11* jdm fehlt etw
landline *74* Festnetzanschluss
language, body ~ *15* Körpersprache; **programming ~** *125T* Programmiersprache; **~ class** *119* Sprachkurs
lap *58* Schoß
large-scale flow *111P* großer Zustrom
to **last** *96* halten
last but not least *82T* zu guter Letzt
lastly *75* zuletzt, als Letztes
latecomer *32T* Nachzügler/in
lately *103* in letzter Zeit
latest *40* jüngste/r/s, aktuell
to **launch sth** *53* etw *(Aktion usw.)* starten, etw *(Unternehmen usw.)* gründen
laundry *57* Wäsche
law *12* Gesetz; **~ enforcement** *39* Rechtsdurchsetzung
to **lay sb off** *126* jdn (betriebsbedingt) entlassen
lay-off *126* (betriebsbedingte) Kündigung
layout *12* Gestaltung, Aufmachung, Layout
laziness *100V* Trägheit, Faulheit
lazy *100V* träge, faul
to **lead to sth** *42* zu etw führen
leader, team ~ *45T* Gruppenleiter/in
leaf (*pl* **leaves)** *97P* Blatt
lean *98* mager

learning: ~ difficulties *pl* 8 Lernschwierigkeiten; **~ disability** 43T Lernbehinderung
least, at ~ 8 mindestens; 127 wenigstens, zumindest; **last but not ~** 82T zu guter Letzt
leave, to **take ~** 115 Urlaub nehmen
leaver, school ~ 9 Schulabgänger/in
legal(y) 39 legal, rechtmäßig; **~ advice** 121 Rechtsberatung, juristischer Rat; **~ problem** 73 juristisches Problem
legalization 39 Legalisierung
to **legalize sth** 39 etw legalisieren
legumes *pl* 98 Hülsenfrüchte
leisure 8 Freizeit
length 24 Länge
lesbian 94 lesbisch
to **lessen sth** 100V etw verringern, etw vermindern
letter, business ~ 74 Geschäftsbrief; **capital ~** 14 Großbuchstabe; **cover ~** 6 Anschreiben, Begleitschreiben
letterhead 84 Briefkopf
level 11 Niveau, Pegel; 38 Stand; **blood glucose ~s** *pl* 99 Blutzuckerwerte; **cholesterol ~s** *pl* 98 Cholesterinwerte; **stress ~** 124 Stressbelastung, Stressniveau; **on a peer-group ~** 11 unter Kollegen und Kolleginnen; **~ teaspoonful** 97P gestrichener Teelöffel
lewd 122 anzüglich, obszön
to **liaise with sb** 106 mit jdm in Kontakt sein
licence, driving ~ 8 Führerschein
to **lie** 104 lügen
life: ~ expectancy 100 Lebenserwartung; **~ skills** *pl* 34T lebenspraktische Fertigkeiten, Lebenskompetenz; **a matter of ~ and death** 67 lebensbedrohliche Situation, Frage von Leben oder Tod; **throughout sb's ~** 99 jds ganzes Leben lang; to **make sb's ~ hell** 123T jdm das Leben zur Hölle machen
lifestyle 33 Lebensweise
lift, to **give sb a ~** 32T jdm (mit dem Auto) fahren/bringen, jdm mitnehmen
to **lighten the load for sb** 35 jdn entlasten
likely 16 wahrscheinlich, aussichtsreich; to **be ~ to do sth** 40 etw wahrscheinlich tun (werden)
limb 42 Gliedmaß, Extremität
to **limit sth** 42 etw beschränken, etw einschränken
limited 41 begrenzt, eingeschränkt
line, subject ~ 77T Betreffzeile; **~ of work** 11 Beruf, Branche; **~ manager** 134 direkte/r Vorgesetzte/r; **on the ~** 81 *(Telefon:)* in der Leitung, am Telefon; **between the ~s** 123 zwischen den Zeilen; to **stand in ~** 126 Schlange stehen, anstehen; to **be in ~ with sth** 103T mit etw übereinstimmen, sich mit etw decken
lipid counts *pl* 100V Lipidwerte
lipoprotein, low-density ~ 99 Lipoprotein niedriger Dichte
list, price ~ 77 Preisliste; **shot ~** 73 Liste der Einstellungen
listener 15V Zuhörer/in
listing, job ~ 24 Stellenanzeige
lit, well ~ 58 gut beleuchtet
Lithuania 103T Litauen
to **live rough** 36 auf der Straße leben
livestock 96 Vieh, Nutztiere
living, activities *pl* **of daily ~** 58T Aktivitäten/Verrichtungen des täglichen Lebens; **assisted ~ facility** 56 (Einrichtung für) betreutes Wohnen; **~ arrangement** 56 Form des Wohnens, Wohnkonzept
load, to **lighten the ~ for sb** 35 jdn entlasten
to **loaf around** 100V herumhängen, herumgammeln
local: ~ authority 29T Kommune, Gemeinde(verwaltung); **~ government** 35V Kommunalverwaltung
location 9 Standort, Ort
locker 35 Schließfach, Spind
logical 83P logisch
long, as ~ as 43T solange
long-lasting 43 langanhaltend, dauerhaft
long-term 8 langfristig, chronisch; **~ care** 56 Langzeitpflege; **~ care home** 56 Langzeitpflegeeinrichtung
to **look: ~ after sb/sth** 10 sich um jdn/etw kümmern; **~ at sth closely** 38T sich etw näher/genau ansehen; **~ forward to sth** 14 sich auf etw freuen; **~ into sth** 130 etw untersuchen, sich um etw kümmern; **~ sth up** 82 etw *(in einem Wörterbuch)* nachschlagen
to **lose weight** 97 abnehmen
loss, hearing ~ 42 Hörverlust, Hörschädigung; **~ of earnings** 127 Verdienstausfall, Einkommenseinbußen; **~ of hearing** 56 Schwerhörigkeit, Hörverlust; **~ of movement** 56 Bewegungseinschränkungen, Mobilitätsverlust; **~ of sight** 56 Erblindung, Erblindungserscheinungen
lounge *BE* 35V Wohnzimmer
loved ones *pl* 62 Angehörige, Nahestehende
to **lower sth** 97 etw senken
luck: Good ~! 75 Viel Erfolg! Viel Glück!
luckily 109 zum Glück, glücklicherweise
lunch, packed ~ 61 Lunchpaket

M

machine, vending ~ 84 (Verkaufs-)Automat
madam: Dear Sir or M~ 14 *(Brief, E-Mail:)* Sehr geehrte Damen und Herren
magazine 28 Zeitschrift
mail 77T Post
to **mail sth to sb** 80 jdm etw (mit der Post) schicken
main: ~ purpose 31 Hauptanliegen, Hauptziel; **~ subject** 13 Hauptfach
mainly 11 hauptsächlich
mainstream 41 regulär
to **maintain sth** 23 etw aufrechterhalten; 33 etw *(Daten usw.)* pflegen, etw instandhalten
major 64 groß, wichtig, bedeutend
majority 34T Mehrheit, Großteil
to **make: ~ sth** 12 etw ausmachen; **~ sb do sth** 17T jdn (dazu) veranlassen, etw zu tun; **~ sth up** 37 sich etw ausdenken; **~ sure** 12 dafür sorgen(, dass ...); sicherstellen(, dass ...); **~ up one's mind** 36 sich entscheiden, sich entschließen; to **be made up of sth** 82T aus etw bestehen
male 35P männlich
to **manage: ~ sth** 28 etw verwalten, etw leiten, etw organisieren, etw managen; 34T etw steuern, etw beherrschen; 63V etw bewältigen; 99 mit etw zurechtkommen, etw in den Griff bekommen; **~ to do sth** 54 es schaffen, etw zu tun
management 87 Geschäftsleitung; **anger ~** 34 Agressionsbewältigung; **conflict ~** 128 Konfliktbewältigung, -bearbeitung, -management; **crisis ~** 30 Krisenmanagement
manager, case ~ 37 Fallbearbeiter/in, Case Manager/in; **HR ~** 126 Personalchef/in, Personalleiter/in; **line ~** 134 direkte/r Vorgesetzte/r; **office ~** 33 Büroleiter/in; **sales ~** 85 Vertriebsleiter/in, Verkaufsleiter/in; **sales ~** 85 Vertriebsleiter/in, Verkaufsleiter/in; **senior ~** 127 leitende/r Angestellte/r
manipulation, genetic ~ 96 Genmanipulation
manipulative 104 manipulativ

manner, in a … ~ 122 auf … (Art und) Weise
manual 109 Handbuch, Leitfaden
manufacturer 119 Hersteller/in
to **marginalize sb** 105T jdn ausgrenzen
mark 34T Note
market 126 Markt; **flea ~** 109T Flohmarkt; **labour ~** 26 Arbeitsmarkt
marriage 69 Ehe; **~ guidance** 69 Eheberatung
married, to **be ~ to sb** 69 mit jdm verheiratet sein; **~ couple** 30 (Ehe-)Paar
marrow, bone ~ 97T Knochenmark
to **marry** 102 heiraten
mass, muscle ~ 100V Muskelmasse
massive 39 groß, gewaltig, massiv
to **master sth** 67 etw beherrschen
match 120 Entsprechung
to **match** 24 zueinanderpassen, übereinstimmen; **~ sth** 17T zu etw passen, einer Sache entsprechen; **~ sth** to **sth** 8 etw einer Sache zuordnen
mate *BE* 18V Kumpel
maternity ward 9 Entbindungsstation *(im Krankenhaus)*
maths 18V Mathe(matik)
to **matter** 52 wichtig sein, von Belang sein
matter 128 Angelegenheit, Sache; **a ~ of life and death** 67 lebensbedrohliche Situation, Frage von Leben oder Tod; **as a ~ of fact** 32T tatsächlich, sogar; **no ~** 29T egal, ganz gleich, unabhängig davon; **subject ~** 77T Thema, Thematik, Inhalt
matter-of-fact 58 sachlich, nüchtern, direkt
maximum 50 höchstens, maximal
me: It's ~. 34T Ich bin's.
meal 29T Mahlzeit, Essen
mealtime 29T Essenszeit, Mahlzeit
meaning 42 Bedeutung; 100V das heißt
meaningful 16 wichtig, bedeutsam
means of communication 74 Kommunikationsmittel
measure 83 Maßnahme; **a small ~** 35V ein geringes Maß; to **take ~s** 83 Maßnahmen ergreifen
to **measure sth** 100 etw messen
meat 96 Fleisch
mechanism 100V Mechanismus
mechatronics 35P Mechatronik
media attention 27 Medieninteresse, Berichterstattung in den Medien
to **mediate** 49 vermitteln
mediation 16 Vermittlung, Mediation, Moderation
medical 11 ärztlich, medizinisch, Medizin-; **~ adviser** 107P medizinische/r Berater/in; **~ care** 56 medizinische Versorgung; **~ check-up** 107P ärztliche Untersuchung; **~ condition** 56 Krankheit; **~ devices/equipment** *pl* 63V Medizingeräte, Medizintechnik; **~ officer** 82 Betriebssanitäter/in; **~ problem** 36 Gesundheitsproblem; **~ records** *pl* 107P Patientenakte; **~ room** 45T Sanitätsraum, Erste-Hilfe-Raum; **~ supplies** *pl* 63V Sanitätsartikel, Medizinbedarf
to **medicate sb/sth** 97T jdn/etw medizinisch behandeln
medication 36 Arzneimittel, Medikamente
medicine 57 Medikament
to **meditate** 46 meditieren
to **meet: ~ requirements** 43T Anforderungen erfüllen; **~ sb's needs** 34T jds Bedürfnisse erfüllen, jds Bedürfnissen entsprechen; **Pleased/Nice to ~ you.** 19 Schön, dich/Sie/euch kennenzulernen.
meeting 45T Sitzung, Besprechung; to **call a ~** 109 eine Sitzung einberufen, eine Besprechung ansetzen; to **hold a ~** 118 eine Sitzung/Besprechung abhalten
member 19 Mitglied, Angehörige/r *(einer Gruppe)*; **~ state** 103T Mitgliedsstaat
memo 109 (Gesprächs-)Notiz, Mitteilung
memorable 62 einprägsam
mental 11 psychisch, mental, geistig; **~ abuse** 104 psychischer Missbrauch; **~ capacity** 42 geistige Leistungsfähigkeit; **~ disorder** 38 psychische Erkrankung; **~ problems** *pl* 28 psychische Probleme; **~ state** 100V Befindlichkeit, seelische Verfassung
to **mention sth** 9 etw erwähnen, etw nennen
mentor 112 Mentor/in
mentoring 9 Begleitung, Betreuung (durch eine/n Mentor/in), Mentoring
merely 100V lediglich, bloß, nur
message, recorded ~ 119 (automatische) Ansage, Bandansage; **text ~** 74 SMS, Textnachricht; to **take a ~** 75 *(Telefon:)* jdm etw ausrichten
to **metabolize sth** 100V etw verstoffwechseln
to **microwave sth** 87 etw in der Mikrowelle erhitzen
microwave oven 87 Mikrowelle(nherd)
midwife (*pl* **midwives**) 9 Hebamme
midwifery 9 Geburtshilfe
migrant 95 Migrant/in
to **migrate** 111 auswandern, migrieren
mild 42 *(Krankheit usw.:)* leicht
to **mind** 88 etw dagegen haben
mind, to **keep sth in ~** 59 etw beachten, an etw denken; to **make up one's ~** 36 sich entscheiden, sich entschließen; to **stick in sb's ~** 43T bei jdm hängen/haften bleiben
minimum 94 Mindest-
minority 30 Minderheit
minute, in a ~ 32T gleich, sofort
to **miss: ~ sth** 64 etw verpassen; **~ sb/sth** 126 jdn/etw vermissen
missing, to **be ~** 35V fehlen
mission 30 Aufgabe, Auftrag, Ziel; **~ statement** 49 Leitbild
mistaken, to **be ~** 127 sich täuschen
to **misunderstand sth** 65T etw missverstehen, etw falsch verstehen
misunderstanding 130 Missverständnis
misuse 38T Missbrauch
to **mix** 110 *(Party usw.:)* sich kennenlernen, miteinander in Kontakt kommen; **~ sth** 97P etw mischen, etw vermengen
mix-up 130 Durcheinander, Verwirrung
mobility: ~ assistance 127 Mobilitätshilfe; **~ problems** *pl* 28 Mobilitätseinschränkungen
model release 73 Modelvertrag, Model Release
moderate 43T gemäßigt, leicht
moderate 101 mäßig, gemäßigt
money, to **generate ~** 51 Geld erwirtschaften, Einnahmen erzielen; to **raise ~** 51 Geld beschaffen; **gift of ~** 31 Geldgeschenk; **good value for ~** 92 preiswert, günstig
to **monitor sth** 63V etw beobachten, etw überwachen
mood 54 Stimmung, Laune
moreover 36 außerdem, darüber hinaus
Morocco 111P Marokko
most recent 12 jüngste/r/s, neueste/r/s
mother, biological ~ 107G leibliche Mutter; **~ tongue** 110 Muttersprache
to **motivate sb** 34T jdn motivieren
motivated 8 motiviert
motor: ~ ability 42 motorische Fähigkeit; **~ neuron disease** 42 Motoneuron-Krankheit

to **open a door of opportunity for sb** *35V* jdm eine (einmalige) Möglichkeit eröffnen
open day *22* Tag der offenen Tür
opening *43T* freie Stelle; **~ hours** *pl 61* Öffnungszeiten
to **operate** *17T* geschäftlich tätig sein, operieren
opinion, in my ~ *11* meiner Ansicht/Meinung nach
opportunity *8* Chance, Möglichkeit; **career development ~ies** *pl 24* berufliche Entwicklungsmöglichkeiten; **equal ~ies** *pl 26* Gleichstellung, Gleichbehandlung, Chancengleichheit; **equality of ~** *40* Chancengleichheit; to **open a door of ~ for sb** *35V* jdm eine (einmalige) Möglichkeit eröffnen; to **present an ~** *65T* eine Gelegenheit bieten; to **take the ~** *15V* die Gelegenheit ergreifen
opposed, as ~ to *42* im Gegensatz zu
opposite *45T* gegenüber (von)
option *10* (Wahl-)Möglichkeit, Option
optional *12* fakultativ
oral *13* mündlich
order *12* Reihenfolge; *45T* Auftrag, Bestellung; to **place an ~** *75* eine Bestellung aufgeben, einen Auftrag erteilen; **in ~ to** *31* um … zu
to **order sth** *50* etw bestellen
organic *86* Bio-
organism *100V* Organismus
organization *6* Unternehmen, Organisation; **business ~** *75* Wirtschaftsunternehmen, Unternehmensform
orientation, sexual ~ *42* sexuelle Orientierung
origin, national ~ *42* nationale Herkunft
original(ly) *29T* ursprünglich
to **originate** *42* entstehen
other, each ~ *31* einander, gegenseitig; **on the ~ hand** *31G* andererseits
out of office *119* nicht am Platz, außer Haus
outcome *83* Ergebnis, Resultat
outdoors *33* draußen
outfit, carnival ~ *88* Karnevalskostüm
outing *56* Ausflug
to **outline sth** *12* etw umreißen, etw skizzieren
outreach: ~ centre *27* Sozialzentrum, Begegnungsstätte, Bürgerbüro; **community ~ worker** *33* Sozialarbeiter/in für gesellschaftliche Randgruppen
outside firm *45T* externe Firma, Fremdfirma
to **outsource sth** *126* etw auslagern
outstanding *60* hervorragend, herausragend
oven *97P* Ofen; **microwave ~** *87* Mikrowelle(nherd)
over, all ~ … *34T* in ganz …; **all ~ again** *65* von neuem, von vorn; **~ and ~ again** *66T* (immer und) immer wieder
overall score *124P* Gesamtpunktzahl
to **overcome sth** *34T* etw überwinden, etw bewältigen
overdose *39* Überdosis
overheads *pl 84* Betriebskosten, Gemeinkosten
overseas *127* im/ins Ausland, in/nach Übersee
oversight *130* Flüchtigkeitsfehler, Versehen
overtime, to work ~ *126* Überstunden machen
overview *11* Überblick
overweight *67P* übergewichtig; *96* Übergewicht
overwhelming *108* überwältigend
overworked *132* überarbeitet
own, of one's ~ *104* eigene/r/s; **on one's ~** *59* allein, selbst
to **own sth** *35V* etw besitzen

P

pace *83* Geschwindigkeit
pack *87* Packung, Beutel
to **pack** *82* packen; **~ sth** *45T* etw verpacken
package *76* Paket; **hassle-free ~** *76* Rundum-Sorglos-Paket; **service ~** *63* Leistungspaket; **severance ~** *126* Abfindung
packaging *45T* Verpackung
packed lunch *61* Lunchpaket
paediatric assistant *28* Pflegefachkraft mit Vertiefung Pädiatrie
pain, stomach ~s *pl 124* Magenschmerzen, Bauchschmerzen
painful *105T* schmerzhaft
painkiller *82T* Schmerzmittel
to **paint** *29T* malen
painting *45T* Gemälde, Bild; **face ~** *76* Kinderschminken
to **pair up** *110* sich paarweise zusammentun
palm oil *86* Palmöl
palsy, cerebral ~ *41* Zerebralparese
paperwork *23* Formulare, Unterlagen; *33* Schreibarbeit, Formalitäten
paragraph *12 (Text:)* Absatz
paraplegia *42* Querschnittslähmung
parent *67P* Elternteil; **single ~** *29T* Alleinerziehende/r
part, on our ~ *130* unsererseits; to **take ~ in sth** *8* an etw teilnehmen
participant *34* Teilnehmer/in
to **participate in sth** *80* an etw teilnehmen
participation *40* Teilhabe, Teilnahme
particular *31* bestimmte/r/s, besondere/r/s, speziell; **in ~** *35G* insbesondere, besonders; **nothing in ~** *100* nichts Besonderes
particularly *14* insbesondere, besonders
party: all ~ies concerned *41* alle Beteiligten, alle Betroffenen
to **pass: ~ sth on** *81T* etw weitergeben; **~ sth on genetically** *107P* etw (genetisch) vererben; **~ an exam** *34T* eine Prüfung bestehen
past *11* Vergangenheit
paste, tomato ~ *97P* Tomatenmark
pastry *86* Gebäck
to **pat** *58* tupfen, abtupfen
path, career ~ *9* Karriere, Berufsweg
patience *29T* Geduld
patient *39* Patient/in
patient(ly) *46* geduldig
patriarchal *102* patriarchalisch
pattern *65T* Muster; **behaviour(al) ~** *104* Verhaltensmuster
pay, severance ~ *133* Abfindung
to **pay: ~ attention to sth** *66* auf etw achten
payment *8* Zahlung
to **peak** *38T* den Höchststand erreichen
pedometer *100V* Schrittzähler
peer-group, on a ~ level *11* unter Kollegen und Kolleginnen
to **peer-review sth** *135* etw (unter Kollegen und Kolleginnen) bewerten
penicillin *83P* Penicillin
pension, state ~ *35V* staatliche Rente
per: ~ cent *29T* Prozent; **~ capita** *101* pro Kopf; **~ item** *86* pro Stück
to **perceive sth** *123* etw wahrnehmen
percentage *34* Anteil, Prozentsatz
perfectionism *43T* Perfektionismus
to **perform** *19* (leistungsmäßig) abschneiden, gut/schlecht sein
to **perform sth** *71* etw aufführen, etw spielen; *107G* etw durchführen, etw ausführen
performance *15C* Darbietung; *71* Aufführung; *100V* Leistung
period *57* Zeitraum, Zeitspanne
permanent *55T* dauerhaft

permission *12* Erlaubnis, Genehmigung
permit, work ~ *111P* Arbeitserlaubnis
person, in ~ *18* persönlich, unter vier Augen
personal *7* persönlich, privat; **~ care** *30* Körperpflege, Unterstützung der Selbstversorgung; **~ details** *pl* *12* persönliche Angaben, Angaben zur Person; **~ hygiene** *35G* Körperpflege
personality *12* Persönlichkeit; **~ changes** *pl* *64* Persönlichkeitsveränderung(en)
to **personalize sth** *76* etw individuell anpassen/gestalten
perspective, career ~s *pl* *8* berufliche Perspektiven, Aufstiegschancen
to **persuade sb to do sth** *36* jdn von etw überzeugen, etw zu tun; jdn dazu überreden, etw zu tun
persuasion *36* gutes Zureden
pesticide *97T* Schädlingsbekämpfungsmittel
pet *23* Haustier
petroleum *97T* Erdöl
pharmaceutical *97T* Arzneimittel
physical(ly) *8* körperlich; **~ abuse** *65* (körperliche) Misshandlungen, Schläge, Übergriffe; **~ activity** *96* körperliche Betätigung; **~ force** *10* körperliche Gewalt
physiotherapist *28* Physiotherapeut/in
to **pick: ~ sth** *6* sich etw aussuchen; **~ on sb** *105T* an jdm herumnörgeln, auf jdm herumhacken; **~ sth out** *71* etw hervorheben; **~ sb up** *35P* jdn aufgreifen
piece of advice *111T* Ratschlag, Rat
pill, contraceptive ~ *83P* Verhütungspille, Antibabypille; **sleeping ~** *66* Schlaftablette
pin, rolling ~ *97P* Nudelholz; **safety ~** *82* Sicherheitsnadel
to **place: ~ sb/sth** *59* jdn/etw platzieren; **~ sb somewhere** *107P* jdn irgendwo unterbringen; **~ an order** *75* eine Bestellung aufgeben, einen Auftrag erteilen
place: ~ of worship *110* Gebetsstätte, Gotteshaus; **in ~ of** *39* anstelle von; **in the first ~** *34T* eigentlich (erst)
placemat *92* Tischset
placement, work ~ *6* Praktikum
plan, action ~ *118* Aktionsplan, Maßnahmenkatalog; **diet ~** *98* Diätplan, Ernährungsplan; **floor ~** *45* Grundriss, Lageplan; **treatment ~** *54* Behandlungsplan, Therapiekonzept
plant *45T* Pflanze
plastic tub *84* Kunststoffschale, -becher
plate *59* Teller
to **please sb** *64* es jdm recht machen, jdn zufriedenstellen
pleased, to **be ~** *78* sich freuen; **P~** to **meet you.** *19* Schön, dich/Sie/euch kennenzulernen.
pleasure: My ~. *81T* Gern geschehen.
point, bullet ~ *70* Stichpunkt; **~ of view** *29T* Perspektive, Blickwinkel, Standpunkt; **at one ~** *109T* irgendwann; **I see your ~.** *92* Ich verstehe, was Sie meinen. **That's a good ~.** *48* Das ist ein interessanter Punkt. Da ist was dran.
to **point sth out** *43* etw darlegen, auf etw hinweisen
poisoning *34T* Vergiftung
Poland *111P* Polen
policy *39* Strategie, Vorgehen, Linie, Politik; **cancellation ~** *129* Stornierungsbedingungen; **drug ~ies** *pl* *39* Drogenpolitik
Polish *13* Polnisch
polite(ly) *19* höflich
politeness *79* Höflichkeit
political *112* politisch
pollen *83P* Pollen
polythene foam *82T* Polyethylen-Schaumstoff
to **pool sth** *43* etw zusammenlegen
poor vision *59* Sehschwäche
population *40* Bevölkerung
position *9* Stelle, Stellung, Position
possession *39* Besitz
possibly *105T* womöglich
to **postpone sth** *81* etw *(Termin usw.)* verschieben
potential *43T* potenziell
to **pour sth** *97P* etw gießen, etw schütten
poverty *11* Armut
powerful *70* stark
practical *7* praktisch
practice *11* Praxis; *58T* Gewohnheit, Sitte; to **be common ~** *12* allgemein üblich sein; **P~ makes perfect.** *16* Übung macht den Meister.
to **practise (sth)** *7* (etw) üben, (etw) trainieren; *52* etw praktizieren, etw ausüben
practitioner, general ~ (GP) *66* Hausarzt/-ärztin
pragmatic *29T* pragmatisch
to **praise sb/sth** *39* jdn/etw loben
prediabetes *99* Prädiabetes
to **predict sth** *30* etw voraussagen, etw vorhersagen
to **prefer sth** *9* etw vorziehen, etw gern/lieber tun
preferably *97T* vorzugsweise, am liebsten
preference *8* Vorliebe, Neigung, Präferenz
pregnancy *95* Schwangerschaft
pregnant *28* schwanger
to **preheat sth** *97P* etw vorheizen
prejudice *43* Vorurteil(e)
prejudiced *43T* voreingenommen, vorurteilsbehaftet
premature *111P* vorzeitig
preparation *21* Vorbereitung
to **prepare: ~ for sth** *18* sich auf etw vorbereiten; **~ sth** *13* etw erstellen, etw vorbereiten; *86* etw *(Essen usw.)* zubereiten, etw kochen
prepared *16* vorbereitet, gerüstet
preschool children *pl* *29T* Kinder im Vorschulalter
present *67* anwesend
to **present: ~ sth to sb** *9* jdm etw vorstellen, jdm etw präsentieren; **~ an opportunity** *65T* eine Gelegenheit bieten
presentable *35V* ansehnlich, vorzeigbar
to **preserve sth** *40* etw bewahren, etw schützen
pressure *9* Druck; **blood ~** *63V* Blutdruck
to **pressure-steam sth** *87* etw im Druckdampfgarer zubereiten
pre-teen *96 Kind im Alter von 9–12 J.*
to **pretend** *123T* so tun, als ob
pretty *10* ziemlich
to **prevent sth** *11* etw verhindern, einer Sache vorbeugen
prevention *39* Prävention
previous *69* vorherig, vorig
previously *100V* vorher, zuvor
price list *77* Preisliste
priced, to **be ~** *86* kosten, (preislich) liegen
primary school *13* Grundschule
principal diagnosis *83P* Erstdiagnose
principle *40* Grundsatz, Prinzip
print ads *pl* *53* Anzeigen in Printmedien
to **print sth off** *54* etw ausdrucken
printout *44* Ausdruck
priority, to **be sb's ~** *34T* für jdn an erster Stelle stehen
prison *37* Gefängnis; to **send sb to ~** *123T* jdn ins Gefängnis werfen, jdn zu einer Haftstrafe verurteilen
privacy *59* Privatsphäre; **~ rights** *pl* *73* Persönlichkeitsrechte; **in ~** *36* diskret, vertraulich

private: ~ individual *31* Privatperson; **~ setting** *59* ungestörter/vertraulicher Rahmen
privately *36* nicht öffentlich, diskret, vertraulich
proactive, a ~ individual *9* jd mit Eigeninitiative
probably *11* wahrscheinlich
probation, to **put sb on ~** *35P* jdn auf Bewährung verurteilen; **~ officer** *35P* Bewährungshelfer
problem, digestive ~s *pl* *124* Verdauungsprobleme; **legal ~** *73* juristisches Problem; **medical ~** *36* Gesundheitsproblem; **mental ~s** *pl* *28* psychische Probleme; **mobility ~s** *pl* *28* Mobilitätseinschränkungen; **respiratory ~** *114* Atemwegserkrankung; to **fix a ~** *128* ein Problem lösen/beheben
procedure *58T* Vorgang, Prozedur
to **proceed** *106* vor sich gehen, laufen
process *16* Verfahren, Ablauf, Prozess; **recovery ~** *54* Genesung, Genesungsprozess; **work ~es** *pl* *53* Arbeitsabläufe; to **be in the ~ of doing sth** *36* dabei sein, etw zu tun
processed food *96* verarbeitete Lebensmittel
professions, caring ~ *7* Berufe im Pflege-, Sozial- und Gesundheitsbereich
professional *9* Fachkraft; *10* professionell, beruflich; **care ~** *27* Pflegefachkraft, Fachkraft im Sozial- und Gesundheitswesen; **~ standards** *pl* *11* berufliche Anforderungen, (einheitliche) Berufsnormen; **supervised ~ care** *56* Pflege/Betreuung unter fachkundiger Leitung
professor, visiting ~ *13* Gastprofessor/in
profile *12* Porträt, Profil
programme, degree ~ *11* Studiengang; **education ~** *33* Bildungsangebot, -programm
programming language *125T* Programmiersprache
progress *23* Verlauf, Fortgang; *34* Fortschritt(e)
projection *96* Prognose
promiscuity *104* Promiskuität, wechselnde Sexualpartner/innen
promise *125P* Versprechen
to **promise** *129P* versprechen
to **promote sth** *27* für etw werben, etw fördern
promotion *125* Beförderung
promotional *53* Werbe-
prompt *47* Stichwort
to **proofread sth** *22* etw Korrektur lesen
proper(ly) *43T* richtig, sachgerecht, ordentlich
property *34G* Eigentum, (Grund-) Besitz, Immobilie(n)
proportion *103T* Anteil
proposal *84* Angebot; **grant ~** *80* Zuschussantrag, Förderantrag
to **propose sth** *132* etw vorschlgen, etw beabsichtigen
pros and cons *pl* *107G* Argumente dafür und dagegen, Vor- und Nachteile
prospect (of sth) *35V* Aussicht (auf etw)
prospective *63* potenziell, interessiert
prostitute *35P* Prostituierte/r
to **protect sb/sth (from sth)** *11* jdn/etw (vor etw) schützen
protection, data ~ *12* Datenschutz; **youth ~ service(s)** *66* Jugendamt
protein *98* Eiweiß, Protein
proud (of sb/sth) *34T* stolz (auf jdn/etw)
to **prove sth** *43T* etw nachweisen, etw belegen; *123T* etw beweisen
to **provide sth** *9* etw bieten, etw zur Verfügung stellen, etw liefern
provider *119* Anbieter; **service ~** *75* Dienstleister/in
to **provoke: ~ sth** *45* etw hervorrufen; **~ sb/sth** *65* jdn/etw provozieren
psychiatric: ~ assistant *28* Medizinische/r Mitarbeiter/in, Assistent/in in der Psychiatrie; **~ unit** *29T* Psychiatrie, psychiatrische Abteilung
psychiatry, adolescent ~ *29* Jugendpsychiatrie
psychological *64* psychologisch
psychologist *52* Psychologe/-in
psychology *11* Psychologie
public *62T* öffentlich; **~ health** *39* Gesundheitswesen, Volksgesundheit; **in ~** *64* in der Öffentlichkeit, unter Leuten
to **punch** *65* (mit der Faust) schlagen
punctual *18V* pünktlich
to **punish sb/sth** *39* jdn/etw bestrafen
purpose *27* Absicht, Ziel, Zweck; **main ~** *31* Hauptanliegen, Hauptziel; **on ~** *34* absichtlich, vorsätzlich; to **have a sense of ~ (in sth)** *45T* einen Sinn in etw sehen, Tatkraft spüren
to **push oneself to do sth** *18V* sich dazu zwingen, etw zu tun
to **put: ~ sth off** *81* etw *(Termin usw.)* verschieben; **~ sb through** to **sb** *81T* *(Telefon:)* jdn mit jdm verbinden; **~ yourself in sb's shoes** *71* sich in jds Lage versetzen; **~ sb in touch with sb** *34T* jdm einen Kontakt zu jdm vermitteln; **~ sb on probation** *35P* jdn auf Bewährung verurteilen; **~ sth into action** *44* etw in die Tat umsetzen

Q

quadriplegia *42* Tetraplegie
qualification *12* Qualifikation, Abschluss, Ausbildung
qualified *11* ausgebildet, qualifiziert, examiniert; **well-~** *10* gut ausgebildet; **~ nurse** *36* examinierte/r Krankenschwester/-pfleger
quality *6* Eigenschaft
quantity *84* Menge
query *61* Frage, Rückfrage, Anfrage
questionnaire *43T* Fragebogen
to **quit** *125T* kündigen; **~ sth** *107P* mit etw aufhören
quite *18V* ziemlich
quitter *62* *jd, der leicht aufgibt*
quota *47* Anteil, Quote
quote *52* Zitat

R

R&D (research & development) *122* Forschung(s-) und Entwicklung(sabteilung)
race *42* Rasse; **costumed ~** *51* Kostümwettlauf
racial discrimination *121* Rassendiskriminierung
racism *103G* Rassismus
rafting, white-water ~ *80* Rafting, Wildwasserfahren
rail, to **go off the ~s** *34T* auf die schiefe Bahn geraten
to **raise: ~ sth** *96* *(Tiere:)* etw züchten, etw aufziehen; **~ money** *51* Geld beschaffen
range *34T* Spektrum, Angebot; **free-~ eggs** *pl* *96* Eier aus Freilandhaltung
to **range: ~ between … and …** *86* sich zwischen … und … bewegen; **~ from … to …** *28* von … bis … reichen, sich von … bis … erstrecken
to **rank sth** *60* etw einstufen, etw (der Rangfolge nach) ordnen
to **rape sb** *66* jdn vergewaltigen
rarely *54* selten, kaum
rascal, little ~ *75* Bengel
rash *58* Hautausschlag

residential home 56 Wohnheim, Seniorenheim
resignation, inner ~ 121 innere Kündigung
resistant, insulin ~ 100V insulinresistent
to **resolve sth** 128 etw lösen, etw (auf)klären
resources *pl* 41 Mittel, Ressourcen; **human ~ (HR)** 121 Personal(abteilung)
respect (for sb) 29T Achtung (vor jdm), Respekt (vor jdm)
to **respect sb** 31 jdn achten, jdn respektieren
respectable 103G respektabel, anständig, ehrbar
respected, to **be highly ~** 10 großes Ansehen genießen, hoch angesehen sein
respectful 58 respektvoll, pietätvoll
respiratory problem 114 Atemwegserkrankung
to **respond to sth** 17 auf etw reagieren, auf etw antworten
response 20 Reaktion, Antwort; **in ~ to** 24 als Antwort auf
responsibility 8 Aufgabe, Zuständigkeit; 124 Verantwortung
responsible, to **be ~ for sth** 97P für etw zuständig/verantwortlich sein
responsiveness (towards sb) 42 (feinfühliges) Eingehen (auf jdn)
rest time 29T Ruhezeit, Pausenzeit
to **restrict sb/sth** 64 jdn/etw einschränken, jdn/etw einengen
restrictive 39 restriktiv
to **restructure** 127 umstrukturieren
restructuring 121 Umstrukturierung
result 34T Ergebnis, Resultat; **as a ~** 36 daher, infolgedessen; 39 als Folge von
to **result: ~ from sth** 42 auf etw zurückzuführen sein; **~ in sth** 108 etw zur Folge haben, zu etw führen
to **retain sth** 36 etw bewahren, etw behalten
retention 87 Erhaltung, Bewahrung
to **retrain sb** 126 jdn umschulen
return, in ~ 35V als Gegenleistung, im Gegenzug
to **return sth** 131 etw zurücksenden, etw zurückschicken
reunification 111P Wiedervereinigung
to **reunite sb with sb** 34T jd mit jdm zusammenbringen/-führen
to **reveal sth** 101 etw aufdecken, etw enthüllen, etw zeigen
revenge 109 Rache
reverse 12 umgekehrt
review 63 Kritik, Rezension, Besprechung
to **review sth** 54 etw (erneut) prüfen, etw nochmals durchgehen
reviewer 63 Rezensent/in
to **revise sth** 70 etw überarbeiten, etw revidieren
rewarding 55 lohnend, bereichernd
to **rewrite sth** 39 etw umformulieren, etw ändern
rid, to **get ~ of sb/sth** 34 jdn/etw loswerden
riding accident 83P Reitunfall
right: ~ (to sth) 27 Recht (auf etw); **privacy ~s** *pl* 73 Persönlichkeitsrechte; **human ~s violations** *pl* 112 Menschenrechtsverstöße; to **get sth ~** 18 etw (gut) hinbekommen, etw richtig machen
rights-free 73 lizenzfrei, *(D:)* GEMA-frei
rigid 82T steif, fest
to **rise** 38 steigen, ansteigen; 97P *(Teig:)* gehen, aufgehen
rise (in sth) 102 Anstieg (von etw), Zunahme (von etw)
risk, increased ~ 99 erhöhtes Risiko; to **be at ~** 11 gefährdet sein
rival 126 Konkurrent/in
robbery 105P Überfall
rock 83 Stein, Fels
role 22 Funktion, Stellung
rolling pin 97P Nudelholz
Roman Catholic 106 römisch-katholisch
Romania 108 Rumänien
room, medical ~ 45T Sanitätsraum, Erste-Hilfe-Raum
rough, to **live ~** 36 auf der Straße leben; to **sleep ~** 34T auf der Straße schlafen
round table 127 Gesprächsrunde, Runder Tisch
routine, daily ~ 8 Tagesablauf
to **rub** 97P reiben
rude 105P unverschämt, unhöflich
rule 12 Regel, Vorschrift
rumour 132 Gerücht
to **run: ~ sth** 27 *(Firma usw.:)* etw führen, etw leiten, etw betreiben; **~ out of sth** 89 etw nicht mehr haben; **~ an event** 76 eine Veranstaltung durchführen
rush hour 65T Hauptverkehrszeit
Russia 10 Russland
Russian 109T Russe/-in; Russisch

S

safe 87 ungefährlich
safety pin 82 Sicherheitsnadel
sake, for heaven's ~ 124P verdammt nochmal
sales manager 85 Vertriebsleiter/in, Verkaufsleiter/in
salon 34T (Kosmetik-, Friseur-) Salon
salutation 77T *(Brief, E-Mail:)* Anrede
SAM splint 82 Alu-Polsterschiene, SAM-Schiene
same: S~ here. 6 Ich auch. Geht mir genauso.
same-sex 103G gleichgeschlechtlich
Santa 45T Nikolaus, Weihnachtsmann
to **satisfy sb** 124 jdn zufriedenstellen
satnav 32T Navi
to **save sb/sth** 82 jdn/etw retten
say, to **have a ~ in sth** 124 ein Mitspracherecht bei etw haben
scale 35V Skala; **large-~ flow** 111P großer Zustrom
to **scan sth** 8 etw *(Text)* überfliegen
scar 64 Narbe
scared, to **be ~** 65T Angst haben
scary 16 furchteinflößend
to **scatter sth** 97P etw verteilen, etw verstreuen
scene 95 Szene
to **schedule sth** 62 etw *(Termin usw.)* ansetzen, etw vereinbaren
schedule 37 Zeitplan, Stundenplan, Dienstplan; **work(ing) ~** 37 Arbeitszeit, Arbeitsplan
scheduling 53 Planung, Terminplanung
school, comprehensive ~ 18V Gesamtschule; **nursery ~** 28 Kindergarten, Kita; **primary ~** 13 Grundschule; **secondary ~** 13 weiterführende Schule; **vocational ~** 81 Berufsschule; **after-~ care centre** 49 Schulhort, Nachmittagsbetreuung; **nursery ~ teacher** 28 Erzieher/in; **~ leaver** 9 Schulabgänger/in; to **enter ~** 108 in die Schule kommen, eingeschult werden
schooling 108 Schulbildung, Schulunterricht
schoolmate 96 Schulkamerad/in, Mitschüler/in
scissors *pl* 82 Schere
sclerosis, multiple ~ 42 Multiple Sklerose
score, overall ~ 124P Gesamtpunktzahl
to **scrape** 97T schaben, kratzen
to **scratch** 82T sich kratzen
scratch, to **start from ~** 35V ganz von vorn / bei Null anfangen; **from ~** 97 ganz von vorn, komplett
script 23 Manuskript, Drehbuch

scripted 117 mit Drehbuch
to **search for sth** 43T etw suchen
seat, to **take a ~** 18V Platz nehmen
seated 73 sitzend
seating area 45T Sitzgelegenheiten
secondary school 13 weiterführende Schule
secret, in ~ 115 heimlich
section 12 Teil, Abschnitt
sector 8 Bereich, Branche, Sektor; **industrial ~** 111P Industrie
security 35V Sicherheit
to **see: I ~.** 17T Verstehe. Aha. **I ~ your point.** 92 Ich verstehe, was Sie meinen.
seeds *pl* 98 Samen, Körner
to **seek sth** 13 etw suchen
see-through 45T durchsichtig, Klarsicht-
segment 53 Teil(stück), Abschnitt, Segment
to **select sth** 92 etw auswählen
self-confidence 45T Selbstvertrauen
self-conscious 109T gehemmt, befangen, unsicher
self-esteem 44 Selbstwertgefühl
self-harm 34 Selbstverletzung
self-help group 66T Selbsthilfegruppe
senior 30 leitend, vorgesetzt; **~ manager** 127 leitende/r Angestellte/r; **~ supervisor** 45 Leiter/in
sense, to **make ~** 111T vernünftig sein, einleuchten; to **have a ~ of purpose (in sth)** 45T einen Sinn in etw sehen, Tatkraft spüren
sensitive: ~ (to sth) 29T verständnisvoll, taktvoll, feinfühlig, sensibel (für/bezüglich etw); **culturally ~** 30 kulturell angepasst, kultursensibel; **socially ~** 127 sozialverträglich
sensitivity 105T Sensibilität
sentence, closing ~ 14 Schlusssatz
to **separate** 105T sich trennen
separate 134 separat, eigen, einzeln
separation 102 Trennung
sequence 135 Abfolge, Folge
series 104 Serie, Reihe
serious 10 ernst, ernsthaft
seriously 18V ernsthaft, im Ernst; to **take sth ~** 29T etw ernst nehmen
to **serve: ~ sb** 31 jdm dienen; **~ sth** 46 etw servieren
service 27 Dienstleistung, Dienst, Hilfe, Service; **care ~s** *pl* 52 Pflegeleistungen, Pflegedienste; **emergency ~** 66 Notdienst, Rettungsdienst; **National Health S~ (NHS)** 29 *staatlicher Gesundheitsdienst in Großbritannien;* **social support ~** 28 Sozialdienst, soziale Einrichtung; **support ~** 56 Betreuungsdienst(leistung); **youth protection ~(s)** 66 Jugendamt; **~ package** 63 Leistungspaket; **~ provider** 75 Dienstleister/in; to **do community ~** 107P Sozialstunden ableisten
serving 98 Portion
session 60 *(Betreuung, Unterricht usw.:)* Stunde, Tag; **music ~** 56 Konzert, gemeinsames Musizieren; **therapy ~** 37 Therapiesitzung; **training ~** 80 Schulung; **trial ~** 61 Probestunde, Probetag
set 12 fest, festgelegt, starr; **~ of values** 111T Werte
to **set: ~ sth out** 90 etw darlegen, etw aufstellen; **~ sth up** 17T etw gründen, etw einrichten
set-up 102 Rahmen, Konstellation
setting 75 Situation, Rahmen, Umfeld; **care ~** 56 Pflegeumfeld, Pflegesituation, Pflegeeinrichtung; **private ~** 59 ungestörter/vertraulicher Rahmen
to **settle** 108 sich niederlassen; **~ down** 111T zur Ruhe kommen, sich beruhigen
several 28 mehrere
severance: ~ package 126 Abfindung; **~ pay** 133 Abfindung
severe(ly) 26 *(Krankheit usw.:)* schwer, stark, heftig
sex 35P Geschlecht
sexual: ~ abuse 34T sexueller Missbrauch; **~ harassment** 121 sexuelle Belästigung; **~ intercourse** 105T Geschlechtsverkehr; **~ orientation** 42 sexuelle Orientierung
sexually suggestive 122 anzüglich, aufreizend
shape 82T Form, Gestalt
to **shape sth** 97P etw formen
to **share (sth) with sb** 8 mit jdm (über etw) sprechen, jdm von etw erzählen
to **share sth** 103T sich etw teilen
shared flat *BE* 35P Wohngemeinschaft
sharp 108 drastisch, stark, plötzlich
sheet, info ~ 56 Informationsblatt
shelf, top ~ 97P oberste Schiene *(im Backofen)*
shelter 36 Unterkunft, Unterstand, Quartier; 47 Obdachlosenunterkunft
sheltered accommodation 34T betreutes Wohnen
shift 18V Schicht; **night ~** 45T Nachtschicht
to **shift the blame** 65T die Schuld jd anderem zuschieben
shoe, to **put yourself in sb's ~s** 71 sich in jds Lage versetzen
to **shoot** 53 *(Film usw.)* drehen
shooting 73 *(Film usw.:)* Dreh, Drehen
shortage, labour ~ 111P Arbeitskräftemangel
shot 73 *(Film usw.:)* Einstellung; **exterior ~** 73 Außenaufnahme; **interior ~** 73 Innenaufnahme; **~ list** 73 Liste der Einstellungen, Shotlist
to **shout sth at sb** 117 jdn (lautstark) mit etw beschimpfen
show, reality ~ 95 Reality-TV-Sendung/-Serie
to **show sb around** 45 jdn herumführen
siblings *pl* 104 Geschwister
sick, to **be off ~** 43T krankgeschrieben sein, *(am Arbeitsplatz)* fehlen
side, to **take ~s** 67 Partei ergreifen
sight, loss of ~ 56 Erblindung, Erblindungserscheinungen
to **sign** 73 unterzeichnen, unterschreiben; **~ off** 77T sich verabschieden, Schluss machen
sign, warning ~ 64 Anzeichen, Hinweis
signature 84 Unterschrift
significant(ly) 40 erheblich, bedeutend
to **signify sth** 100V etw bedeuten, für etw stehen
silence 67 Stille
silicone 97T Silikon
silly 125P albern
similar (to sb/sth) 11 (jdm/einer Sache) ähnlich
similarity 11 Ähnlichkeit, Übereinstimmung
similarly 107G ebenso, in gleicher Weise
simulated 23 gespielt, simuliert
since then 123T seitdem
sincerely: Yours ~ 14 *(Brief, E-Mail:)* Mit freundlichen Grüßen
single parent 29T Alleinerziehende/r
sir: Dear S~ or Madam 14 *(Brief, E-Mail:)* Sehr geehrte Damen und Herren
to **sit in on sth** 47 bei etw dabei sein, an etw teilnehmen
site, building ~ 35P Baustelle
situated, to **be ~** 68 liegen
sketch 70 Skizze
to **ski** 83 (Ski) fahren
skiing, cross-country ~ 80 Skilanglauf

skill *6* Fähigkeit, Kompetenz; **interpersonal ~s** *pl* *9* soziale Kompetenz; **life ~s** *pl* *34T* lebenspraktische Fertigkeiten, Lebenskompetenz
skilled, highly ~ *30* hochqualifiziert
skillful *62* geschickt, gekonnt
to **skim a text** *30* einen Text überfliegen
skin *58* Haut
to **sleep rough** *34T* auf der Straße schlafen
sleeping pill *66* Schlaftablette
sleepover *41* Pyjamaparty
slice *97P* *(Pizza, Kuchen usw.:)* Stück
slide *77* Rutsche, Rutschbahn; **water ~** *77* Wasserrutsche
slight(ly) *38T* leicht, geringfügig, ein wenig
slippery *58* rutschig
slogan *50* Motto, Werbespruch, Slogan
sluggish *114* träge, schwerfällig
smart *126* intelligent, schlau
smoker *107P* Raucher/in
to **smooth sth** *97P* etw glattstreichen
smooth(ly) *49* reibungslos; *97P* glatt, geschmeidig
snorkeling *129T* Schnorcheln
so, in ~ doing *35V* auf diese Weise; **I'm afraid ~.** *105T* Leider ja. **~ far** *65T* bisher, bislang
so-called *43T* sogenannt
sociable *46* gesellig, umgänglich
social *8* gesellig, sozial; **~ administrator** *28* Sachbearbeiter/in, Beamte/r in der Sozialverwaltung; **~ care** *28* Sozialhilfe, Sozialleistungen; **~ and health care** *8* Gesundheit und Soziales, Sozial- und Gesundheitswesen; **~ education worker** *29* Sozialpädagoge/-in; **~ interaction** *42* Umgang mit anderen, soziale Interaktion; *57* Geselligkeit, geselliges Miteinander; **~ occasion** *64* geselliges Treffen, private Zusammenkunft; **~ studies** *pl* *13* Sozial- und Erziehungswissenschaften; **~ support service** *28* Sozialdienst, soziale Einrichtung; **~ work** *10* Sozialarbeit; **~ worker** *10* Sozialarbeiter/in
socially sensitive *127* sozialverträglich
society *30* Gesellschaft
sodium *99* Natrium
soft *58T* *(Musik usw.:)* leise, sanft; **~ toy** *45T* Stofftier, Kuscheltier
software testing *43T* Softwareprüfung, Softwaretests
solidarity *111P* Solidarität
solution (to sth) *35V* Lösung (für etw)
to **solve sth** *10* etw *(Problem usw.)* lösen
Somali *109T* Somalier/in
sometime *113T* irgendwann (einmal)
somewhat *100V* ein wenig, irgendwie
sort *34T* Art
to **sort sth out** *34T* etw klären, etw regeln
to **sound** *9* klingen
sound, to make ~s *123T* Laute von sich geben
source *48* Quelle
to **speak: ... speaking.** *17* *(Telefon:)* Sie sprechen mit ..., ... am Apparat; **as we ~** *128* gerade, in diesem Moment
speaker, native ~ *13* Muttersprachler/in
special: ~ classes *pl* *108* Sonderklassen; **~ needs** *pl* *26* Förderbedarf, Behinderung; **~ teacher** *41* Fachlehrer/in
specific *12* bestimmt, speziell; *77T* konkret; **from the general to the ~** *111T* vom Allgemeinen zum Konkreten
spectrum, autism ~ disorder *43T* Autismusspektrumstörung
speech *50* Rede, Ansprache; *71* (Art zu) Sprechen, Redestil; **~ impairment/impediment** *42* Sprachbehinderung, Sprechbehinderung; **~ therapist** *54* Logopäde/-pädin
to **speed sth up** *54* etw beschleunigen
to **spell sth** *81P* etw buchstabieren
spelling *24* Rechtschreibung
to **spend** *34* *(Zeit:)* verbringen; **~ sth on sth** *84* etw *(Geld usw.)* für etw ausgeben
spice *99* Gewürz
to **spill sth** *59* etw verschütten, kleckern
to **split sth** *102* etw teilen, etw aufteilen
spokesperson *132* (offizielle/r) Sprecher/in
sponge *58* Schwamm; to **do a ~ bath** *58* (jdn) mit dem Schwamm (im Bett) waschen
spoon *97P* Löffel
spouse *65T* Ehepartner/in, Ehegatte/-gattin
sprain *82* Verstauchung, Verrenkung
to **sprinkle sth** *97P* etw streuen
square, to **be back to ~ one** *126* wieder ganz am Anfang stehen
to **stab sb** *35P* auf jdn einstechen
to **stabilize sth** *82* etw stabilisieren
stable *30* stabil
staff *10* Personal, Belegschaft, Mitarbeiter/innen; to **reduce ~** *120* Personal abbauen
stage *65* Phase, Stadium, Schritt
stainless steel *97T* (aus) Edelstahl
stairs *pl* *105P* Treppe
to **stand: ~ by** *105T* zusehen, dabeistehen; **~ out from the crowd** *63* sich von der Masse abheben; **~ in line** *126* Schlange stehen, anstehen
standard, academic ~ *11* Ausbildungsniveau; **professional ~s** *pl* *11* berufliche Anforderungen, (einheitliche) Berufsnormen
to **stare** *122* starren; **~ at sb** *109T* jdn anstarren
start, from ~ to finish *76* von Anfang bis Ende
to **start: ~ sb off** *114* jdm Starthilfe geben; **~ from scratch** *35V* ganz von vorn / bei Null anfangen; **~ a business** *127* ein Unternehmen gründen
to **~ with** *109T* am Anfang, anfangs
started, to **get ~** *7* loslegen, anfangen
to **state sth** *14* etw angeben, etw sagen, etw feststellen
state *52* Zustand; *111P* Bundesland; **member ~** *103T* Mitgliedsstaat; **mental ~** *100V* Befindlichkeit, seelische Verfassung; **~ pension** *35V* staatliche Rente
state-run *29T* staatlich
statement *10* Aussage, Stellungnahme; **mission ~** *49* Leitbild
statistical *33* statistisch
statistically *102* statistisch gesehen
statistics *pl* *27* Statistik(en)
status *131* Stand (der Dinge), Lage, Zustand; **health ~** *63V* Gesundheitszustand
stay *38* Aufenthalt
to **stay** *36* bleiben; **~ in touch** *35V* in Verbindung bleiben
to **steal** *35P* stehlen, rauben
steel, stainless ~ *97T* (aus) Edelstahl
step *16* Schritt, Stufe; to **take ~s** *119* Schritte unternehmen, Maßnahmen ergreifen; to **go one ~ further** *43T* einen Schritt weiter gehen
to **step into sth** *58T* in etw gehen, in etw steigen
stepchild *102* Stiefkind
stepdad *34T* Stiefvater
stepfamily *102* Stieffamilie
stepfather *106* Stiefvater
stepmum *96* Stiefmutter

stepparents *pl* *102* Stiefeltern
stepping stones *pl* *35V* Sprungbrett, (wichtige) Schritte
stereotype *43T* Rollenklischee, Vorurteil, Stereotyp
to **stick: ~ to sth** *29T* sich an etw halten; **~ in sb's mind** *43T* bei jdm hängen/haften bleiben
sticky note *41G* Haftnotiz, Klebezettel
stimulation *42* Reiz(e), Anregung(en), Stimulation
sting *82* (Insekten-)Stich
stomach pains *pl* *124* Magenschmerzen, Bauchschmerzen
stone, stepping ~s *pl* *35V* Sprungbrett, (wichtige) Schritte
to **stop at sth** *111T* bei/vor etw Halt machen
storage *45T* Aufbewahrung, Lagerung
to **store sth** *87* etw lagern, etw aufbewahren
storeroom *45T* Lagerraum, Lager
storyboard *73 (Film usw.:)* Szenenbuch, Storyboard
straight *54* direkt, sofort; **~ away** *128* sofort
strange, in a ~ way *34* seltsam
strategy *26* Strategie
straw *59* Strohhalm
strength *16* Stärke
stress: ~ level *124* Stressbelastung, Stressniveau; **~ test** *100V* Belastungstest
stressful *104* belastend, anstrengend, stressig
strict *39* rigoros, strikt
strict(ly) *29T* streng, strikt
strip *82T* Streifen
to **strive to do sth** *49* sich bemühen, etw zu tun; danach streben, etw zu tun
stroke *54* Schlaganfall
strong *22* gut, stark
structure *12* Aufbau, Konstruktion, Struktur
to **structure sth** *29T* etw strukturieren, etw aufbauen
to **struggle** *95* kämpfen, zu kämpfen haben, sich abmühen
studies *pl* *11* Studium; **health ~** *13* Gesundheitswissenschaften (mit Pflege); **social ~** *13* Sozial- und Erziehungswissenschaften
to **study: ~ sth** *30* sich etw genau durchlesen/ansehen; **~ sth closely** *38T* sich etw näher/genau ansehen
subheading *70* Zwischenüberschrift
subject *77* Thema, *(Brief, E-Mail:)* Betreff; *100V* Versuchsperson; **main ~** *13* Hauptfach; **~ line** *77T* Betreffzeile; **~ matter** *77T* Thema, Thematik, Inhalt
to **submit sth to sb** *83* etw bei jdm einreichen
substance *39* Droge; **~ abuse** *34T* Drogenmissbrauch
subtitle *101* Untertitel
success rate *34T* Erfolgsquote
to **suffer** *41* leiden, Schaden nehmen; **~ from sth** *124* an/unter etw leiden
sugary *84* zuckerhaltig
to **suggest sth** *23* etw vorschlagen; *107P* auf etw hindeuten, etw nahelegen
suggestion *50* Vorschlag
suggestive *122* anzüglich, aufreizend
suicidal, to be ~ *64* Selbstmordgedanken haben, selbstmordgefährdet sein
suicide *62* Selbstmord
to **suit sb/sth** *9* für jdn/etw geeignet sein, (zu) jdm/etw passen
suitable *9* geeignet, passend
to **sum up: to ~** *11* zusammenfassend
to **summarize sth** *9* etw zusammenfassen
summary *12* Zusammenfassung
sunflower *29* Sonnenblume
to **supervise sb/sth** *29T* jdn/etw beaufsichtigen, jdn/etw betreuen
supervised professional care *56* Pflege/Betreuung unter fachkundiger Leitung
supervision *8* Betreuung, Supervision
supervisor *124P* Vorgesetzte/r; **senior ~** *45* Leiter/in
supplier *75* Lieferant/in, Zulieferer
supplies *pl*, **medical ~** *63V* Sanitätsartikel, Medizinbedarf
to **support: ~ sb** *8* jdm helfen, jdn unterstützen, jdn fördern; **~ sth** *48* etw *(Argument usw.)* untermauern, etw stützen
support *8* Hilfe, Unterstützung, Förderung; **carer ~** *30* Unterstützung für pflegende Angehörige; **home ~** *30* häusliche Unterstützung; **relationship ~** *30* Partner- und Familienberatung; **~ centre** *31G* Hilfsstelle, Hilfszentrum; **family ~ centre** *105* Familienhilfe, Familienhilfezentrum; **~ service** *56* Betreuungsdienst(leistung); **social ~ service** *28* Sozialdienst, soziale Einrichtung; **community ~ worker** *28* Sozialarbeiter/in
supportive *46* unterstützend, hilfsbereit
to **suppose: I ~ …** *18V* wohl, vermutlich
supposed, to **be ~ to do sth** *129T* etw (eigentlich) tun sollen
sure, to **make ~** *12* dafür sorgen(, dass …); sicherstellen(, dass …)
surface *97P* Oberfläche, Arbeitsfläche
to **surface** *107G* auftauchen, auftreten
surge of energy *65T* Energieschub
surname *133* Nachname
to **survive** *109T* überleben
survivor *127* Überlebende/r
suspected, to **be ~ to do sth** *100V* im/unter Verdacht stehen, etw zu tun
suspicious, to **be ~ of sb** *36* jdm misstrauen
sustainable *86* nachhaltig
to **swallow** *59* schlucken
to **swap** *61* tauschen, vertauschen
sweat: No ~! *16* Kein Ding! Kein Problem!
symptom *82* Anzeichen, Erscheinung, Symptom
syndrome, Down's ~ *41* Down-Syndrom
Syria *108* Syrien
system, education ~ *34T* Bildungssystem

T

tablespoon *97P* Esslöffel
taboo *110* Tabu; tabu
to **tackle sth** *36* etw *(Problem usw.)* angehen, etw bekämpfen
to **take: ~ over (from sb)** *55T* (von jdm) übernehmen; **~ sth** *36* etw benötigen, etw erfordern; **~ sb on** *15V* jdn einstellen; **~ sth over** *120* etw übernehmen; **~ sth up** *34T* etw anfangen; **~ sides** *67* Partei ergreifen; **~ sth seriously** *29T* etw ernst nehmen; **~ turns** *9* sich abwechseln
talk *125T* Gespräch; to **give a ~ (on sth)** *11* einen Vortrag (über etw / zum Thema …) halten
to **talk highly of sb/sth** *63* sich anerkennend über jdn/etw äußern
talkative *46* geschwätzig
tape, adhesive ~ *82* Heftpflaster
target group *31* Zielgruppe
to **target sb/sth** *72* jdn/etw ins Visier nehmen, jdn ansprechen
task *8* Aufgabe
taste *61* Geschmack
tasty *86* schmackhaft, lecker
teacher, assistant ~ *113T* (Aus-) Hilfslehrer/in, Assistenzlehrer/in; **head ~** *67P* Schuldirektor/in;

nursery school ~ *28* Erzieher/in; **specialist ~** *41* Fachlehrer/in
team leader *45T* Gruppenleiter/in
to **tease sb** *109T* jdn aufziehen, jdn provozieren, jdn scharfmachen
teaspoonful, level ~ *97P* gestrichener Teelöffel
technical college *108* Berufskolleg, Fachhochschule
technique *62T* Technik, Praktik, Methode
technology *21* Technik
telephone counsellor *28* Telefonseelsorger/in
telework *126* Telearbeit
teleworker *126* Telearbeiter/in
teleworking *127* Telearbeit
temporary *13* befristet
to **tend to do sth** *45T* dazu neigen, etw zu tun
tendency *111T* Neigung, Tendenz
tenderness *52* Güte, Wärme, Zärtlichkeit
tense *124P* angespannt
tension, muscle ~ *124* Muskelverspannung(en)
term *36* Begriff; *BE* *105P* Trimester; **in ~s of** *34T* hinsichtlich
termination *106* Schwangerschaftsabbruch
terminology *42* Begriffe, Terminologie
test, stress ~ *100V* Belastungstest
testing, software ~ *43T* Softwareprüfung, Softwaretests
text message *74* SMS, Textnachricht
texture *87* Konsistenz
that: ~ way *54* auf diese Weise; **that's why** *11* daher, deshalb; **That's it.** *111T* Genau!
theme *50* Thema
theory *11* Theorie
therapist *33* Therapeut/in; **occupational ~** *28* Ergotherapeut/in, Beschäftigungstherapeut/in; **speech ~** *54* Logopäde/-pädin
therapy, one-to-one ~ *34T* Einzeltherapie; **~ session** *37* Therapiesitzung
to **think: ~ about sth** *7* über etw nachdenken, sich über etw Gedanken machen; **~ sth up** *69* sich etw ausdenken, etw erfinden
thorough(ly) *116* gründlich
though *10* aber, jedoch, allerdings, doch; **even ~** *16* obwohl
thought, food for ~ *97T* Denkanstöße, Stoff zum Nachdenken
to **threaten sb** *109* jdn bedrohen
thriving *30* florierend, lebendig
through *61* bis
throughout sb's life *99* jds ganzes Leben lang
to **throw sb out** *34T* jdn hinauswerfen, jdn rauswerfen
thus *36* folglich
time, nap ~ *57* Mittagsschlaf; **rest ~** *29T* Ruhezeit, Pausenzeit; **full-~** *29* Vollzeit(-); **on ~** *18V* pünktlich; **at the ~** *107P* seinerzeit; **at ~s of crisis** *30* in Krisen(zeiten); **at all ~s** *58T* stets, immer; **waste of ~** *124T* Zeitverschwendung; to **have ~ off** *124T* frei haben
timely *86* rechtzeitig, pünktlich
tin *97P* Dose
tiring *55* anstrengend, ermüdend
title, job ~ *12* Stellenbezeichnung
togetherness, feeling of ~ *45T* Zusammengehörigkeitsgefühl
tolerance *103G* Toleranz
tolerance: ~ (of sth) *39* Duldung (von etw); **zero ~** *39* null Toleranz
to **tolerate sth** *120* etw dulden, etw tolerieren
toll, to **take its ~ on sth** *100V* seinen Tribut von etw fordern, etw (gehörig) mitnehmen
tomato paste *97P* Tomatenmark
tone *72* Ton, Tonfall, Unterton
tongue, mother ~ *110* Muttersprache
tonne *84* Tonne *(1000 kg)*
tool *127* Werkzeug
top, on ~ of sth *61* über etw hinaus(gehend), zusätzlich zu etw
topic *41* Thema; **on assigned ~s** *33* zu bestimmten Themen
topping *97P* *(Pizza:)* Belag
torn *67P* zerrissen, zerfetzt
torture *112* Folter
total *38T* Gesamt-; *42* völlige/r/s, vollständig; **a ~ of** *105P* insgesamt
touch, to **be/get in ~** *17T* sich (bei jdm) melden; to **get in ~ with sth** *66* mit etw in Kontakt kommen; to **put sb in ~ with sb** *34T* jdm einen Kontakt zu jdm vermitteln; to **stay in ~** *35V* in Verbindung bleiben
touching *122* Berührung(en), Anfassen
tough *33* hart
tour *44* Rundgang, Besichtigung
toy, soft ~ *45T* Stofftier, Kuscheltier
trace *97T* Spur, Rückstand
track, to **get sth back on ~** *35V* etw wieder auf Kurs bringen
traditional *102* hergebracht, traditionell
tragically, to **die ~** *84* auf tragische Weise ums Leben kommen
to **train to be sth** *24* eine Ausbildung zu etw machen
trained *9* ausgebildet, geschult, qualifiziert
trainee *8* Auszubildende/r
trainer *67* Dozent/in, Ausbilder/in
training *6* Ausbildung; *17T* Schulung; **on-the-job ~** *9* Ausbildung am Arbeitsplatz; **~ session** *80* Schulung
tranquilizer *124* Beruhigungsmittel
transfer, bank ~ *133* Überweisung
to **transform sth** *100V* etw verwandeln, etw umwandeln
to **translate** *119* übersetzen
translation *97P* Übersetzung
transport *78* Beförderung, Transport
trap, to **set a ~** *65* eine Falle stellen
traumatic *106* traumatisch
traumatized *112* traumatisiert
to **travel** *36* fahren
travel: ~ agency *129T* Reisebüro, Reiseagentur; **~ contract** *129T* Reisevertrag
tray, baking ~ *97P* Backblech
treasure *78* Schatz; **~ hunt** *76* Schatzsuche, Schnitzeljagd
to **treat sb/sth** *10* jdn/etw behandeln
treatment *35V* Behandlung; **fertility ~** *107P* Kinderwunschbehandlung, künstliche Befruchtung; **~ plan** *54* Behandlungsplan, Therapiekonzept
trend *38* Tendenz, Trend
trial session *61* Probestunde, Probetag
to **trial sth** *87* etw testen, etw erproben
trip to the countryside *45T* Fahrt/Ausflug aufs Land
trisomy 21 *41* Trisomie 21
trouble, to **be in ~** *26* in Schwierigkeiten sein
truant, to **play ~** *104* die Schule schwänzen
true *10* zutreffend, wahr; to **be ~ for sb/sth** *39* auf etw zutreffen, für jdn/etw gelten
trust *36* Vertrauen
to **trust sb** *36* jdm vertrauen
tub, plastic ~ *84* Kunststoffschale, -becher
tube *82T* Rohr, Röhre
Tunisia *111P* Tunesien
to **turn: ~ to page X** *11* Seite X aufschlagen; **~ sb/sth into sth** *100* etw aus jdm/etw machen, jdn/etw zu etw machen, jdn/etw in etw umwandeln
turn, to **take ~s** *9* sich abwechseln
tweezers *pl* *82* Pinzette

twice *54* zweimal
twins *pl* *105P* Zwillinge
type *8* Art
to **type** *128* tippen
typically *100V* normalerweise
typing error *133* Tippfehler

U

Ukrainian *113T* Ukrainisch
unable, to **be ~ to do sth** *105P* nicht in der Lage sein, etw zu tun; etw nicht tun können; to **feel ~ to do sth** *107G* sich nicht in der Lage sehen, etw zu tun; sich nicht trauen, etw zu tun
unacceptable *34G* inakzeptabel
unbelievable *129T* unglaublich, unerhört
uncertain *35V* unsicher, ungewiss
unclean *23* schmutzig
uncomfortable *34G* ungemützlich, unangenehm
underage person *73* Minderjährige/r
understaffed *133* unterbesetzt
understanding *105T* Verständnis
to **undertake sth** *30* etw übernehmen, etw durchführen
unemployed *40* arbeitslos; to **be made ~** *126* arbeitslos werden
unfair(ly) *10* ungerecht, unlauter
unforgettable *76* unvergesslich
unfortunately *36* leider, unglücklicherweise
unhappy *64* unzufrieden, unglücklich
unhealthy *84* ungesund
uninteresting *55* uninteressant
unit *29T* Spezialabteilung, Station *(im Krankenhaus usw.)*; **psychiatric ~** *29T* Psychiatrie, psychiatrische Abteilung
unpleasant *105T* unangenehm, unerfreulich
unreasonable *111G* unvernünftig, abwegig
unreliable *43T* unzuverlässig
unresolved *121* ungeklärt, ungelöst
to **unroll sth** *82T* etw entrollen, etw aufrollen
unspoken *64* unausgesprochen
unstable *63V* instabil
unsure *77* unsicher
untidy *23* unordentlich, unaufgeräumt
until recently *115* bis vor kurzem
unusual *103* unüblich
unwelcome *120* unerwünscht
unwilling, to **be ~ to do sth** *36* nicht bereit sein, etw zu tun
up, to **be ~ to sb** *124P* jdm überlassen bleiben, jds Entscheidung sein
upbringing *107G* Erziehung, Elternhaus
upcoming *53* bevorstehend, demächst stattfindend
update *37* Aktualisierung
to **update sth** *55T* etw aktualisieren, etw auf den neuesten Stand bringen
to **upload sth** *48* etw hochladen
upset *128* verärgert, aufgebracht; to **be/get ~** *58* sich aufregen
urgent(ly) *39* dringend
use *42* Verwendung, Gebrauch, Nutzung; **drug ~** *39* Drogenkonsum
used, to **be widely ~** *42* weit verbreitet sein, häufig verwendet werden
usefulness *65* Nutzen
user, drug ~ *39* Drogenkonsument/in
usually *10* normalerweise, gewöhnlich
utensils *pl*, **wide-grip ~** *59* Besteck mit breitem Griff

V

vacancy *10* freie/offene Stelle
vaccinated, to **get ~** *62T* sich impfen lassen
vaccine *97T* Impfstoff
valuable *20* wertvoll
value *49* Wert; **set of ~s** *111T* Werte; **good ~ for money** *92* preiswert, günstig; to **add ~ to sth** *21* eine Bereicherung für etw sein
vandalism *107P* (mutwillige) Sachbeschädigung
to **vandalize sth** *34T* etw mutwillig beschädigen
variety *111G* Vielfalt
to **vary** *12* sich unterscheiden, variieren
vegan *87* vegan
vegetarian *87* vegetarisch; Vegetarier/in
vending machine *84* (Verkaufs-) Automat
venue *50* Veranstaltungsort
verbal abuse *106* Beschimpfungen, Beleidigungen
via *35P* über, mittels
victim *11* Opfer
view: ~ (on sth) *11* Ansicht (über etw), Meinung (zu etw); **in my ~** *11* meiner Ansicht/Meinung nach
to **view sb as sth** *36* jdn als etw betrachten
viewer *22* Zuschauer/in
vigorous *101* energisch, kräftig
violation, human rights ~s *pl* *112* Menschenrechtsverstöße
violence *10* Gewalt; **domestic ~** *55T* häusliche Gewalt
violent *10* gewalttätig, brutal
visible *42* sichtbar, erkennbar
vision *30* Vorstellung(en), Vision; **poor ~** *59* Sehschwäche; **~ impairment** *42* Sehbehinderung, Sehschwäche
visiting professor *13* Gastprofessor/in
visual *15* visuell, optisch; **~ impairment** *42* Sehbehinderung, Sehschwäche
visuals *pl* *48* Bildmaterial, Bilder
vital *99* unerlässlich, unverzichtbar
vocational: ~ college *12* Fachoberschule; **~ school** *81* Berufsschule
voicemail *89* Anrufbeantworter, Mailbox
voluntary *12* ehrenamtlich, freiwillig
volunteer *9* Freiwillige/r, ehrenamtliche/r Mitarbeiter/in
to **volunteer** *18V* ehrenamtlich tätig sein, (freiwillig) arbeiten/helfen

W

wages *pl* *35P* Lohn
war *108* Krieg
ward, maternity ~ *9* Entbindungsstation *(im Krankenhaus)*
warning *34T* Verwarnung, Ermahnung; **~ sign** *64* Anzeichen, Hinweis
washcloth *58* Waschlappen
waste *84* Abfall, Müll; **~ of time** *124T* Zeitverschwendung
to **waste sth** *97T* etw vergeuden
water: ~ cooler *124P* Wasserspender; **~ slide** *77* Wasserrutsche
wave *108* Welle
way, that ~ *54* auf diese Weise
weakness *16* Schwäche
to **wear off** *65T* abklingen, nachlassen
weekday, on ~s *34T* werktags, unter der Woche
weekly *55* wöchentlich
weight *98* Gewicht; to **gain ~** *98* zunehmen; to **lose ~** *97* abnehmen; **~-reducing products** *pl* *114* Schlankheitsprodukte
welcome, to **be ~ to do sth** *61* gern etw tun können; **You're ~.** *17T* Bitte (sehr). Gern geschehen.
welfare, child ~ *28* Kindeswohl, Kinder- und Jugendschutz; **child ~ worker** *28* Jugendamtsmitarbeiter/in, Kinderschutzfachkraft
well, as ~ as *9* sowie, und
well-being *10* Wohl, Wohlbefinden, Gesundheit
well lit *58* gut beleuchtet

well-qualified *10* gut ausgebildet
wheelchair *42* Rollstuhl; ~ **accesss** *45T* rollstuh-/behindertengerechter Zugang
whether *21* ob
whichever *77T* welche/r/s (auch immer)
while *123T* Weile
white-water rafting *80* Rafting, Wildwasserfahren
whoever *82T* wer auch immer
whole grains *pl* *99* Vollkorngetreide
wide *60* breit
wide-grip utensils *pl* *59* Besteck mit breitem Griff
widely, to **be** ~ **used** *42* weit verbreitet sein, häufig verwendet werden
willing, to **be** ~ **to do sth** *9* bereit/willens sein, etw zu tun
willingness *128* Bereitschaft
wish: Best ~es *pl* *77T (Brief, E-Mail:)* Viele Grüße
withdrawn *64* verschlossen, introvertiert
within *19* innerhalb (von), binnen
witness *123T* Zeuge/Zeugin
women's refuge *55* Frauenhaus
to **wonder** *82T* sich fragen
woodlands *pl* *78* Wälder
to **work** *30* funktionieren; ~ **on sth** *16* sich mit etw befassen, sich mit etw auseinandersetzen; *121* etw erarbeiten, an etw arbeiten; ~ **long hours** *29* lange arbeiten, Überstunden machen; ~ **overtime** *126* Überstunden machen
work, social ~ *10* Sozialarbeit; ~ **contract** *126* Arbeitsvertrag; ~ **experience** *9* Praktikum, Berufserfahrung; **line of** ~ *11* Beruf, Branche; ~ **permit** *111P* Arbeitserlaubnis; ~ **placement** *6* Praktikum; ~ **processes** *pl* *53* Arbeitsabläufe; ~ **schedule** *127* Arbeitszeit, Arbeitsplan; ~**-related** *74* arbeitsbezogen, berufsbezogen
worker, case ~ *38* Sozialarbeiter/in; **child welfare** ~ *28* Jugendamtsmitarbeiter/in, Kinderschutzfachkraft; **community outreach** ~ *33* Sozialarbeiter/in für gesellschaftliche Randgruppen; **community support** ~ *28* Sozialarbeiter/in; **social** ~ *10* Sozialarbeiter/in; **social education** ~ *29* Sozialpädagoge/-in
working: ~ **class** *108* Arbeiterklasse; ~ **conditions** *pl* *10* Arbeitsbedingungen; ~ **schedule** *37* Dienstplan, Arbeitsplan
workplace *26* Arbeitsplatz, Arbeitsstätte; ~ **harassment** *121* Mobbing am Arbeitsplatz; to **enter the** ~ *43* in die Arbeitswelt einsteigen
workshop *27* Kurs, Schulung, Workshop; *45* Werkstatt
World Health Organization (WHO) *96* Weltgesundheitsorganisation
worrying *103T* bedenklich, beunruhigend
worship, place of ~ *110* Gebetsstätte, Gotteshaus
worth *62T* wert
worthwhile *29T* lohnenswert, wertvoll, interessant
wound *82* Wunde; ~ **care** *82* Wundversorgung
written *13* schriftlich
writing, in ~ *73* schriftlich, in Schriftform

XYZ

xenophobia *111P* Fremdenfeindlichkeit
yeast *97P* Hefe
young offender institution *35P* Jugendstrafanstalt
yours: Y~ faithfully *14 (Brief, E-Mail:)* Mit freundlichen Grüßen; **Y~ sincerely** *14 (Brief, E-Mail:)* Mit freundlichen Grüßen
youth *36* Jugendliche/r; ~ **court** *34T* Jugendgericht; ~ **protection service(s)** *66* Jugendamt
Yuck! *97T* Bäh! Igitt!
Yugoslavia *111P* Jugoslawien
zero tolerance *39* null Toleranz

be	was/were	been	*sein*
beat	beat	beaten	*schlagen, besiegen*
become	became	become	*werden*
begin	began	begun	*anfangen, beginnen*
bend	bent	bent	*(sich) beugen*
blow	blew	blown	*wehen, blasen, ziehen*
break	broke	broken	*brechen*
breed	bred	bred	*sich vermehren, sich ausbreiten*
bring	brought	brought	*(mit)bringen*
build	built	built	*bauen*
burn	burnt/ burned	burnt/ burned	*(ver)brennen*
buy	bought	bought	*kaufen*
catch	caught	caught	*fangen, fassen, erreichen*
choose	chose	chosen	*(aus)wählen*
come	came	come	*kommen*
cost	cost	cost	*kosten*
cut	cut	cut	*schneiden*
deal (with)	dealt (with)	dealt (with)	*sich kümmern um, umgehen mit*
dig	dug	dug	*graben*
do	did	done	*tun, machen*
draw	drew	drawn	*zeichnen*
dream	dreamt/ dreamed	dreamt/ dreamed	*träumen*
drink	drank	drunk	*trinken*
drive	drove	driven	*fahren*
eat	ate	eaten	*essen*
fall	fell	fallen	*fallen*
feed	fed	fed	*füttern, ernähren*
feel	felt	felt	*(sich) fühlen, empfinden*
fight	fought	fought	*kämpfen*
find	found	found	*finden*
fit	fit/fitted	fit/fitted	*passen, anbringen, entsprechen*
fly	flew	flown	*fliegen*
forbid	forbade	forbidden	*verbieten*
forget	forgot	forgotten	*vergessen*
get	got	got (AE gotten)	*bekommen*
give	gave	given	*geben*
go	went	gone	*gehen, fahren*
grow	grew	grown	*wachsen*
hang	hung	hung	*hängen*
have	had	had	*haben*
hear	heard	heard	*hören*
hide	hid	hidden	*(sich) verstecken*
hit	hit	hit	*schlagen*
hold	held	held	*halten, festhalten*
hurt	hurt	hurt	*verletzen*
keep	kept	kept	*behalten*
know	knew	known	*kennen, wissen*
lay	laid	laid	*legen*
lead	led	led	*führen*
lean	leant/ leaned	leant/ leaned	*sich lehnen, sich beugen*

learn	learnt/ learned	learnt/ learned	*lernen*
leave	left	left	*abfahren, verlassen, weggehen*
let	let	let	*lassen*
lie	lay	lain	*liegen*
light	lit	lit	*anzünden, beleuchten*
lose	lost	lost	*verlieren*
make	made	made	*machen*
mean	meant	meant	*meinen, bedeuten*
meet	met	met	*treffen*
pay	paid	paid	*bezahlen*
put	put	put	*setzen, stellen, legen*
quit	quit/ quitted	quit/ quitted	*verlassen, aufhören*
read	read	read	*lesen*
ride	rode	ridden	*reiten, fahren*
ring	rang	rung	*anrufen, läuten*
rise	rose	risen	*(an)steigen*
run	ran	run	*laufen, rennen*
say	said	said	*sagen*
see	saw	seen	*sehen*
seek	sought	sought	*suchen*
sell	sold	sold	*verkaufen*
send	sent	sent	*senden, schicken*
set	set	set	*setzen, stellen*
shake	shook	shaken	*schütteln*
shine	shone	shone	*scheinen, glänzen*
show	showed	shown	*zeigen*
shrink	shrank	shrunk	*schrumpfen, zurückgehen*
shut	shut	shut	*schließen*
sing	sang	sung	*singen*
sink	sank	sunk	*sinken*
sit	sat	sat	*sitzen*
sleep	slept	slept	*schlafen*
slide	slid	slid	*(ab)rutschen, (ab) sacken*
smell	smelt/ smelled	smelt/ smelled	*riechen*
speak	spoke	spoken	*sprechen*
spell	spelt/ spelled	spelt/ spelled	*buchstabieren*
spend	spent	spent	*ausgeben, verbringen*
spread	spread	spread	*(sich) verbreiten*
stand	stood	stood	*stehen*
steal	stole	stolen	*stehlen*
swim	swam	swum	*schwimmen*
take	took	taken	*nehmen*
teach	taught	taught	*unterrichten, beibringen*
tell	told	told	*sagen, erzählen*
think	thought	thought	*denken*
throw	threw	thrown	*werfen*
understand	understood	understood	*verstehen*
wake	woke	woken	*aufwachen, -wecken*
wear	wore	worn	*tragen*
win	won	won	*gewinnen*
write	wrote	written	*schreiben*

Titelfoto: Shutterstock.com / Timurpix

S. 6: *(1)* Shutterstock.com / Robert Kneschke; *(2)* Shutterstock.com / Rawpixel.com; **S. 7:** *(1)* Shutterstock.com / Photographee.eu; *(2)* Shutterstock.com / fizkes; **S. 8:** Shutterstock.com / wavebreakmedia; **S. 9:** *(1)* Shutterstock.com / Travel Stock; *(2)* Shutterstock.com / The Creative Guy; **S. 10:** Shutterstock.com / antoniodiaz; **S. 11:** *(1)* Shutterstock.com / Avatar_023; *(2)* Shutterstock.com / jordisalas.net; **S. 15:** Shutterstock.com / ProStockStudio; **S. 16:** *(1)* Shutterstock.com / Dean Drobot; *(2)* Shutterstock.com / boonchoke; **S. 17:** Shutterstock.com / Prostock-studio; **S. 18:** Cornelsen / Rockfinch / Claire Cunningham, Dublin; **S. 19:** Shutterstock.com / Jacob Lund; **S. 22:** *(1)* Shutterstock.com / Gonzalo Aragon; *(2)* Shutterstock.com / Photology1971; *(3)* Shutterstock.com / dizain; *(4)* Shutterstock.com / Igor Levin; **S. 23:** *(1)* Shutterstock.com / Grzegorz Petrykowski; *(2)* Shutterstock.com / dizain; *(3)* Shutterstock.com / Ford Contributor; *(4)* Shutterstock.com / Pormezz; **S. 24:** *(1)* Shutterstock.com / Rawpixel.com; *(2)* Shutterstock.com / Rafal Olechowski; **S. 25:** *(1)* Shutterstock.com / Trueffelpix; *(2)* Shutterstock.com / pathdoc; **S. 26:** *(1)* Shutterstock.com / Monkey Business Images; *(2)* Shutterstock.com / New Africa; **S. 27:** *(1)* Shutterstock.com / Halfpoint; *(2)* Shutterstock.com / Roman Zaiets; **S. 28:** Shutterstock.com / StockCanarias; **S. 29:** *(1)* Shutterstock.com / Syda Productions; *(2)* Shutterstock.com / Krakenimages.com; *(3)* Shutterstock.com / mimagephotography; **S. 30:** *(1)* Shutterstock.com / Rob Marmion; *(2)* Shutterstock.com / Prostock-studio; **S. 31:** stock.adobe.com / zinkevych; **S. 32:** *(1)* Shutterstock.com / garetsworkshop; *(2)* Shutterstock.com / mentatdgt; *(3)* stock.adobe.com / fizkes; **S. 33:** Shutterstock.com / mentatdgt; **S. 34:** *(1)* Shutterstock.com / stockfour; *(2)* Shutterstock.com / Lena Pan; **S. 35:** *(1)* Shutterstock.com / Sabphoto; *(2)* Shutterstock.com / ALFATEH PAL; **S. 36:** Shutterstock.com / Pressmaster; **S. 38:** Shutterstock.com / Juice Flair; **S. 40:** Shutterstock.com / Astafjeva; **S. 41:** Shutterstock.com / Monkey Business Images; **S. 42:** *(1)* Shutterstock.com / Maliutina Anna; *(2)* Shutterstock.com / myphotobank.com.au; *(3)* Shutterstock.com / DGLimages; *(4)* Shutterstock.com / AA.Shkob; **S. 43:** *(1)* Shutterstock.com / StockCanarias; *(2)* Shutterstock.com / Krakenimages.com; **S. 44:** *(1)* Shutterstock.com / SeventyFour; *(2)* Shutterstock.com / Firma V; **S. 45:** Shutterstock.com / Tyler Olson; **S. 47:** Cornelsen / D 'Avila Illustration Agency; **S. 49:** stock.adobe.com / 2014 Olesia Bilkei / Olesia Bilkei; **S. 52:** *(1)* Shutterstock.com / ALPA PROD; *(2)* Shutterstock.com / oliveromg; **S. 53:** *(1)* Shutterstock.com / Monkey Business Images; *(2)* Shutterstock.com / fizkes; **S. 54:** Shutterstock.com / JPC-PROD; **S. 55:** *(1)* Shutterstock.com / petrroudny43; *(2)* Shutterstock.com / Drazen Zigic; **S. 56:** *(1)* Shutterstock.com / Photographee.eu; *(2)* Shutterstock.com / Dmytro Zinkevych; **S. 57:** *(1)* Shutterstock.com / matsabe; ; *(2)* Shutterstock.com / sakmeniko; **S. 58:** *(1)* Shutterstock.com / Atiketta Sangasaeng; *(2)* Shutterstock.com / Lisa-S; *(3)* Shutterstock.com / Robert Kneschke; *(4)* Shutterstock.com / BrAt82; **S. 60:** *(1)* Shutterstock.com / Robert Kneschke; *(2)* Shutterstock.com/Aniroot M; *(3)* Shutterstock.com / Laura Appena; **S. 61:** *(1)* Shutterstock.com/yusufdemirci **;** *(2)* Shutterstock.com / wavebreakmedia; *(3)* Shutterstock.com / Robert Kneschke; **S. 62:** Cornelsen / D 'Avila Illustration Agency; **S. 63:** Shutterstock.com / Syda Productions; **S. 64:** Shutterstock.com / rawf8; **S. 65:** *(1)* Shutterstock.com / archivector; *(A-E)* Cornelsen / D 'Avila Illustration Agency; **S. 66:** *(1)* Shutterstock.com / Pormezz; *(2)* Shutterstock.com / Littlekidmoment; *(3)* Shutterstock.com / SpeedKingz; **S. 70:** Shutterstock.com / Trueffelpix; **S. 71:** *(1)* Shutterstock.com / Atstock Productions; *(2)* Shutterstock.com / Ana Blazic Pavlovic; **S. 72:** Shutterstock.com / lemono; **S. 73:** Shutterstock.com / Viktoriia Hnatiuk; **S. 74:** *(1)* Shutterstock.com / Monkey Business Images; *(2)* Shutterstock.com / Monkey Business Images; *(3)* Shutterstock.com / Creative Stall; *(4)* Shutterstock.com / APVCTR; *(5)* Shutterstock.com / Pro Symbols; *(6)* Shutterstock.com / Lyudmyla Kharlamova; *(7)* Shutterstock.com / Graphic Idenic; **S. 75:** *(1)* Shutterstock.com / Mansoreh; *(2)* Shutterstock.com / MaximP; *(3)* Shutterstock.com / notbad; **S. 76:** *(1)* Shutterstock.com / Sergey Novikov; *(2)* Shutterstock.com / Prostock-studio; **S. 80:** Shutterstock.com / Umomos; **S. 81:** Shutterstock.com / Roman Samborskyi; **S. 82:** *(1)* Shutterstock.com / GenOMart; *(2)* Shutterstock.com / PRESSLAB; **S. 83:** Shutterstock.com / Dragana Gordic; **S. 84:** Shutterstock.com / Kzenon; **S. 86:** *(1)* Shutterstock.com / margouillat photo; *(2)* Shutterstock.com / Studio Peace; *(3)* Shutterstock.com / navorolphotography; *(4)* Shutterstock.com / PhotoSongserm; *(5)* Shutterstock.com / g_dasha; **S. 87:** *(1)* Shutterstock.com / AikStudio; *(2)* Shutterstock.com / Prostock-studio; **S. 90:** Shutterstock.com / RAGMA IMAGES; **S. 91:** Shutterstock.com / Monkey Business Images; **S. 92:** Shutterstock.com / Rawpixel.com; **S. 93:** Shutterstock.com / ALPA PROD; **S. 94:** *(1)* Shutterstock.com / NDAB Creativity; *(2)* Shutterstock.com / Photographee.eu; **S. 95:** *(1)* Shutterstock.com / Monkey Business Images; *(2)* Shutterstock.com / Prostock-studio; **S. 97:** *(1)* Shutterstock.com / StockCanarias; *(2)* Shutterstock.com / Elnur; **S. 98:** Shutterstock.com / VectorMine; **S. 99:** Shutterstock.com / Kanel Bulle; **S. 100:** Shutterstock.com / Photographee.eu; **S. 104:** Shutterstock.com / Gavrilo Stanojevic; **S. 105:** *(1)* Shutterstock.com / StockCanarias; *(2)* Shutterstock.com / AJR_photo; **S. 106:** Shutterstock.com / Photographee.eu; **S. 107:** *(1)* Shutterstock.com/Olena Yakobchuk; *(2)* Shutterstock.com / marvent; *(3)* Shutterstock.com / mavo; **S. 108:** Shutterstock.com / Monkey Business Images; **S. 109:** Shutterstock.com / Monkey Business Images; **S. 110:** *(1)* Shutterstock.com / Tirachard Kumtanom; *(2)* Shutterstock.com / goodluz; *(3)* Shutterstock.com / Billion Photos; **S. 111:** *(1)* Imago Stock & People GmbH / UIG; *(2)* Imago Stock & People GmbH / Werner Schulze\r; **S. 113:** Shutterstock.com / Pablo Eder; **S. 116:** Shutterstock.com / Monkey Business Images; **S. 119:** Shutterstock.com / Cozine; **S. 120:** *(1)* Shutterstock.com / Antonio Guillem; *(2)* Shutterstock.com / Prostock-studio; **S. 121:** *(1)* Shutterstock.com / Drazen Zigic; *(2)* Cartoonstock / Jonny Hawkins; **S. 122:** Shutterstock.com / Zholobov Vadim; **S. 123:** Shutterstock.com / Zholobov Vadim; **S. 124:** Shutterstock.com / AlexTanya; **S. 125:** Shutterstock.com / fizkes; **S. 126:** *(1)* Shutterstock.com / Rido; *(2)* Shutterstock.com / pixelheadphoto digitalskillet; *(3)* Shutterstock.com / Monkey Business Images; *(4)* Shutterstock.com / Rido; *(5)* Shutterstock.com / mavo; **S. 129:** Shutterstock.com / YanLev; **S. 136:** *(1)* stock.adobe.com; *(2)* Shutterstock.com / Inspiring; **S. 137:** Shutterstock.com / fizkes; **S. 151:** Shutterstock.com / TarikVision; **S. 152:** Cornelsen / D 'Avila Illustration Agency; **S. 153:** Cornelsen / D 'Avila Illustration Agency